A Collector's Identification and Value Guide
North American
INDIAN ARTIFACTS

5th Edition
by Lar Hothem

BOOKS AMERICANA
INC.

ISBN-0-89689-101-1

i.

DEDICATION

To the North American Indian artisans of whatever time and place — And to the collectors of today who value what they made.

Three Nez Perce men, with tipis to side and background. Note the fine necklaces and blankets; photo taken at Colville, Washington, ca. 1904.

Photographer, Dr. E. H. Latham; courtesy Photography Collection, Suzzallo Library, University of Washington.

AUTHOR'S NOTE: This book is intended as a guide to many kinds of artifacts and in a variety of value ranges. It is for general education and information purposes only. Neither the author nor the publisher will be responsible for any transactions based on the values listed herein. This includes profits, losses and trades.

ACKNOWLEDGEMENTS

It is the usual practice for a writer to thank those for without whose help the book could not have been completed. For this project, the writer acknowledges over fifty persons, without whose assistance and encouragement the book would not have gone beyond the early stages of research.

This is not the definitive book on all American Indian collectibles and their values, for such will never be compiled by anyone. It is, however, as comprehensive as possible, including many examples both common and rare.

The book is also authoritative, for many of the contributors are highly knowledgeable and experienced in their respective fields — as will be obvious on even a casual reading. The book, in short, goes far beyond single-individual approach and comprehension.

The persons who provided photographs from private collections are thanked, and their photographs and valuations appear throughout the book. They are, in each case, credited to the sender. The extent of individual contributions, and my thanks, will be evident.

However, there were some who made available photographs that were outstanding in both quantity and quality. They are: John W. Barry, Tom Browner, H. Jackson Clark, Kenneth R. Canfield, Marguerite Kernaghan, Harvey and Rose King, Wayne Parker, Bill Post, and Summers Redick.

Thanks also to Howard Popkie and Robert C. Calvert, for an extended look at some scarce Canadian artifacts. In some cases, collectors and dealers had professionals photograph items, and thanks for that fine work.

A number of institutional or governmental sources were drawn upon for excellent photographs of historic significance. These illustrate a variety of scenes, from contemporary activities to prehistoric ruins. They are:

Florida Division of Tourism
National Photography Collection, Public Archives of Canada
Nebraska State Historical Society, John A. Anderson Collection
South Dakota State Historical Society
Photography Collection, Suzzallo Library, University of Washington
U.S. Department of the Interior, National Park Service
Utah State Historical Society, Collection of Smithsonian Institution

Thanks are due, very much so, to the various Indian art galleries and dealers that kindly permitted reprinting. This was of descriptions and prices of selected artifacts and artworks from their catalogs and listings. They are:

W.J. Crawford, The Americana Galleries, Phoenix, Arizona James O. Aplan, Midland, South Dakota
Pierre and Sylvia Bovis, Winona Indiana Trading Post, Santa Fe, New Mexico
Kenneth R. Canfield, Plains Indian Art, Kansas City, Missouri
Barry Hardin, Crazy Crow Trading Post, Denison, Texas
Hyde's, Santa Fe, New Mexico
Sam and Nancy Johnson, Caddo Trading Company and Gallery, Mufreesboro, Arkansas
Manitou Gallery, Cheyenne, Wyoming
Armand Ortega, Indian Ruins Trading Post, Sanders, Arizona
R.G. Munn, Whispering Pines Gallery, La Mesa, California

Other specialty listings were used, and are noted and credited throughout the book.

Thanks are due to auction houses which allowed item descriptions from catalogs and results from bid-sheets. Appreciation to:

Col. Doug Allard, St. Ignatius, Montana
Tom King and Tom Porter, Garth's Auctions, Inc., Stratford Road, Delaware, Ohio
Jan Sorgenfrei, Old Barn Auctions, Findlay, Ohio
Rod Sauvageau, Trade Winds West Auction Gallery, Portland, Oregon

Various private collectors sent thorough descriptions of items, placing a fair market value on some of their prize specimens. Very special thanks, also, to those who went considerably out of their way to provide detailed chapter introductions, namely: Tom Browner (Bannerstones), Dick Weatherford (Baskets), and John Barry (Pottery).

Respects to several gentlemen who contributed literature and all possible help on the Federal level. Robert G. Hart, General Manager, Indian Arts and Crafts Board, U.S. Department of the Interior, Washington, D.C., gave personal help and literature. Also, Charles Dailey, Museum Director, Institute of American Indian Arts (Bureau of Indian Affairs, U.S. Department of the Interior), Santa Fe, New Mexico, for pertinent literature and personal help. Further, to Lloyd New, former Director of the Institute of American Indian Arts, for his excellent summary regarding the state of Indian Art.

Acknowledgement goes to the Executive Director of the Indian Arts and Crafts Association, this in two directions. First for the literature and reprint permission, and second, for personal correspondence that aided greatly in an area of sensitive coverage.

Ultimate gratitude to Sue McClurg Hothem, who assisted in suggestions, paperwork and fine moral support throughout. And the same to Adena and Hopewell, for understanding. Deep thanks to Ronald E. Hothem, Attorney-at-Law, San Francisco, for legal counsel in several areas of importance.

Lar Hothem

TODAY, AMERICAN INDIAN ART RIDES AT THE PINNACLE OF APPRECIATION. WORKS WHICH ONLY A DECADE OR TWO AGO WERE VIEWED GENERALLY AS THE CURIOUS OUTPUT OF AMERICA'S ABORIGINAL WAGON TRAIN RAIDERS HAVE SUDDENLY BEEN ACCORDED SUPER-STATUS. THIS PHENOMENAL RISE IN ACCEPTANCE IS MANIFEST IN THE VIRTUAL CRAZE ON THE PART OF THE PUBLIC FOR INDIAN ARTS AND CRAFTS TODAY, NOT ONLY IN TRADITIONAL MODES, BUT IN IN- NOVATIVE STYLES AS WELL. INDIAN ARTS AND CRAFTS ARE NOW TREATED WITHIN THE SAME ELITIST EXHIBITION AND MARKETING CHANNELS AS THOSE PREVIOUSLY RESERVED FOR THE FINEST ART FROM OTHER SOURCES THROUGHOUT THE WORLD.

From *One With The Earth,* catalog of the Traveling Exhibit; by Lloyd New, Director, Institute of American Indian Arts, Bureau of Indian Affairs, Santa Fe, New Mexico.

TABLE OF CONTENTS

TABLE OF CONTENTS

TABLE OF CONTENTS

INTRODUCTION

Fascination with things American Indian is deeply ingrained in our culture. It began with childhood games, Cowboys and Indians. It is continually reinforced by advertising symbols, company names, movies, television, everyday conversation.

No American needs to ask the meaning of these phrases: "Burying the hatchet"; "Smoke the peacepipe"; "Indian Summer". And how many low-ranking military personnel have complained about "Two many chiefs, not enough Indians"? The American Indian or Amerind presence is everywhere, and a healthy part of our national existence.

This partly explains the present fascination with objects made by Indians. There are today probably well over two-and-a-half million persons who collect Indian goods or are in other ways involved in the vast area.

There are certain characteristics of Amerind collectibles. One is that they are almost always made from natural materials and substances, whether plant, animal or mineral. Another is that all, or almost all, of the work required to complete the object is done by hand, slowly and carefully.

Yet another characteristic is workstyle, with the object being shaped into a form familiar to the Amerind lifeways. It is decorated, if at all, with designs that have their origin in the timeless North American past.

The essence of the Amerind art form — be it utensil, tool, weapon, ornament, whatever — is uniqueness. For all authentic pieces there was, and is, no such "improvement" as assembly-line mass production. And no two objects are ever totally alike, no matter how much they may resemble one another. The pieces are as varied as the individuals that made them; each is a sole creation.

Perhaps still another hallmark of Amerind works, and one that appeals highly to collectors, is the "utility-plus" factor. A great percentage of Amerind objects were made far better than necessary to merely complete a task. Much loving skill and attention to detail were added.

Amerind art and artifacts have long been admired and collected in European countries and elsewhere. Americans, pioneer and recent, have largely failed to understand or appreciate the field. Only within the last few years has there been a broad groundswell of interest and attention, but Americans have now begun to accept good Amerind material as good art.

Native American art, sometimes primitive, sometimes amazingly sophisticated, has gone (in regard to marketability) far beyond the flash and fad stages. It has become a major field to be in, a heritage to be knowledgeable about, **the** collectibles to have.

Some preliminary explanations and comments are in order. There are terms used throughout this Guide that are important. "Prehistoric" means before-writing, or the arrival of Europeans to record events. Prehistoric also means cultural items designed by Amerinds alone, without ideological contamination from European sources and generally this means all human-occupied North American time **before** about AD 1500.

"Historic", as used here, means heavy cultural contact with Europeans and Russians, in a time zone broadly ranging from AD 1500. "Recent", is here considered to be from 1900 to 1980. "Contemporary" indicates years from 1980 to the present. These time-zones are open to debate, but if the meaning is clear they remain sufficient and descriptive.

This book is a **Guide** to American Indian Collectibles and their values. It identifies and describes major collecting areas available today. Representative prices, or close price ranges, are accurately given.

It should be noted that the listed value — whether for item description or photograph — is not an ultimate valuation. It does not usually constitute an offer to sell. It does not represent an appraisal. Instead, it is judged by the possessor to be a fair market value. Information is given for the sake of knowledge.

To a certain extent, the chapter lengths reflect the quantity of that sort of American Indian material available to the collector. It is to a degree a guide to the amount of material on the market.

For example, for every, say, presentation-grade pipe tomahawk, there are many thousand flint projectile points. For every Plains Indian beaded dress in ultra-fine condition, there are hundreds of other beaded clothing items, more available and less expensive.

Don't be upset by what may seem to be high prices; don't feel that American Indian items are beyond your financial reach. A major and long-term effort has been made, for this book, to secure listings and photographs of some of the top collector pieces in North America. They are here for your study.

These are very good examples, for the most part, of material you will see and have the opportunity to purchase. Bargains can still be picked up at auctions, flea markets and antique shops, providing you know what you are looking at and have some idea of the market value.

And while the Guide should be a general help in acquiring good pieces at reasonable prices, there is yet no substitute for personal knowledge and experience. The more you know about what you decide to collect, the better will be your Amerind collection.

Key letters preceding price figures: The source
A) Auction   D) Dealer
C) Collector   G) Gallery

Consider the value of knowing Indian Collectibles values:

A rancher finds a prehistoric flint artifact which a neighbor tells him is incomplete because it does not have notches. The rancher sells it for $10, which is about what the neighbor tells him it is worth. Later, the rare Paleo-period fluted-base point is sold for $175.

A box of old costume jewelry in an antique shop attracts the attention of a buyer at $12.50. Among the items is a heavy trade-era silver beaver-shaped pendant and a handful of glass trade beads. Once a necklace, the set is now insured at $500.

A man at a Midwestern farm auction pays a few dollars for what the auctioneer called "an old hatchet". It is that and more. The collector who now owns the late-1700s pipe-tomahawk with original handle has twice refused offers of $600 or over.

A "musty old leather thing" is *donated* to a cheritable organization and passes through several hands. The last owner refuses to part with the piece; it is a fine Plains Indian pipebag with exquisite bead and quillwork designs. It is valued, conservatively, at $950, because there was also a genuine two-piece pipe inside.

An old Indian weaving is obtained for a nominal sum at a flea market. A knowledgeable dealer and collector is intrigued; he flies halfway across the country to take a look. He obtains the item, a fine late-phase Chiefs' blanket worth many thousand dollars.

ALLARD AUCTION

Col. Doug Allard, Flathead Indian and well-known auctioneer of Amerind material, presided over a recent auction featuring 1550 fine Indian-related lots. (The Allard catalogs alone have become collector items). Some 90-plus listings and twelve photographs (by Jeanine Allard) are reprinted here, by permission of the Allards. This three-day auction took place March 20-22, 1992, and was known as the Million Dollar III auction.

In-depth coverage is accorded these objects for several reasons. One is the high quality of the items, most being in the advanced-collector category. Another is the great range of artifacts, from many tribes, geographic regions and time-periods. This provides a broad-spectrum look at Amerind works.

Criteria used to select objects for inclusion here included: Types collectors will likely encounter, unusual pieces, or those which due to rarity are not covered elsewhere in this book. All listings included here would of course carry the "A" designation.

My sincere thanks to Col. Allard for permission to reprint selected auction results from this event. For those wishing further information, the address is: Col. Doug Allard, P.O. Box 460, St. Ignatius, Montana, 59865. Phone number is (406) 745-2951. Toll-free, (800) 821-3318.

Peace medal, silver, round John Adams Indian peace medal ¼ x 3 in., dated 1797. $250

Basketry hat, Hupa, classic twined women's hat with geometric designs, 3½ x 7 in., ca. 1920. $325

Ledger drawings, four drawings done by Koba, who was a Kiowa, four pieces, ca. 1890. $200

Moccasins, Cheyenne, rare fully beaded (including soles) ceremonial, sinew-sewn on buffalo, 2½ x 7¼ in., ca. 1890. $750

Jewelry set, Zuni four-piece, choice turquoise and silver pettit-point bracelet, ring and earring set, all signed, ca. 1975. $300

Lithograph, R.C. Gorman, hand-signed Limited Edition (54/70) colored lithograph, "Mother and Child", 22 x 30 in., 1972. $300

Necklace, turquoise nugget, three-strand, Santo Domingo spider web nuggets with sterling silver cones, 30 in., ca. 1990. $150

Basket, Maidu, large oval coiled bowl with red "stars" overall, 5½ x 12 in., ca. 1920. $300

Knife case, Cheyenne, beautiful sinew-sewn full-beaded rawhide case with tin and horse-hair drops, 3 x 15 in., ca. 1890. $1200

Necklace, Navajo, coin silver squash blossom with hand-made beads of Mercury dimes, 8 Morgan dollars, and heavy naja, large, ca. 1940. $400

Beadwork, Crow, Civil War cartridge case with Morning Star and stylized crossed American Flags beaded on flap, 9 x 10 in., ca. 1870. $750

Basket, Pima, small very finely coiled negative image "Man in the Maze" motif, ½ x 4 in., ca. 1940. $250

Basket, Pima, huge coiled storage basket with geometric design, 9 x 22 in., ca. 1920. $600

Allard Auction / Million Dollar III - 1992

Hide-scraper, Plains, rare scraper made from a gun barrel, 10 in. long, late 19th century. $175

Rug, Navajo, large four-figure Yei rug in near-mint condition, 45 x 63 in., ca. 1940. $425

Trade rifle, beautiful Indian rifle with brass inlay and fine burl wood stock, 4½ x 47 in., ca. 1820. $700

Necklace, Zuni, classic design with excellent silverwork and over 350 turquoise stones, 28 in., ca. 1935. $550

Whale effigy, stone, Chumash early Pacific Coast artists of southern California, connected with fishing ceremonies, 1½ x 3½ in., ca. 1600. $570

Belt, Great Lakes, beautiful large full-beaded ceremonial belt with geometric designs and wool fringe, 4 x 44 in., ca. 1900. $425

Moccasins, Santee Sioux, choice buckskin moccasins with muslin high tops and fine floral beaded toes, 7 x 10½ in., ca. 1910. $600

Pottery, Mimbres, deep black on white inside geometric design, 3 x 7 inches, prehistoric. $300

3

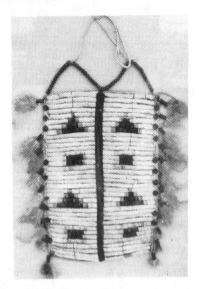

Breastplate, Sioux, fully quilled breastplate in glassed frame, with shell and feather appendages, size 7 x 11 in., ca. 1880. $1100

Allard Auction / Million Dollar III - 1992

Teepee ornament, fully quilled disc on buffalo hide, 7 inches in diameter, ca. 1860. $450

Allard Auction / Million Dollar III - 1992

Tobacco bag, Sioux, choice old buffalo hide bag with geometric beadwork and quilled suspensions with horsehair and tin cones, 9 x 15 in., ca. 1880. $1400

Breastplate, Plains, with 74 bone hairpins interspersed with brass and cobalt glass trade beads, 10½ x 18 in., ca. 1880. $950

Beaded bag, Wishram, early contour beaded bag with rare stylized Elk Dreamer Society design, 9 x 11 in., ca. 1870. $450

Concho belt, Navajo, man's hand-wrought belt with nine conchos and buckle set with turquoise, 3 x 42 in., ca. 1940. $250

Beaded crown, Yoruba, rare excellent condition beaded crown with beaded bird and human figures, 7 x 16½ in., ca. 1910. $500

Belt, silver and gold, containing 17 silver dollars from the 1890s and an 1894 twenty-dollar gold piece set in a silver buckle, 2¼ x 34 in., ca. 1900. $750

Dolls, Seneca, two very old handmade dolls with cornhusk faces and classic clothing, one man and one woman, ca. 1900. $350

Basket, Eskimo, baleen, round twined basket with lid and ivory handle, 3¼ x 3½ in., ca. 1930. $725

Basket, Mission, choice polychrome coiled bowl with star design in center, 3 x 14½ in., ca. 1920. $900

Cradle, Paiute, twined basketry baby carrier with beaded and fringed buckskin cover, 10 x 32 in., ca. 1910. $450

Pipe, Catlinite, red hatchet-shaped pipe with beautiful carved Catlinite stem, 6 x 14 in., year 1892. $175

Pipe tomahawk, rare and fine brass head on carved and tacked wooden handle, with silver mouthpiece and end, rare museum piece, 7 x 20 in., ca. 1860. $2200

Vest, Sioux, early child's vest with beading sinew-sewn on buffalo, excellent condition, museum quality, 15 x 16 in., ca. 1870. $2100

Quirt, Crow, early hand-carved tacked quirt with great patina, 17 in. long, 1870. $350

Ivory doll, Eskimo, carved fossil ivory Shaman's doll, Dorset Culture human effigy, ½ x 3 in., AD 1200. $575

Rattle, Pueblo, fine painted gourd ceremonial rattle with carved and twisted wooden handle, 4 x 20 in., ca. 1920. $125

Parfleche, Nez Perce, rectangular geometric painted rawhide carrying case with flap and brilliant colors, 8 x 12 in., ca. 1910. $400

Basket, Pomo, large, round single-rod coiled basketry bowl with reddish triangulated design, 3½ x 12 in., ca. 1910. $400

Bowl, Pima, basketry, rare with fret design and squares, braided rim, 4½ x 9 in., ca. 1930. $300

Quiver, Crow, very rare otter skin quiver with fully beaded flaps, complete with beaded drops, strap, bow and arrows, 38 in., long, 20th century. $6250

Strike-a-lite, Kiowa, rare early genuine sinew-sewn strike-a-lite pouch on hard leather, 5½ x 6 in., ca. 1860. $600

Allard Auction / Million Dollar III - 1992

Canoe, Salish, carved cedar model with classic painted decorations, 5½ x 24 in., ca. 1930. $250

Rug, Navajo, early natural wool Crystal pictorial with feathers within the design, 50 x 69 in., ca. 1930. $1200

Gun case, Eskimo, large hide case with hair on, collected in 1905, 9½ x 44 in., ca. 1900. $325

Pottery, Mesa Verde, large beautiful bowl with curvilinear and fine line designs painted on the inside; unrestored, 5 x 9 in., prehistoric. $500

Necklace, Blackfoot, outstanding 13-loop tile and brass bead Warrior's necklace, museum quality, 9 x 16 in., ca. 1870. $1050

Basket, Apache, round coiled basketry tray with black geometric designs, 11 in. in diameter, ca. 1920. $250

Kayak, Eskimo, small hide-covered Eskimo model kayak, 18 in., long, ca. 1900. $150

Basket, Washo, finely woven basketry bowl with fret pattern, mint condition, 3 x 6 in., ca. 1930. $500

Basket, Tlingit, rare and finely woven polychrome rattle-top basket, 3¼ x 6¼ in., ca. 1900. $850

Drum, Taos, Pueblo drum in very fine condition, 8 x 24 in., ca. 1930. $275

War lance, Indian, extremely rare hand-forged long-bladed lance, 7 in. by 7 ft. long, ca. 1850. $1200

Teepee, Sioux, very old model hide tepee with beaded design and tin cone suspensions; set on display base with two dolls, ca. 1880. $800

Flute, Iowa, rare early example hand-carved six-hole courting flute in working order, 12 in. long, 19th century. $500

Leggings, Arapaho, sinew-sewn on buffalo hide with tent canvas tops, mint condition, 6 x 20 in., ca. 1870. $1100

Yoke, Blackfoot, huge full-beaded yoke with basket beads and tubular beads, 18 x 19 in., ca. 1890. $800

Holster, Sioux, very rare Eastern Sioux beaded holster on painted buffalo hide parfleche with Tree of Life design, 4 x 10 in., ca. 1860. $1500

Badge, star-shaped brass, "Indian Police — Arizona Territory", 3 in. in diameter, ca. 1910. $150

Armbands, Sioux, geometrically beaded hide bands with long quilled drops, each 2 x 9 in., ca. 1935. $225

Bag, Plateau, contour beaded floral Sally bag with beaded fringe and trade cloth back, 10 x 10 in., ca. 1880. $550

Olla, Apache, excellent condition basket, Apache polychrome olla with negative and positive Crown Dancer figures, 19½ x 22 in., ca. 1900. $11,500

Pottery, Sikyatki, rare brown on buff pre-Hopi bowl with geometric designs inside and out, 4 x 6 in., prehistoric. $250

Choker, Sioux, hand-carved bone hair pipe choker with brass beads and leather spacers, in frame, 1 x 14½ in., ca. 1890. $250

Cradle, Crow, extremely rare full-size sinew-sewn cradle, beadwork on buckskin with six flaps and tailpiece, museum quality, 10½ x 46 in., ca. 1880. $7500

Knife, Plains, fantastic "stabber" or "beavertail" trade knife with painted and engraved handle, provenance attached, 2½ x 15 in., ca. 1835. $7250

Peace medal, George Washington oval medal dated 1789, with emblem of America on obverse, 2¾ x 4 in.. $300

Quirt, Crow, rare early hand-carved painted and tacked quirt, with original beaded handle, 17 in. long, ca. 1870. $900

Canteen, Cochiti, fine old effigy canteen, featuring a lizard, turtle and frog, 5 x 6 in., 20th century. $125

War shirt, Sioux, choice muslin shirt with full-beaded strips and long fringe; pawned in a Rapid City shop in 1910, medium size, ca. 1890,
Allard Auction / Million Dollar III - 1992 $2250

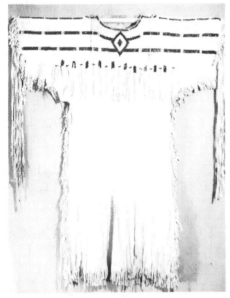

Dress, Nez Perce, fine buckskin dress decorated with beads and long fringe, medium size, ca. 1915. $1000
Allard Auction / Million Dollar III - 1992

Parfleche, Crow, very old buffalo hide rawhide fold-over with classic painted designs, 13 x 27 in., ca. 1880. $700
Allard Auction / Million Dollar III - 1992

Beads, amber, long strand of huge graduated trade beads, 37 in., long, ca. 1860. $250

Yoke, Mojave, rare and beautiful old Mojave fully beaded ceremonial yoke in blue and white, 8 x 19 in., ca. 1890. $425

Basket, Salish, rectangular embricated huckleberry basket with original carrying straps, 10 x 12 in., ca. 1900. $200

Rug, Navajo, very large vegetable dye floor rug with unusual and interesting design, from Chinle; size, 71 x 92 in., ca. 1975. $950

Rifle scabbard, Crow, rare piece beaded on buckskin in classic design, 42 in. long, ca. 1890. $800

Rug, Navajo, Western Reservation floor rug with serrated diamond design, 35 x 51 in., ca. 1940. $300

Pottery, Maria, very early all black jar with original signature "Marie", 4 x 7 in., ca. 1920. $400

Beadwork, Assiniboine, set of two dance cuffs and two fully beaded armbands with matching designs, ca. 1940. $325

War shirt, Kootenai, rare hide shirt with floral beaded bib and beaded fringe, owned by Chief Phillips of the Tobacco Valley band in Grasmere, Alberta, Canada; medium size, ca. 1900. $2700

Basket, Washo, very fine coiled small bowl with polychrome stylized "butterfly" design, 3 x 4 in., ca. 1920. $400

Pipe bag, Sioux, classic yellow ochred hide bag with geometric beadwork and quilled and fringed bottom, 6 x 22 in., ca. 1900. $1250

Amulet, Sioux, small umbilical cord holder beaded in turtle form, 2 x 4 in., ca. 1890. $150

Basket, Papago, coiled basketry olla with vertical connected arrowhead design, 9 x 9 in., ca. 1930. $150

Awl case, Sioux with beaded drops from top to bottom, ¾ x 13 in., ca. 1890. $200

Pottery, Mesa Verde, black on white pottery olla with geometric and fine line designs, 14 x 14 in., prehistoric. $150

Moccasins, Kiowa, choice high-top sinew-sewn yellow ochred hide moccasins with geometric beadwork, brass buttons and fringe, 3½ x 9 x 19 in., ca. 1920. $950

Bags, Sioux, rare pair of Santee Sioux family quilled bags with beaded stars on back, 10 x 10 in., ca. 1870. $2500
Allard Auction / Million Dollar III - 1992

Cuffs, Wishram, early contour beaded cuffs with Ghost Dance design from very old Columbia River culture, ca. 1870. $650
Allard Auction / Million Dollar III - 1992

Rug, Navajo, large early homespun Teec-Nos-Pos with outlined "sawtooth" dividers, 35 x 98 in., ca. 1930. $800
Allard Auction / Million Dollar III - 1992

Shirt, Nez Perce, child's shirt with beaded strips on red stroud, rare piece, small size, ca. 1880. $800
Allard Auction / Million Dollar III - 1992

Basket, Klickitat, fine embricated design from the Bert Robinson collection, excellent condition, 10 x 12 in., ca. 1900. $525

Dye chart, Navajo, framed Navajo rug with all the vegetable dye colors shown coming from the original plant material, color by color, 16 x 19 in., ca. 1950. $175

Pottery, Maria, small black on black pottery jar, signed "Marie" (Maria Martinez), 3 x 4¾ in., ca. 1940. $550

Necklace, heshi, superfine ten-strand necklace with award ribbons, done by Percy Reano, 22 in., year 1972. $375

Drum, Plains, round hide-covered hand drum with painted star and with beater, 2½ x 12 in., ca. 1900. $250

Basket, Pit River, choice large twined bowl with striking reddish geometric designs, 7 x 11 in., ca. 1920. $325

Photograph, Indian, framed original photo of a large group of Sioux Indians in full ceremonial costume, 11 x 13 in., ca. 1915. $125

Teepee bags, matched pair of sinew-sewn buffalo hide possible bags with quilled fronts and beaded sides, 12 x 19 in., ca. 1890. $1200

Knife case, Sioux, rare Santee Sioux beaded case made from calvary tent canvas and containing an old hand-made knife, 2½ x 10 in., ca. 1890. $275

Peace medal, Franklin Pierce silver medal on old hair pipe bone necklace, 3 x 27 in., year 1853. $400

Bandolier, Chippewa, outstanding full-beaded shoulder bag with stylized floral and foliate designs and with beaded fringe, 16 x 38 in., ca. 1890. $3000

Rug, Navajo, huge vegetable dye pictorial with many birds and corn stalks, in mint and beautiful condition, 15 ft. 7 in. by 16 ft. 10 in., ca. 1960. $7000

Blanket, Navajo, choice Third Phase Navajo Chief's blanket with classic design, 64 x 70 in., ca. 1930. $1250

Doll, Plains, female doll with full-beaded dress, belt, human hair and moccasins, rare "Two Faces", 6 x 11 in., ca. 1910. $500

Allard Auction / Million Dollar III - 1992

Ivory, Eskimo, superb huge scrimshawed walrus ivory cribbage board with animals, 2½ x 23 in., ca. 1910. $1500

Basket, Chemeuvi, fantastic coiled basketry bowl with two lines of geometric design, 3 x 12 in., ca. 1920. $1350

Club, Wasco, ancient black stone "Salmon Packer" with carved hands at the top, 2½ x 18 in., ca. 1700. $350

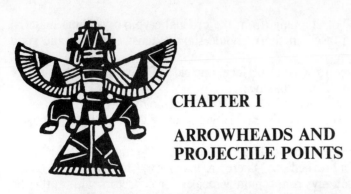

CHAPTER I

ARROWHEADS AND PROJECTILE POINTS

The small chipped points of ancient times are among the most collectible of Amerind artifacts. They exist in one form or another over all of North America, and many types are still very reasonably priced.

Projectile points — the term means both arrowheads and lanceheads — are often the earliest signs of humans on the land. It has long been agreed that people came from Asia, via the Bering Straits, in excess of 20,000 years ago.

Some of the flint artifacts, including those found by archaeologists along the Alaskan Pipeline right-of-way, may be even older. Such chipped tools and weapons may well be the oldest cultural debris in The Americas.

The much-admired fluted-base points are up to 11,000 years old, though related varieties were made until about 5000 or 6000 BC. Points were chipped until the coming of European Whites, the Metal People, when iron and steel points were either traded or made from White-supplied materials.

Until about AD 500, the chief weapon in North America was the Atl-atl, a hand-held wooden lance-thrower, itself a very rare item today. It acted as an extension of the human arm, providing leverage, flinging the lance or javelin further and harder. Many of the existing prehistoric lances had a short and thin foreshaft. This was apparently left in the target animal, and the valuable feather-vaned main shaft was retrieved.

It is not always easy to tell the difference between a lancehead and an arrowhead. One guideline is that most lanceheads **average** about 2 in. (50mm) in length, and ½ in. (12mm) between basal notches. Arrowheads tend to be closer to 1 in. (25mm) or slightly longer, and be about ¼ in. (7mm) between basal notches. Arrowheads are also proportionately thinner and much lighter in weight than the typical Atl-atl point.

Projectile points were made by various chipping processes, by controlled blows that flaked off unwanted material. Bone and antler chipping rods and billets were used. Hammerstones helped create the rough blank. Then, percussion flaking worked the material into a preform, similar in size and shape to the finished artifact.

The preform was further reduced by a process called pressure flaking, which added basal notches, and retouched and evened all edges. Final steps might include basal grinding, when sharp lower edges were dulled. This was probably done so that binding thongs of sinew were not cut through.

Many different types of material could be chipped, most of them being classed as "crypto-crystalline quartz". This includes the common names, flint, chalcedony, chert, jasper, and so on, many with regional names. Obsidian — natural volcanic glass — was widely used, especially in Western areas.

Other materials were used, like petrified wood (Southwest), agatized coral (Southeast) and many types of quartz (Eastern). Even though brittle, the better grades of material are extremely hard. Many varieties will actually scratch plate glass.

Determinants of point value to both dealer and collector involve over half a dozen factors. Size is important, with a larger point being worth comparatively more than a smaller point, other factors assumed equal. Material is a key element; dull and coarse quartzes are less admired than higher, more nearly pure grades. Color is important, with some collectors preferring bold or subtle hues.

Workstyle means the manner in which any one projectile point was fasioned. Desirable qualities would be the thinness and uniformity of the finished point, plus the number and regularity of pressure-chipping scars. Workstyles range from poor to superb, with an infinite number of in-between grades.

Condition of the point refers to any damage sustained by the piece, no matter when such damage occurred. For example, many points being picked up today show the typical sharp-edged breaks caused by agricultural equipment and construction machinery.

Even minor damage can detract greatly from point value, though each instance is of course judged by itself. Perfect specimens are the most avidly sought and command the higher values.

Point-type — there are close to 500 regional main and sub-group point varieties in North America — is a determinate of value, with many collectors willing to pay more for a variety that they admire. One key factor here could be called "intricacy", meaning the delicate and accurate chipping skill evidenced by the point. Examples might be an obsidian fluted Paleo point from the Pacific Northwest, or the rare Midwestern fractured-base point. The last, by the way, refers to a manufacturing technique, not damage.

The final two value determinants are related. One is the "mirror-image" examination, and simple means how much the point obverse resembles the reverse. Or, are both point sides or faces pretty much the same? If there are startling differences in chipping patterns or one side has areas "bare" of chipping (from the original crypto-crystalline material from which the point was made) this lowers the value. Both faces, in short, should show extensive, similar and good workmanship.

Symmetry, as the writer uses the term, means the degree to which one face, one side of the point resembles the other. Looking at either the left or right side there should be visual "balance".

All the determinants add up to a quality that can be called esthetics — how pleasing the point is in an artistic sense. While collectors will place different weight on the various determinants, all or most will be considered in regard to collector desirability, hence value.

Fakes are a real problem today. And the person who believes that only the ancients could chip flint well is likely to be surprised at the skill with which modern points are being turned out. There are many ways to tell good (original) points from the bad, but the beginner is advised to purchase only from reputable dealers or collectors with authentic material. And if a price appears too good to be true, it very possibly is.

Most importantly, talk with knowledgeable people. Learn as much as possible about authentic specimens, and study broken points to see how they were made. Before long, modern-made points will begin to stand out.

EASTERN POINTS

Folsom-type fluted point, 1⅞ in. long, found on New York ocean beach Paleo site. Well-fluted both sides, nearly to tip. All edge treatment extremely well done, with minute chipping. Material, an out-of-state dark flint.   C—$150

Arrowheads from Connecticut, average 2 in. long.
D—$3-6 each

Fine white 1 in. **beveled-edge arrowhead,** undoubtedly made in post-AD 500 times, apparently from the tip of an Archaic beveled edge blade. Portion of base missing. Unusual.
C—$8

Florida **gempoint** made of translucent material called agatized coral. Stemmed point is 1¾ in. long, and ¾ in. wide at sloped shoulders. High colors, fine chipping. C—$60

Frame of 24 **arrowheads** and projectile points, from James River, Virginia, area.   D—$75

Cahokia gempoint, Illinois, amber and white flint, 1⅜ in. long. Notched on sides, notched at base center, very delicately chipped. Mississippian period.   C—$50

Set of 3 **Paleo points** from near Hartford, Connecticut.
D—$55

Stemmed **projectile point,** chipped from white flint, 2½ in. long, from Virginia. Wide stem has the base bifurcated, that is, deeply incurvate in base center.   D—$12

Wide and **shallow-notched point** or blade, Alabama, 2⅜ in. long, possibly Woodland period. Black flint, low grade.
D—$10

Unusual Paleo **Folsom-type fluted point,** 1⅞ in. long, but channel-fluted to tip on both sides. Found near Mississippi River, in state of that name. Perfect condition. C—$150

Triangular point, Alabama, made of a gray chert material, and 1¼ in. long. Perfect condition.   D—$5

POINT OR BLADE made of black flint, 3 in. long and 1¼ in. wide at shoulders. Serrated edges are still sharp; piece was found in southcentral Tennessee.   C—$40
Photo courtesy of Jim Northcutt, Jr., Corinth, Mississippi.

BLADE OR PROJECTILE POINT, 2½ in. long and 1¼ in. wide, found in Prentis County, Mississippi. A Benton type point, it has good symmetry.   C—$25
Photo courtesy of Tracy Northcutt, Corinth, Mississippi.

Common flint **arrowhead,** late prehistoric, and 1 in. long, stemmed, of white low-grade material. Chipping haphazard and uneven, and foreign inclusion makes part much thicker. One notch smaller than the other.   C—$2

Triangular flint **point,** 1¼ in. wide at base. Very thin. Made of black and pink flint, unknown origin. Found in North Carolina and may have been traded there. Base has bottom edges ground, very unusual for the type.   C—$17

Lovely **pentagonal point** or blade, 2 in. long, pink and cream high-quality flint. Corner-notched, ¼ in. of tip missing also one base corner. (Perfect, would have been a $20 point). With damage and as-is, valued less.   C—$12

HARDIN BARBED POINT, found in Adams County, Illinois; Burton Creek area. It is 2¾ in. long and 1½ in. wide at shoulders. From Early Archaic times, approx. 7500 BC. The unique characteristics of this point is that the serrations point forward instead of backward or out to sides.
Photo courtesy of Pat Humphrey, Westcentral Illinois.   C—$165

HOPEWELLIAN PROJECTILE POINTS, showing an interesting range of size and styles. The two specimens on right are both of high grade. Flintridge material. Values, from left to right:

Private collection

C—1st point, $4
2nd point, $12
3rd point, $25
4th point, $9

Side-notched Archaic point, gray-brown flint, 1¾ in. long, ½ in. wide. Chipping average-good, no major damage.
C—$8

Triangular arrowhead, straight base, 1¼ in. long, late prehistoric, found in New York state. Point in ⅝ in. wide at straight base.
C—$4

Small quartzite **arrowhead,** "sugar" or opaque white type, from near Washington, D.C.; 1⅛ in. long. Corner notches are wide and shallow.
C—$4

Corner-notched point, New Jersey, made of a rough material, collected (according to accompanying card) on an archaeological survey as a university project. Point broken near tip.
C—$3

Four smaller sugar quartz **projectile points** or arrowheads from coastal Virginia, average about 1½ in. in length. No damage, but workmanship about average.   D—$2 each

Small white flint **Hardin barbed point,** Illinois, 2¼ in. long and 1¼ in. wide.
G—$50

Quartzite **stemmed point,** from Maine coastal site and probably Archaic period. Point is 1¾ in. long, thick, with short sturdy stem. Rough-chipped due to nature of material.
C—$2

Hopewellian point or blade, 3 in. long, notching fine and medium-depth. Damage to one shoulder tip and one corner of base but very minor. Excellent chipping. A—$20

Corner-notched serrated-edge point, probably Archaic, 1½ in. long, glossy black flint, from Indiana. Well-notched.
C—$17

Paleo period PROJECTILE POINTS from West Texas surface sites, Edwards Plateau flint. Points are 1 in. to 4 in. in length, of following types:
Top row: Clovis, Fishtail Yuma, Fishtail Yuma, Yuma, Yuma.
Middle: Hell Gap, Clovix, Meserve, Plainview, Agate Basin.
Bottom: Folsom, Folsom, Sandia, Sandia, Sandia. $75-$400

Private collection

Unusual prehistoric salvage work: An **Archaic point** of black flint has typical corner notches and serrated edges, measures about 2 in. long. Obverse shows fine percussion and pressure flaking. Reverse has a long channel, averaging ½ in. wide, running from point base to tip. Without doubt, one of the early Paleo-period fluted points was found much later by an Archaic Indian and reworked to present form. Double-worked.   C—$55

Top row, left to right: ASHTABULA-TYPE POINT, dark gray flint.C—$6
CORNER-NOTCHED POINT of blade, black and cream flint. C—$70
CORNER-NOTCHED POINT from Indiana Archaic period site, of translucent pinkish material. Flintridge.   C—$6
Large WHITE CHERT KNIFE, blade from Kansas: stemmed variety, 4¼ in. long. Private collection.   C—$13

STEMMED POINT of blade, well-flaked and thin, of Quitaque flint quarried in the Texas Panhandle. Found in New Mexico. Piece would be more valuable if not for missing portion on right side above shoulder. Point is 2¾ in. long.   C—$45

Photo courtesy of Ralph W. White, Oklahoma

Thin Illinois **side-notched point,** Kramer type, of white flint. Point is 2¾ in. long and 1 in. wide.   G—$14

Small **"birdpoint" arrowhead,** late Woodland or Mississippian period, ⅞ in. long, ½ in. wide, with crisp and well-done basal notches.   C—$5

WESTERN POINTS

Arkansas **Dalton-type point,** deeply basal-notched, edges heavily serrated, perfect condition. Point is 1⅞ in. long, very well proportioned and balanced; basal grinding. C—$65

Very delicate **Northwest coast arrowhead,** translucent red and orange gem point. Point is ⅞ in. long, notched from bottom, with wide stem. Shoulders drop below stem base. Point almost resembles swallow in flight. Excavated find, state of Washington.   D—$40

Frio point from Texas, 2¼ in. long and ¾ in. wide, of pinkish white material.   G—$7

Extra-delicate **Columbia River gem point,** triangular form, reddish translucent chalcedony, square-stemmed; shoulders barbed with tips that extend ⅛ in. below stem. Point is 2¹⁄₁₆ in. long and perfectly symmetrical; also equally attractive obverse and reverse. Perfect condition.   C—$150

Steuben point, of good gray flint, classic shape. It is 2¾ in. long and ⅜ in. wide.   G—$12

SIX FLINT POINTS from a surface site in West Texas, showing long barbs. They are 2 in. to 3 in. long. These are similar to the Calf-Creek points, but have not been named or classified yet in Texas. Archaic period. Five of the points are of Edwards Plateau flint, while middle point, top row, is made of Tecovas jasper.   C—$55-$70

Photo courtesy of Wayne parker, Texas

SMALL SCOTTISBLUFF PALEO POINT, made of brown petrified wood. Material has black streaks and black specs throughout. Artifact has nice form, is of unusual material; it is 2⅛ in. long, from Oklahoma.C—$50-$60

Photo courtesy of Ralph W. White.

Reverse of a fine DALTON-TYPE POINT, found in Adams County, Illinois. Of high-grade white flint, the point is nearly 3 in. long and perfect condition. Point probably dates to the early Archaic, and lasted thousands of years. Age: 7000 BC to about 5000 BC.   C—$150

Photo courtesy of Pat Humphrey Westcentral Illinois.

Oregon arrowhead, chipped from petrified wood, red and yellow striped colors, 1 in. long, stemmed and barbed. Very well chipped. C—$20

Small slightly damaged **Arkansas Dalton,** white and pink material. Piece is 2 in. long and ¾ in. wide. G—$11

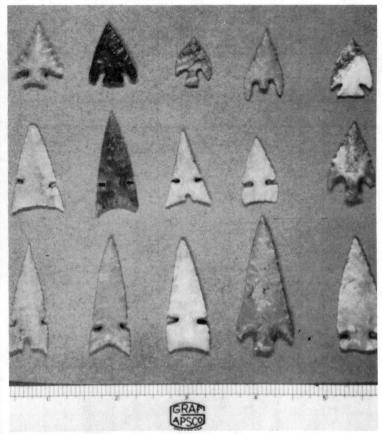

Small ARROWPOINTS from West Texas Surface sites. These are the more common types found in the Panhandle and West Texas. Late prehistoric, they are classified as Scallorn, Harrell, Bonham, Perdiz and Rockwall. C—$30-$75

Photo courtesy of Wayne Parker, Texas.

FLINT DARL POINTS, average length 2¼ in. These were surface finds in central Texas, and are made of Edwards Plateau flint. The points all have right side bevels, and are from the Archaic period. C—$35

Photo courtesy of Wayne Parker, Texas.

Small **Epps point** from Missouri, classic type, and made of gray flint. It is 2 in. long and 1 in. wide. G—$9

Agate arrowhead from Columbia River Valley, beautifully colored and translucent material. Reddish color, 1½ in. long. C—$55

Red **gem point,** Oregon, 1⅛ in. long, stemmed, down-swept shoulders reach same distance as stem base. Very balanced. C—$35

Sandia-type point, heavy-duty and notched on only one side; found by New Mexican rancher in dry cave near arroyo. Point is exactly 2 in. long, rough-made in classic Sandia-II form. C—$120

Two nice **Alba-type Caddo points,** white and gray flint, and averaging 1 in. in length. G—$13

Ornate black **obsidian point,** base deeply indented to "V" shape, high side notches, base ends form curved tangs. Point is 1⅞ in. long, and just over 1 in. wide at tangs. Very symmetrical and perfect condition. C—$40

Side-notched **Godar-type point,** from Arkansas, made of pink flint. It is 2¾ in. long and 1½ in. wide. G—$21

White **Dalton point** from Arkansas, 1¾ in. long and ¾ in. wide, very nice. G—$22

Birfurcated-base **Archaic period point,** reddish obsidian, 2 in. long, corner-notched. About ⅛ in. of tip gone C—$8

Scarce **Hohokam arrowhead,** from Arizona, 2⅞ in. long, made from a white flint. Very narrow, with 3 deep indentations along lower base sides. Condition perfect, fine chipping. C—$80

Hohokam point, 1½ in. long, very narrow, edges deeply serrated and undamaged. C—$60

Dalton-type point, serrated edges, ground base sides and bottom, 1½ in. long, perfect, from Louisiana. C—$33

Clovis-type point, 3 in. long, found in Minnesota, made of a regional chert. Fluted both sides. C—$90

Paleo-period **flint point,** from prehistoric lake (now dried) in Nevada, and 2 in. long, made of a dull chert. Has rounded base, excurvate sides. No damage, but not too artistic. C-$20

Fluted-base Clovis-like point, found in Montana, 2⅜ in. long. Material a colorful, quality chert. Chipping very distinct, flute-channels deep. Said to have come from a "buffalo-jump" site. C—$100

Gem point, of black obsidian, found in Nevada. Corner-notched, bifurcated base. Piece is 2⅞ in. long, translucent, probably Archaic. D—$50

13

Small **obsidian arrowhead,** ¾ in. long, ⅜ in. wide at base, triangular form with no notches. C—$7

Deep-notch Texas **projectile point,** 2¾ in. long, 1¼ in. wide, and of gray flint. G—$14

Brownish **obsidian point,** from northern California, 2 in. long, side-notched. C—$17

Evans point from Yell County, Arkansas; length is 3 in. and width is 1¼ in. pink color, double notches. G—$16

Frame of **arrowheads,** all fine obsidian point from Nevada. They (25) range in length from ½ in. to 2 in. G—$90

Decorative white flint **Texas "birdpoint",** serrated edges, small squared notches, base very concave, length 1 in. and very thin. Made of a glossy red flint with superb chipping. D—$40

Frame of **arrowheads;** frame size 8 in. by 10 in. There are 30 fine obsidian points, with 6 damaged. Range in size from ½ in. long to 2½ in. long. G—$60

Rare **crystal quartz arrowhead,** Arkansas, ¾ in. long and ¼ in. wide. G—$40

Three **Caddo arrow points,** two of novaculite, one of brown chert. Average length is ¾ in. G—$16

Frame of 20 **leaf-shaped arrowheads** from near Twin Falls, Idaho. D—$75

Frame of **arrowheads,** all obsidian, and 21 points. Several styles, and most are perfect. Size range from 1 in. long to 2¼ in. long. G—$110

Clovis-type fluted point, from New Mexico, made of high-quality translucent agate-flint, gray and green, unusual. Point is 2⅞ in. long, has two opposite small nicks on sides, probably from being wired to a frame by early collector. Well-fluted both sides, and very attractive piece. D—$300

Beveled-edge shouldered point, from Iowa, 2½ in. long and 1½ in. wide. G—$25

Fluted Clovis-type point, Oregon, obsidian, fluted on only one side and very thin. Perfect, and 3 in. in length. C—$115

Washington state coastal-site **chalcedony point** or blade, 2¼ in. long, black obsidian, perfectly symmetrical. Shoulder tips even with flatish base, and is diagonally bottom-notched. Regular chipping with very tiny flakes removed. C—$85

CANADIAN POINTS

Frame of 9 **arrowheads** from central Canada, from 1⅛ in. to 2½ in. in length. Most are chipped from a gray flint; all in perfect condition. There are 7 notched types and 2 triangular forms, all probably Woodland and later in time. C—$60

Side-notched point, central Canada, gray flint, 2⅛ in. in length. Archaic period. C—$17

Triangular point, chipped from argillite, from British Columbia, Canada. Piece is 1½ in. long, blackish C—$7

Small **projectile point,** from Saskatchewan, Canada, Paleo period. Unfluted, has the concave base and good chipping; 2⅜ in. long. C—$55

Small-notched point, New Brunswick, Canada, made from a white material, and 2 in. long. Edges are lightly serrated. C—$12

Suggested reading

Bell (& Perino), *Guide to the Identification of Certain American Indian Projectile Points,* Special Bulletins No. 1-4; Oklahoma Anthropological Society, Oklahoma City, Oklahoma.

Folsom, Franklin, *America's Ancient Treasures,* University of New Mexico Press, Albuquerque, 1983.

Basic CLOVIS-TYPE PROJECTILE POINT, a Paleo variety often found around Debert in Nova Scotia. In the opinion of a Canadian researcher, this point would be about 11,000 years old; it may have been picked up and modified by later Amerinds, as the edge serrations help make this a unique point. Piece is 2¼ in. long, and less than ¼ in. thick. C—$115

Photo courtesy of Howard Popkie, Arnprior, Ontario, Canada.

FINE FOLSOM POINT, 2¼ in. long, ⅞ in. wide. Very nicely chipped artifact, as are most Folsoms. From an old Canadian collection in Canada. Folsom points are generally found on the High Plains of Alberta. C—$115

Photo courtesy of Howard Popkie, Arnprior, Ontario, Canada.

CANADIAN PROJECTILE POINT, found at Woodstock, Ontario. Piece is 1¾ in. long, and is a side-notched variety somewhat resembling U.S. Woodland-era points.

C—$8

Photo courtesy of Howard Popkie, Arnprior, Ontario, Canada.

CANADIAN PROJECTILE POINT, found near Dundas. Ontario, Point is 1½ in. long and is probably an Archaic variety. Made of a green flint. C—$8

Photo courtesy of Howard Popkie, Arnprior, Ontario, Canada.

Top, very thin blade with long base, possibly an Adena Waubesa type. It is 2¹⁵⁄₁₆ in. long, from Benton County, TN, and made of Dover flint. Ex-coll. Mark Clark. $30-$50

Bottom: Adena point or blade, with tapered stem, very thin and well-made from Dover flint. From Benton County, TN, and ex-coll. Mark Clark. $200-$250

John M. Maurer collection, Ft. Campbell, Kentucky; photograph by Dan Privett.

CANADIAN POINT or blade, believed to be Archaic but possibly Paleo era, and picked up near Moose Jaw, Sask. Artifact is 2½ in. long, and made of a brown flint or chert. C—$9

Photo courtesy of Howard Popkie, Arnprior, Ontario, Canada.

FRAME OF PREHISTORIC POINTS AND BLADES, plus a design of shell beads. All from Ontario, Canada. Longest piece is just over 3 in. Material priced without frame. C—$400-$600

Photo courtesy Robert C. Calvert, London, Ontario, Canada.

Lanceolate, Late Paleo, from Tuscarawas County, Ohio. Length is 5¾ in. and material is Coshocton flint. This lance has fine parallel percussion flaking and is in fine condition. $300-$400

Alvin Lee Moreland, Corpus Christi, Texas

FRAME OF ARTIFACTS, with small flaked tools and scrapers from prehistoric times, plus clay pipe and fine strand of trade beads. Material priced without frame. C—$125-$150

Photo courtesy of Robert C. Calvert, London, Ontario, Canada.

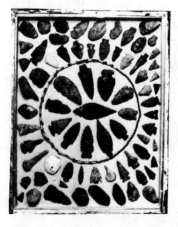

Fine FRAME OF ARTIFACTS, containing prehistoric points and blades, plus French trade beads. Age of chipped artifacts range from Paleo to late Woodland and Mississippian times, and cover some 10,000 years. Material priced without frame. C—$500-$650

Photo courtesy Robert C. Calvert, London, Ontario, Canada.

Rare Cumberland points, pictured elsewhere in book. The left example is Kentucky blue flint and was found in Steward County, Tennessee. $380-$500

Right: Ft. Payne chert, from Montgomery County, Tennessee. $250-$300

John M. Maurer collection, Ft. Campbell, Kentucky; photograph by Dan Privett

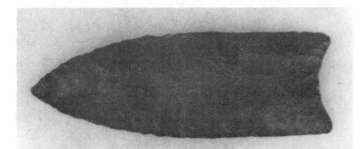

This Clovis point is known as the "Red Cedar Clovis" and is made of oolitic hematite of Canadian origin. It is 1 x 3⅛ in. and is from Barron County, Wisconsin. Until 1987, there was no known Early Paleo material from the county; as a first, this piece has attracted considerable attention.

Mert Cowley collection, Chetek, Wisconsin $500

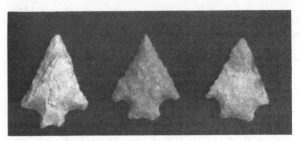

Stanly points or blades, from North Carolina and Virginia. Materials are quartzite and silicified shale. $5 each

Rodney M. Peck collection, Harrisburg, North Carolina

Clovis (Early Paleo) points, all from North Carolina and made from silicified shale. $200-$300 each

Rodney M. Peck collection, Harrisburg, North Carolina

Wisconsin chipped artifacts in colorful materials. Various time periods are represented.   Collection, $225-$350

Robert D. Lund collection, Watertown, Wisconsin

Clovis point (Early Paleo), museum-quality piece, made of brown jasper. It is from Bladen County, North Carolina. $800

Rodney M. Peck collection, Harrisburg, North Carolina

Cumberland point, from the Mammoth Cave region, Kentucky, made of Dover flint. This rare early artifact is 3½ in. long. $1000-$1200

Rodney M. Peck collection, Harrisburg, North Carolina.

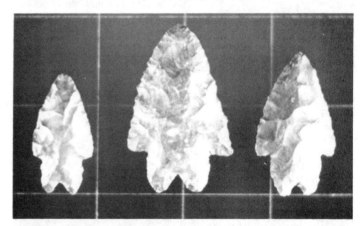

Bifurcated or split-base blades, Early Archaic period, all Ohio. Material is Upper Mercer in several shades of blue. One inch background grid gives scale.   Left: $12-$15
                    Center: $30-$35
Private collection, Ohio   Right: $15-$20

Agate Basin, Late Paleo/Early Archaic, from Pike County, Illinois. This exceptional point or blade is 5¾ in. long and very well-made. $800

L.M. Abbott, Jr. collection, Texas

16

Paleo points, various types.
Left two: multiple flutes, 2¼ in., found by Geoff Ransford in Christian County, Kentucky. $100
Next: Montgomery Co., TN, ex-coll. Clark. $150
Right: unfluted Clovis from Logan County, Kentucky.
$50

John M. Maurer collection, Ft. Campbell, Kentucky; photograph by Dan Privett

Woodland point or blade, possibly a Hopewell variant, 1½ in. long. From Vinton County, Ohio, material is jewel amber-colored translucent Flintridge. $25

Private collection, Ohio.

Adena point or blade, translucent Flintridge, from Washington County, Ohio. At 1½ x 2 1/16 in., the relatively short length for basal size indicates extensive prehistoric resharpening. $35

Private collection, Ohio

Late Paleo / Early Archaic point, a Dalton-Colbert, 2½ in. long. From Benton County, TN, it is thin with heavy basal grinding and with basal thinning. Ex-coll. Mark Clark, this piece is lightly serrated. $150

John M. Maurer collection, Ft. Campbell, Kentucky; photograph by Dan Privett

Fluted points, Paleo period. Left, Redstone fully fluted, dark patinated Dover flint, found by Adrien Boudoin in Todd Co., KY. $550 plus
Right: Redstone-like fluted point, found by Dennis Drugman in Christian Co., Kentucky. The missing ear was salvaged in that area after prehistoric damage. $150

John. M. Maurer collection, Ft. Campbell, Kentucky; photograph by Dan Privett

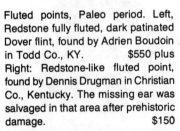

Quad point or blade, Late Paleo / Early Archaic, 3⅛ in. long. It is made of tan flint, is thin, with heavily ground hafting region. From middle Tennessee, it is ex-colls. Clark and Ransford. $300

John M. Maurer collection, Ft. Campbell, Kentucky; photography by Dan Privett

17

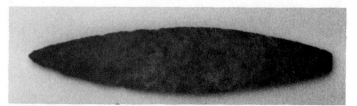

Lanceolate point, Late Paleo, from Hancock County, OH. It is made from Upper Mercer flint, Coshocton variety, in white, gray, blue-black, and with reddish spotting. Size, 1⅜ x 6³⁄₁₆ in.; G.I.R.S. authentication number C88-27. This is one of the largest and finest lances to be found in the state. $1000 plus

Collection of David G. & Barbara J. Shirley

Dalton point or blade, Pike County, IL. At 5½ in., it is made of gray-tan high quality chert. Late Paleo / Early Archaic, this piece has very fine flaking. $400-$500

Alvin Lee Moreland, Corpus Christi, Texas

Points or blades from the Coles Creek culture, Mississippi / Louisiana state line region. These are very high quality artifacts. $15-$100 each

Wilfred A. Dick collection, Magnolia, Mississippi

Expanded-stem point or blade, golden Hixton quartzite, from Barron County, WI. It is ¾ x 1¹³⁄₁₆ in. long. $20-$25

Mert Cowley collection, Chetek, WI.

Cumberland points, Late Paleo period.
Left: small fluted point from Todd County, KY; found by owner. $50
Next: KY blue flint, Steward County, TN, ex-coll. Mark Clark. $380-$500
Next (center): Ft. Payne chert, Montgomery Co., TN, ex-coll. Boudoin. $250-$300
Next: unfluted Cumberland, KY blue flint, western KY, ex-coll. Clark. $125-$175
Right: thin and fully fluted. $50-$100

John M. Maurer collection, Ft. Campbell, KY; photograph by Dan Privett

Late Archaic / Early Woodland point or blade, white Hixton quartzite, from Dunn County, WI. Size is ¹¹⁄₁₆ x 1⅝ in. and type is Durst-stemmed. $15-$18

Mert Cowley collection, Chetek, WI

Late Archaic / Early Woodland point or blade, golden Hixton quartzite, from Barron County, WI. Size is ¾ x 1⅝ in. $15-$20

Mert Cowley collection, Chetek, WI

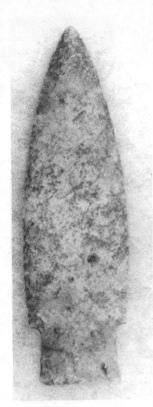

Harrell point, late prehistoric Caddoan, and a classic example. It is from Runnels County, Texas, and 1½ in. long. $50-$75

Grady McCrea collection, Miles, Texas

Known as "The Glacial Lake Scottsbluff", this fine Late Paleo lanceolate has been pictured in the "Creme de la Creme" section of *Indian Artifact Magazine*. This piece is made of chert with crystalline inclusions and was found in northern Wisconsin, rare for the region. Size, 1¼ x 4³⁄₁₆ in. $450-$500

Mert Cowley collection, Chetek, WI

Washita point, late prehistoric Caddoan, found in Runnels County, Texas. Made of translucent gemgrade flint, this piece is 1¼ in. long. $50

Grady McCrea collection, Miles, Texas

Paleo period points and blades. Top to bottom, rows left to right. Clovis, Dover chert, from Tennessee, 5 inches, $500; Clovis, McIntosh County, Oklahoma, 3¾ in., $250; Clovis, Illinois, 3¾ in., $300; Clovis, Taney County, Missouri, 3¾ in., $350; Midland point, Midland, Texas, 2 inches, $150; cast replica of Folsom, Custer County, Oklahoma, Edwards Plateau chert, 2¼ in., original point $450; Folsom, quartzite, Blain County, Oklahoma, 1⅝ in., $450; Clovis, 2¾ in., St. Clair, Illinois, $175; Clovis, McIntosh County, Oklahoma, 2½ in., Boone chert, $150; Center, St. Louis type Clovis, 5¾ in., Hickman County, Kentucky, Indiana hornstone; $650. Folsom, 1¼ in., jasper from Arnold County, Nebraska, $250; Clovis, 3¾ in., Boone County, Illinois, Knife River flint, $650; Cumberland, Hamilton County, Tennessee, 3¼ in., $350; Clovis, Flintridge flint, 2⅞ in., Tuscarawas County, Ohio, $350; Clovis, 3¼ in., Alibates flint, $250; Quad type, Morgan County, Alabama, Fort Payne chert, 2⅜ in., shown in *Story in Stone*, $150; Clovis, 2 in., $100; Clovis, Miami, Texas, 5 in., $500; Clovis, St. Clair, Illinois, 4½ in., $250; Ross County type Clovis, Callaway County, Missouri, $325.

Larry Merriam collection, Oklahoma City, Oklahoma

Dalton points or blades, Late Paleo / Early Archaic period.
Left side top to bottom: Northeast Arkansas, 6½ in., Cherry Hill style, $650; Adams County, Illinois, 6 in., $450; Benton County, Arkansas, 6¼ in., $475; Jefferson County, Missouri, 5 in., $275. Center, Howard County, Missouri, 6¾ in., $650.
Lower center: Cherry Hill Dalton, 5 in. $250.
Right side top to bottom: Pike county, Arkansas, 6⅛ in., $325; Boone County, Missouri, 6 in., $300; Ripley County, Missouri, 6½ in., $650; Saline County, Missouri, 5 in., $350.

Larry Merriam collection, Oklahoma City, Oklahoma

Perdiz point or blade, very thin and with fine flaking. The classic Texas example is 2¾ in. long. $125

Grady McCrea collection, Miles, Texas

Perdiz point, late prehistoric period, from Runnels County, Texas. This specimen is 1½ in. long.
                              $35
Grady McCrea collection, Miles, Texas

Angostura point or blade, Texas, made of Edwards Plateau flint. This very rare specimen has the remains of the original flint nodule or cortex at the base bottom. It is 4 in. long. $400-$750

Grady McCrea collection, Miles, Texas

Lott point, very late prehistoric, with delicate chipping. It is made of Edwards Plateau flint and is 1¾ in. long.
                              $75-$100
Grady McCrea collection, Miles, Texas

20

Obsidian and quartz points, all from Box Elder County, Utah. The small size of these artifacts suggests they may be true arrowheads of later prehistoric times, except for the top center piece which may be older.
Group, $30

Randall Olsen collection, Cache County, Utah

Barber point, Early Archaic, made of unknown material. It is from Upshur County, Texas. $250

L.M. Abbott, Jr. collection, Texas

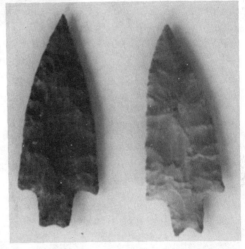

Pontchartrain points made of an unusual material, petrified wood. They are from Angelina County, Texas.
Right: 3 in. $65
Left: 3½ in. $80

L.M. Abbott, Jr. collection, Texas

Meserve point, from Polk County, Texas, 4¼ in. long.
L.M. Abbott, Jr. collection, Texas $275

Darl dart or lance point, Edwards Plateau chert, from Coryell County, Texas. It is 4 in. long. $80

L.M. Abbott, Jr. collection, Texas

Pedernales points, Late Archaic, both made from Edwards Plateau chert. Each is 4¼ in. long. $125 each

L.M. Abbott, Jr. collection, Texas

Pedernales, made of Edwards Plateau flint, from Coryell County, Texas. A good type example, it is 4¼ in. long. $150

L.M. Abbott, Jr. collection, Texas

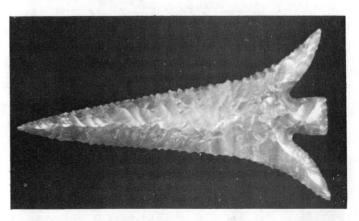

Gunther point, 1 x 1⅞ in., made of Oregon gem material. It is from the Columbia River area, Washington. This is one of the finer Northwest Coast gempoints. $235

Larry Lantz, First Mesa, South Bend, Indiana

Texas points and blades, high-quality flints and cherts, with half a dozen different types represented. There are 192 pieces in the frame.

Individual: $25-$175
Total: $5000

Larry G. Merriam collection, Oklahoma City, Oklahoma

Points or blades from North Dakota, found by Steve Childress and made of Knife River flint. These are high-grade pieces made of a gem material.

Each $35

Larry G. Merriam collection, Oklahoma City, Oklahoma.

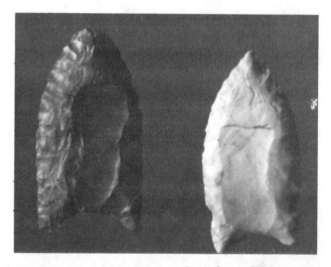

Folsom (Late Paleo) points. Left, from Cedar Creek, Oklahoma, a personal find of the owner. It is 1⅜ in. and made of Edwards chert; found in two pieces. $250

Right: Folsom variant with slight side-notches (may be a newly recognized type) also 1⅜ in. and also found by owner. The material (white) is unknown. $350

Larry G. Merriam collection, Oklahoma City, Oklahoma

Point or blade, Agate Basin of Late Paleo / Early Archaic period. It is made of brown jasper and is 4½ in. long. It came from Platte County, Wyoming $250

Steven D. Kitch collection, Pueblo, Colorado

Point, Hell Gap, Late Paleo / Early Archaic, made of highly patinated Knife River flint. It is 3½ in. long and from Pueblo County, Colorado.$200

Steven D. Kitch collection, Pueblo, Colorado

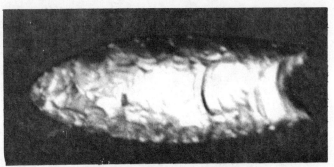

Scottsbluff point or blade, Late Paleo / Early Archaic, Zafala County, Texas. At 4½ in. long, material is a glossy blue-green to gray flint. Flaking is parallel to collateral. $400

Alvin Lee Moreland, Corpus Christi, Texas

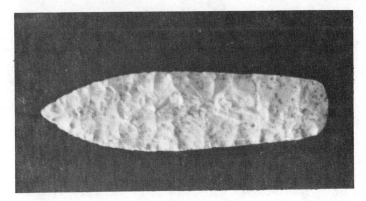

Agate Basin point, Late Paleo / Early Archaic period, made of a gem material, dendritic (branching minerals) jasper. It is 3⅛ in. long and from Saguache County, Colorado. $400

Steven D. Kitch collection, Pueblo, Colorado

Eden point or blade, Late Paleo / Early Archaic, made of a fine translucent amber-brown flint. It has parallel flaking and no damage. This is a scarce type, from Texas. $400

Alvin Lee Moreland, Corpus Christi, Texas

Agate Basin point or blade, Alibates flint, from Baca County, Colorado. Late Paleo / Early Archaic, this fine piece is 3⅛ in. long. $300

Steven D. Kitch collection, Pueblo, Colorado

Scottsbluff point or blade, Late Paleo / Early Archaic, from southern Texas. It is 4³⁄₁₆ inches long and material is pink, cream and red chert. This is a fine piece with oblique and transverse flaking. $250-$350

Alvin Lee Moreland, Corpus Christi, Texas

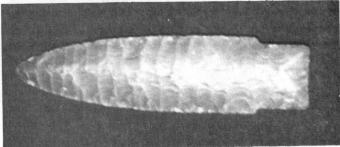

Scottsbluff point or blade, Late Paleo / Early Archaic, from Texas. Material is a brown translucent flint. It has collateral flaking and highly unusual hafting residue. $300-$400

Alvin Lee Moreland, Corpus Christi, Texas

Clovis point or blade, Early Paleo period, from the Council Bluffs area, Iowa. At 3½ in. long, the piece is made from Knife River flint, amber with white cloudy inclusions. It is fluted on both faces, ½ and ⅔ length, respectively.$350-$450

Alvin Lee Moreland, Corpus Christi, Texas

Collection of artifacts from Ontario, Canada, very high quality pieces. Included are three birdstones, a humped adz (top right), a pipe, a gorget, a hafted blade and two Early Paleo Clovis or Clovis-like points.   Unlisted

Robert C. Calvert, London, Ontario, Canada

A fine collection of artifacts from Ontario, Canada. Included are two birdstones (Late Archaic), three pipes, two gorgets, several knives and a pendant.   Unlisted

Robert C. Calvert, London, Ontario, Canada

24

Puye Cliff Dwellings, Santa Clara Indian Reservation, New Mexico. This is a series of cave-like rooms excavated into the canyon wall. Additional ruins are on the mesa top, while the cave-rooms extend for nearly a mile. Puye was settled in the early to mid AD 1500s.

Lar Hothem photo

Interior of Far View Ruins, Mesa Verde National Park, Colorado. The very large structure was made of above and below-ground rooms, carefully walled with fitted stone blocks.

Lar Hothem photo

25

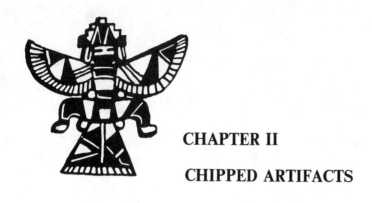

CHAPTER II

CHIPPED ARTIFACTS

Chipping was one, and the first, of the three great prehistoric and early historic tool-shaping methods.

For the first chapter, projectile points were arbitrarily grouped as about 3 in. (75 mm) or under in length. There is some debate in the area, and undoubtedly some of the artifacts listed were actually blades or small knives.

In general, the various other chipped artifacts were made of the same crypto-crystalline materials as were the projectile points. The two requirements seem to have been that the flint or chert chipped well, and had few foreign inclusions, bad spots, to interfere with that chipping.

Some of the value factors for the projectile points are relevant here, like the emphasis on quality material, workstyle, size and condition. There is the added factor of a rare class. There have never been many notched hoes, for example, so an artifact in that category is more highly valued than, say, a crude chopper.

Here, other chipped artifacts are described and listed; there are a number of them, so rather than attempt to introduce and list them all, each sub-group has a brief preface.

Knives or blades are usually medium to large-size chipped tools, apparently used as cutting instruments. They are in many shapes, and no one definition covers them all. If there is a generalization it is that blade edges were more important than the tip; these areas often show minor work-breaks and heavy wear.

Some blades had serrated or saw-tooth edges, while others were sharply angled or beveled. And others had nondescript edge treatment, and may have been multi-purpose knives. The base is usually fairly sturdy, and the distance between notches, or the width of the basal stem, may be an inch (10 cm) or so an average. Other blades do not show specific chipping for hafting, and it is unknown how the handle, if any, was attached.

All the valuation factors mentioned for projectile points apply to symmetrical blades. Length is of special importance, and large authentic pieces command much collector attention. Condition is vital, for larger artifacts are difficult to locate in absolutely perfect form.

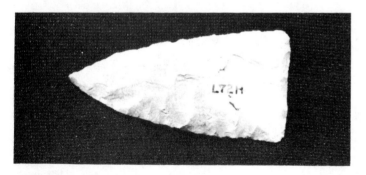

TRIANGULAR BLADE, 3½ in. long and 1½ in. wide at base. This is a very thin piece, ³⁄₁₆ in. thick. Other artifacts found on the same site include a fluted point and an Atlatl weight. Found in southern Tennessee.
C—$45

Photo courtesy of Jim Northcutt, Jr., Corinth, Mississippi.

EASTERN CHIPPED BLADES

Base-notched **translucent blade,** of a high-quality light-transmitting flint, from Florida. Point is 3⅜ in. long, perfect in all details; notches thin and well-made. C—$80

Oval-shaped **cache blade,** unfinished, Indiana. Probably Woodland, 5¼ in. long, 3 in. wide, gray flint. D—$21

Osceola blade, Illinois, made of a reddish and white high-grade flint. Piece is nearly 6 in. long, about 2¼ in. wide; colors form artistic pattern. Only slight original wear shows on blade sides; base fully ground. No damage. D—$495

Side-notched blade, probably Archaic, small but deep notches put in about ½ in. from base bottom. Sides are about straight, and then incurvate to tip. Blade is 4½ in. long. A—$80

Archaic **bifurcated-base blade,** blue-gray flint, 3½ in. in length, 1½ in. wide. Base bottom is indented to same degree as corner notches. Small side serrations. A—$40

Large **Dovetail or St. Charles blade,** damage to one corner of base, otherwise fine condition and just under 5 in. A good specimen for restoration. A—$165

Dovetail of Carter Cave flint, Kentucky, 5 in. long, and 1¾ in. wide. G—$75

Large **blade** or knife, uncertain period, may be Archaic. Base-stemmed, with base bottom slightly incurvate. Blade sides are slightly excurvate, serrated edges. Piece is 6¼ in. long. A—$265

PROBLEMATICAL ARTIFACTS, from Prentis County, Mississippi. Largest piece in photos is 1 in. by 2 in. Over 100 have been found on just one village site, and have been associated with Benton points. These seem to have once been blades or points, were broken, and then were smoothed on all sides and faces. These are not water-worn, but abrasion or smoothing was intentional.

C—No value listed.

Photo courtesy Jim Northcutt, Jr., Corinth, Mississippi.

SERRATED EDGE BLADE, 1½ in. wide and 3 in. long, Mississippian period and found in southcentral Tennessee. Base with missing corner has been ground smooth and cutting edges clearly show retouching or resharpening.

C—$16

Photo courtesy Retha D. Northcutt, Corinth, Mississippi.

Quartzite **blade,** Pennsylvania, 7 in. long.   D—$50

Serrated blade, found in Ohio near West Lafayette in 1953 on site that produced Archaic and Woodland periods material. Piece is 3⅛ in. long, wide-stemmed, thin, of red and white flint. Extremely fine chipping, glossy surface, no wear.   C—$80

Pentagonal blade, 3¼ in. long, made of Ohio Flintridge multicolored material. Small section missing from one barbed shoulder, hardly noticeable.   D—$26

Hopewellian point or **blade,** Kentucky, 3⅞ in. long, 2⅛ in. wide, of a glossy black flint. Perfect.   D—$85

Large **Adena blade,** Woodland period, made of a fine light-colored flint, and 5½ in. long, 2⅛ in. wide at shoulders; well stemmed. Slight damage to one corner of stem, small nick from one side halfway to point tip, possible equipment strike.   A—$120

Barb-shouldered **blade,** of high quality, from Alabama. Probably Archaic, and found on site that has produced such artifacts. Piece is 3½ in. long, perfect condition.   C—$35

Archaic **beveled-edge blade,** symmetrical, of a mixed dark and light brown flint in pleasing bands. Notches deep and regular, base well-notched and edges ground. Perfect, and 4½ in. long.   A—$250

Fine leaf-shaped **Adena cache blade,** of translucent Flintridge material. About 6 in. long by 3 in. wide. A—$225

Ashtabula-type blade, of a gray, nondescript flint, 4⅞ in. long, and from Indiana.   C—$75

Expanded-notch or **E-notch blade,** 3⅛ in. long, perfect, from Illinois. Edges worn but overall good lines.   C—$65

Alabama **blade,** whitish chert, 5¼ in. long, side-notched. Shaped solely by percussion flaking, no edge retouch.   C—$40

Dovetail or St. Charles blade, exceptional piece, large and perfect. Piece is 5¾ in. long, 3 in. wide, no damage anywhere. Basal notches deep, base edges ground. Made of translucent multi-hued Flintridge material; from an old collection.   A—$500

Blade, from New Jersey, chipped from black chert and 4 in. long. Leaf-shaped, no edge retouch, average workstyle.   C—$12

Archaic **beveled-edge blade,** finely chipped base with deep notches; 5¾ in. long, and surface is nicely patinated to a pale cream. Damage: About ½ in. missing from tip, exposing lighter-colored interior. As is, a superb example of prehistoric flint-knapping. Easily restored.   C—$235

Fluted **Clovis-like blade,** Florida, from a black high-grade material. Point is 3⅜ in. long, deeply fluted both sides, perfect, ground basal edges.   C-$135

Large **Turkey-tail blade,** light gray shade of Indiana hornstone flint, found in West Virginia. Blade may have once been part of cache or underground deposit of artifacts, as accompanying card in old-style handwriting states "1 of 13". Blade is 5⅛ in. long.   C—$175

Tennessee **blade,** triangular, beveled edges, no stem or notches. Piece is 5¼ in. long.   A—$90

Fluted point from lower Michigan. 4⅛ in. long, made of black Coshocton County (Ohio) flint. Average wear on all sides, base not ground, no damage. Fluting channels extend for approximately 2 in. up both base sides. D—$295

Five FLINT CORES, the portion remaining after thin flake knives have been knocked off. Highest grade Ohio Flintridge material, very colorful and glossy. Per each. C—$9
Private collection.

Left to right, rough-chipped FLINT CELT, age unknown. Midwestern; about 6 in. in height. C—$12
Rough-chipped FLINT AXE, age unknown. Midwestern; about 7 in. in height. Some collectors feel these may be of Paleo origin, but proof is lacking. C—$18
Private collection

WESTERN CHIPPED BLADES

Corner-notched blade, base excurvate and well-ground, sides deeply serrated, Archaic period. Artifact is 3½ in. long, well balanced, both sides or faces equally good. From Iowa. A—$115

Shouldered blade from Arkansas, 3½ in. long, blue-white flint. G—$13

Chipped **obsidian blade,** from Santa Catalina Island, southern California cultural area, and 4⅛ in. long. Leaf-shaped and undamaged; unusual locale. C—$80

Kansas flint blade, unusual form, 2¹⁵⁄₁₆ in. long. Large side notches halfway between tip and base; base bottom deeply indented (bifurcated) which gives blade a tri-notched appearance. Damage to one side near tip minor. C—$45

Unusual blade, certainly Paleolithic period, non-fluted piece of a superior flint, origin unknown. Found in Oklahoma in 1972 by a camper. Point is 3⅜ in. long, and expands from a forked base about 1 in. wide and very thin. Chipping, especially pressure retouch, is regular and excellent. Type not mentioned in any of the standard reference works; may be regional sub-variant. C—$230

Corner-tang blade from Oklahoma Panhandle region, lower blade slightly excurvate, 4⅛ in. long, larger than usual for type. Notching is deep, remaining section forms triangular stem, yellowish flint of unknown quarry site. D—$175

Eden-type blade, 4⅛ in. long, evidencing parallel flaking, gray flint. Found in a wind-erosion "blowout", Nebraska, in 1951. Perfect condition, flint high grade, well made. C—$375

Sedalia-type blade, Missouri, squared base, excurvate sides tapering to very sharp tip. Piece is 8⅛ in. long, widest measurement is 2¼ in. from the tip. Pale white chertish material, and excellent chipping overall. Perfect condition. C—$325

Plains-Midwestern (?) **concave-conves sided blade,** resembling a dagger. Piece 7¼ in. long, 1⅜ in. wide at squared base. Haft area incurvate; working edges excurvate. This type of flint artifact is not often found intact due to size and brittle nature of flint. Perfect condition. C—$475

Leaf-shaped blade, Woodland period, of mottled white and dark flint. Not notched or stemmed. Base casually rounded, blade presents an ovate appearance. Piece is 5½ in. long. A—$140

Wide-shouldered **point or blade,** wide stem, whitish flint, possibly Woodland and resembles Snyder type. Exactly 3 in. long. C—$33

Chumash **point or blade,** diamond-shaped, 3½ in. long, of a low-grade material. From southern California, site on coast, excavated find. D—$17

Pedernales-type blade, from central Texas, with sharply indented base and sharply barbed shoulders, edges finely serrated. Perfect condition, and 3¼ in. long. C—$130

Large **obsidian blade,** 9¼ in. long, 2⅛ in. wide at base near small corner notches. Backside of knife straight-edge, working edge convex and mild wear shows authenticity. Excavated from early Colorado site. D—$220

Late Paleo **lanceolate blade,** chert, Colorado, good form but material not of best quality. Piece is 4⅞ in. long. A—$27

Large 6 in. **cache blade,** ovate, rough, found in northern Georgia and made of gray Indian hornstone. Part of a deposit of over 50 blades said to have been found by a fisherman along a river. C—$44

ANGULAR KNIFE, left, 2¼ in. (5.5 cm) by 4½ in. (11.5 cm). Archaic period. Flint is blue-black and condition is perfect.   C—$15

DOVETAIL BLADE, right, 1⅜ in. (3.5 cm) by 2½ in. (6.0 cm) long. Archaic period and with heavy basal grinding. Blue-black flint with white and gray mottling; Dovetails are increasingly rare finds.   C—$75

Photo courtesy of Mark Hersman, Lucas, Ohio.

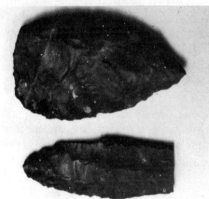

CACHE BLADE, top, 3½ in. (9.0 cm) in length, made of black flint with gray flecks; probably a Woodland-era piece.   C—$17

DOUBLE-FLUTED PALEO POINT, 3⅛ in. (8.0 cm) long, made of brown-black flint and with lateral grinding. Basal section broken.   C—$18

Photo courtesy of Mark Hersman, Lucas, Ohio.

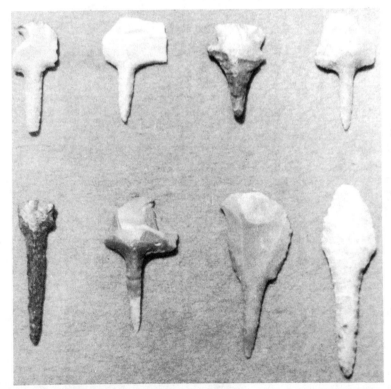

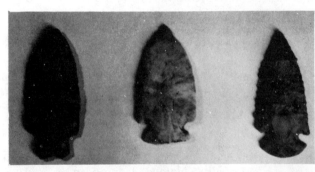

Three Midwestern blades; left. HEAVY-DUTY blade 3¼ in. long, of black Coshocton flint, one minor area of damage in left side, otherwise fine.   C—$35

LARGE BLADE, probably Woodland and late prehistoric, perfect, edges worn.   C—$35

Midwestern BEVEL-EDGE BLADE, quality gray flint, serrated edges. One tip of left shoulder missing, minor damage, could be restored. Basal area heavily ground.   C—$65

Private collection

Eight FLINT DRILLS, from different sections of Texas. Archaic and late prehistoric periods. They range in length from 1¼ in. to 3 in.   C—$35-$55 each

Photo courtesy of Wayne Parker, Texas.

Very fine and CLASSIC CLOVIS POINT, made of Edwards Plateau flint. Point is 3½ in. long, and dates from early Paleo times. 10,000 to 15,000 BC.   C—$500

Photo courtesy of Wayne Parker collection.

Pink **novaculite blade,** from Arkansas, 3¼ in. long.
G—$27

Obsidian blade, excurvate sides with ends nearly identical, duo-tipped, from Washington state. Exactly 4½ in. long.
A—$38

Base-notched point or **blade,** Missouri, white flint and 7¾ in. in length. It is 2¼ in. wide at shoulder tips, same measurement at expanded sides near tip. Finely chipped, with flake removal regular and consistent. Perfect.C—$500

Large **flint blade,** extreme western Midwest, unknown period but probably Archaic because of fine edge retouching and basal grinding and serrated edges. Resembles a cross between Godar and Gravel Kame types; 6⅜ in. long, notches deep and perfectly matching. Inside of notching heavily ground, bottom of base not. C—$600

Large **duo-tipped blade,** Oregon, and piece is 9⅝ in. long. Obsidian of a reddish hue, and surface find from beach area that has produced late Paleo and early Archaic materials. Rather thick, but good chipping. C—$195

Black **obsidian blade,** Nevada, 4½ in. long, 1 in. wide at mid-length. Concave base, side-notched, and very symmetrical blade. Notches narrow and shallow. C—$95

Large and **wide blade,** 3½ in. long, 1¾ in. wide, ovate, no notches or stem, well-chipped. C—$17

Long Missouri **Dalton-type blade,** white flint, smooth edges, 3¼ in. long. One minor chip from blade edge; easily and quickly restored with minimum of detraction from form.
D—$37

Base-notched blade, 3½ in. long, from Oregon. Reddish flint of good quality. Notches ¼ in. deep. D—$18

CANADIAN CHIPPED BLADES

Obsidian blade found in British Columbia, Canada, 4⅞ in. long, 1⅜ in. wide, and leaf-shaped. Perfect. C—$65

Diamond-shaped blade, of pinkish chert, from Canada's Great Slave Lake region. Believed to be very early, possibly Paleo, edges worn and never resharpened (rechipped). Blade is 3⅝ in. in length. C—$10

Large **argillite blade,** made of the black material that can be both carved and chipped. From western Canada, 7½ in. long. C—$33

Flaked blade, British Columbia, Canada, made of a light chert-like material. Blade is 7¾ in. long and leaf-shaped.
C—$65

Chalcedony blade, 3⅜ in. long, found in southwestern British Columbia, Canada, and gem quality. Basal notched.
C—$100

Knife **blade,** from Nova Scotia, Canada, 4¼ in. long, made from quartzite. Found on coastal site, middle Archaic period. Rough-chipped but with good overall form.C—$15

Fluted Paleo point or **blade,** from central Canada near Regina, made of fine-grained quartz. Piece is 4⅛ in. long, perfect, with flutes extending over 1 in. (25mm) on both base sides. Good form, but rough due to average-quality material. C—$75

Agate Basin type PALEO POINT, found in Adams County, Illinois, in 1975. Piece is 4¼ in. long and ⅞ in. wide, and evidences very fine flaking and good basal grinding.
C—$400-$600

Photo courtesy of John P. Grotte, Illinois.

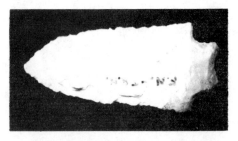

PROJECTILE POINT, 1¼ in. wide and 3 in. long, from Tennessee. Point is probably a Benton type, and 1000-2000 BC. Perfect condition. C—$25-$40

Photo courtesy Flint Na Mingo Northcutt, Corinth, Mississippi.

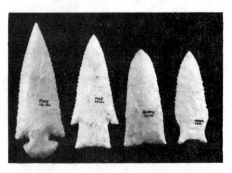

Four blades or points, all from Illinois: left to right:
DOVETAIL (St. Charles) BLADE
C—$300-$500

HARDIN BARB with fine serrated edges
C—$250

PLAINVIEW variant   C—$85
DALTON POINT   C—$110

Photo courtesy of Pat Humphrey, westcentral Illinois.

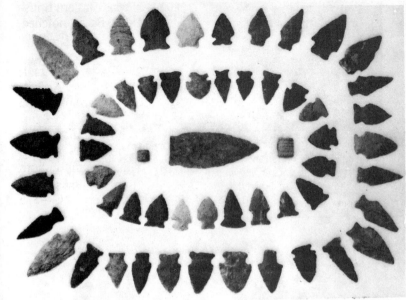

A nice FRAME OF PROJECTILE POINTS, ranging in length from 1 in. to 2¼ in. These range in time from Archaic to Mississippian times, although long point or blade in center may be late Paleo. All found in Pennsylvania; material is flint, rhyolite, jasper, quartz and chalcedony.
C—$200 frame

Photo courtesy of Jonas Yoder, Jr., McVeytown, Pennsylvania

From left to right:

PROJECTILE POINT OR BLADE, 3¼ in. long and 1 in. wide. Very detailed chipping, dark red and white material. Somewhat resembles Paleo points but may be early Archaic. Found in Tishomingo County, Mississippi near the (future) Tennessee-Tombigbee Waterway.
C—$30

Fine HARDIN BARBED POINT or blade, found in Pike County, Illinois. Note the fine and regular serrations on both edges, and the excellent symmetry.
C—$250

Photo courtesy of Pat Humphrey westcentral Illinois.

A very fine CORNER-TANG KNIFE of blade, found in Texas County, Oklahoma. It was made from a blue-gray Alibates flint and is larger than average for the type. The blade is 3¾ in. long.
C—$400

Photo courtesy of Ralph W. White, Oklahoma.

CHIPPED DRILLS

Drills have been used in North America for at least 10,000 years, and fine specimens have been found on many late-Paleo sites. They range in length from ½ in. to specimens over 4 in., though the longer types are rare.

This particular tool was used to make holes in bone, shell, hard-stone, banded slate, wood and rock crystal. Drills were turned with fingers, attached to a rod and twirled between the palms, and secured below the flywheel of the bow-turned drill-set. Because they are long and slender they are fairly fragile, and perfect artifacts of this type command a premium.

Small **drill,** 1¼ in., from Maine. Side-notched, and chipped from a white flint. Perfect condition.
C—$13

Large ceremonial **drill,** 4¼ in. long, "T"-shaped top, said to have been a mound recovery in northern Kentucky. Adena or Hopewell periods. Made of a black, glossy flint with thin "lightning" streaks of white. No signs of wear or use.
C—$425

Cylindrical **drill** from southern Canada, 2¼ in. long, made from a brown flint. Tip worn from use, but perfect. C—$18

Flint **drill,** American southwest, 1½ in. long, of a good flint; perfect condition, base notched.
D—$16

Flint **drill,** 3 in. long, wide base and drill-shaft thin and very well chipped. Pink-white material, glossy. C—$55

Drill from Missouri, oval base with flaring barbs, and 2⅞ in. long.
G—$11

Fine flint **drill,** "T"-shaped top, dark flint of good quality, and 3½ in. long. Found in Illinois.
C—$36

Miniature flint **drill,** just under 1 in. long, with notched base. From Oklahoma.
A—$9

Fine **drill** of multicolored Flintridge material, translucent, 3⅛ in. long. Very fine chipping, no damage. D—$130

Rounded-top **drill,** 2⅜ in. long, well-chipped. C—$15

Flint **drill,** made from an earlier Paleo point, with basal flute still extending on both sides of drill base. Rare. Drill is just 3 in. (75mm) long. Yellow-white material, perfect.
C—$75

Small flint **drill,** cylindrical form, 1½ in. long, tip shows considerable wear.
C—$11

Drill, 2⅛ in. long, wide-notched base, perfect.
C—$13

Drill, Kentucky Carter Cave flint, 1⅞ in. long, with wide base. Found in central Indiana; possibly Woodland-era.
C—$27

Quartzite **drill,** North Carolina, probably Archaic and 1¾ in. long. Roughly notched at base.
D—$7

Early **drill,** found in southern Michigan on site that has produced Aqua-Plano material, about 7-8000 BC. Drill is 3⅝ in. and with a narrow "T"-shape top, ⅜ in. wide. Exceptionally fine chipping, extremely smooth and glossy surface. Balanced.
C—$240

OTHER CHIPPED ARTIFACTS

Scrapers, for hide preparation, and perforators, for piercing materials, and gravers, for scoring bone — all are frequent finds on early Amerind sites. There is, however, not much market activity for such artifacts, and most would fall in the five-dollar range or below. They are, nonetheless, excellent examples of the daily prehistoric lifeway; tools reflect the times.

CHIPPED SPADES

A generally large artifact, spades typically have a smaller often squared end, and a larger, heavier end with the semblance of a digging blade. Other than traditional value factors, such as size and shape and material, collectors value more highly spade examples with heavy use-polish on the working blade edge. The better the polish the more desired is the object — at least to many Midwestern collectors. Most spades, and hoes, are from this region.

Spade, 8 in. long and 5 in. wide, with outstanding bit polish; fine example.
D—$200

Illinois **spade,** from St. Clair County, Illinois, 11¼ in. long and 4¼ in. wide.
G—$350

Spade, from Schuyler County, Illinois, 11½ in. long and 4½ in. wide.
G—$300

Unusual shovel-nose type **spade,** with well-shaped bit and heavy polish. Piece is 8½ in. long, 5½ in. wide. G—$250

Spade over 7 in. long, from Jefferson County, Missouri.
D—$125

UNFLUTED CLOVIS-TYPE PALEO POINT, made of a fine quality brown flint; a purple stripe runs from near the base almost to the tip. Piece is 4½ in. long and 1⅜ in. wide at shoulders. A very colorful point, it was found in Pike County, IL.
C—$425

Photo courtesy John P. Grotte, Illinois

Paleo-period point converted in prehistoric times to a BEVELED-EDGE KNIFE. Blade is made of blue banded Alibates flint, and is from the neo-American period, 900-1300 AD. Blade is 3½ in. long and well-chipped.
C—$90

Photo courtesy of Wayne Parker Collection.

BEVELED BLADE, four edges and in diamond shape. It is of a reddish Alibates (?) flint and large for the type. Blade is 6 in. long, while average size is closer to 2½ in. or 3 in. Found in Texas County, Oklahoma. One shoulder has some battering, but minor.
C—$200

Photo courtesy Ralph W. White, Oklahoma.

LARGE CLOVIS-TYPE POINT or blade, made of a light gray quartzite, fine-grained material. Beautifully flaked point is 4⅝ in. long, and from New Mexico. Basal edges are heavily ground as is common for the type.
C—$375

Agate Basin type PALEO POINT, found in Adams County, Illinois, in 1974. It is 4³⁄₁₆ in. long and 1 in. wide, and displays superb workmanship and fine flint-knapping. It would be from the late Paleo or Early Archaic period.
C—$450

Private collection

Four BEVELED-EDGE KNIVES from Texas, and 4 in. to 6 in. in length. These date from AD 900-1300, and came from a Panhandle Pueblo site.
C—$175-$300

Photo courtesy of Wayne Parker, Texas

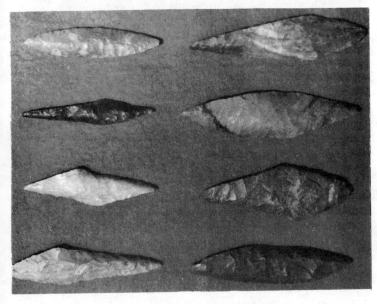

EIGHT BEVELED KNIVES, from South Texas Plains region, and from 3½ x 4½ in. in length. Left column, all of Edwards Plateau flint. Right, column, top to bottom: Alibates flint, Alibates flint, Tecovas jasper, Edwards Plateau flint. All were surface finds, from late prehistoric times.
C—$175-$300

Photo courtesy of Wayne Parker, Texas

Large and fine flint **spade,** 13 in. long and 5¾ in. wide at curved bit; good polish in blade region. Some small damage to spade base in handle attachment region, minor.
D—$350

Good Arkansas **spade,** 9 in. long and 5¼ in. wide, made from a brown chert. Has polished bit.
G—$200

Very fine **spade,** with extra-heavy polished bit. Piece is 12 in. long and 4⅝ in. wide; found in Hickman County, Kentucky.
G—$500

Oval-type **spade,** good polish, fine condition, measuring 8¼ in. long and 5½ in. wide.
G—$195

Flint **spade,** very thin and with good polish, 9¼ in. long and 5 in. (12.5cm) wide.
G—$250

Polished flint **spade,** from Missouri, not too thin but nice; piece is 7¼ in. long and 4¼ in. wide.
G—$95

Extra-long unnotched flint **spade,** from eastern Missouri, and 14 in. in length. Very thin, fine chipping, good polish.
C—$450

Shovel-nose **spade,** Missouri, 7½ in. long, just under 5 in. in width. Heavily used, some breaks on working edge.
C—$90

CHIPPED HOES

Compared to spades, hoes tend to be smaller, and many varieties have notched bases for a right-angle handle attachment. Bit polish adds to value, as does blade thinness and traditional factors of size, workstyle and quality of material. Late prehistoric, and generally used with the development of agriculture and permanent village sites.

Small **hoe (?)** from eastern Ohio, fine-grade blue-white flint, made from a very large flake. Piece is 4¼ in. wide and 3½ in. high, with no prominent notches. Well pressure-flaked around all four sides and edges.
C—$24

Large notched **hoe,** from Tennessee, 7½ in. long and 5½ in. wide.
G—$2000

Square-back **hoe,** from Arkansas, 5½ in. long 2½ in. wide; made from a pink chert.
G—$65

Fine notched flint **hoe,** from Missouri, 6 in. long and 3⅞ in. wide, highly polished blade area. Made from a pink and brown glossy flint; thin, good workstyle.
C—$215

Hoe, with polished working edge, 5¼ in. long and 4¼ in. wide. Good quality black flint, notched at base.
C—$110

Brown flint **hoe,** not notched, but upper portions are narrowed, 5⅛ in. long, 3¼ in. wide, Midwestern.
C—$90

Ornate white flint **hoe,** strangely notched with two shallow notches at top sides, one at top center. Piece is 5½ in. long, well made, with use-polish on bit.
C—$285

OTHER CHIPPED TOOLS

Flint **spud,** (sharp, narrow spade) classic shape and with wide flaring bit, much polish. From Union County, Illinois, it is 9 in. long and 4 in. wide.
G—$500

Flaked **celt** (ungrooved axe) Arkansas, 3½ in. long, good shape.
G—$30

Duo-bladed flint **axe,** 6 in. long, blades semicircular with nice curves, flint unremarkable. Percussion chipping average; large notches in sides, no blade polish, unknown period.   C—$35

Cache of 15 **digging tools,** average length 3½ in. all made of white and gray flint.   D—$70

Unusual **eccentric flint** chipped in the form of a half moon. Piece is 1 in. long and ½ in. wide, authentic.   G—$15

Fine polished flint **spud,** from Johnson County, Illinois. Made of white flint, 8 in. long, and 3½ in. wide. It has the flared bit and polished for entire length.   G—$600

Flaked **celt,** from Missouri; 5 in. long and 3 in. wide, made from brown flint.   G—$30

Flint **celt,** white flint, very good lines; 5 in. long, 2⅛ in. wide, no damage. Polish over the entire surface that has largely obliterated original chipping scars.   C—$200

Suggested Reading:

Whiteford, Andrew H.; *North American Indian Arts,* Western Publishing Co., Inc., New York, 1970.

FLARED-BIT SPADE, made of brown Mill Creek tabular flint. It is 8⅜ in. long and 5⅜ in. wide at bit. Found in Madison County, Illinois, it may be Cahokian, from the Mississipian period.   C—$450

Photo courtesy of John P. Grotte, Illinois.

DRILL, chipped from black flint, and 3 in. in length, 1¼ in. wide at notch protrusions. This would be late prehistoric, probably Woodland. Found in Mifflin County, Pennsylvania.   C—$90

Photo courtesy of Jonas Yoder, Jr., McVeytown, Pennsylvania.

Three very interesting FLARED-BIT SPADES, with large central specimen over 3 in. wide at top, over 5 in. wide at bottom. It is 9 in. long, and all have heavily polished bits. These were part of the largest CACHE of spades ever found. There were 108 specimens; they were found in 1971, in Pointset County, Arkansas. C—$350-$600

Photo courtesy of Pat Humphrey, Westcentrl Illinois.

OVAL-BIT SPADE of tabular flint, with markings indicating Muskatine County, Iowa, as the source. It is Mississippian culture, and found rather far north for the type. Heavy use polish on rounded blade.   C—$125-$150

Photo courtesy of Pat Humphrey. Westcentral Illinois.

Large FLINT SPADE, made of a brown Mill Creek tabular flint, and is from the Mississippian culture and period. Piece is 11½ in. long and 4¾ in. wide; it was found in Madison County, Illinois.   C—$100-$175

Photo courtesy of John P. Grotte, Illinois.

Fine SPADE OR HOE, 8¾ in. long and 4 in. greatest width. From the Mississippian culture, it is highly polished for nearly half of length. Spade is made of a conglomerate that is pink, gray and yellow in color. C—$125-$200

Photo courtesy of Jim Northcutt, Jr., Corinth, Mississippi.

SANDSTONE SPADE or agricultural implement, 8½ in. long and 4½ in. wide. Piece was rough-flaked into form; found in Mifflin County, Pennsylvania. This may be a Woodland-era object. C—$35

Photo courtesy of Jonas Yoder, Jr., McVeytown, Pennsylvania.

TWO POLISHED HOES, each 3¼ in. by 7½ in. in size. Example on left contains a visible seashell fossil at the top right and center of back side. C—$125-$200

Photo courtesy of Bob Brand Collection, Pennsburg, Pennsylvania.

Paleo points and blades, Late Paleo period.

Top row, tips downward, left to right: Pike county type, 4¼ in., $225; Agate Basin, 4 in., Maury County, Tennessee, $250; Plainview, from Kansas, 3⅝ in., $200; Allen, colorful material, High Plains region, 3⅜ in., $375; Eden made of Knife River flint, Cody, Wyoming, 3½ in., $225; Beaver Lake, $3½ in., from Illinois, $275.

Second, semicircular row, tips upward, left to right: Holland type, from Missouri, 3¾ in., $225; Agate Basin, 4⅛ in., Illinois, $200; Scottsbluff, from Missouri, 5¼ in., $275; Agate Basin, from Illinois, 5⅞ in., $450; Paleo knife, 6¾ in., St. Charles county, Missouri, $300; Scottsbluff, Pike County, Illinois, 5½ in., $375; Eden, from McIntosh County, Oklahoma, 5½ in., $475; Eden, 5 in., from Cherokee County, Oklahoma, $350; Eden, 4½ in., from the Arkansas-Louisiana-Texas region, nice piece, $450.

Bottom center piece, Agate Basin or Eastern lanceolate, Marion County, Ohio, 4¾ in., $300.

Larry Merriam collection, Oklahoma City, Oklahoma

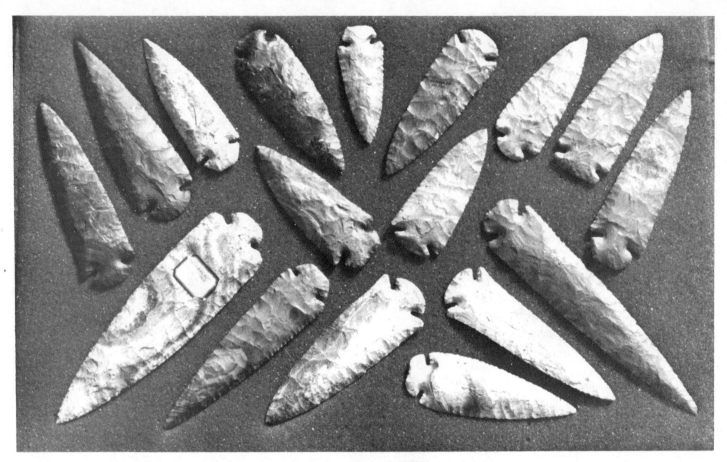

Dovetail or St. Charles blades, mainly Midwestern. Three points or blades upper left corner, lower left to upper right: Black flint, provenance unknown, $500; chert, from Tennessee, 5 in., $250; light material, from Howard County, Missouri, 3¾ in., $150.

Lower left corner, left to right: Small-base or button-tang Dovetail, Putnam County, Indiana, $700; Kentucky, 5¼ in., $275; St. Clair County, Illinois, $475.

Upper right corner three blades, left to right: Flintridge, Ross County, Ohio, 3⅜ in., $250; chert, 4¼ in., Callaway County, Missouri, unlisted; beveled-edge blade, 4⅞ in., Kentucky, $250.

Lower right corner, top to bottom: Chert Dovetail from Tennessee, 6⅞ in., $750; Clark County, Arkansas, 4¾ in., $275; Greene County, Missouri, 4⅛ in., $250.

Five blades, clockwise from top center: Cooper County, Missouri, 3 in., $150; Schuyler County, Illinois, 4⅜ in., $350; Pike County, Missouri, 3½ in., $225; St. Louis County, Missouri, 4 in., $275; Upper mercer flint, Ross County, Ohio, 4¼ in., $325.

Larry Merriam collection, Oklahoma City, OK

Early Archaic Dovetail or St. Charles blade, large-base type, made of very colorful Flintridge material. It is from Ohio and 5 in. long. Dovetails have long been one of the most collectible of early flint types.

Museum quality

Bill & Margie Koup collection, Albuquerque, New Mexico; Bill Koup photograph.

Very early type points and blades. Daltons are from MO, IL, KY, TN and FL. $75-$250 each
Decatur, top center, KY. $150
Greenbriar, second from top on right, Tennessee. $100
Scale, bottom center 4 in.

Pocotopaug Trading Post, South Windsor, Connecticut

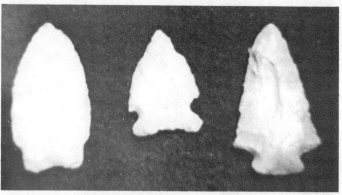

Early Woodland blades, various regions, all left to right:
Cresap Adena, Union Co., Ohio $100
Robbins blade, Upper Mercer material, Meigs Co., Ohio

$175
Robbins, Delaware Co., Ohio $200
Waubesa Adena, Shuyler Co., IL $500
Marion, agatized coral, central Florida, 6⅜ in. $800
Pocotopaug Trading Post, South Windsor, Connecticut

Flint blades, all Eastern Midwest, the three in lighter shades of material. Example on left is about 2½ in. long. The three, $35-$55
Private collection

Alamance point or blade, Late Paleo / Early Archaic period, made of silicified shale. It is from Alamance County, North Carolina. $200

Rodney M. Peck collection, Harrisburg, North Carolina

Point or blade, Hardaway-Dalton and Late Paleo / Early Archaic. It is made of silicified shale and is a scarce very early type. This piece is from Moore County, North Carolina. $200

Rodney M. Peck collection, Harrisburg, North Carolina

Hardaway side-notched point or blade, Late Paleo / Early Archaic period, from Union County, North Carolina. It is made of silicified shale. $100

Rodney M. Peck collection, Harrisburg, North Carolina

Hardaway-Dalton point or blade, Late Paleo / Early Archaic, from Stanly County, North Carolina. It is made of silicified shale. $100

Rodney M. Peck collection, Harrisburg, North Carolina

Morrow Mountain point or blade, Middle Archaic period, from Virginia. $150-$200

Rodney M. Peck collection, Harrisburg, North Carolina

Dovetail or St. Charles blade with probable shoulder notching, from Ohio. Material is an attractive Flintridge in gray translucent chalcedony with dark blue tip and blue streak. Size is 1⅜ in. x 3¾ in., exceptionally thin. G.I.R.S. authentication number C889-19. $700

Collection of David G. & Barbara J. Shirley

Turkeytail or Red Ochre blade from the Early Woodland, black to dark gray and tan Indiana hornstone. It is very thin and measures 1¾ x 4¹³⁄₁₆ in. It is ex-coll. Dean Driskill. $1500

Collection of David G. & Barbara J. Shirley

Dovetail or St. Charles blade, from Montgomery County, Ohio. It is made of Coshocton flint in gray, tan and black and is 1¹¹⁄₁₆ x 4⅝ in. Ex-coll. Wachtel, it has G.I.R.S. authentication number C88-17. $700

Collection of David G. & Barbara J. Shirley

Turkeytail (Red Ochre) blade from the Early Woodland, 1¾ x 5¹⁄₁₆ in., long. Made of blue Indiana or Kentucky hornstone, this came from Marion County, Indiana. This is a very fine piece, with all Turkeytail characteristics desired. Ex-colls. Cline and Cameron Parks. $475

Private collection, Ohio

Archaic blade, concave-base corner-notch type, 3⅛ in. long. Made of caramel and blue Upper Mercer, the piece is from Perry County, Ohio. $65

Private collection, Ohio

Archaic side-notch blade, 4⅞ in. long. Material is a high-grade mixed brown flint of unknown origin. This exceptional early piece is from Licking County, Ohio. $175

Private collection, Ohio

Woodland-era point or blade, from the Eastern Midwest, 2½ in. long. Material is a yellow-tan chert or flint; narrowness of the blade portion suggests heavy prehistoric resharpening. $10

Private collection, Ohio

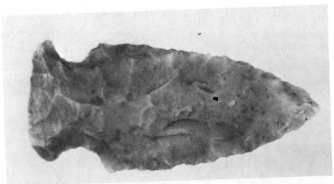

Hopewell (Middle Woodland) blade, from Licking County, Ohio. It is made of translucent gray Flintridge, a typical high-quality Hopewellian material. Size, 2⅝ in. $40

Private collection, Ohio

38

Archaic corner-notch blade, material an unknown gray banded flint. From Fairfield County, Ohio, size is 2½ in. long. In many ways this is a typical Archaic piece. $18

Private collection, Ohio

Dovetail or St. Charles blade, blue Upper Mercer flint, from Vinton County, Ohio. At 1¾ in. x 4⅜ in., this artifact evidences the rough usage (edge wear and chipping) typical of knives. $225

Private collection, Ohio

Early Archaic blade, deep-notch beveled type, 2½ in. long. It came from Fairfield County, Ohio, and is made of a cream translucent material that is either Upper Mercer or Flintridge. Nice specimen. $55

Private collection, Ohio

Morrow County lanceolate, Late Paleo, 1½ x 3⅝ in. This type has a definite stem but no shoulders, expanding gradually to greatest width near mid-length. Material is blue Upper Mercer flint and the stem sides and base are ground. This is a good type specimen, from Morrow County, Ohio. $225

Private collection, Ohio

Indented-base Archaic beveled blade, material is a dark blue Upper Mercer flint with many brown inclusions and several small lightning lines or quartz veins. From Coshocton County, Ohio, size is 1¾ x 3½ in. $150

Private collection, Ohio

Base-notch, Early Archaic period, a fine long blade in mottled blue Upper Mercer flint. From Licking County, Ohio, it measures 1⅝ x 4⁷⁄₁₆ in. A far-above-average specimen. $250

Private collection, Ohio

Archaic side-notch, from Licking County, Ohio. Material is a medium blue Upper Mercer and the artifact is 3 in. long. This blade has a balanced mix of percussion and pressure flaking typical of the Archaic. $40

Private collection, Ohio

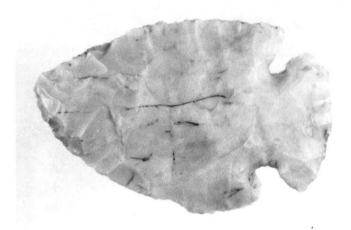

Thebes family Archaic bevel made of translucent jewel Flintridge. From Licking County, Ohio, size is 1¾ x 2⅝ in. $40

Private collection, Ohio

Thebes family Archaic upswept notch style blade, 2½ in. long. Material is a fine caramel and green Flintridge variety; from Fairfield County, Ohio. $55

Private collection, Ohio

Ledbetter points or blades, Early Woodland period, from Benton County, Tennessee. These are ex-coll. Mark Clark; longest piece here is 4⅜ in. $225, Group

John M. Maurer collection, Ft. Campbell, Kentucky; photograph by Dan Privett

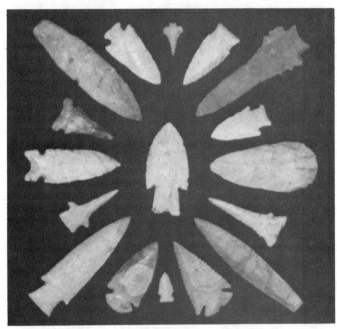

A fine flint collection, Late Paleo through Archaic times. These are from Illinois, Missouri, and Tennessee. For scale, the numbered boxes are one inch square. The small Fox Valley at 12 o'clock was gift to the owner while serving in Saudi Arabia during Operation Desert Storm.

Group, $2300 plus

John M. Maurer collection, Ft. Campbell, Kentucky; photograph by Dan Privett

Benton points or blades, all four made of Dover flint. These examples are from western to central Tennessee. $25-$75 each

John M. Maurer collection, Ft. Campbell, Kentucky; photograph by Dan Privett

Big Sandy type points or blades, Middle / Late Archaic period. Example on far right is from Montgomery Co., TN, while the others are from Christian Co., Kentucky. This is a good type grouping. $115, Group

John M. Maurer collection, Ft. Campbell, Kentucky; photograph by Dan Privett

Early Archaic notched-base made of blue Upper mercer material, 1½ x 2⅞ in. long. From Licking County, Ohio, it has very large serrations (sawtooth edging) for size. This was a personal find by the owner in 1980. $125

Larry Garvin collection, Ohio

Early Archaic notched-base made of blue Upper Mercer flint, 1⅝ x 3 in. long. The type may be related to Dovetails (St. Charles) but is a distinct type. From Licking County, Ohio. $150

Larry Garvin collection, Ohio

Adena stemmed blade, from St. Joseph County, Michigan. Material is gray/tan Flintridge and size is 2 x 5⅜ in. This superb artifact bears G.I.R.S. authentication number C88-21. $900

Collection of David G. & Barbara J. Shirley

Archaic blade, deep corner-notch type, made of blue Upper Mercer flint. It measures 2 x 3⅛ in. and is very thin for size. It was found in Muskingum County, Ohio. $175

Larry Garvin collection, Ohio

Hopewell (Middle Woodland) blade, made of gray translucent Flintridge chalcedony. Possibly from Ohio, it measures 2 1/16 x 4 3/16 in. $500

Collection of David G. & Barbara J. Shirley

Dovetail or St. Charles blade, from Indiana and made of Indiana hornstone. It is gray and light tan, and 1 7/16 x 4⅝ in. This is an excellent Early Archaic piece. $300

Collection of David G. & Barbara J. Shirley

Hopewellian (Middle Woodland) blade or knife, found in northeastern Ohio in the 1960s. Made of multi-colored high-grade Flintridge, this piece is thin and very well-made. It is 5½ in. long. $550 plus

Private collection; photograph by Rick Foster

Cache blades, from Michigan. A photo of these artifacts appeared in Moorehead's *Prehistoric Implements,* p. 23, when they were in the Mitchell collection. $100 each

Wilfred A. Dick collection, Magnolia, Mississippi

Prehistoric blades, various regions, all left to right:
Hopewell(?), Knife River flint,
Ross county, Ohio $125
Corner-notch, Livingston Co., NY $100
Hopewell, Middle Woodland, 3⅜ in., IL $175
Motley cache blade, 4¼ in., from KY $300

Pocotopaug Trading Post, South Windsor, Connecticut

Fluted points, Early Paleo period, top left Clovis, 3¼ in., agatized coral, from Columbia County, Florida. $225
Top right: Redstone, Coshocton flint, from Ross County, Ohio, tip restored, 3¼ in. $200
Bottom row, left to right:

Clovis, Hixton quartzite, Wisconsin. $350
Clovis, 4 in., Dover flint, TN. $500
Clovis, 4¾ in., hornstone, KY. $800
Clovis, gem hornstone, 4⅛ in., KY. $600
Clovis, Harrison Co., KY, 3⅝ in. $250

Pocotopaug Trading Post, South Windsor, Connecticut

Late Paleo points and blades, various regions.
Top left: stemmed lanceolate, Ford County, IL, 3 in., collateral flaking. $95
Top right: Plainview, jasper, transverse flaking, Wyoming, 3 in. $250
Lower, left to right:
Eastern Scottsbluff or stemmed lanceolate, 3¼ in., Warsaw, OH $125
Angostura, Cooper County, MO, heat-treated Burlington chert, oblique transverse flaking, 4⅛ in. $300
Lind Coulee, oblique transverse flaking, red and black jasper, southeastern WA, 3⅞ in., rare piece. $500
Plainview, oblique transverse flaking, red Alibates flint, Moore Co., TX, 4¼ in. $350
Scottsbluff, Missouri, collateral flaking, 3⅝ in., fine piece. $400

Pocotopaug Trading Post, South Windsor, Connecticut

Dovetail or St. Charles blade, Early Archaic and ca. 7500 BC, from Ohio. Material is Flintridge in creams, yellows, tans and pinks. Length is 4⅜ in. and a crystal quartz eye appears on both faces. Slight basal damage. $500

Alvin Lee Moreland, Corpus Christi, Texas

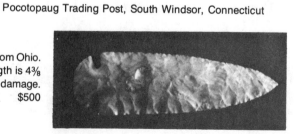

Hardin-barbed, Early Archaic, from IL. It is 7⅛ in. long and made of white to cream chert with red inclusions and a reddish base with a red stripe. This is large for a Hardin and the piece has fine flaking. $950

Alvin Lee Moreland, Corpus Christi, Texas

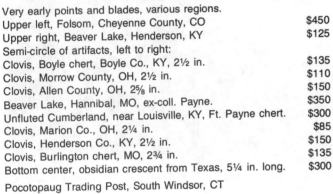

Very early points and blades, various regions.

Upper left, Folsom, Cheyenne County, CO	$450
Upper right, Beaver Lake, Henderson, KY	$125

Semi-circle of artifacts, left to right:

Clovis, Boyle chert, Boyle Co., KY, 2½ in.	$135
Clovis, Morrow County, OH, 2½ in.	$110
Clovis, Allen County, OH, 2⅝ in.	$150
Beaver Lake, Hannibal, MO, ex-coll. Payne.	$350
Unfluted Cumberland, near Louisville, KY, Ft. Payne chert.	$300
Clovis, Marion Co., OH, 2¼ in.	$85
Clovis, Henderson Co., KY, 2½ in.	$150
Clovis, Burlington chert, MO, 2¾ in.	$135
Bottom center, obsidian crescent from Texas, 5¼ in. long.	$300

Pocotopaug Trading Post, South Windsor, CT

Dovetail, Early Archaic and ca. 7500 BC, from Ohio. Material is Flintridge in multicolored hues; this piece has gem-quality material and fine overall flaking obverse. $500

Alvin Lee Moreland, Corpus Christi, Texas

Alabama blade types, made of colorful flints and cherts. This is a very good regional collection.

Individual, $7.50-$35

Larry G. Merriam collection, Oklahoma City, OK   Total, $500

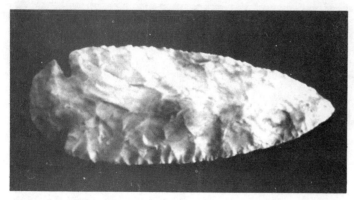

Dovetail, reverse shown, Early Archaic, from Ohio. This is a fine, large blade. $500

Alvin Lee Moreland, Corpus Christi, Texas

This stemmed Late Archaic / Early Woodland point or blade is made of golden Hixton quartzite and came from Barron County, Wisconsin. Size is 13/16 x 2¼ in. This material is sometimes referred to as "brown sugar" quartzite. $20-$25

Mert Cowley collection, Chetek. Wisconsin

Button-base or small-base Dovetail (St. Charles) blade, Early Archaic and ca. 7500 BC. Length is 5 in., from Preble County, Ohio; material is pink and cream Flintridge with pink stripes. $500

Alvin Lee Moreland, Corpus Christi, Texas

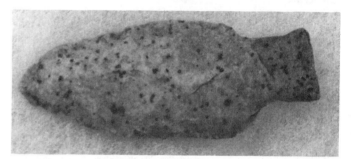

Woodland blade or point, made of oolitic chert, from Dunn County, Wisconsin. It measures 15/16 x 27/16 in. $25-$30

Mert Cowley collection, Chetek, Wisconsin

Preble County, Ohio, Dovetail (reverse view). Made of jewel-grade Flintridge from Ohio's Licking County, this is an exceptional early blade. $500

Alvin Lee Moreland, Corpus Christi, Texas

Sloan Dalton, IL, 11-plus in. long. Made of high-grade translucent white flint, transverse flaking is present. This is an important Late Paleo / Early Archaic piece, very rare. $15,000-$20,000

Alvin Lee Moreland, Corpus Christi, Texas

Sloan Dalton, IL, 11-plus in. long, reverse view. (See other photo for obverse.) This superb blade has a slight reddish-orange cast from soil contact and iron oxide deposits. This artifact is extremely rare. $15,000-$20,000

Alvin Lee Moreland, Corpus Christi, Texas

Waubesa point or blade, contracting stem, Early Woodland period. It is 1 1/16 x 2⅜ in. and is made of cream/tan flint. From Barron County, Wisconsin, this comes from a verified Early Woodland site that is 150 miles further north than any previous Early Woodland sites registered in the state. $75

Mert Cowley collection, Chetek, Wisconsin

Late Paleo points and blades; Left, top to bottom:

Sloan Dalton, Worland, Missouri, 4¾ in.	$225
Holland point, McIntosh County, Oklahoma, 3 in. long.	$175
Sloan Dalton, Clark County, AR, Burlington chert, 4¾ in.	$225

Second row from left, top to bottom:

Dalton, 2½ in., McIntosh County, OK, white Boone chert.	$150
Paleo knife, unknown type, 6¼ in., Greene County, IL.	$250
Dalton variant, Boone chert, McIntosh County, OK, 2¼ in.	$50

Center column, top to bottom:

Cherryhill Dalton variety, Arkansas novaculite, Pike Co., AR, 2 in.	$100
Dalton variant, Burlington chert, Poplar Bluff, MO, 3¾ in.	$225
Dalton, 2 in. long, McIntosh County, OK.	$100

Second column from right, top to bottom:

Dalton, McIntosh County, OK, very thin, 2½ in. long.	$125
Dalton knife, 5¾ in., Crescent chert, St. Charles Co., MO.	$450
Dalton, Crescent chert, from Missouri, 2½ in., left-hand bevel.	$125

Right-hand column, top to bottom:

Sloan Dalton from Arkansas, 4¾ in.	$175
Dalton, Burlington chert, McIntosh County, OK, 2⅞ in.	$125
Sloan Dalton, Stuttgart, Arkansas, 5⅝ in.	$275

Larry G. Merriam collection, Oklahoma City, Oklahoma

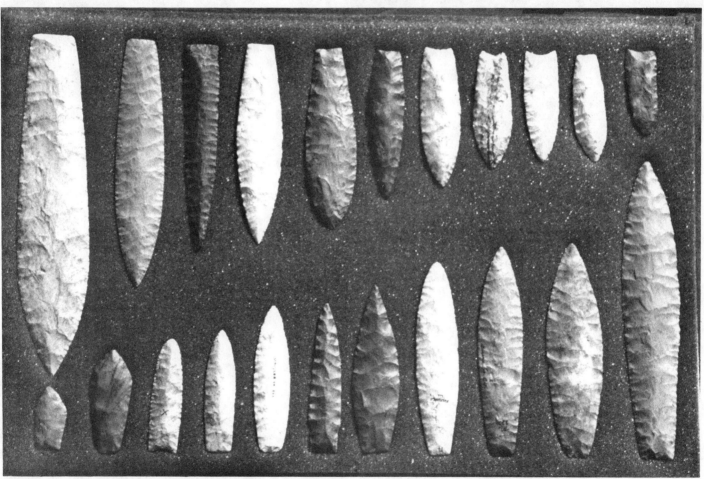

Lanceolates, mainly Late Paleo, superb frame, upper row left to right:

Wadlow knife, 8¼ in., fine large blade, from Missouri.	$350
Agate Basin, from North Dakota, 6 in. long, excellent chipping.	$300
Eden, Knife River flint from Wyoming, 5 in. long.	$500
Sedalia/Nebo Hill from Marion County, Missouri, 4⅞ in.	$375
Point resembling a Hell Gap, 4½ in. long, Adams County, IL.	$175
Angostura, from Texas, 3⅞ in. long.	$175
Agate Basin, Late Paleo, 3½ in., from Pike County, Missouri.	$150
Unknown type, Alibates flint, northwestern Oklahoma, 3 in. long.	$150
Plainview, from Missouri, 2⅞ in.	$125
Agate Basin, rather rough, from Missouri, 2¾ in.	$75
Plainview, made from petrified wood, Maverick Co., Texas, 2¼ in.	$70

Bottom row, left to right:

Agate Basin, exhausted condition, Edwards chert, Texas, 1½ in.	$50
Possible Lake Mohave point, 2½ in., from Southwest U.S.	$100
Plainview, banded Florence chert, 2¾ in., Howard Co., MO	$125
Agate Basin, 2⅞ in., from southwestern Missouri.	$125
Agate Basin, 3½ in., from Schuyler County, IL	$175
Texas Eden, 3½ in. long, made from Edwards Plateau chert.	$175
Eastern lanceolate, 4 in. long, from Kentucky	$200
Agate Basin, extremely fine, 4⅝ in., Fulton County, IL.	$350
Agate Basin, from Greene County, Arkansas, 5 in. long.	$350
Agate Basin, southeastern Colorado, 5¼ in. long.	$250
Agate Basin, Cass County, Missouri, 7⅛ in. long.	$275

Larry G. Merriam collection, Oklahoma City, Oklahoma

Texas chipped artifacts, all material various grades of Edwards Plateau flints.

Three blades far left, top to bottom: San Saba, dark material, 6 in. long, Medina County, Texas, $275; Pedernales, 4⅜ in., light-colored material, $250; Montell, 4⅛ in., light-colored, Coryell County, $225.

Second row left top piece, base-tang knife, curved blade, tan chert, Waco, TX, 6¼ in., unlisted.

Second row left second piece from top, 3 in., Bandy Creek (?), Bandera County, TX, $150.

Center row top to bottom: Base-notched ovate blade, central Texas, 4½ in., $275; corner-tang knife, 4½ in., $375; untanged corner-tang (bottom middle), 6¼ in., unusual, use-marks and beveled, central Texas, $325.

Second row from right, top piece: Knife, heavy white patina on one side with lighter material on opposite, 5¼ in., central Texas, $175. Second row from right, middle piece, Uvalde, 3¼ in., thin with heavy patina, from Gillespie County, TX, $125.

Far right row, top to bottom: Base-notched knife, 6½ in., Bandera Co., TX, $325; Montell, 4½ in., nice thin piece from near Temple, TX, $225; Castroville, 4 in., from central Texas, $225.

Overall, this is a fine representative selection of large and superior Texas blades.

Larry Merriam collection, Oklahoma City, OK

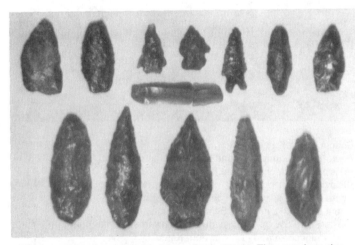

Knives and blades, black obsidian, 1¼ to 3¼ in. They are from the Western U.S.

$140 Group

Pat & Dave Summers, Native American Artifacts, Victor, New York

This fine blade was found by an archaeologist near Durango, Colorado. Very well-chipped, it is 5⅛ in. long.   Museum quality

Grady McCrea collection, Miles, Texas

A superb frame of flint, time-period ranging from the Early Paleo into the Archaic. Shown are point or blade examples of the following types: Daltons, Allen, Eden, Pike County, Agate Basin, Clovis, Alberta and unnamed types. Examples shown are from the states of Colorado, Missouri, Illinois, Arkansas and Montana. The value range here is from $25 to $600.

Larry Merriam collection, Oklahoma City, OK

An extremely fine frame of points and blades from the Central United States region, most being Dalton cluster pieces plus related subtypes. These are from the states Arkansas, Texas, Oklahoma, Louisiana, Missouri, Illinois and Ohio. The San Patrice points or blades (some with bifurcated bases and serrated edges) are from Texas, Arkansas, Missouri and Oklahoma.

The frame examples show a wide variety of styles, sizes and materials. The value range per each is from $25 to $250, depending on size, material, the workmanship quality and overall appearance.

Larry Merriam collection, Oklahoma City, OK

Base-tang knife or blade, found in Runnels County, Texas. This piece is quite thin, with excellent flaking overall. $275

Grady McCrea collection, Miles, Texas

Early Paleo and Early Archaic pieces. Left, Ross County Clovis, Gregg County, Texas. $250
Right, Calf Creek with shoulder missing, probably removed during resharpening, Gregg County, TX. $125

Willie Fields collection, Hallsville, Texas

Prehistoric artifacts, all Texas
Left, Ouachita (related to the Little River), Calf Creek top center, and small Plainview to right. Bottom center, a White River and bottom right, a Barber (Clovis-related).

$1000, Group

Willie Fields collection, Hallsville, Texas

High Plains knife, found in 1991 in Box Elder County, Utah. Material is unknown, while the type is probably ca. 3000 BC. This is a fine, large blade at 2 x 5 in. $200

Randall Olsen collection, Cache County, Utah

Corner-tang knife, white Georgetown flint, Coryell County, Texas. The color, size, shape, workstyle and condition make this a very rare piece, and a very expensive one.

Museum quality

L.M. Abbott, Jr. collection, Texas

Double-pointed blade, Georgetown flint, from Bell County, Texas. This is a large and fine piece, measuring 4½ x 9 in., $1200

L.M. Abbott, Jr. collection, Texas

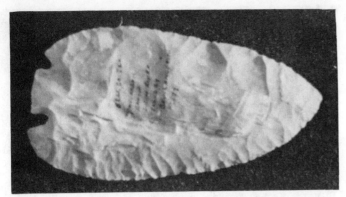

Base-tang knife, from Bell County, Texas, 3 x 5¾ in. Material is a cream Edwards Plateau chert or flint. $700

L.M. Abbott, Jr. collection, Texas

Harahey knives, Neo-Indian period or very late prehistoric period, all found in Runnels County, Texas. This is a fine selection showing the type in different stages of being resharpened, wide to narrow. $100-$275 each

Grady McCrea collection, Miles, Texas

Angostura blade or knife, ca. 7000 BC, Edwards Plateau chert, from Comanche County, Texas. Size is 2⅜ x 6¼ in. $475

L.M. Abbott, Jr. collection, Texas

Corner-tang blade or knife, 3⅜ in. long and very thin. This scarce type is Late Archaic and is widely distributed in Texas. $275

Grady McCrea collection, Miles, Texas

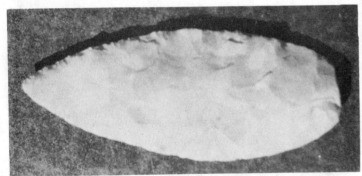

Large Caddo blade, late prehistoric, from Henderson County, Texas. This fine piece is 6¾ in. long. $775

L.M. Abbott, Jr. collection, Texas

Late Paleo knife, Chillicothe, Missouri. It is made of tan and brown flint and is 1³⁄₃₂ x 5¹⁄₃₂ in. This exceptional piece has G.I.R.S. authentication number C89-40. $900

Collection of David G. & Barbara J. Shirley

Gahagan blade or knife, Edwards Plateau chert, from Hamilton County, Texas. Size is 4¼ in. long. $250

L.M. Abbott, Jr. collection, Texas

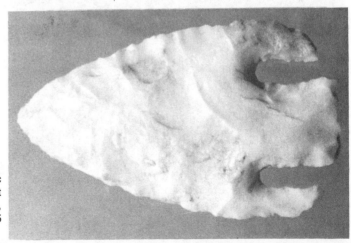

Calf Creek type blade, 3½ in. long, found by C.W. Womack in Pontotoc County, Oklahoma. This is ca. 7000 BC and is made of Frisco chert in creamy white. (A cast replica is available from Peter Bostrom, Troy, IL). $225

Courtesy C.W. Womack collection

Hell Gap point or blade, from Pueblo County, Colorado. It is made of black basalt and is 4¼ in. long. $300

Steven D. Kitch collection, Pueblo, Colorado

Knife, Harahey, made of weathered quartzite. This is an attractive piece with good workstyle, 6½ in. long. It is from Elbert County, Colorado. $200

Steven D. Kitch collection, Pueblo, Colorado

Scottsbluff point or blade, Late Paleo / Early Archaic, found in Cheyenne County, Colorado. It is made of Knife River flint and is 3 in. long. $200

Steven D. Kitch collection, Pueblo, Colorado

Plainview point or blade, Early Archaic and ca. 7500 BC. This fine artifact was found near Lander, Wyoming and has a Perino paper of authentication. Length, 2 in. $150

Steven D. Kitch collection, Pueblo, Colorado

Eden point or blade, Late Paleo / Early Archaic period, from Pueblo County, Colorado. It is made of an unusual material, petrified bone. This scarce artifact is 4 in. long. $350

Steven D. Kitch collection, Pueblo, Colorado

Castroville, Late Archaic period, from Dimmit County, Texas. It is made of Edwards Plateau flint in browns and tans, 4⅛ in. long. This is the scarce squared-barb type with needle tip. It has random flaking and deep notches. $300-$400

Alvin Lee Moreland, Corpus Christi, Texas

Hell Gap point or blade, found in Crowley County, Colorado. It is 3 in. long and is made of purple quartzite. $200

Steven D. Kitch collection, Pueblo, Colorado

San Saba base-tang drill, made of Edwards Plateau chert, from Coryell County, Texas. This superb piece is 4¾ in. long. $650

L.M. Abbott, Jr. collection, Texas

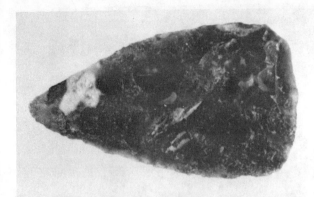

Triangular blade, probably Woodland and a possible cache piece, from Licking County, OH. It is made of translucent gray Flintridge and is 2⅜ in. long. $15

Private collection, Ohio

Hoe or spade, from Pike County, Indiana. It is made of Mill Creek chert, a whitish-gray high-grade material. Size is 5¼ x 11⁹⁄₁₆ in. and the lower, wide end has polish. This is pictured in *Who's Who in Indian Relics No. 3*. $700

Collection of David G. & Barbara J. Shirley

This hafted scraper is very thin and well-made; from Runnels County, Texas. $75-$100

Grady McCrea collection, Miles, Texas

Spade made of Dover flint, 11½ in. long, from Benton County, Tennessee. This Mississippian period artifact is ex-coll. Mark Clark. This is a high-grade large artifact in top condition. $500

John M. Maurer collection, Ft. Campbell, KY; photograph by Mike Maurer

Spade or hoe, flint, well-polished edge. It is 8½ in. long and from Massac County, IL. $90

Pat & Dave Summers, Native American Artifacts, Victor, New York

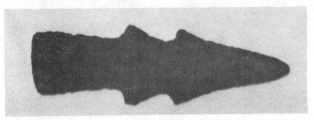

Dagger, double-barbed, a very rare Mississippian period artifact, made of Dover flint, the classic material. It is either from Kentucky or Tennessee, and is shown in *Stone Age in North America*, Vol. I, p. 235. Ex-colls. Young and Smail.

Museum quality

John M. Maurer collection, Ft. Campbell, Kentucky; photograph by Dan Privett

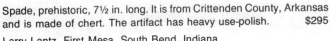

Spade, prehistoric, 7½ in. long. It is from Crittenden County, Arkansas and is made of chert. The artifact has heavy use-polish. $295

Larry Lantz, First Mesa, South Bend, Indiana

Frame of Wisconsin artifacts, including points, blades, scrapers and drills.　　Collection, $300-$400

Robert D. Lund collection, Watertown, Wisconsin

Notched hoe from St. Louis County, IL. Material is a white-gray chert with sections of the original brown exterior. Size, 5½ x 6 in. This Mississippian piece is pictured in *Who's Who in Indian Relics No. 1*

Collection of David G. & Barbara J. Shirley　　　$800

Rare early ovoid knife, Paleo period, from Perry County, IL. It is made of white Illinois flint and measures 2⅞ x 6⁷⁄₁₆ in. This piece bears G.I.R.S. authentication number C88-15.　　　$1000

Collection of David G. & Barbara J. Shirley

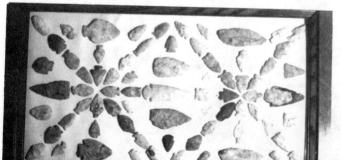

Frame of Wisconsin points and blades, mainly from the Archaic period. The white Dovetail at center is of interest;

Collection, $500-$700

Robert D. Lund collection, Watertown, Wisconsin

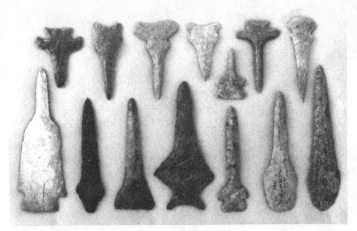

Points and blades, various periods and locations.
Top row, left to right:

Lost Lake, Kentucky	$25
Plainview (Late Paleo / Early Archaic), TX	$125
Thebes blade, Early Archaic, Kentucky	$100
Pine Three auriculate, Archaic, Kentucky	$20
Side-notch drill, Kentucky.	$25
Decatur or fractured-base drill, KY	$75
Dovetail or St. Charles, exhausted, KY	$65

Bottom row, left to right:

Etley, 4¾ in., Missouri, drill-top	$65
Adena (Early Woodland), New York	$40
T-drill, Arkansas (or expanded-base)	$75
Susquehanna, New York state	$125
Corner-notch, Tennessee	$85
Sedalia, Illinois	$60
Beaver-tail Adena, 4¾ in., KY	$125

Pocotopaug Trading Post, South Windsor, CT

Collection of points and blades from Mississippi, Louisiana, Texas and Arkansas. Many different types and materials are represented. $25-$125 each

Wilfred A. Dick collection, Magnolia, Mississippi

Hopewell (Middle Woodland) blades, all left to right:

Jefferson County, New York	$125
Knox County, Indiana, Coshocton flint	$125
Near Elizabethtown, KY, 4⅛ in.	$185
Normanskill flint, New Haven, CT	$300
Allegany County, New York, 4⅝ in.	$150

Pocotopaug Trading Post, South Windsor, CT

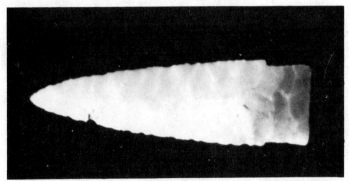

Scottsbluff point or blade, Late Paleo / Early Archaic period, from Adams County, Colorado. This artifact is made of gem material, translucent white and orange agate. This fine piece is 3½ in. long. $400

Steven D. Kitch collection, Pueblo, Colorado

Late Woodland blade, from Fairfield County, OH. Material is blue-gray Upper Mercer and length is 3⅜ in. This piece has restoration in two places, at the lower blade edge and basal corner. $25

Private collection, Ohio

Harahey knife, made of Alibates flint. It is from Pratt County, Kansas, and is 5 in. long. This is an excellent example of a four-way bevel. $150

Steven D. Kitch collection, Pueblo, Colorado

Plains Indians in Montana, date unknown. Note the fine baby carrier woman carries between tipis, and dramatic feather headdress worn by standing man.

Photographer, Roland Reed; courtesy Photography Collection, Suzzallo Library, University of Washington.

CHAPTER III

ARTIFACTS OF ORGANIC MATERIALS

Artifacts made from mammal and shellfish parts were widely common in prehistoric times. Relatively few of the objects survive to the present. Such organic materials, like wood artifacts, have largely disappeared due to the combined actions of time, moisture and bacteria.

Antler, from deer and elk, was a much-used raw material for tools and weapons. Flaking rods of antler helped make the incredible numbers of chipped objects, and deer tines were often used for projectile points. Antler, due to the hardness and availability, was used in much of North America, including all of the Continental U.S.

Horn, usually from the so-called buffalo (the American bison), was made into ladles, spoons, and ceremonial objects. In the northern reaches of the Rockies, horn also came from mountain goats and bighorn sheep. Horn strips were sometimes used to reinforce bows, and the material was made into knife handles and charms and decorations.

Ivory had been widely used in the Alaskan region (see later Chapter) and northern Canada. Ivory artifacts form a scarce class, especially for prehistoric items in the adjoining United States. Among animals that provided ivory are the walrus and narwhale, a mammal with a single twisted tusk and which may have inspired the unicorn legend.

To a limited degree ivory also came from the twin tusks of long-dead mastodon and mammoths, preserved in permafrost. Smaller objects made from the teeth of other sea creatures are sometimes referred to as ivory.

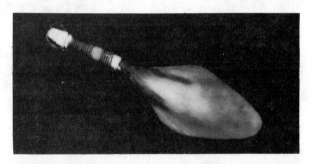

HORN SPOON, 8 1/16 in. long, with sinew sewn beaded handle in colors white, green, yellow and blue. Material is cow horn, and piece is ca. 1910.
Photo courtesy of Crazy Crow Trading Post, Denison, TX. $225

Six DEER-ANTLER TOOLS, from Archaic site in Kentucky near Ohio River. Excavated from rock shelter, longest piece is just over 4 in. It is believed these are flint-chipping tools; all six sections, in good condition.   All, $15

Private collection

Antler, Horn and Ivory Artifacts

Plains Indian **horn spoon,** unusual carved handle, cow horn, and 10 in. long. Probably 19th Century.   G—$125

Buffalo horns from old headdress, Taos Pueblo, ca. 1800s.   D—$95

Elk horn point, from southern Oregon, 3¼ in. long, thinly notched at base. Narrow, may be an arrowpoint.C-$35

Horn spoon, large 11 in. in length, with curved handle done in quill-work. Probably recent, but good piece.   C—$95

Plains Indian spoon or ladle, of bison horn, 12 in. long, no damage, some painted designs on handle portion.D—$95

Deer-antler arrowpoint, Kentucky rock shelter, 2¼ in. long; base hollowed out for arrow shaft.   C—$8

Wide-bowled horn spoon, or ladle, 7 in. long, 4 in. wide at shallow bowl. Northwest Coast, probably historic and late 1800's.   C—$135

Nez Perce deep **horn ladle or dipper,** 8¾ in. long, of bent and shaped horn. No decoration, but good lines.C—$125

Elkhorn scraper, 13 in. long with right-angle curve; has a snub-nose scraper of quartz still in position. Held by rawhide bindings and pitch. Horn polished by much use; condition good.   D—$230

Incised ivory bar, western Canada, 3½ in. long, about ¼ in. thick. Both sides have a series of zigzag lines, in parallel rows of 3. Possibly a gaming token or marker; actual use unknown. Golden brown with slight age cracks.C—$160

Hand-carved Sioux **horn spoon.**   D—$50

Freshwater pearls, evidently **necklace beads,** probably Hopewellian, approximately 70 drilled pearls, none in good condition.   C—$95

Set of 7 **elk teeth,** drilled at bases for suspension.C—$42

Antler Atl-atl hook, rare piece, removed from North Carolina rock shelter. Piece is 6¾ in. long, averages 1 in. in diameter, material in medium-good condition. Notched at end to receive lance base.   C—$225

Ivory pendant, northern California; may have been made from walrus ivory, but uncertain. Drill hole at one end; 2¾ in. in length. Oval shape.   C—$130

Plains Indian horn spoon; 11 in. overall length; and has beaded handle. Pre-1900.   G—$195

Antler pick, from prehistoric period, probably 4000 years old. Tip shows polish from long use, but rest of material is chalk-like. Piece is 13 in. long; may once have had wood handle.   C—$70

Adz with wooden handle and **elk horn blade.** Piece is 12 in. long, good condition.   G—$195

Elk horn hide scraper, ivoryized from much use, good condition.   G—$215

BEAR CLAW NECKLACE, with longest claw 5 in. long. Inside of claws is painted with vermillion; the necklace was made from the now-extinct prairie grizzly. Piece is Northern Plains and ca. 1870.Museum quality
Nedra Matteucci's Fenn Galleries, Santa Fe, New Mexico

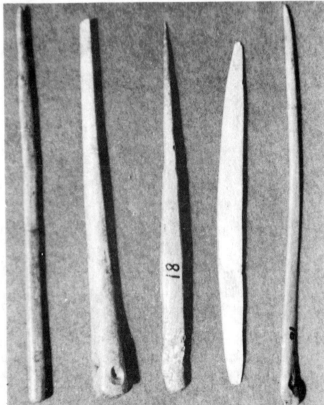

Five long BONE AWLS, from Texas sites, and late prehistoric era. These were excavated from a Panhandle Pueblo site along with 2-notch and 3-notch Harrell points. Awls are 6 in. to 7 in. in length   C—$35-$60
Photo courtesy of Wayne Parker, Texas

BONE ARTIFACTS

Bone items were made from the skeletal material of many animals, from raccoons to whales. They were less common in the American southwest, but other regions had a wide variety of such artifacts. These ranged from turkey wing-bone flutes to deer-bone awls to elk-horn hoes. Flint and obsidian blades shaped the bone.

Bone hoe, made from bison shoulder blade, with original handle.   D—$200

Bone awl, from New York, 4⅝ in. long, made of splintered deer bone. From late prehistoric site.   C—$28

Tennessee **bone whistle,** 3⅛ in. long. Has incised lines in spiral design around sides.   D—$65

Bone comb, probably Iroquois, with rounded comb teeth that resemble outstretched fingers of the hand. Piece is 4½ in. high; two effigies on top, resembling facing animals, species unknown.   C—$265

Bone hide scraper, Mesa Verde area of Colorado, and made ca. 1900. Piece is 7½ in. long, perhaps bison bone, with working edges smoothed by use; has quartzite blade.   C—$110

Necklace elements, consisting of 8 bone beads, each about 1 in. (25mm) long, and 3 bear canine teeth, averaging about 2½ in. in length. Canines drilled at rear; fangs and beads in good condition. Age unknown; from Wyoming dry cave.   C—$145

Raccoon **penis-bone perforator,** from Georgia, 3⅛ in. long. Knobbed at one end, smaller and has been sharpened by abrasion. Piece in outline forms part of an "S" curve. Found on late prehistoric site.   C—$13

Hupa **ceremonial ladle,** 11 in. long, carved from bone; handle decorated with central cutouts and expanded serrations just above bowl. Used for important feast occasions.   C—$210

Bone flaking tool, broken and reglued. Piece is 5½ in. long and 1½ in. wide.   G—$14

Bone whistle, emits a single-pitch tone, 7 in. in length. Made from deer or antelope bone. Piece collected in California, early 1900's.   D—$80

Elk-bone perforator, 3⅞ in. in length, one tip ground to sharp point. Shows much use; surface very smooth.   C—$11

Deer bone awl from Mimbres, New Mexico.   D—$18

Bone fish hook, from Alabama coastal site, 1¼ in. long, fine condition.   D—$12

Long POLISHED-BONE HAIRPIN, 5⅞ in. long, light incised lines along shank sides.   C—$55
Portion of BONE FLUTE or whistle, said to have been recovered from Kentucky.   C—$65
BONE SPATULA or hide-working tool, tapers to sharp rounded blade at end, shows heavy polish in lower regions. Old label states it is from Henderson, Kentucky.   C—$30
Private collection

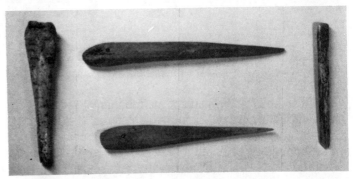

Long wide turkey BONE AWL, in two sections left to right, each about 3 in. long and polished from much use.
Center, two fine BONE AWLS or needles, all from West Virginia rock shelter, longest about 5 in. long. The small holes are modern-drilled, by an earlier collector, who secured pieces together with cord.   G—$28
Private collection

Polished **bone awl** from Missouri, 3 in. long, and ¼ in. in diameter.   G—$16

Decorated **bone hairpin,** 7½ in. long, nearly pointed at tip, expanded at base end. Designs of crossed and dotted lines for about half distance from base to tip. Highly polished overall; has a yellow-brown color.   C—$100

Excavated **bone awls** or quill flatteners.   G—$7 each

Bone fish-shaped wand, Tlinget, 15½ in. long, recent and still used in ceremonies.   C—$60

Bone harpoon tip, Oregon river valley, 4 in. long, double barbs on each side; socketed base for insertion into long wooden shaft. Base has knobs or protusions for securing line that was fastened to the tip.   D—$95

Split bone awl, Missouri, 3¾ in. long.   G—$14

STRAND OF ASSORTED BEADS, made of bone and shell, with largest bead ¾ in. in diameter. These are probably prehistoric.   C—$35-$45

Photo courtesy of Robert C. Calvert, London, Ontario, Canada

COLLECTION: A fine assemblage of shell artifacts in central frames, with flint points. Surrounding artifacts include stone celts, axes, flint blades, gorgets, discoidals, plummets and a spatulate form. All pieces are from Tennessee.   C—Not listed

Photo courtesy of Joseph D. Love, Chattanooga, Tennessee

Polished **bone needle,** from Dickerson Cave, Kentucky. Piece is 4 in. long and ¼ in. in diameter.   G—$18

Bone fish-killer club, made of marine animal bone, 19¼ in. long. Plain, heavy, 2⅞ in. in diameter at striking end. Handle end has circular extension like a baseball bat for non-slip hold. Weathered a bleached pale gray, but good condition.   D—$300

Polished **bone needle** from Kentucky, 4½ in. long and ½ in. in diameter.   G—$20

Woodlands region **bone comb** or hair decoration, historic Indian, probably Iroquois. About 2½ in. wide at base, part of human figure effigy on comb back. Figure would have stood about 5 in. high, but head broken off. Several teeth missing from comb but a fine example.   D—$185

Bone **fish hook,** 1½ in. long, very thin, of deer bone. Highly polished; line end has groove near top.   C—$15

Blackfoot **bone scraper,** 12 in. long. Piece has original metal scraper blade. This is 19th Century.   G—$140

Polished **bone bead,** probably part of a necklace, 1 in. long and ½ in. wide; well-drilled. Faint circular incised lines on surface, now almost obliterated.   C—$8

End-drilled pieces of polished bone, probably **necklace segments** or miniature pendants. Probably deer bone, from Colorado rock shelter. Bone pieces are nearly matching in size, averaging 2⅛ in. long. There are 14 in all. D—$90

Long **bone needle,** from Todd County, Arkansas, it is 5 in. long and ¼ in. in diameter. Good polish and with a perforated eye.   G—$35

Bone pendant, Louisiana, about 2 in. wide and 3½ in. long, end-drilled with a single hole. Rectangular form, age unknown, incised with series of x-like marks on one side.   C—$65

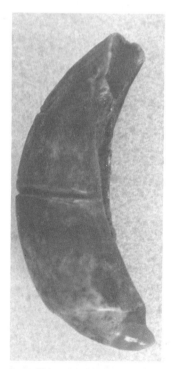

Bear canine tooth, from Shiawassee County, Michigan. Such objects were often used for decorative artifacts.

$45

Collection of David G. & Barbara J. Shirley

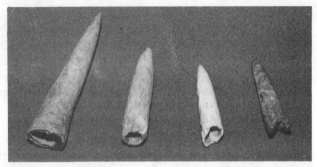

Deer antler projectile tips or points, all from Mississippi. $25 each
Wilfred A. Dick collection, Magnolia, Mississippi

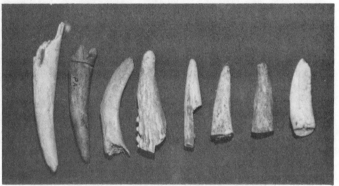

Deer antler tines showing prehistoric working and cuts for snapping off.
One is from Pennsylvania and others from Mississippi.
Wilfred A. Dick collection, Magnolia, Mississippi $5 each

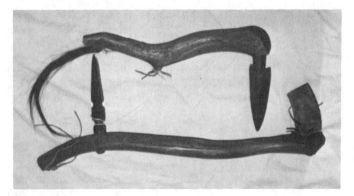

Elkhorn clubs, Arapaho.
Top, horn with metal point, horse-hair drop, hide wrist-band, and paint
in colors of yellow, red and green. The upper example is ex-coll. Green.
These are ca. 1840-60. $1000 each

Private collection, photo by John McLaughlin

Unusual artifact, a bone arrow-shaft straightener. It was found in Haskell
County, Oklahoma, by the owner. $95

James Bruner collection, Oklahoma

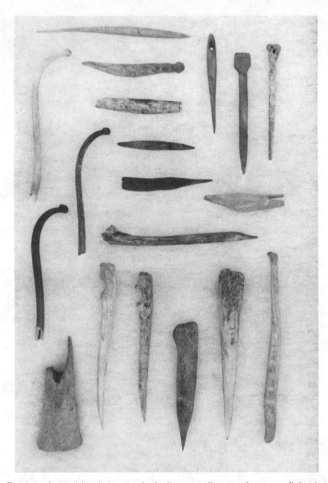

Bone tools and implements, including needles, perforators, fish-pins,
awls, hair-pins, etc. These came from the Columbia River area and are
ca. 1850-1900. $150

Morris' Art & Artifacts, Anaheim, California; Dawn Gober photograph

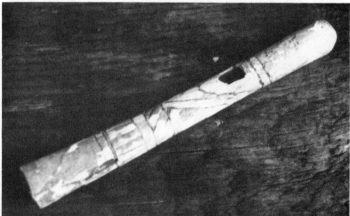

Bone whistle, Archaic period and ca. 2000 BC, from Lewis County, New
York. It is geometrically incised. Size, ½ x 6 in., scarce artifact. $125

Frank Bergevin, Port of Call, Alexandria Bay, New York

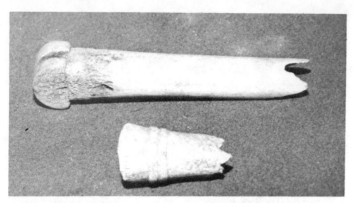

End fragments of carved bone artifacts, both from Kentucky.

Wilfred A. Dick collection, Magnolia, Mississippi   Study value

Bone and shell artifacts, prehistoric.

Bear canine teeth, KY	$20-$45
Bone awls, KY	$5 each
Needles, lower right, ME	$5
Elk teeth, shell crescent, from NY	$20
Center shell gorget, from CT	$15

Pocotopaug Trading Post, South Windsor, CT

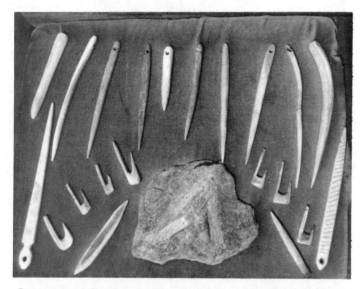

Bone artifacts. These include fish hooks, awls and needles and hairpins. A well-used sandstone sharpening slab is included.$20-$125 each

Private collection

SHELL ARTIFACTS

Shell, the exo-skeletons of a multitude of fresh and salt water species, had a long and extensive period of usage for artifacts. Amerinds used shell, with some minor changes, for spoons, containers and hoes. Other shell portions became pendants and bracelets.

Tiny shell segments of larger shells became the disc and tubular beads of early and historic times. The well-known "wampum" beads served as a medium of exchange even to the first Colonists in New England.

Shell—like some high grades of flint, copper and other desired materials — is an example of far-flung trade in prehistoric times. Gulf of Mexico conch shell was used by Ohio's Gravel Kame Indians 4000 years ago. Pacific abalone shell was traded into the Southwest at the close of the BC years. Other bivalve halves were even, by the legendary Hohokam, treated with pitch and saguaro cactus acid to become the first etchings in the world.

Two **shell rings** and two **shell pendants,** from Arizona, average diameter 1 in.   G—$30 for the four

Fort Ancient, late prehistoric, **shell effigy gorget** illustrating the human face with weeping-eye motif. Specimen is 4⅛ in. high and 3⅛ in. wide, with some parts missing at lower shell fringes or "chin" area.   C—$350

Complete **shell dipper or spoon** from a shell-mound site in Kentucky. Dipper is mussel-shell, 5 in. long by 3¼ in. wide. One long side has been notched in early times.C—$55

Marine **shell gorget,** Mississippi culture, found in Georgia. Piece is 5 in. high, inscribed with "eagle warrior" motif, lines not all clear. Depiction is faded and shell not in good condition.   C—$325

Necklace of prehistoric **graduated-size shell beads,** disc-shaped, about 21 in. long. Largest discs in center measure ⅝ in. There are approximately 140 beads in the strand.   C—$200

Shell bead strand, tube type, length 26 in. Material is from Arkansas.   G—$75

Shell necklace with drilled cougar fang pendant, probably Mississippian, late prehistoric. There are 17 freshwater mussel beads, pendant drilled very much off-center, all in fair condition. Beads average ¾ in. in length; pendant is 1⅛ in. long.   C—$75

Large Arkansas **shell beads,** disc and barrel types, and length is 20 in.   C—$60

Shell beads and pendant, which is carved in the form of an animal; strand is 17 in. long.   G—$50

Mississippian period **engraved shell gorget,** 4 in. by 4¾ in. Central motif depicts man dancing or flying. Excellent condition, some surface flaking due to age.   C—$595

Prehistoric shell beads and necklace of beads and bear teeth.

Left, necklace	$125-$200
Center, bear-tooth necklace	$250-$350
Right, necklace	$125-$200

Philip L. Russo collection, Danbury, CT

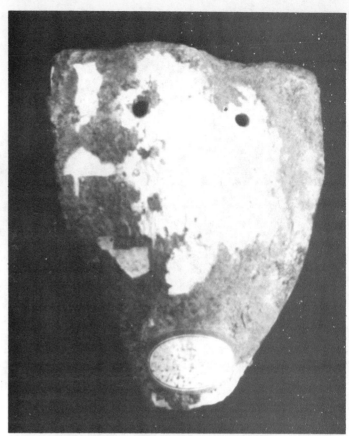

Mask, made of marine shell, from Smyth County, Virginia. Mississippian in origin, these are rare in good condition. $300

Rodney M. Peck collection, Harrisburg, North Carolina

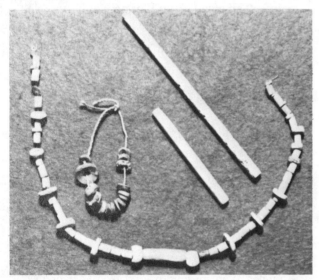

Shell ornaments, from Pennsylvania and New York, ca. 1550-1700s. Long tubular "hair pins", small strand of circular disk "wampum", large strand of shell disk beads and "European" wampum, barrel-shaped.

Hair pipes	$25-$75
Wampum strand this size	$10-$20
Large mixed strand	$50-$75

Gary L. Fogelman collection, Pennsylvania

Shell fish hook, made of abalone shell, coastal California. Piece is 1½ in. long, nice curve, good condition, notched for string, excavated find.   C—$17

String of early Indian **shell heishi,** restrung to be worn.   G—$300

Strand of documented **Spiro Mound shell beads,** disc and barrel types, 37 in. in length.   G—$95

Decorated **abalone shell pendant,** 4⅛ in. long, about 2 in. average width. Single drill-hole at one end; scalloped cut-outs at other end; from California.   C—$100

Shell pendants, large pendant 6 in. long. Small examples are abalone, from the Channel Islands, California. $100

Morris' Art & Artifacts, Anaheim, California; Dawn Gober photograph

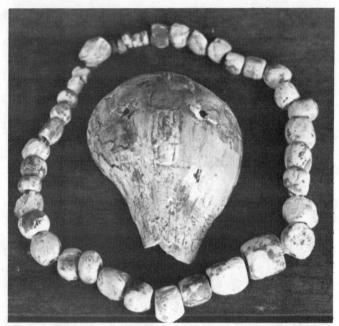

Center, Mississippian shell mask with bas-relief and drilled features, 3 x 4 in. Ca. AD 1200-1600, Arkansas. $700
Necklace, Mississippian period, 39 beads with largest ¾ in. This shell strand is 18 in. long. $125

Frank Bergevin, Port Of Call, Alexandria Bay, New York

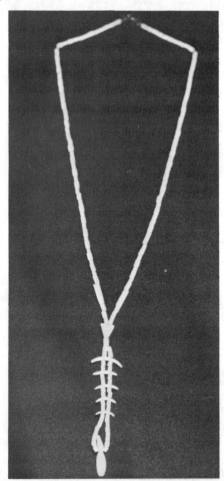

Trade wampum necklace, rare Seneca origin and Dutch-made with five crescents and a shell bird or duck effigy pendant, 25 in. plus 5¼ in. drop. From near Lima, New York, these are ca. 1640-1660 and ex-coll. Wray. $2500

Pat & Dave Summers, Native American Artifacts, Victor, New York

Strand of shell beads, graduated sizes and well-shaped beads, with 40 in. length. G—$210

Polished **shell pendant,** one side with heavy polish, drilled with three holes. It is 1¾ in. long and 1½ in. wide, from Virginia. G—$14

Graduated **strand of shell beads,** well shaped and 19 in. in length; from Tennessee. G—$75

Shell hoe, Virginia, 4 in. long 2½ in. wide. Made from shell of a freshwater mussel. Single hole in thick central portion for handle. Shell somewhat deteriorated. C—$19

Effigy shell head of alligator; strange piece excavated in Arkansas; it is undrilled and 2 in. long. G—$45

Northern California **tube shell beads,** made by pump-drilling abalone shell. G—$150

Conch shell plummet, from Florida, double grooved at the top. Piece is 4¼ in. long, slender, about 1 in. in diameter at center. Lower end tapers to near-point. Discolored with age. C—$60

Otter hide necklace with large **sea shell ornament,** possibly a personal amulet. G—$95

Grooved shell bead, perforated at each end to be worn as a pendant. From Tennessee, it is 3¾ in. long. G—$22

String of **marine shell beads,** approximately 50, recovered from site in Tennessee. Beads average ¾ in. long and ⅜ in. long and ⅜ in. in diameter. Well preserved necklace. C—$95

Outstanding strand of **shell heishi beads,** prehistoric, very well made; 31 in. in length, and from Arizona. G—$125

Shell ornaments in the shape of birds, from California. Two have holes; the third is undrilled. Average size, 1¼ in. by 1½ in. G—$40 set

Perforated shell disc, with hole in the center; 2 in. in diameter. G—$13

Suggested Reading

Miles, Charles, *Indian & Eskimo Artifacts of North America,* Bonanza Books, New York, 1963

Sioux Indian man performs in the Sun Dance in the Black Hills. Dancer may be blowing on bone whistle or flute.

Photo courtesy South Dakota State Historical Society.

Bell photo of three Sioux Indians dressed for the Sun Dance, probably in Black Hills. Two of the men are wearing large ''sun disc'' pendants.

Photo courtesy South Dakota State Historical Society.

CHAPTER IV

AXE FORMS

Indian axes are a touchmark of prehistoric occupation on the land. Most were made of some type of hardstone which worked well and provided a durable cutting edge and a pounding surface. The first well-made hardstone axes, as opposed to chipped flint, were made about 6000 years ago. Then Amerinds discovered how to shape stone by pounding, grinding and polishing.

Pecking and abrasion are the second of the three great tool-making methods. A stone a bit larger than the axe-to-be was selected. This was struck rapidly and repeatedly with a smaller hammerstone, each blow powdering and removing bits of stone.

Grooves were pecked and ground, except for celts. The axe was then polished, perhaps with sand and leather. Sometimes the entire axe head was so-treated; more often, the lower blade and groove area only were polished.

The groove of course was for the handle, and helped secure the axe while in use. This matter of the groove appears to follow a logical sequence, with the oldest axes being full-grooved, or entirely circled with the handle channel.

Later axes were either three-quarter grooved or half-grooved, depending on period and region. And the most recent axe form, used until the arrival of Whites, was the celt. This was essentially a long and narrow grooveless axe, and was mounted in a hole or socket of a rather thick-ended handle.

Some areas did not follow this exact progression, and the full-grooved axe was used by some later peoples. Whatever the type, the axe heads are scattered over most of North America. There is an interesting theory that a prime use for axes in prehistoric times wasn't for battle, or even for felling trees, though such woodwork was certainly done. Instead, axes were an aid in obtaining sufficient firewood for heat, light and food preparation.

The collecting of axes is a major field. Prices can range from several dollars for a battered, low-grade specimen to $1500 for a fine trophy-grade ceremonial axe.

The rare monolithic (one-stone) axes are late prehistoric copies of the celtiform axe — complete with handle. There's really no top price limit to axes of this type. But the average price for the average axe is probably in the $60 to $125 range.

For the dozens of thousands of collectible axes, a number of guidelines are used to judge axe quality. Material is important, with a compact, close-grained stone most desirable. According to several knowledgeable axe collectors, size and condition are the two key factors, followed by shape or type. Large size is preferred to smaller sizes, because these have more "visual impact" and do in fact represent more workmanship by the prehistoric creator.

As with all early Amerind works, condition — the presence and amount of damage or absence of same — is vital. (A particular perfect axe might be worth $200 to a collector; half the same axe, nothing). Some axe types are considered extra-good, because they have additional, often regional, "extras".

Examples might be the Michigan barbed axes, with the end-projecting grooved ridges, or the fluted Wisconsin varieties. These have various arrangements of shallow channels, usually at an angle to the actual axe groove. The purpose of such varieties is not known; it may have been only decorative.

Still other axe value determinants are overall workstyle and balance and symmetry along several examination planes. The blade edge or bit ought to be regular and without heavy use-damage. Grooved ridges, if present, should be even and similar. Polish adds to value, and the more the better.

Fakes exist in all axe categories, but abound in two. One is the low-cost axe, made of a softer stone (brown and gray sandstone seem to be popular) with the axe made first, then the groove pecked in. Widely sold in the $25 to $100 range, they are fine examples of nothing.

A tougher area is the well-made trophy-grade hardstone axe-head, complete with a few just-still-visible peck marks. Consult with advanced collectors before laying out any large sum, and if the piece is at all questionable, pass it by.

FULL GROOVE AXE, 4 x 6¾ in., and very heavy. Semi-polished, with some nicks, this piece is from Michigan. C—$125

Photo courtesy Bob Brand Collection, Pennsburg, Pennsylvania.

FULL GROOVE AXE, 4¾ x 8¼ in. Unpolished, but a good example of a Pennsylvania axe. From the Delaware River area. C—$85

Photo courtesy Bob Brand Collection, Pennsburg, Pennsylvania

FULL GROOVE AXE, 4 x 7¼ in. and very heavy. Somewhat crude, but an unusual type; semi-polished, and with several nicks. C—$300

Photo courtesy Bob Brand Collection, Pennsburg, Pennsylvania.

FULL—GROOVE AXES

Full-groove axe, Minnesota, 8¼ in. long, about 5 in. wide. Unusual in that groove is very near the center of axe, not closer to pounding poll. Little polish, a very utilitarian form, fine condition. C—$90

Supberb axe from Richland County, Ohio, 7¾ in. long and 3¾ in. wide. Fine condition. G—$295

Miniature Ohio grooved axe, highly polished, 3 in. long and 2 in. wide; material is a dark green color. G—$40

Full-grooved axe, Michigan, and blade tapers to about half of extreme width, 4¼ in. at grooved ridges. Piece is 6½ in. long, made of a white or gray stone. Some original wear on blade edge, but only average. C—$165

Full-groove axe, 5 in. long and 2⅝ in. wide, and a dark brown color. From Iowa. G—$45

Full-groove axe. Arizona, 6 in. long, of a black basaltic rock. Groove is near rounded poll, with long, polished blade and excurvate blade edge. D—$200

Full-groove axe, Missouri, 6¼ in. long, about 4 in. wide. Some damage to lower blade region, probably prehistoric breakage, disfigures piece. C—$35

Miniature full-groove axe, Illinois, 3⅛ in. long, and well-polished over all surface. Shallow groove. C—$65

Large full-groove axe, from Illinois, perhaps ceremonial. Piece is 14½ in. long, 8 in. wide and was a surface find on Archaic site. Well-polished in groove and lower blade regions; peck-marks remain on other surfaces. C—$600

Raised groove dark gray axe, found white excavating for the railroad building in St. Louis. Some damage to bit; piece is 7¼ in. long and 4 in. wide. G—$165

FULL-GROOVED AXE, 4¼ in. long. Archaic, excellent condition. Edge has very mild battering, but piece has overall high polish. C—$65
Private collection.

Full-groove axe, probably Middle Archaic, with pronounced ridge around groove, upper and lower areas. Axe is 10¼ in. long, of dark compact stone; high polish, especially on blade. C—$425

Small black **full-groove axe,** 4⅜ in. high and 2¾ in. wide. Groove is shallow but very regular, good overall polish to piece. Blade edge shows mild battering. C—$50

NOTE: A **full-groove axe,** the midwestern trophy-grade axe, is not represented here. Sometimes these are also **three-fourth groove.** This axe is made of colorful high-grade hardstone, is between 4 in. and 6 in. long, with ridged groove. No dealer had one in stock, and none have been offered at auction recently. The "going rate" for classic specimens is said to be in the $750 to $3000 range. One knowledgeable collector stated that probably no more than three hundred authentic pieces exist.

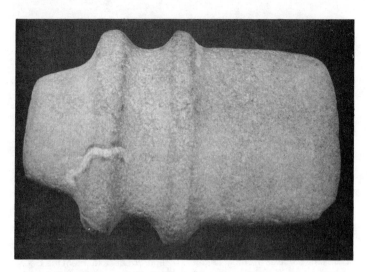

Axe, full or 4/4 grooved, Eastern raised-ridge (or Southern trophy axe), Alleghany County, North Carolina. Made of medium-grained granite, it is 9¾ in. long and weighs 8½ pounds. This is a museum quality axe, very rare. $5000 plus

Rodney M. Peck collection, Harrisburg, North Carolina

FULL-GROOVE ROUND-TOP AXE, 3 in. by 7¼ in. This piece is from New Jersey, unpolished, and with slight nick in the top. C—$100

Photo courtesy Bob Brand Collection, Pennsburg, Pennsylvania.

LIGHTLY GROOVED AXE, full-grooved type, 7 in. long. Almost round, it has an extreme diameter of 2½ in. Found in Mifflin County, Pennsylvania; cutting edge of bit is only ⅞ in. long, and is polished. C—$70

Photo courtesy Jonas Yoder, Jr., McVeytown, Pennsylvania

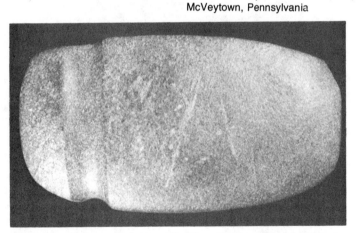

Axe, 4/4 or full grooved, from Pike County, Missouri. Material is a medium-grained granite and size is 8¼ in. long; weight is 5¼ pounds. $400

Rodney M. Peck collection, Harrisburg, North Carolina

Full-groove axe, Archaic, made of porphyry, black with yellow inclusions. Size is 2 x 3½ x 5¼ in. This beautiful example is ex-colls. Scott, Walters and Jardine. $900

Collection of David G. & Barbara J. Shirley

THREE-FOURTH GROOVE AXES
(also called "three-quarter groove")

Black and white granite **three-quarter groove axe,** Brown County, Illinois; 7 in. long, 4 in. wide. An exceptional axe. G—$350

Three-quarter groove axe, from Southwestern cliff dweller site, and with wide, shallow groove near large and rounded poll. Stone head is 6¼ in. long, of black material, with very small cutting edge, 1⅞ in. long, curved. Fine condition. D—$170

Very large **three-quarter groove axe,** Southeastern U.S., possibly ceremonial size. Axe head is 13¼ in. long, and 7 in. wide below groove. Good condition; not polished. A—$220

Full-groove or 4/4 stone axe, Archaic period, with flattened poll. It is made of gray-green hardstone and is from Horseheads, New York state. Size is 1½ x 2½ x 5¼ in. $200

Pat & Dave Summers, Native American Artifacts, Victor, New York

THREE-FOURTH GROOVE AXE, 4 x 6 in. Piece is very good condition, with a small nick on the back; semi-polished.   C—$200

Photo courtesy Bob Brand Collection, Pennsburg, Pennsylvania.

Large **three-quarter groove axe,** 9 in. long, 5½ in. wide, nearly 4 in. thick. Overall high polish.   A—$200

Miniature axe, three-quarter groove, exactly 3 in. long, about ⅝ in. thick. Well-made piece.   C—$80

Large **three-quarter groove axe,** Missouri, 6 in. long and 4½ in. wide.   G—$140

Three-quarter groove axe, about 6 in. long, about 3 in. wide, made of a dark, dense material. High polish in lower blade region.   A—$100

Hardstone **three-quarter groove axe,** Missouri, 4 in. long and 3 in. wide.   G—$70

LEFT:
THREE-FOURTH GROOVE AXE, 3¼ in. by 6½ in. with the Keokuk groove. From Pike County, Illinois, this is a good piece, semi-polished. It was formerly in the E.W. Payne Collection.   C—$250

Photo courtesy Bob Brand Collection, Pennsburg, Pennsylvania

Very fine THREE-QUARTER AXE, Archaic period, made of brown fine-grained stone. It is 8½ in. long and 4½ in. wide; weight is 7 pounds. This axe has exceptionally fine lines, and was found in Illinois.   C—$250-$600

Photo courtesy John P. Grotte, Illinois.

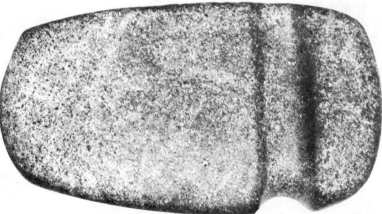

Hohokam **three-quarter groove axe.** Arizona, 9½ in. long, with typical wide and shallow groove. A little over 3 in. wide; stone head tapers to a small, rounded blade edge.   D—$125

Three-quarter groove axe, Western U.S., 5⅜ in. long. Narrow groove is rather deep; perfect condition. High polish in groove and all of blade area. Edge good.   C—$135

Exceptional **three quarter groove axe,** with slight basal flute, from Jersey County, Illinois. Piece is 7 in. long and 3½ in. wide. Material is dark green and white in color.G—$215

Fine Southwestern U.S. **axe,** three-quarter groove, perfect condition. Has made-up (recent) handle for display, but axehead is original and fine.   A—$115

Outstanding **Hohokam axe,** three-quarter groove, 8 in. long and 3 in. wide. Bit is highly polished.   G—$205

THREE-FOURTH GROOVE AXE, 3½ in. by 8 in., from Pike County, Illinois. Material is a greenish-black; piece is semi-polished, fine condition.   C—$350

Photo courtesy Bob Brand Collection, Pennsburg, Pennsylvania

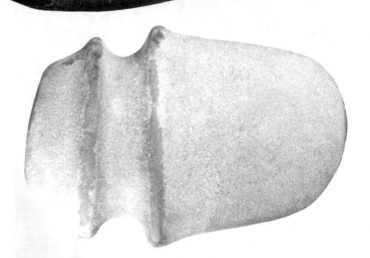

Fine THREE-QUARTER GROOVED AXE, of a granite-like fine grained brown stone. Axe is 8½ in. long, and 4½ in. wide and 2⅝ in. thick. It weighs 6 pounds and was found in Adams County, Illinois; this axe is very finely made.
C—$400-$650

Photo courtesy John P. Grotte, Illinois.

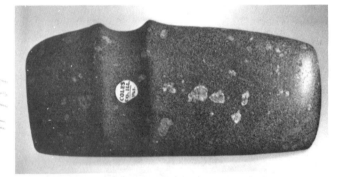

Axe, ¾ grooved, from Coles County, IL. This very fine axe is made from brown porphyry. It is 10¼ in. long and weighs 9 pounds. $3000

Rodney M. Peck collection, Harrisburg, North Carolina

Axe, full or 4/4 grooved, Eastern raised-ridge type, from Sevier Co., Tennessee. Material is a fine-grained granite. Size, 8¾ in. long, weight 5¾ pounds. $600

Rodney M. Peck collection, Harrisburg, North Carolina

Archaic axe, three-quarter grooved, 7½ in. long; weight is 7 pounds. This example is made of a heavy dark hardstone with medium polish. It was found during construction of Mohawk Dam in Ohio.$300-$350

Larry Garvin collection, Ohio

Axe, ¾ grooved, Saline County, Missouri. Material is a fine to medium-grained granite; axe is 8¾ in. long and weight is 7 pounds. $1000

Rodney M. Peck collection, Harrisburg, North Carolina

68

Three-quarter groove axes, dark hardstone, from Wisconsin. These are solid, well-made artifacts from the Archaic period. Axes are difficult to find anymore without implement strikes which produce scratches and scars. $250-$375 the two

Robert D. Lund collection, Watertown, Wisconsin

Prehistoric ¾ x 4/4 groove axes.
Back row, left to right: Illinois, 6 x 8½ in.; Georgia, 4 x 9 in; axe 3½ x 9 in.; Missouri, 4 x 8½ in.
Bottom row, center axe from Arizona is 2½ x 9 in. The two small 4/4 groove axes to either side are from the U.S. Northeast.
$75-$600 each

Philip L. Russo collection, Danbury, Connecticut

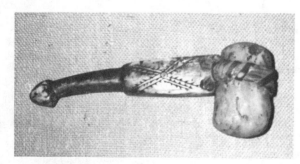

Rare complete club, jade head with carved and decorated ivory handle. The handle is about 10 in. long. This artifact was found in a cave along the Columbia River in Oregon. From an old collection, all parts of the club are original. Museum quality

Philip L. Russo collection, Danbury, Connecticut

HALF-GROOVE AXES

Half-groove axe, 4¼ in. long and 2¾ in. wide, good groove but blade is canted off to one side, giving a lopsided appearance. Made of a close-grained sandstone-like material. C—$37

Half-groove Keokuk-type axe, rectangular outline, 3¾ in. long. Made of a dark compact stone; groove and blade area well polished. Crisp, clean lines on this specimen. C—$85

Half-groove axe from Missouri, well-shaped and polish over entire surface. Edges, front and rear, undamaged. Axe is 7 in. long, 3¼ in. wide. No damage, fine specimen. C—. $300

Unremarkable **half-groove axe,** 4 in. long and 2¾ in. wide. Lacks polish; poll area is battered, blade average. C—$22

Half-groove Keokuk-type axe, made of a highly polished granite-like stone, black and tan color. Axe is 4¼ in. high. From Iowa. Blade edge forms very pleasing excurvate contour. D—$140

CELTS (ungrooved axes)

Large **celt,** from northern Louisiana, 7¼ in. long, 3¼ in. wide, well polished. Made of green and black material, no damage, good lines. D—$95

Large polished **celt.** From Shelby County, Illinois. Piece is 7 in. long and 3¼ in. wide. G—$175

Fine gray stone **celt,** 5 in. long and 2¼ in. wide. No damage. G—$40

Rectangular **Hopewellian celt,** central Ohio, 6 in. long, 2¾ in. wide at blade, both sides flatish. No damage, and made from a yellow and tan stone. Good lines C—$85

Miniature celt, 2 in. long and 1 in. wide. G—$20

Fine speckled granite-like **celt** 10 in. long, about 4 in. wide. Polished cutting edge; celt is cylindrical in shape, and even poll area is well polished. C—$115

Arkansas **Caddoan celt,** dark gray stone; 5 in. long and 1¾ in. wide. G—$30

Hardstone **celt,** average form, late prehistoric, from Illinois. Piece is 5½ in. long, 2¾ in. wide, about 2 in. thick. Several minor plow scars, otherwise good condition. D—$28

Granite **celt,** squared-base type, 5⅞ in. long, 2¾ in. wide. Good polish in lower blade area; two minor plow marks that disfigure blade side. C—$19

Celt from Virginia, 5¼ in. long and 2¼ in. wide. Stone is a light gray color. G—$16

Hopewellian **rectangular celt,** from Illinois, 9¼ in. long, 3¾ in. wide near bit, and evidencing almost perfect balance. All lines pleasing; entire surface area polished to a uniform medium-high gloss. No damage; piece looks as if it has never been used. Granitic stone approaches coal-black.C—$450

Dark greenstone **celt,** outstanding polish, good condition. It is 4¼ in. long and 2¼ in. wide.   G—$65

Miniature celt, 1⅜ in. long, from Iowa, found during tilling of garden. Proportionate to full-size specimens.C—$30

Miniature celt, 2¼ in. long, slightly flared blade corners, found in Missouri. Black and white hardstone. C—$70

Fine polished miniature flare-bit celt, from Oklahoma. It is 2½ in. long and 1½ in. wide.   G—$30

Dark green **celt** from eastern Texas, polished bit, 5 in. long and 2¼ in. wide.   G—$35

Banded slate celt, 6¾ in. long, from Illinois, and exactly 3 in. at greatest width. Cylindrical form, black bands on green back-ground. One agricultural equipment mark toward top of rounded poll, not deep.   C—$50

Granite **celt,** rectangular form, 4 in. long and 2¼ in. wide. High polish overall, and speckled black and white material. No damage; perfect proportions. From Missouri.C—$60

CELTIFORM TOOLS, all from Canada, and averaging 5 in. in length. Piece in center may be unfinished; all in fine condition. C—$10-$40
each
Photo courtesy Robert C. Calvert, London, Ontario, Canada.

Adz blades, all late prehistoric, Adena culture, Midwestern. Top: Lower portion of larger ADENA ADZ, salvaged in rear section, 3¼ in. long, colorful material.   C—$20
Black ADENA ADZ, edge shows heavy wear, good form.   C—$30
Small brown stone ADENA ADZ, exactly to scale of much larger specimens, 3¼ in. long.   C—$25
ADENA ADZ blade, almost identical to black specimen at left; edge is sharp.   C—$30
Private collection.

Three fine Midwestern celts. L to R: Fine late prehistoric HOPEWELLIAN CELT, nicely tapered. Polish on lower blade, 5⅜ in. long.   C—$55
Slender TAPERED CELT, prob. late prehistoric, made of a brownish quartz. Unusual material and good lines to piece.   C—$65
Large HOPEWELLIAN CELT, nearly round at center, heavily polished over entire surface. Brown material, black inclusions, granite-like stone.   C—$85

Private collection.

Small section of late prehistoric artifacts, longest (bot. L.) 3½ in. (Top row, L to R; small CELT).   C—$15
Rectangular HOPEWELLIAN CELT, perfect form and highly polished overall.   C—$40
SLATE CELT, probably Adena, good edge and well-rounded.C—$20
Celt or CHISEL, well-polished overall, two small damaged areas appear as light-colored spots.   C—$15
CHISEL, well-tapered but no polish. May be fragment from larger specimen.   C—$10

Private collection.

Unusual THREE-QUARTERS GROOVED AXE, from Franklin County, Ohio, and 6⅞ in. long, 3⅝ in. wide. Made of grayish quartzite material. Axe has narrow ridge running from front of groove to lower blade, then up rear portion to flatish area behind groove. Also, blade size is small for axe of this size.

C—$225

Private collection.

From left to right:
CELTS AND GOUGES, average-good condition, made of slate and hardstone. All from Canada.

C—$5-$25 each

Large CELTS, possibly Woodland period, one 10 in. long, other 8¾ in. Blade lengths are 2½ in. both from Canada.   Left (longest) C—$30
Right C—$30

Photo courtesy Robert C. Calvert, London, Ontario, Canada.

Fine THREE-QUARTERS GROOVED AXE, 7½ in. long, 3¼ in. wide below notch. Very good condition, some polish, Franklin County, Ohio. Archaic period; axe is made of a compact brownish material. C—$250

Private collection.

Chipped flint artifacts with polished blade areas. L to R:
FLINT CELT about 5 in. long, blade region highly polished. C—$40
FLINT CELT or chisel, lower blade region nicely polished, good edge.
C—$15
FLINT CHISEL, highly polished blade area, small working edge C—$25
Private collection.

AXE VARIETIES

Lightly **grooved celt,** Indiana, with the tapering characteristics of the celt and very light axe-like full grooving. Piece is about 6 in. long, and groove was pecked in at no great depth. Celt head is lightly polished overall except for groove.   D—$65

Porphyry **Michigan barbed axe,** very colorful material. Outstanding specimen that has been pictured in archaeological publications. It is 7¼ in. long and 3¾ in. wide.
G—$800

Very good **flared-bit celt** or spatulate form, nearly 6 in. long and 2½ in. wide at blade-edge tips. Well-contoured and is made of a dark, compact material.   D—$115

Black **stone monolithic axe,** 15¾ in. long, and 6¼ in. high at celtiform head height. Copy is one-piece stone of complete celt-axe with handle. Piece has exceptional polish overall. Very rare; probably no more than a few hundred complete specimens exist. Late prehistoric. (Private collection)
C—$4500

Flare-bit celt, fine condition, polish on blade. Piece is 7½ in. long and 3¼ in. wide.   G—$90

Wisconsin fluted axe, three-quarter groove, with fluting running parallel to groove and lower blade regions. Fluting is very shallow but regular. Axe is 6½ in. long. C—$375

Notched celt, from Indiana, 3½ in. long, and with pecked notches on side edges. Faces polished; interesting specimen and not common.

CELTIFORM TOOLS, hardstone and slate, 4½ in. to 6 in. long. All from Canada, and evidencing varied degrees of workstyle and condition.
C—$5-$30
each
Photo courtesy Robert C. Calvert, London, Ontario, Canada.

Unusual DUO-BLADE CELT, from collection in New Jersey. Material is a light green very compact material almost resembling soapstone. Both edges fine condition, overall polish. Piece is 6¼ in. long, about 3½ in. wide.   D—$45

Private collection.

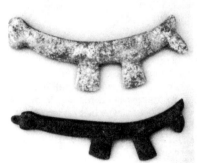

Top "SLAVE-KILLER" CEREMONIAL AXE, 15 in. long. Item was traded for at the mouth of the Columbia River in 1840 by Joseph Moore, Mate of the ship Salem Queen.
Bottom   "SLAVE-KILLER" CEREMONIAL AXE, 15 in. long. This piece was found about 1833 on the Oregon coast.
C—Museum quality; No value listed. S.W. Kernaghan photo; Marguerite Kernaghan Collection.

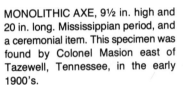

MONOLITHIC AXE, 9½ in. high and 20 in. long. Mississippian period, and a ceremonial item. This specimen was found by Colonel Masion east of Tazewell, Tennessee, in the early 1900's.
C—Museum quality; no value listed.

S.W. Kernaghan photo; Marguerite Kernaghan Collection.

HUMP-BACKED AXE or ADZ, 6½ in. long and 2 in. wide and thick at central ridge. Blade is at wider end, and piece is in excellent condition; not a common artifact. Material is a green hardstone. C—$75-$125

Photo courtesy Robert C. Calvert. London. Ontario, Canada.

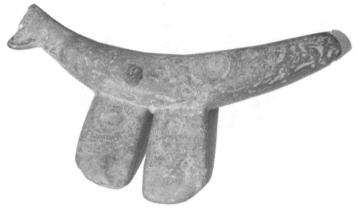

"Slave-killer" axe, from Oregon coastal region, made of hard slate. The neck of the effigy was broken and has been reglued.Museum quality

Private collection

Axe, 4/4 grooved, Eastern raised-ridge type or Southern trophy type. From Granville County, North Carolina, material is a quartz diorite. It is 10 in. long and weighs 9 pounds. This is a rare, museum-quality axe. $3000

Rodney M. Peck collection, Harrisburg, North Carolina

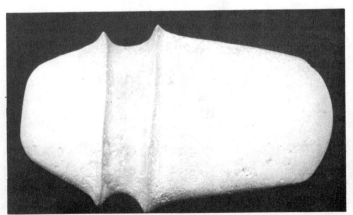

Axe, full or 4/4 grooved, Eastern raised-ridge type from Washington County, Virginia. It is made of a fine-grained granite material; size, 8½ in. long, four pounds in weight. $600

Rodney M. Peck collection, Harrisburg, North Carolina

Axes and celts, at center a trophy-grade axe 10 in. long, ¾ groove with a fine edge. Lower right is a rare pocket axe, 4/4 or full-groove. All are from the Columbia River area. $20-$200 each

Morris' Art & Artifacts, Anaheim, California; Dawn Gober photograph

Full-groove axe found in Oklahoma County, Oklahoma. This interesting artifact is 11 in. long, made from light brown hardstone. $250

Larry G. Merriam collection, Oklahoma City, Oklahoma

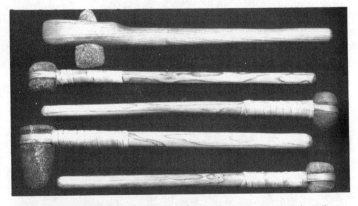

Ancient stone tools with modern museum-demonstration type handles. Shown are three grooved hammerstones and a celt (top) and grooved axehead (bottom). Hafting designs are based on extant specimens found in rock shelters or underwater; hafting done by Deer Creek Enterprises, Ohio.

$235-$295 each

Larry Lantz, First Mesa, South Bend, Indiana

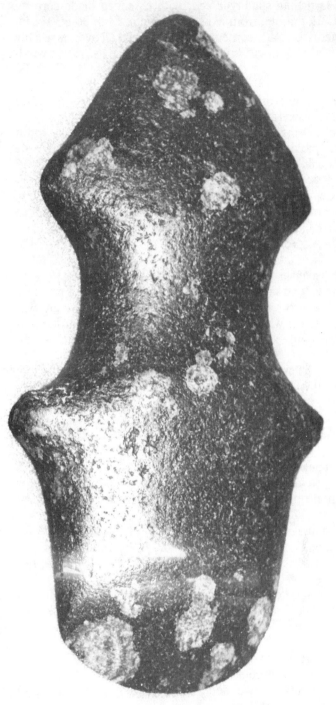

Michigan barbed axe, from Shiawassee County, Michigan. Made of porphyry, it is black and green with tan inclusions. Size is 1⅝ x 3¾ x 6¾ in. and it has G.I.R.S. authentication number 0-6. $2500

Collection of David G. & Barbara J. Shirley

Hardstone spud-type celt, with extended blade corners. Dark granite, from Missouri. Spud is 13 in. long, 3¼ in. across at blade corners. Highly polished all over, especially in blade region. Probably ceremonial; no use marks whatsoever. C—$900

Extremely fine **Michigan barbed-ridge axe,** with groove extensions at both ends, top and bottom. Material is a gray speckled granite, and piece is 8½ in. long, average width for piece. Perfect conditon. Axe poll is almost pointed. Fine polish. D—$650

Celtiform spud or **flare-bit celt,** found in eastern Minnesota. About 8 in. long, 3½ in. wide at blade corners. Each face has 3 shallow grooves, for unknown reasons. Not a common specimen. D—$400

Wisconsin fluted axe, three-quarter groove type, 6½ in. long, with single central flute on each blade side. From this, other grooves radiate. Rounded poll also has two grooves on sides, which follow contour of the top. Unusual, interesting example of multiple fluting. D—$850

Large **flare-bit celt,** blade sides and edge highly polished, body of piece retains some peckmarks. It is 11¼ in. long, and 4⅛ in. across at blade edges. C—$450

Missouri **flare-bit celt,** 6½ in. long and 2½ in. wide. G—$65

Double-groove axe, from northern Missouri, unusual. Piece is 5¾ in. long, about 2½ in. wide, lower groove a bit deeper than upper groove. Green, compact stone. C—$140

Double-groove axe, Iowa, black granitic stone and 6½ in. long, 2⅞ in. wide. Distinct double groove, and lower blade is in perfect condition. Little polish. C—$140

Long-poll celt, Lower Mississippi Valley, 6¼ in. long, 1⅜ in. wide. Fine example and undamaged; unusually slender for type. D—$95

Half-groove axe, Iowa, 3½ in. long and 3¼ in. wide. Well-polished, fine color, perfect condition except for tiny chip from cutting edge, depression polished. C—$90

Hardstone adz, 4⅞ in. long, 1⅞ in. wide at curved cutting edge. Flat bottom, very minor damage to rounded end. D—$60

Three-quarter groove axe, from Arizona, 9 in. long and 3¼ in. wide at groove area. Good polish in groove and on lower blade. Fine overall form. D—$155

Stone artifacts.
Top, axe or hoe, brownstone, from Mississippi. $100
Bottom, graystone axe, from Michigan $100
Wilfred A. Dick collection, Magnolia, Mississippi

Celt made of rock crystal or clear quartz, transparent, 1⁹⁄₁₆ x 4⅛ in. This rare and fine piece is from Hardin County, Ohio, and probably Woodland period in origin. This example is one of a very few ever found in the Eastern Midwest.

Museum quality

Larry Garvin collection, Ohio

Adena celt, Early Woodland, material a gray-green hardstone. Well-polished, this artifact is from Monroe County, Ohio, and is 5⅛ in. long. $70
Private collection, Ohio

Celt, Woodland period, from Midland, Michigan. It is made of brownish-tan banded slate with black banding. Size, ⅝ x 2 x 6⅜ in. Slate is an unusual celt material and this is a scarce artifact. $500

Collection of David G. & Barbara J. Shirley

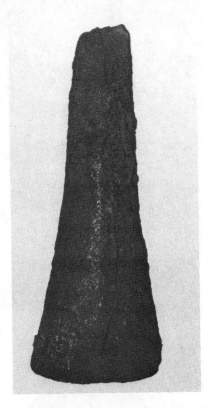

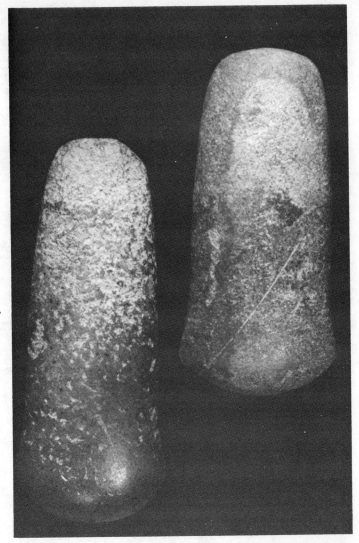

Celts, flared-bit, from Alexander County, Illinois. Material is fine to medium-grained granite.
Left: 8½ in. long. $300
Right: 7½ in. long $300

Rodney M. Peck collection, Harrisburg, North Carolina

Copper celt, Late Archaic Old Copper culture, from Barron County, Wisconsin. A personal find by the owner, it measures 1⁹⁄₁₆ x 4 in. It is in very good condition. $250

Dennis R. Lindblad collection, Chetek, Wisconsin

Celt collection, many sizes, materials and styles. These are from the states of Alabama, Arkansas and Mississippi. $15-$75 each

Wilfred A. Dick collection, Magnolia, Mississippi

Grooved axes, all Archaic period. Five are full-groove with example at top right three-quarter groove. $250-$350 the group

Robert D. Lund collection, Watertown, Wisconsin

Celts or ungrooved axes from the Woodland period, different sizes, styles and materials. Second artifact from the bottom appears to be an adz or gouge. This is a good small collection.   Collection $125-$175

Robert D. Lund collection, Watertown, Wisconsin

Far View Ruins, foreground; background, Pipe Shrine House. Both are on the canyon rim in Mesa Verde National Park, Colorado. Many of the early ruins (including those shown) have been carefully preserved and stabilized to protect them. Both of the ruins shown are Developmental Pueblo period.

Lar Hothem photo

CHAPTER V

STONE COLLECTIBLES

"Stone" here means hardstone, natural rocks commonly used in prehistoric times to make artifacts. This chapter deals with a variety of classes, among them the curious discoidals, food grinders and pulverizers, and the mundane hammerstones. There are effigies, utensils and many others.

For each grouping, a slightly different set of measures determine collector interest and help set fair market values. All of these artifacts are relatively simple in design, except for effigy figures.

Portrayals of human, and animal, figures from early times have always been premium collector items. In all this stone-collectible area, the one aspect to be examined is the nebulous term, "first appearance".

Assuming the article is genuine — and no listing or photograph of a known questionable piece has been but in this book — there are some questions to be considered. Is the artifact pleasing? Why? Does it bother, confuse you? Again why? Is it larger or smaller than usual for the type — and is it too large or too small for your taste? Does it, as is, give a feeling of completeness, of well-accomplished form?

Granted, this is looking at early Indian items as art — but that is what is being done these days. Again, the value-range can be jolting. A plain oval pestle, little more than a natural cobble with some wear-marks, can have literally no market value. A long ceremonial-grade pestle, say from the Northwest U.S. region and evidencing supreme care in the making can easily be in the $1000 to $3000 class.

There is still some diversity of opinion as to what discoidals ("discs" to collectors) are. It is agreed that they are found in the Mississippi watershed area and are late prehistoric. Numerous historic-period reports state they were rolled along the ground and were used as targets for arrows and thrown darts in a game called "Chunkey".

However, the workmanship displayed for many fine examples suggests they were more than utilitarian in nature, at least the better specimens. And there is a definite lack of damage which would have resulted from such violent use. A superb specimen sold a few years ago for $1000, but the average disc price would be nearer $100-$200.

Plummets are still another enigma; few are listed here, as they were commonly made of materials other than hardstone. Plummets are shaped like elongated eggs, with a hole or groove at the smaller end. Most are meticulously made, well proportioned and polished.

For a long time, it was thought they were fishing or net sinkers. New thought is that they were **bolas** weights, and were secured by short thongs in sets of 3 to 5. In use, they were whirled and thrown, to bring down waterfowl or small game.

The following information on spatulates was written by Tom Browner of Davenport, Iowa, who has contributed greatly to the prehistoric section of the book; used with permission.

NORTHERN TRADITION SPATULATE, 9 in. long and 3 in. wide at flared bit. This specimen is one of the finest of the type. Note the lighter hafting band 3½ in. from the bit tip. Rounded bit and oblong poll show it to be from about AD 900. Material is a gray, polished granite; this piece is from Fulton County, Illinois.

C—$1200

Courtesy Ferrel Anderson, photographer; Thomas Browner Collection; Davenport, Iowa.

INTRODUCTION

"Spatulates, commonly known as spuds, probably began around AD 500, having evolved from the Woodland culture's flare-bit celts. Like celts, many spatulates show halfting lines where they were attached to wooden handles. Spatulates continued to evolve until the end of the Mississippian period, about AD 1700.

"It is uncertain where spatulates began; however, the Mississippi River Valley north of St. Louis is an educated guess. This assumption is based on the large numbers of spuds found in the region and the fact that Cahokia seems to be the divisional point between Northern and Southern traditions.

"The heart area" of the Northern Tradition seems to be Illinois, Missouri, Indiana and Ohio. Northern Tradition spatulates are made of fine-grained granites and occasionally slate. The earlier types tend to have thicker bodies like celts, oval cross-sections and rounded bits. As time progressed, the polls became thinner and more rounded. The bits became more elongated and convex. To the North, the polls became shorter; likewise, the further South the longer the polls tend to be.

"Southern Spatulates tend to have rounded and long polls. The material of choice tends to be green-stone or slates. The bits flatten and become almost square in classic types, with tally marks or grooves being common. The Southern Tradition heartland is southern Illinois, Missouri, Kentucky, Tennessee, Georgia, and Alabama, Cahokia, near St Louis, Missouri, seems to be the area where the two traditions met."

Unfortunately, because of space limitations, this section can only give a sampling of the rich and varied field of hardstone Indian collectibles.

LATE SOUTHERN-TYPE SPATULATE or spud from, 5¾ in. by 5⅛ in. A large specimen of a rare type, it lacks the drilled hole common in many pieces. Exfoliation of the surface and large size identify this as authentic. There are generally no genuine artifacts of this type on the market. Specimen is made of red and tan limonite, and is from Woodruff County, Arkansas.   C—$150-$400

Courtesy Ferrel Anderson, photographer; Thomas Browner Collection; Davenport, Iowa.

SPATULATES OR SPUDS

Granite spud, 10 in. long and 1¼ in. wide, made of well-polished material, good overall form. This piece was broken and restored.   A—$150

Elongated spud, 13¼ in. long and 1⅞ in. wide, with good material, blackish fine-grained hardstone. Beautiful form, evenly flared bit, high polish; one slight plow-scar along poll side but barely visible. Rare item in size and shape.   C—$1500

Granite spud, 10 in. long and 2 in. wide at bit. Bit or blade area has softly rounded corners instead of sharp shoulders.   A—$95

Granite spud, 8 in. long and 3 in. wide, well polished and good form. Fine condition.   A—$360

Banded slate spud, 7½ in. long and 1⅜ in. wide, made of a finely banded green and black material. Good shape and overall polish, no damage.   C—$550

DISCOIDALS

Double-cupped discoidal, 3¼ in. wide, 1⅜ in. high, light tan granitic material and overall high polish. Midwestern piece.   C—$155

Tennessee discoidal, uncupped and of a black material. It is 2¼ in. in diameter and 1¼ in. high.   G—$90

Pink and black quartz discoidal, 3½ in. in diameter and 1½ in. high, slightly cupped each side. Piece is from Illinois.   G—$225

Miniature discoidal, 1¼ in. in diameter, ⅜ in. thick, very shallowly cupped, medium-good polish. Rare.   C—$65

Quartz discoidal, cups on each side (double or duo-cupped), and has a golden color. Piece is 2¼ in. in diameter and ¾ in. thick.   G—$160

Hardstone discoidal, made of a light-colored close-grained stone. Cupped on both sides, perfectly round, smooth finish. A bit over 4 in. in diameter, and 1⅜ in. thick at outer rim. Hole at center where the bottom of cups meet.   C—$450

Pink hardstone discoidal, with deep cups, 2¼ in. in diameter and 1¼ in. thick.   G—$260

Quartz discoidal, duo-cupped, nearly 6 in. in diameter and 2⅛ in. in thickness. Polished to a high gloss overall, no damage or imperfection in stone. Piece glitters with quartzite inclusion when strong light strikes it; very pleasing piece.   C—$1300

Discoidal of pottery, only 1½ in. in diameter, and with decorations of incised lines scratched into surface.   C—$10

Discoidal from Tennessee, double-dish (duo-cupped) form, perfectly scooped and "dimple" in center of cup on each side. Piece is 3¾ in. in diameter, made from fine orange-red stone.   C—$420

Double-cupped discoidal, Indiana, 2⅞ in. in diameter and 1¼ in. thick.   D—$110

Biscuit-type discoidal, 2⅛ in. in diameter, made of black and reddish hardstone. Perfect, and polished.   C—$115

Quartzite double-cupped discoidal, 2½ in. in diameter and of a dark green steatite. Outside rim has a single meandering line incised around it.   C—$170

Sandstone discoidal, battered around outside rim, 2¼ in. in diameter.   C—$25

Barrel-type discoidal, 2¾ in. in diameter, 2⅛ in. thick. Average good condition; not much polish.   D—$37

DOUBLE-CUP LATE WOODLAND DISCOIDAL, 2¾ in. in diameter. This specimen is notable for its deep cups, perfect symmetry and polish; even the cups are polished, which is unusual for most discoidals. The piece is from Des Moines County, Iowa, and is made of rhyolite. C—$375

Courtesy Ferrel Anderson, photographer; Thomas Browner Collection; Davenport, Iowa.

Tan and brown striped DISCOIDAL, Jersey Bluff or Cahokia type. It is 3½ in. in diameter and 2 in. high, and from Mississippian times. C—$250

DOUBLE-CUP WOODLAND DISCOIDAL, 4¼ in. in diameter, 2 in. thick. Made of black granite, this is an Ohio piece. The specimen has good size, shape and deep cups. It also lacks color and sharply delineated cup rims; not quite unique enough to command the top discoidal prices of $400-$500. Perfect condition. C—$325

Courtesy Ferrel Anderson, photographer; Thomas Brewer Collection; Davenport, Iowa.

Jersey Bluff type DISCOIDAL, 2⅝ in. in diameter and 1½ in. high. Made of a dark green material, from Adams County, Illinois, and highly polished. Probably from Mississippian period. C—$215

Photo courtesy John P. Grotte, Illinois.

CAHOKIA TYPE DISCOIDAL, 3 in. in diameter. This is a classic Cahokia discoidal with deep cups and prominant rims. When competing local collectors attempt to obtain a limited number of classic artifacts, the prices go up. This piece is made of gray granite and is from Pike County, Illinois. C—$400

Courtesy Ferrel Anderson, photographer; Thomas Browner Collection; Davenport, Iowa.

CAHOKIA TYPE DISCOIDAL. 2¾ in. in diameter, and made of red quartzite. This is a nice intact and colorful specimen, with traceable history. It is from Pike County, Illinois. C—$175

Courtesy Ferrel Anderson, photographer; Thomas Browner Collection; Davenport, Iowa.

STONE DISCOIDAL, Jersey Bluff type (has somewhat flattened portion around both outside rims) and made of an attractive yellow, green, black and pink granite. Discoidal was found in Adams County, Illinois, and is 3¾ in. in diameter, 2¼ in. high. It displays exceptionally fine workmanship. C—$800

Photo courtesy John P. Grotte, Illinois.

Cahokia-type white quartz DISCOIDAL, with outer rim nearly joining central cups on both sides. Found in Madison County, Illinois, this would be a Mississippian period artifact. It is 2⅝ in. in diameter, and 1¼ in. high. C—$495

Photo courtesy John P. Grotte, Illinois.

BISCUIT-TYPE DISCOIDAL, 3¼ in. in diameter. Material is a brown and tan claystone. The piece is from Menard County, Illinois, and very colorful and nicely polished. C—$275

Courtesy Ferrel Anderson, photographer; Thomas Browner Collection; Davenport, Iowa.

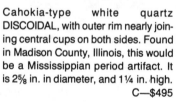

DISCOIDAL, Jersey Bluff or Cahokia type, found in Humphrey County, Tennessee. It is 2⅜ in. in diameter and 1¼ in. high. From Mississippian times, it is made of a colorful reddish purple and gray quartz. C—$425

Photo courtesy John P. Grotte, Illinois.

BISCUIT-TYPE DISCOIDAL, 2⅞ in. in diameter and made of black diorite. The specimen shows high polish, center pecking and very shallow cupping; it was found on an early Woodland site on the bluffs near Quincy, Illinois. C—$350

Courtesy Ferrel Anderson, photographer; Thomas Browner Collection; Davenport, Iowa.

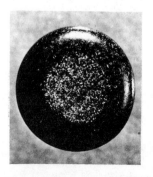

Discoidals or gamestones, Mississippian period. Top row, left to right:
Sandstone, not well-made, MS $15
Pottery, cupped both sides, AR $25
Sandstone, smooth, well-made, AR $40
Sandstone, rough and thick, MS $15
Sandstone, smoothed, AR $25
Center, fine double-cupped disc, nicely shaped and worked, MS$250
Miniature beside coin, Northwest U.S., Snake River area . $75

Wilfred A. Dick collection, Magnolia, Mississippi

Discoidal, perforated with ¼ in. hole, Mississippian period. It is made of cannel coal and is from Trigg County, KY. $250
Marguerite L. Kernaghan collection; photograph by Marguerite L. and Stewart W. Kernaghan, Bellvue, Colorado

Stone artifacts, all from Mississippi. Top, sandstone discoidal $25
Center left, polisher(?), mano(?) $25
Center, brownstone discoidal $50
Center, right, pestle $10
Bottom, well-shaped mano/pestle $35

Wilfred A. Dick collection, Magnolia, Mississippi

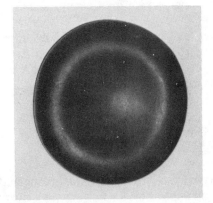

Discoidal, Mississippian period, made of cannel coal. It was found in Trigg County, KY, and is 2½ in. in diameter. $175
Marguerite L. Kernaghan collection; photograph by Marguerite L. and Steward W. Kernaghan, Bellvue, Colorado

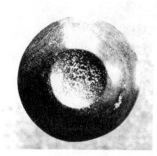

SALT RIVER TYPE DISCOIDAL, 4½ in. in diameter and 2¼ in. thick and a large and colorful specimen. Salt River discoidals vary from other types in that the circumference is not oval, but comes to a fine edge like a "V". They are found in the Mississippi River area above St. Louis, Missouri. This piece is made of red quartzite and came from the LaSalle-Peru area of Illinois. C—$600

Courtesy Ferrel Anderson, photographer; Thomas Browner Collection; Davenport, Iowa.

Mortars or seed-grinding containers, stone, from the Northeastern U.S. Fine examples such as these are not common. $50-$250 each

Philip L. Russo collection, Danbury, Connecticut

DOUBLE-CUP DISOIDAL, sometimes called a "dimple" cup, from the Mississippian era. The disc is 4¾ in. in diameter and is a classic piece. Note the well-defined edges and dimple. Large size, polish and symmetry make this an outstanding artifact. Made of brown granite, this comes from Ohio County, Kentucky.C—$575

Courtesy Ferrel Anderson, photographer; Thomas Browner Collection; Davenport, Iowa.

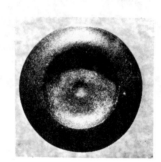

MORTARS & PESTLES (Eastern U.S.)
MANOS & METATES (Western U.S.)

Round boulder **mortar,** from California beach site. It is 9 in. across, and the pounding hole in center is about 4½ in. across. Exterior surface of mortar is fairly smooth. C—$32

Pear-shaped pestle, probably Archaic, 3 in. high, found in Alabama. Made of a dull-colored hardstone. C—$16

Missouri **mano** or hand-held corn-grinding stone, 2 in. high and 3 in. wide. G—$10

Bell-type pestle, 6½ in. high and 3⅝ in. wide at basal diameter. Top expands slightly while central section is about 2 in. in diameter. Piece is made of a yellow-tan material and there is high polish on the central shaft. C—$130

Stone pestle, Oregon, 8 in. high. Cylindrical form, and tapering from top to base. Base has an extended band 2 in. high; top has similar but smaller band. Central portion of cylinder forms a handgrip. C—$135

Roller-type pestle, Vermont, 11½ in. long, about 2 in. diameter. Some polish around circumference, and polished at both ends, rounded in same areas. C—$70

Stone mortar from North Carolina, oblong and about 10 in. long. Top depression for holding seeds averages ¾ in. in depth. Center shows extensive wear. C—$26

Pole-shaped mano, New Mexico, 9½ in. long. Chip on one end, otherwise fine condition. G—$32

Mortar and pestle, mortar height 14 in. and diameter 16 in.; the pestle is 16 in. long and 4 in. in diameter. From the Columbia River area, the artifacts are ex-museum and ca. AD 1600-1800. $350

Morris' Art & Artifacts, Anaheim, California; Dawn Gober photograph

Large round **mortar and pestle,** latter over 14 in. in diameter, 7¾ in. high. Pestle about 10 in. high. (May not have been an original set, but looks like they belong together). Central California origin. C—$110

Metate or grinding slab for the mano; seed-grinder is 19 in. long, large for the type. Made from a loose-grained stone, upper working surface ground down from long use. Northwestern Nevada. C—$60

Flat **stone metate** from Texas, near Mexican border, about 7 in. long. Grinding stone has 3 protrusions on bottom in triangular pattern, like short legs. C—$65

Mano or hand-stone for grinding grain or seeds, oblong, 7 in. in length. Underside flat; may have been used with both hands. Probably prehistoric Hohokam, Arizona, and made from a slate-gray porous volcanic rock. C—$17

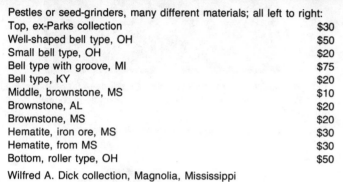

Pestles or seed-grinders, many different materials; all left to right:

Top, ex-Parks collection	$30
Well-shaped bell type, OH	$50
Small bell type, OH	$20
Bell type with groove, MI	$75
Bell type, KY	$20
Middle, brownstone, MS	$10
Brownstone, AL	$20
Brownstone, MS	$20
Hematite, iron ore, MS	$30
Hematite, from MS	$30
Bottom, roller type, OH	$50

Wilfred A. Dick collection, Magnolia, Mississippi

Bird-faced **paint mortar,** Oregon, perhaps depicting a hawk. Piece is 7 in. high, 4 in. in diameter, and in battered but good condition. Made from a rough-grained river boulder. Effigy has indented eyes, projecting beak.   C—$350

Long decorative and cylindrical **stone pestle,** probably Yurok, and 16½ in. in length. Piece is 3¼ in. in diameter at base. Extended ring rear bottom and near top. Fine and highly polished stone.   C—$550

WOODWORKING TOOLS

Grooved stone gouge, New York, 8¼ in. long, 2⅛ in. wide at rounded cutting bit. Groove on underside runs from bit to poll end. (Such length is unusual, as many are only partially grooved). Light tan stone, high polish.   D—$235

Black **hardstone chisel,** 4⅜ in. long, and 1 in. wide, tapered to straight blade at one end, rounded at other. No damage, some heavy use-marks on bit or blade edge.   C—$70

Three-quarter groove adz, from Georgia near Florida line; 9 in. long. Well-finished overall, some use-marks; this is not a particular common type of artifact.   C—$175

Hardstone gouge, New Jersey, 6⅛ in. long, deeply scooped concave groove on underside running half the length of piece. It is 1½ in. wide at the cutting edge.   D—$70

Hump-backed adz, from Indiana, 6¾ in. long, with protruding ridge on topside, evidently to aid hafting. Believed to be a woodworking tool. Made of a gray-black material, and piece is about 2 in. wide. Nice polish, no damage.   C—$395

OTHER STONE ARTIFACTS

Sandstone **shaft smoother,** 4 in. long. The flat stone has a straight groove along the top, about ½ in. across and ⅜ in. deep. From South Dakota.   C—$25

Stone adz handle, from southwestern Washington. It is 11¾ in. long, with a down-curved handle grip. Unusual, but without the once-attached adz head. Well-made piece; well-worn.   C—$155

Rare piece from northern Alabama; **hardstone bowl,** 9⁵⁄₁₆ in. in diameter, nearly 3 in. high. Polished inside and out. Pink, close-grained stone, but not Catlinite. Probably a ceremonial item; possibly Mississippian period in origin.   C—$560

"Donut stone", California, 3½ in. in diameter, and with central hole 1 in. across. Made of a compact hardstone, no damage, highly polished piece. May have been a clubhead.   C—$150

Historic **Sioux food pulverizer,** stone head 4 in. high, flat bottom, used for tenderizing meat, crushing seeds and making pemmican. An all-purpose tool, with plain wrap-around leather covered handle 14 in. long.   D—$125

Small **stone bowl,** from Oregon, 2¼ in. high, about 5 in. in diameter, of smooth brown stone. Edges chipped in a number of places.   A—$75

Sandstone spool, very late prehistoric (Woodland), and from Ohio. Piece is 3⅛ in. long, and has incised wavy lines on central part of cylinder, which is concave. It is thought that sandstone spools were used with pigment to ceremonially decorate the body.   C—$800

Clear rock crystal pebble pendant or bead, smoothed almost flat on one side, left naturally rounded on the other. Hole had been drilled in one end, but had broken through. Very small hole 1/16 in. had been drilled in opposite end. Period unknown; picked up on Midwestern site that has produced Archaic and Woodland artifacts. C—$45

Sandstone awl-sharpener, 3 in. long, with several thin grooves on upper surface. Believed to be "needle tracks". C—$13

Ceremonial club, from British Columbia, Canada. Piece is 16 in. long, and with human head at base of handle. Blade has a blunt cutting edge; weight is just over 4 pounds, and made of a compact dark gray stone. C—$950

Hardstone pendant, 2¾ in. long, 1⅜ in. wide, made of a fine-grained salt and pepper colored hardstone. Single hole drilled in smaller end, from both sides. Surface hole drilled in smaller end, from both sides. Surface is highly polished. Perfect condition, from Illinois. C—$500

Plain stone club, of the "fish-killer" type, **miniature** form, only 7½ in. long and ⅞ in. in diameter. Quite unusual, and has small hole drilled in handle end. C—$350

Steatite or soapstone bowl, 12 in. by 16 in. and about 5 in. deep. Exterior walls about 1½ in. thick. Recovered from central California, and in undamaged condition except for extreme wear on upper edges. A rare item. C—$650

Cupstone, about 12 in. long and 4 in. wide, with 2 depressions in top about the size of a silver dollar. Common on Archaic sites in Midwest, purpose uncertain. C—$10

Plummet, from Archaic site, 2¾ in. long, 1 in. in diameter. Made of pink sandstone, top grooved. Perfect. C—$23

Plummet, granite, 1½ in. long and ⅝ in. in diameter. Very shallow groove about in middle. C—$26

Drilled stone tube, 3⅞ in. long, flat on bottom, highly polished surface. Piece has a central hole and about ½ in. in diameter. Stone mottled green and white, one small scratch across top. C—$165

Sandstone scooped bowl, Massachusetts, 9 in. in diameter and about 3 in. high. Rounded base, and vessel is rather roughly made, time period unknown; much damage to rim area. C—$85

Hammerstone, ungrooved, 3½ in. high, well polished overall. Both ends evidence some battering. This was a tool used to make other tools. C—$3

Fully grooved hardstone maul or club head, 4½ in. high and over 2 in. thick. Groove about ¼ in. deep; this could be considered a heavy-duty hammer-stone. D—$42

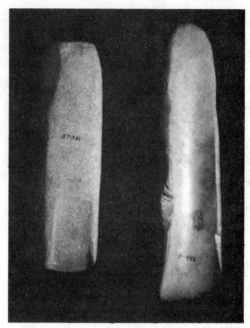

Gouges, hardstone, both from the New England area. Left example is concave for several inches while the right example is concave nearly full-length. $150 each

Rodney M. Peck collection, Harrisburg, North Carolina

Adena (Early Woodland period) adz-blade, black tool-grade hematite, from Belmont County, Ohio. It is 1¾ in. long and very highly polished overall. Nice piece. $25

Private collection, Ohio

Faceted or beveled-face adz, Archaic period, from Muskingum County, Ohio. Material is a blue-gray hardstone, possibly diorite. Size is 1¾ x 4⅝ in. $90

Private collection, Ohio

Notched celt, probably Woodland period, with material a fine-grained gray hardstone. This piece is from Mercer County, Pennsylvania and is 4⅞ in. long. Notched celts are scarce wherever found. $50

Private collection, Ohio

Hardstone tools, all from Wisconsin. Types include cupstones or miniature mortars and pestles or mauls.

$125-$175 the group

Robert D. Lund collection, Watertown, Wisconsin

Stone turtle effigy paint bowl, contemporary, made of gray hardstone. From Minnesota, the bowl is 3⅛ in. long. $160

Michael F. Slasinski, Saginaw, Michigan

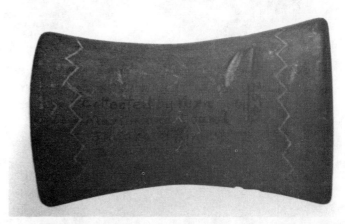

Spool made of tan sandstone, from Brown County, Ohio. It is 1⅛ x 2⅛ x 3⁷⁄₁₆ in. and is well-shaped, with incised zigzags. It was assigned G.I.R.S. authentication number C89-33. $1000

Collection of David G. & Barbara J. Shirley

Stone book effigy, found in Saginaw, Michigan, in 1930. Made of close-grained gray hardstone, it dates from the 1700s. Size, ⅞ x 1⁹⁄₁₆ x 2⅝ in. $130

Michael F. Slasinski, Saginaw, Michigan

Three-quarter groove hammerstone, 1¾ in. high and 1¼ in. wide. Well polished, perfect condition, from Pennsylvania. Groove area has very smooth finish.   C—$35

Kneeling figure, sandstone, undoubtedly Mississippian, from Georgia. An old excavated find, it depicts a clothed woman; figure is 15½ in. high, and weight is over 15 pounds. Well-detailed, especially face. (Private collection)Museum quality

Pelican-stone charm, effigy figure, California. It somewhat resembles the neck, head and beak of that bird. Piece is 4⅞ in. high with extended base.   C—$475

Hardstone drilled object, purpose unknown, 2½ in. high and 1½ in. wide at flattish base. Smaller, rounded top was drilled from both ends and shows much wear. Unpolished.
C—$70

Squared/rectangular pestle (a scarce type compared with the usual rounded "roller" type pestles) from the Wills Creek area, Coshocton County, Ohio. It is made of yellow and tan hardstone and measures 2¼ x 1⅝ x 8¾ in. Surfaces are highly polished. $35

Private collection, Ohio

Incised stones, probably Late Archaic and Desert culture, with polish and shallow line. Size range is from 1 to 1½ in., and all are from Cache County, Utah. These may be broken Atl-atl stones, but this is far from certain. Very interesting examples.   Museum quality

Randall Olsen collection, Cache County, Utah

Rounded gamestones, both Texas. Left, hematite, Harrison Co. $35
Right, Ogallala chert, Gregg County. $15

Willie Fields collection, Hallsville, Texas

Effigy bowl (?), gray stone, well-made, top scooped, bird head at one end. The artifact has tally marks on the sides and is nicely polished. It is from Mississippi. $500

Wilfred A. Dick collection, Magnolia, Mississippi

Incised stone, purpose unknown, from Cache County, Utah. While the time-period is unknown, Pinto points were found on the same site, suggesting Desert Late Archaic after 3000 BC. It measures 1½ x 2 in.   Museum quality

Randall Olsen collection, Cache County, Utah

Stone artifacts, left to right:
Anvil, brownstone, LA $25
Smoothed and polished anvil or polisher, well-made, MS $25
Anvil, brownstone, LA $25

Wilfred A. Dick collection, Magnolia, Mississippi

Handled pestle made of volcanic rock, probably Western U.S. $75
Private collection

Stone bowl, reddish interior, well-shaped and finished, from Arizona.$85

Wilfred A. Dick collection, Magnolia, Mississippi

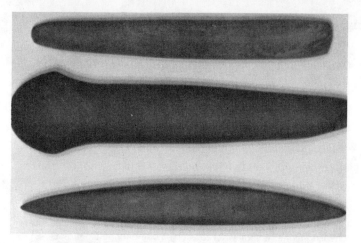

Large and fine artifacts, various periods. Top, Mississippian chisel, 8¼ in., Tennessee. $500
Well-polished slate spud, Mississippian period, Spencer County, IN, 9⅝ in. $1500
Bottom, very fine Late Woodland ceremonial pick, blue and black slate, 1⅛ x 9 in., from western New York state. $800

Pat & Dave Summers, Native American Artifacts, Victor, New York

Notched flint hoe, with lower edge polished from use. This artifact is from northern Alabama. $200

Private collection

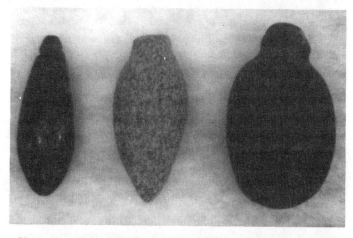

Plummets or plumb-bobs, Late Archaic and Early Woodland, left to right:
Hematite plummet, Schuyler County, IL, 2⅝ in. $200
Granite plummet, South Windsor, CT, 2¾ in. $90
Fairly rough plummet, 3 in., from Massuchusetts. $30

Pocotopaug Trading Post, South Windsor, CT

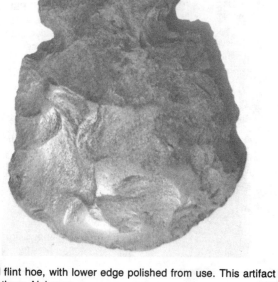

Spade blade, flint, from northern Alabama. The wide lower working edge is polished from use. $300

Private collection

L to R: DRILLED PEBBLE, unknown use. Good drilling, but rest of stone rough, medium polish only. C—$10
DO-NUT STONE, California, 3⅓ in. across, very fine central hole. High polish overall. May have been a club head. C—$125
Unusual SLATE CUTTING TOOL, or for chopping tasks; has characteristics both of notched celts and three-quarter grooved axes. Good edge, probably Archaic period. Midwest. C—$25

Private collection.

From left to right:
RARE STONE OBJECT, fully drilled and 2 in. long. Stone still retains painted brown bands, marking this item as probably used in historic times. Exact purpose of item unknown, but may be a medicine man's healing stone. It somewhat resembles ball bannerstones.   C—$175

Photo courtesy Robert C. Calvert, London, Ontario, Canada.

UNKNOWN STONE OBJECT, probably prehistoric, found near London, Ontario. Piece is 4½ in. long and has a hole ½ in. deep at one end, with incised marks along end sides. Unfinished pipe? Effigy form? C—$60

Photo courtesy Robert C. Calvert, London, Ontario, Canada.

UNUSUAL STONE OBJECT, purpose unknown, 4 in. long. Item may be a preform, but appears to be a complete artifact. Made of a compact green stone, and found near Komoka, Ontario. This has been identified as a monolithic Adz handle.   C—$250

Photo courtesy Robert C. Calvert, London, Ontario, Canada.

Left, concretion cup CONTAINER, may have been for paint, about 2 in. in diameter, center worn smooth.   C—$20
Right, notched pebble NET-SINKER, though exact use of these artifacts is not known. Frequently found near streams in the Midwest.   C—$8
Bottom, small concretion cup cup CONTAINER, dark brown stone. Outside has also been nicely rounded, central depression is absolutely circular.   C—$22
Private collection

Hematite CONE, 1⅝ in. in diameter and ¾ in. high. It is from Adams County, Illinois, of a colorful red hematite. This piece is flatbased.   C—$200
Photo courtesy John P. Grotte, Illinois

Left TEAR-DROP PLUMMET, 4⅜ in. long and 1⅛ in. wide. Made of pink and black mottled granite, this item is from the Los Angeles area of California.   C—$400
Middle TEAR-DROP PLUMMET, 4⅞ in. long, made of a black and red mottled granite. It is from the Sacramento area of California.   C—$500
Right DRILLED PLUMMET, 4⅜ in. long and 1 in. in extreme diameter. Made of a yellow and brown granite, this too is from the Sacramento, California area.   C—$400

Courtesy Ferrel Anderson, photographer; Thomas Browner Collection; Davenport, Iowa.

Hematite CONE, measuring 1⁷⁄₁₆ in. in diameter and ⅞ in. high. It has a small concave dimple on the flat bottom center. Piece is from the river bottoms of Adams County, Illinois, and probably dates from Woodland times. The surface of this cone is partially exfoliated or in the process of flaking.   C—$250
Photo courtesy John P. Grotte, Illinois.

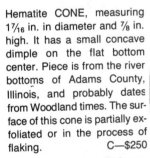

PLUMMET of hardstone, drilled and grooved at one end. It is 3 in. in length, and 1½ in. in diameter. Object almost resembles an effigy form, perhaps of a manatee, but resemblance is probably accidental. Found in Fairfield County, Ohio.   C—$50

Photo courtesy Bob Champion, Ohio.

Grouping of PLUMMETS, all three quite different L to R:
Polished HARDSTONE PLUMMET, 2⅜ in. long, glossy surface. C—$40
Small egg-shaped HEMATITE PLUMMET, very shallowly grooved near top.   C—$30
Fine-grained SANDSTONE PLUMMET, grooved near top for attachment.   C—$25

Private Collection.

An 1891 photo taken by Gravill of Deadwood, with original caption: "Home of Mrs. American Horse. Visiting women at Mrs. A's home in hostile camp". Note the proliferation of White-made goods throughout the encampment. Interestingly, one of the more valued things in nearly treeless regions were the long poles for the tepees.

Photo courtesy of South Dakota State Historical Society.

CHAPTER VI

BANNERSTONES
AND RELATED OBJECTS

The introduction to this chapter was written by Thomas E. Browner, officer of the Central States Archaeological Societies, Inc., and a man thoroughly knowledgeable in the field; used with permission.

"Bannerstones are a loose category of Archaic artifacts. In outline, bannerstones or banners are symmetrical, usually winged artifacts possessing a drilled center hole or notches. Large numbers of blending forms in a great variety of stones lead to difficulties in classifications as well as value.

Begining in the Southeast portion of the United States, bannerstones over a period of centuries migrated North and Westward. Evolving with territorial expansion into more eccentric forms and utilizing finer grades of stone, some of the banners are top collectors pieces today.

As Atl-atl weights, bannerstones were simple tubular forms. Later, the advanced types were too large and thin to take the pressures of hard everyday use. Theories of social status emblems and tribal or religious significance have been placed on the later types.

As in any commerce, a tangible object must be matched with an intangible concept called value for it to change ownership. Artifacts like bannerstones are one-of-a-kind. Each is different, and therefore values as absolutes do not exist. An artifact is only worth what an individual collector is willing to pay for it. Such a value must be viewed as an extension of the collector's personality, thus reflecting his personal taste, interest and income.

One collector alone can set the price for a particular class of artifacts by purchasing all that are presented at a higher than normal market value. However, this is unusual as market value is normally determined by the demand of larger groups of collectors, all bidding for a limited number of genuine artifacts.

In 1912, Warren K. Moorehead stated, "the farther away from the source of supply the more valuable the material — shell, copper, hematite". Of course, he was referring to the economic importance to the Indians. It is interesting to note that the finished artifact today is worth the most in its region of origin. Local artifacts, being the most prized by local collectors, command premium prices.

Besides demand and location of origin, artifacts generally follow a broad range based, in order of importance, on these factors:

1. Rarity of type
2. Perfection
3. Workmanship
4. Material
5. Size
6. Color
7. Pedigree

These are self-explanatory, with the possible exception of pedigree. By pedigree is meant a traceable history, beginning with a list of previous owners and ending with photographs in various publications and books. It is a line of ancestry.

Unfortunately, fakes and fakers do exist. A pedigree does not guarantee genuineness, but it does increase the collector's chances. Many of the fraudulent specimens being produced today are so realistic that they almost defy detection.

Therefore, only purchase what you know about, and then only from reputable dealers and collectors. Never buy if you have any doubts about a piece. Ask to take the artifact on approval for a reasonable time. This will allow you the opportunity to trace the history and secure other opinions.

There are no experts, only collectors like yourself with more knowledge and experience. Anyone can be fooled. Unfortunately, one of the byproducts of this situation is that the unknown, the slightly out-of-type, and the unusual are characteristically branded as frauds. The final forms are much treasured and therefore do not tend to change hands as often.

In choosing a bannerstone, a collector must check the planes, drillings, patination, manufacturing techniques, etc. Many old pieces were scrubbed to bring out the ancient color. The Indians salvaged many specimens. Thus a double crescent banner could end up as a butterfly type. Therefore, even genuine specimens may not be without recent fault or ancient change or profile.

Are the planes normal for the type? Is the patination even, including edges and salvaged sides? Are the drillings tapered? Has the surface defoliated? Are there any so-called 'worm marks'? Once authenticity has been established, merit as to value must be made on the basis of type, perfection, size, color and so forth.

Unusual range highs and lows may be caused by some of the following factors. Obvious bleaching, scrubbing, or the use of oil, shellac or other caustic agents may lower the value of an artifact by as much as 50%. On the other hand, a good pedigree could increase the asking price by 20%. Buying an artifact in its home locality might cost an extra 30%.

The finest artifacts of a type could demand a price two or three times the going range high. Prices are generally higher at shows than in homes. However, travel expenses and the reluctance of collectors to sell cherished pieces often makes the dealer's price the only price available.

Unlike some other collectibles, there are a very limited number of genuine, intact Indian artifacts. Many of these have gone into the vaults of museums and schools and civic organizations and are not readily available for study. In many cases the pride of ownership, more than the object's true value, is a prime objective of the collector.

Finally, common artifacts remain common.

The increase in the number of collectors has driven the prices of better grade specimens higher each year. Therefore, buy for the long range appreciation of your investment by selecting the best of what is offered to you. Rare specimens will only become more valuable with time."

(T.E.B.)

Bannerstones

Slate banner, butterfly type, not drilled in center, but nicely grooved either side, perfect. Wings are 4¼ in. wide from tip to tip. From Michigan.   C—$600

Geniculate bannerstone, banded slate, some minute original damage in hole region. It is 3¼ in. long, 2 in. high, of very colorful blue-black material. Illinois.   C—$450

Pick banner, worked so that bands converge near center, adding to attractiveness. Some battering to slate near one end of central drill hole, unimportant to overall appearance. Somewhat crescentic form, and 3⅞ in. long.   A—$200

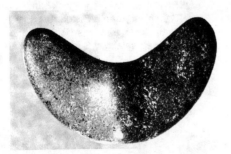

CRESCENT BANNER, hardstone, 3¾ in. by 2½ in. and illustrated in INDIAN AND ESKIMO ARTIFACTS OF NORTH AMERICA. Material is a brown, fine-grained granite.   C—$600
Courtesy Ferrel Anderson, photographer; Thomas Browner Collection; Davenport, Iowa.

Double crescent banner, 5 in. wide, 3⅛ in. high, some damage to 3 of the 4 arms or wings. Central portions, including hole, are fine. Retains good polish; ideal for restoration.   C—$600

Fine **geniculate banner** of banded slate, size about 3 in. by 3 in., pristine condition and a scarce Archaic form. All corners well-rounded, oblong hole, and extension comes to a rounded tip.   A—$470

Large **winged banner,** of banded slate, remaining portions measuring 5 in. by 3 in. Lower wing edges broken in prehistoric times, and piece was salvaged by grinding down broken areas to balance the appearance. Salvaged regions not quite as well done as original edges.   A—$300

Winged banner, banded slate, of a type sometimes called "butterfly". Piece is 3⅛ in. wide and 1⅛ in. high. Finished on exterior; cane-drilled hole not quite completed.C—$250

Pick banner, curved and 4¼ in. long, 1 in. wide, with the slate a banded black, and gray background.   D—$245

Chlorite pick banner, hardstone, 2⅜ in. long 1¼ in. wide at center. Completely drilled and color an amber-yellow, hard to describe. Very minor surface scratches here and there, original, with polish extending into the scratches, which are really only faint lines.   C—$800

Tubular banner, Kentucky, rounded top and sides, flat bottom, drilled for entire length, which is 2¾ in. Material a dark gray unbanded slate.   A—$185

Winged banner, Wisconsin, hardstone and made from a material resembling granite. Piece is 3¾ in. wide and 2⅛ in. long. Undrilled, but highly polished specimen.C—$300

Fluted ball banner, Ohio, 1⅞ in. long and 1⅛ in. wide. Very colorful green slate with red and black bands. Some very slight original damage around one end of drill-hole.C—$120

Rare **notched-ovate banner,** Midwestern Archaic, banded slate, 5⅜ in. long, 3¼ in. wide. Some restoration to two of the curved tips. Notched in center of convex edges. C—$900

Winged bannerstone, 4⅛ in. between tips. About 1 in. of one wing has been carefully restored. Reddish slate with black bands, colorful. C—$475

Pick banner, a hardstone similar to diorite, smooth-grained, good polish. Piece is 4⅞ in. long and slightly pointed on one end, slightly flattened on other. No damage; unusual. C—$350

Duo-tipped slate pick, from Canada, 5¼ in. long and ⅞ in. wide. Material is a dark gray slate, not banded. Piece is well-shaped but undrilled. C—$200

Fine **panel banner** of very attractive, thinly-banded slate, good condition. Edges have regular tally notches. As is common for the form, one end of the banner is slightly larger than the other. Central hole runs lengthwise; piece is 3½ in. long. A-$300

Hardstone banner, 2⅜ in. wide, 1⅞ in. long, Midwestern origin, made of chlorite (?), well-drilled, no damage. Small but perfect; highly polished buff-coloed surface.C—$700

Quartz bannerstone, 1⅞ in. wide and 2¾ in. long. Made of a well polished translucent quartzite having black inclusions. Perfect condition, but undrilled; drill-hole was just started, never completed. C—$250

Cresentic pick banner, 3½ in. long, with central hole ½ in. in diameter. Very symmetrical, nicely polished, made of dark, close-banded slate. From an old collection.A—$170

Lunate banner, about 5 in. across at the tips, which lack the typical notches or grooves. One arm is slightly shorter than the other and projects at a different angle than does its twin. No restoration and unusual in an unbroken or damaged condition. A—$245

From left to right:
Unfinished BUTTERFLY BANNERSTONE, from Chenango County, New York. It is 6 in. wide and 2¾ in. long. Not completed because the drilling missed and bypassed. Shape only fair, and a wing chip breaks the outline. Made of a green and black banded site.

C—$300-$550

Courtesy Ferrel Anderson, photographer; Thomas Browner Collection; Davenport, Iowa.

BUTTERFLY BANNERSTONE, brown and black banded slate, 4½ in. wide and 2 in. long. Two minor edge nicks do no major harm to this banner. Note also the light "worm trail" from left to right on specimen, moving down at about 45-degree angle. Such markings are within the natural material. C—$500-$750

Courtesy Ferrel Anderson, photographer; Thomas Browner Collection; Davenport, Iowa.

End-view of a fine HOURGLASS-TYPE BANNERSTONE. Made of a colorful rose quartz, piece was reed-drilled approximately half way through center. Length is 2⅜ in. and width is 1⅛ in.; artifact was found in Adams County, Illinois. C—$600

Photo courtesy John P. Grotte, Illinois.

HOURGLASS BANNERSTONE, from Fulton County, Illinois. It is 2¹⁵/₁₆ in. long and 1¾ in. wide, made of a fine grade of quartz. Drilling is slightly broken out at one end, color is not evenly distributed, nor vivid. It is yet a good, acceptable artifact; if everything were perfect, it could be worth closer to $1000. C—$600

Courtesy Ferrel Anderson, photographer; Thomas Browner Collection; Davenport, Iowa.

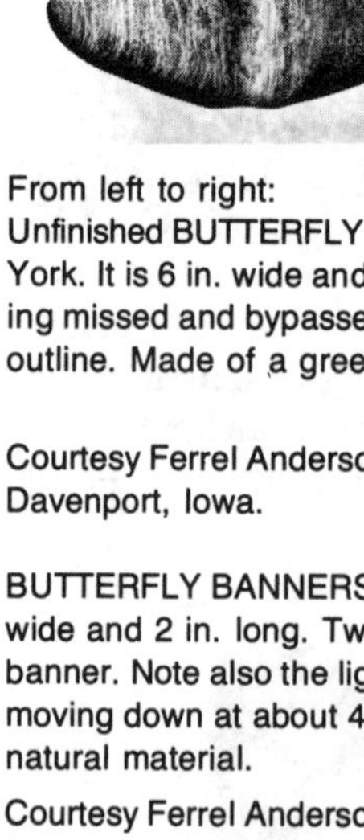

BALL BANNERSTONE, 1⅝ in. by 1½ in. from Bureau County, Illinois, piece is made of green and black banded slate. Note high degree of polish on this well-banded banner.

C—$350

Courtesy Ferrel Anderson, photographer; Thomas Browner Collection; Davenport, Iowa.

From left to right:
QUARTZ BUTTERFLY BANNERSTONE, 3 in. wide and 1⅝ in. long. It is from Cedar County, Missouri, made of white quartz with reddish tinges. Perfect in every detail, it lacks only color and more size to command the highest prices. Edges are nicely rounded and wings are porportionate to the size of the barrel.　　　　C—$1000-$1800
Courtesy Ferrel Anderson, photographer; Thomas Browner Collection; Davenport, Iowa.

UNDRILLED FETISH KNOBBED LUNATE BANNERSTONE, made of brick-colored hematite. It is 2⅞ in. wide and 1⅝ in. long. This specimen is rather crude in form, but does represent a one-of-a-kind object. It is from Hudson County, Tennessee.

C—$250

Courtesy Ferrel Anderson, photographer; Thomas Browner Collection; Davenport, Iowa.

WISCONSIN WINGED BANNERSTONE, from Clark County, Missouri. It measures 3¾ in. by 2 in. and is made of a black and white porphyry. This specimen was expertly restored in one corner; in 1956 it was purchased for $300. The exceptional color and workmanship make this artifact a rare collector's item.　　　　C—$1000-$1800

Courtesy Ferrel Anderson, photographer; Thomas Browner Collection; Davenport, Iowa.

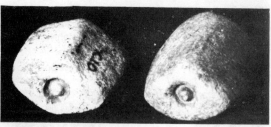

UNFINISHED BANNERSTONES, each measuring 2 in. by 2 in. These clearly show the drilling (hollow cane type), with central "islands" protruding about ¼ in. Both are Archaic and found in northeast Mississippi. The C10 piece is made of quartz material.　　　　C—$80 each

Photo courtesy Jim Northcutt, Jr., Corinth, Mississippi.

From left to right:
DOUBLE-BITTED AXE BANNERSTONE, from Pope County, Indiana. It is 5½ in. wide and 3¾ in. long, and made from green and black banded slate. Exceptional shape; note the even color and the centered eye (in banding). Both size and color help make this specimen one of the finest of the type.　　　　C—$1000-$1800
Courtesy Ferrel Anderson, photographer; Thomas Browner Collection; Davenport, Iowa.

BUTTERFLY BANNERSTONE, 5 in. wide and 1⅞ in. long from Miami County, Ohio. Material is a green and black banded slate. An earlier collector scrubbed the piece with steel wool to bring out the colors, but destroyed the surface patina. This should never be done.
C—(without scrubbing) $300-$400
C—(after scrubbing) $125-$175
Courtesy Ferrel Anderson, photographer; Thomas Browner Collection; Davenport, Iowa.

SALVAGED DOUBLE-CRESCENT BANNERSTONE, 4⅜ in. long and 1½ in. wide. Piece is from Kent County, Illinois. Current appearance of this banded-slate artifact is that of a butterfly or double-bitted axe banner form; crescentic extensions were ground off in prehistoric times.　　　　C—$400-$600
Courtesy Ferrel Anderson, photographer; Thomas Browner Collection; Davenport, Iowa.

SALVAGED DOUBLE-CRESCENT BANNERSTONE, 3⅞ in. wide and 3⅛ in. long. Material is a green and black banded slate. One prong was broken in ancient times, and the other three ground down to create a symmetrical piece.　　　　C—$700-$1200

Courtesy Ferrel Anderson, photographer; Thomas Browner Collection; Davenport, Iowa.

RECTANGULAR BARRELED BANNERSTONE, 4⅛ in. by 2¾ in. The symmetry and raised barrel are the major features of this artifact. Material is a pink and black granite. It is from Preble County, Ohio. Most bannerstones offered for sale can be considered in the more common classes.　　　　C—$1000-$1400
Courtesy Ferrel Anderson, photographer; Thomas Browner Collection; Davenport, Iowa.

TUBE TYPE BANNERSTONE, 1¼ in. wide and 2½ in. long, made of a green stone material. Hole measures ½ in. at both ends; tube has a flat bottom. Archaic, it was found near the Hatchie River in Alcorn County, Mississippi.   C—$400

Photo courtesy Jim Northcutt, Jr., Corinth, Mississippi.

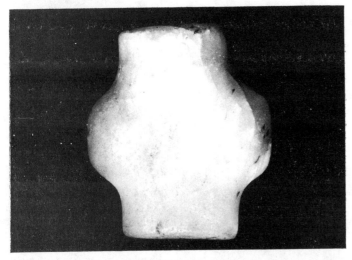

BIFACE BOTTLE BANNERSTONE, 2½ in. by 2 in. It is a fine white quartz with small black inclusions. Though small, it is well-documented since the beginning of the 1900's; most collectors will pay more for a traceable artifact. From southern Indiana.   C—$1200-$1800

Courtesy Ferrel Anderson, photographer; Thomas Browner Collection; Davenport, Iowa.

HOURGLASS BANNERSTONE, from Adams County, Illinois and made of green quartzite. It is 2 in. long nd 1¹⁵/₁₆ in. wide, and might be considered a common specimen. Browner: "Size is small and shape only fair; with most of its history lost, it is reduced to an orphaned piece of common art".   C—$600-$900

Courtesy Ferrel Anderson, photographer; Thomas Browner Collection; Davenport, Iowa.

TRIANGULAR DUAL BANNERSTONE, from Hancock County, Illinois. It is 4¼ in. long and 2⅞ in. wide, made of mottled granite. This is both a rare piece and somewhat controversial, in that only a portion of its history has been traceable. So...if you collect, you must catalog and trace and record all findings. This means authentic specimens are fully documented.
          C—$1500-$2000

Courtesy Ferrel Anderson, photographer; Thomas Browner Collection; Davenport, Iowa.

PEBBLE BANNERSTONE, from Boone County, Missouri. It is 2½ in. wide and 1½ in. long, made of a tan sandstone. Bannerstones began like this, a simple perforated pebble around 4000 BC. This specimen was only shaped slightly by flattening the circumference. Many banners are believed to have been Atl-atl weights.   C—$80

Courtesy Ferrel Anderson, photographer; Thomas Browner Collection; Davenport, Iowa.

SINGLE-FACE BOTTLE BANNERSTONE, from Lincoln County, Missouri, and 3 in. long. Note the flared lips forming mini-rectangles at both ends. Topside is gracefully rounded, bottomside is flat. The material is red quartzite.   C—$1200-$1500

Courtesy Ferrel Anderson, photographer; Thomas Browner Collection; Davenport, Iowa.

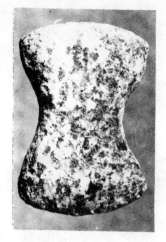

UNDRILLED WISCONSIN WINGED BANNERSTONE, 2½ in. by 1¾ in. From Illinois, it is made of mottled granite. The specimen is a bit thick and lacks good polish.　C—$100

Courtesy Ferrel Anderson, photographer; Thomas Browner Collection; Davenport, Iowa.

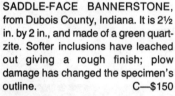

SADDLE-FACE BANNERSTONE, from Dubois County, Indiana. It is 2½ in. by 2 in., and made of a green quartzite. Softer inclusions have leached out giving a rough finish; plow damage has changed the specimen's outline.　C—$150

Courtesy Ferrel Anderson, photographer; Thomas Browner Collection; Davenport, Iowa.

Left to right:

Drilled center BANDED SLATE BANNERSTONE, Archaic times, and 4½ in. in length. Found near Pembroke, Ontario, Canada. C—$300

Photo courtesy Howard Popkie, Arnprior, Canada.

KNOBBED LUNATE BANNERSTONE, from Delaware County, Ohio. It is 5⅞ in. long and 2 in. wide. Piece is made of green and black banded slate.　C—$900-$1300

Courtesy Ferrel Anderson, photographer; Thomas Browner Collection; Davenport, Iowa.

WINGED BANNERSTONE, 4½ in. long; from near Pond Mills, near London, Ontario. While not shown in photo, piece is fully drilled.　C—$200-$250

Photo courtesy Robert C. Calvert, London, Ontario, Canada.

HOURGLASS BANNERSTONE, 3 in. long and 2¼ in. wide, and from Randolph County, Illinois. Has the classic shape. At some early time, a person scratched the initial "W" on it; this fault would be penalized to some degree by different collectors. Made of reddish-brown slate; material could be better for the artifact type.　C—$700-$1100

Courtesy Ferrel Anderson, photographer; Thomas Browner Collection; Davenport, Iowa.

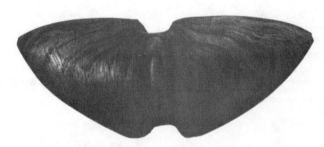

Winged bannerstone, from Branch County, Michigan, in light brown banded slate with darker brown bands. It is ⅞ x 2 x 5³⁄₃₂ in., and bears G.I.R.S. authentication number C89-32.　$2000

Collection of David G. & Barbara J. Shirley

Bannerstone, tubular with reverse groove, from Hopkinsville, KY. Made of green and black banded slate, size is 1 x 1¹³⁄₁₆ x 3¼ in.

$500

Collection of David G. & Barbara J. Shirley, Michigan

Pick-type bannerstone, light green to medium green mottled chlorite, Archaic period. From Fairfield County, Ohio, it is ex-colls. Dr. Copeland and Dr. Meuser. With good design, finish and coloring, this is a small but top piece. Size, 1⁵⁄₁₆ x 2¹⁵⁄₁₆ in.　$2500-$3200

Private collection, Ohio

Pick-type bannerstone, from Ohio, made of green banded slate. It is 4¾ in. long and ex-coll. McNight. The fine specimen has had the slate worked so that the concentric bands accent the central drill-hole.

Museum quality

Bill & Margie Koup collection, Albuquerque, New Mexico; Bill Koup photograph

Pick bannerstone, Archaic period, material a dark green chlorite with small black specks. Size is 1½ x 4⅟₁₆ in. It is from Marion County, Ohio, and ex-coll. Dr. G.F. Meuser. This is a very collectible and well-made specimen. $2500-$3300

Private collection, Ohio

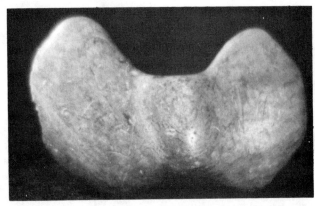

Winged bannerstone, green and black hardstone, from Bedford County, Pennsylvania. It is 1 x 2¾ x 4¼ in. and ex-coll. Foote. $300

Pat & Dave Summers, Native American Artifacts, Victor, New York

Tube-type bannerstone, made of tan banded slate, 3⅝ in. long. It was found near Ft. Ancient in Warren County, Ohio, and is from the Archaic period. This is a solid old piece with good patination.

$225

Larry Garvin collection, Ohio

Winged bannerstone Type A, from Midland County, Michigan. Made of gray banded slate with darker bands, it is 2½ x 4⅟₁₆ in. This is one of the top five of the type. It has G.I.R.S. authentication number 221.

$2500

Collection of David G. & Barbara J. Shirley

Winged bannerstone, Cass County, Michigan. It is made of fractured banded slate, greenish-gray with dark banding. Size is 1¼ x 3³⁄₁₆ x 4¾ in. The banner is pictured in *Prehistoric Artifacts*. $1000

Collection of David G. & Barbara J. Shirley

Shuttle-type bannerstone, very thin for size, 2½ in. wide. It is unusual for the area where found, Pickaway County, Ohio, near Circleville. Circleville itself was named for a prehistoric Hopewellian earth-work. Ex-colls. E. Good and Dr. G. Meuser (number 3211 over 5).

Museum quality

Bill & Margie Koup collection, Albuquerque, New Mexico; Bill Koup photograph

Panel bannerstone, gray banded slate with black banding. It measures ⅝ x 2¹⁄₁₆ x 2⁷⁄₁₆ in. Panels are scarce banner types. This artifact was pictured in *Central States Archaeological Journal*, 1988, Vol. 35 No. 3. It is from the Midwest. $800

Collection of David G. & Barbara J. Shirley

Expanded-center Adena gorget, Early Woodland period, material a translucent tan-cream quartzite. It is 1⅞ x 4⅝ in., from Knox County, Ohio, and ex-coll. R. Leatherman. It is undrilled but appears finished, a rare gorget type in this material. $450-$500

Private collection, Ohio

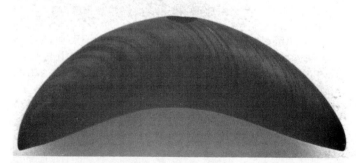

Curved pick bannerstone, Midwestern, gray banded slate with dark banding. It measures 1¼ x 6¹⁵⁄₁₆ in. This is a fine old piece, ex-colls. Dr. Bunch, Payne, McClain and Smith. It has G.I.R.S. authentication number C88-14. $1800

Collection of David G. & Barbara J. Shirley

Loafstones, Archaic period, both from Ohio.
Left, cream-colored quartzite, Crawford County, ex-coll. A.T. Wehrle, 1½ x 2⅛ in.
Right, tan-cream banded quartzite, 1⅝ x 2⁵⁄₁₆ in., from Ross County. $175-$275 each

Private collection, Ohio

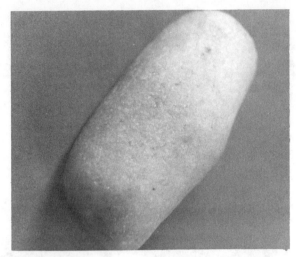

Humped center bar amulet, Early Woodland period, made of cream-colored quartzite. This interesting piece was found near Volney, Michigan and is 1³⁄₁₆ x 2¹¹⁄₁₆ in. long. The end-drilling was started but not completed, possibly due to the extreme hardness of the material.

Private collection, Ohio $300-$450

Humped-center bar amulet, Early Woodland period, material a translucent tan-cream quartzite. From Logan County, Ohio, hole-drilling was started at each end but not completed. The base of this 1³⁄₁₆ x 4¹⁄₈ in. specimen is scooped or concave. $450-$650

Private collection, Ohio

Boatstone, Woodland period, scooped on reverse (shown). It is drilled with two ³⁄₈ in. holes. This polished piece is from Calloway County, KY.
$450

Marguerite L. Kernaghan collection; photograph by Marguerite L. and Stewart W. Kernaghan, Bellvue, Colorado

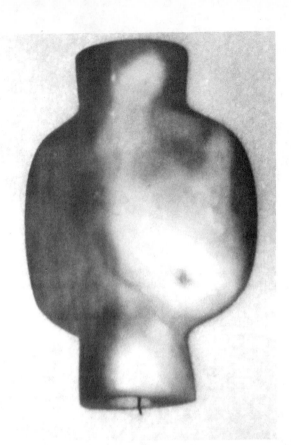

Bannerstone, highly developed bottle shape, ferruginous quartzite. It is 2¼ x 3¾ in. and is from KY. $1000

Marguerite L. Kernaghan collection; photograph by Marguerite L. and Stewart W. Kernaghan, Bellvue, Colorado

ATL-ATL WEIGHTS

There is considerable evidence that at least some bannerstones served as Atl-atl weights. It is easy to imagine some of the heavier and more compact forms employed in this manner, more difficult in the case of the large, thin-winged types.

Banners, already described, can be quickly (and incompletely) summarized. They are artifacts with a single large round or ovate central hole, and with symmetrical protrusions on both sides of that hole. Only a form like the atypical geniculate family alters this "rule"; even then, set on edge, the symmetry is regained.

There is a whole other great collecting field, that of the Atl-atl weights. These generally lack a large central hole and tend to be flat or concave on the bottom. As a broad class, they are long, narrow, and may have squared or rounded sides and top. Many forms have grooves or drill-holes for attachment.

It is believed weights were both functional and ornamental. Functional, because the weight would have given some added impetus to the lance-throw. They also would have served as a counter-balance when the flint or obsidian-tipped lance was in place.

Ornamental, because many varieties are extremely well made, small works of fine porportions and high polish and static grace. Some were effigy forms, adding perhaps luck and magic to the hunter's foray.

Atl-atl weights were used over the entire Continental U.S., plus into Canada and Mexico. It is believed the weights were used from early Archaic times until around AD 500, giving the Atl-atl/lance weapons system perhaps 8000 and more years of dominance. Early weights were somewhat plain and crude, little more than flattened rocks that could easily be glued or fastened to the wooden lance-thrower.

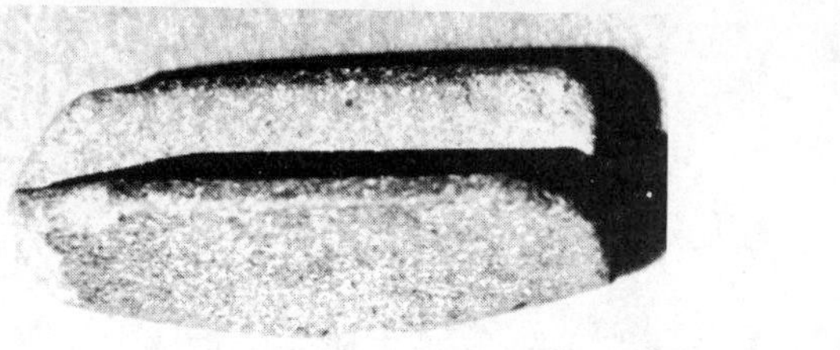

STONE ATL-ATL WEIGHT, excavated from a cave shelter in Arkansas. Found in the same occupational zone as Gray points, and from the Archaic period. Weight is 2½ in. long.

C—$75

Photo courtesy Wayne Parker, Texas.

What is, and what is not, a weight will no doubt be as hotly debated in the future as it is today. New thought is that any prehistoric Amerind artifact that is long, thick flat-bottomed — and served no other obvious function — may well have been a weight. The writer leaves it at that.

Because many of the weights are highly collectible, and these may include some slate and hardstone gorget and boatstone forms, the fakers have been at work. Some of the fraudulent specimens go back to the early years of the century and are now beginning to look old.

There are so many classes of weights that is is difficult to give guidelines on what to watch out for. Drill-holes for weights should be conical, from the tapered flint drills, and not of uniform diameter. Note that drilling, good drilling, adds much to the value of a piece.

One of the more difficult fakes to deal with is the authentic-improved piece, an old artifact that has been recently drilled to increase the value. In most cases, this will be obvious; after all, a semi-skilled person is working on an object that is thousands of years old. The marks of steel tools are not the same as those made by prehistoric implements.

Generally, the patina, the microscopically thin surface layer, is disturbed. If in doubt, do not collect the piece.

Stone **Atl-atl weight,** Klamath River area of Oregon, 3 in. long, 1⅝ in. high, speckled white stone. Flat bottom, piece nicely grooved front the back and across the center. Surface well-polished. D—$235

Boatstone, Arkansas, 3¾ in. long, 1¼ in. wide. Bottom side, flat on edges, and deeply hollowed out or scooped. Good workstyle, high polish overall, perfect condition. D—$270

Shaped shell **Atl-atl weights,** set of 9, from northern Kentucky. Each has a basic triangular shape, corners rounded; each is drilled with central hole about ⅝ in. in diameter. Placed together and approximating original positions, set is about 4 in. long and 1¼ in. wide. Segments evidence polish, and each is carefully made. C—$240

Hardstone, **Atl-atl weight,** state of Washington, 3⅜ in. long. Bottom is flat, top has two longitudinal grooves, and is highly polished. Made of a compact tan stone. C—$195

Sandstone weight, from Scioto River Valley, Ohio. It is 3½ in. long and 1⅝ in. wide, about ⅜ in. thick. Perfect, and an early specimen. Unremarkable. C—$30

Drilled and scooped banded-slate **boatstone,** Indiana, 3⅞ in. long, 1⅛ in. wide. Flattish base has been scooped to a depth of nearly ½ in. Some battering on the ends, but shallow and polished over. C—$195-250

Dark-colored slate **bar amulet,** 4½ in. long and 1⅝ in. wide. From Michigan. D—$250

Bar-type grooved Atl-atl weight, 4 in. long, ⅞ in. wide, and made of a blackish slate. Bottom flat, top rounded, with two thin grooves about ⅜ in. from each end. Unusual and well-finished piece. C—$265

Layer-slate weight, from New York, 2¾ in. long, 1 in. wide, with rounded top. Rough finish. C—$55

Grooved weight, 3⅛ in. long, ⅞ in. wide, and of a light-colored slate. Bottomside flat, top rounded, wide groove across the center. Semi-polished, good condition. D—$115

NOTE: There are other forms that are almost certainly weights, although currently called by other names. These are covered in other chapters consistent with nomenclature. Such artifacts include some late Archaic Glacial Kame gorgets and some Woodland (Adena) bi-holed forms, which are in fact often undrilled.

Suggested Reading

Knoblock, Byron W., *Bannerstones of the North American Indian;* Privately published, La Grange, Illinois, 1939

The archaeological societies quarterly journals are excellent sources. See last Chapter.

Pick-type bannerstone, from Logan County, Ohio, one of the state's better examples. Material is gray and green banded slate with dark gray banding, and size is 1 1/16 x 1 x 5 in. Pictured in *Who's Who in Indian Relics No. 1* (p. 118), it has G.I.R.S. authentication number 203.$1500

Collection of David G. & Barbara J. Shirley

Bannerstones, Archaic period, top row left to right:

Hematite, drilled, MS	$100
Saddle type, drilled, MS	$250
Winged, brownstone, drilled, MS	$75
Second row left to right:	
Broken half, polished, MS	$20
Hematite, polished, undrilled	$50
Broken polished section	$20
Bottom from MS, polished	$20

Wilfred A. Dick collection, Magnolia, Mississippi

Sioux ration camp in Nebraska. Meat, probably beef or bison meat, dries on racks out of reach of camp dogs. Indians gathered periodically to receive U.S. government food supplies. Photo courtesy of John A. Anderson Collection, Nebraska State Historical Society.

Spruce Tree House, Mesa Verde National Park, Colorado. This is one of the better-preserved Anasazi cliff-dwellings or cliff-villages, being protected from much of the weather by the rock overhang.

Lar Hothem photo

101

CHAPTER VII

BANDED SLATE ORNAMENTS AND OBJECTS

In a vast region ranging from the Mississippi watershed area East to the Atlantic Coast and from North of the Great Lakes South nearly to the Gulf, slate was a favorite material in prehistoric times. Much of this slate was of glacial origin, and the slate was traded far into non-glaciated areas. The slate was compact and colorful, and it worked well.

The beauty of banded slate certainly attracted prehistoric crafts-people, just as the finished artifacts attract collectors today. Very simple methods were used to turn out some very well-designed and executed objects. The peck-and-abrasion method was employed, basically the same used for making hardstone tools.

When the final form was approached, the piece was ground against loose-grained stone, and some very delicate work could be done in this fashion. And last, the surface was polished and any drilling put in.

For slate artifacts, determinants of present-day value include size of the artifact and the condition. The greater the damage, the greater the loss of value. Collectors seek symmetrical slate, and the pattern, regularity and boldness of the bands count for much.

Especially admired are pieces where the slate has been worked so the bands are either in harmony with the artifact's lines, or emphasize a key part of the artifact. An example is a panel banner with the slate bands all at the same angle on the top surface. Another is when bands converge to emphasize the eye region of a birdstone.

Slate surfaces should be highly polished and have no serious scratches, either from prehistoric use or today's agriculture equipment. (A surprising amount of breakage and damage occurs when unknowing people acquire fine artifacts and treat them as mere stones). In the general slate categories of pendants and gorgets, drilling is important. Pendants generally have one hole, gorgets two or more. Both tend to be long and flat, with a varied width.

All holes should be artistically placed and the same space from sides for pendants, the same from sides and ends for most gorgets. While some collectors admire very thin slate pieces for the workmanship involved, others seek thick slate for the weight and contoured three-dimensional artistry.

Fakes exist. In the more valued classes, like birdstones, several knowledgeable people have stated there are probably more fraudulent than genuine pieces. There **are** lucky occurrences. One man bought a box of junk at a farm sale for the bag of nails he saw at the top. After getting it home, he discovered something else on the bottom. His cost was a dollar. His prize was a hardstone, perfect-condition birdstone, worth in excess of one thousand dollars.

Another man bought two birdstones from a pawnshop owner, because they looked good and were priced at only $300 each. With the average "bird" selling in the $1,500 range, they were a bargain providing they were authentic. They were neither.

For the average slate pendant, gorget, birdstone or effigy, the prices listed here are about market, but many examples can be obtained for far less. A good slate artifact collection can be put together, made up of under $100 pieces, but it is still buyer beware. Know your seller or get a written guarantee that the piece can be returned for a refund if it proves to be questionable.

SLATE PENDANTS

One-holed slate pieces, if they are in fact completed by drilling, are termed pendants. It is believed they were worn around the neck like a large medallion. As prehistoric decorative items, great care seems to have been used in making many of them, though their relative thinness — ⅛ in. to ⅜ in. — makes them rather fragile.

Anchor-type **slate pendant,** 5 in. long and 1½ in. wide at expanded lower base. One anchor prong is a bit smaller than the other.   A—$150

Biconcave pendant, made in gorget form, but centrally drilled with single hold instead of usual two holes. Exactly 4 in. long and 1⅞ in. wide at ends; from Missouri. Material is a green slate with green bands.   C—$175

Rectangular banded slate pendant, 2 in. wide by 5 in. long. Single large hole drilled from both sides, about 1¾ in. from one end. Very nice black bands against a reddish slate.   C—$260

Anchor-shaped pendant, 4¼ in. long and 1½ in. wide, with minor damage.   G—$135

Trapazoidal slate pendant, 5 in. long, 2 in. wide at base, and 1¼ in. wide at top, with single suspension hole. Perfect condition, good polish, very symmetrical.   A—$285

Adena bell-shaped pendant, large central hole in upper portion, and with tally marks (regular incised lines) at pendant top; piece about 4 in. long.   A—$175

Slate pendant, 3½ in. long and 1½ in. wide at base. Nicely balanced pendant; partly restored.   A—$40

Slate shovel-shaped pendant, 4½ in. long and 1¾ in. wide; very good lines to this piece.   A—$100

Keyhole pendant, Adena culture, from Christian County, KY. It is gray banded slate with darker bands and measures 2⁷⁄₁₆ x 4⁹⁄₁₆ in. It is pictured in *Prehistoric Men of Kentucky*, 1910, p. 202. It has G.I.R.S. authentication number C88-12. $2500

Collection of David G. & Barbara J. Shirley

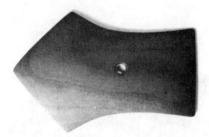

Very unusual Hopewellian SHIELD-SHAPED PENDANT, of fine banded slate, piece is ⅛ in. short of 5 in. Topside is slightly convex; underside is very slightly concave. Very symmetrical and an outstanding type specimen.   C—$2500

Private collection.

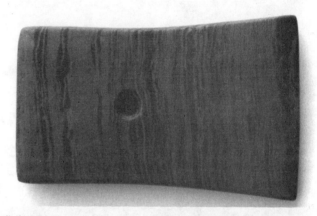

Bell-shaped pendant, Woodland period, Ashland County, Ohio. Material is gray banded slate with dark banding and size is ³⁄₁₆ x 2⅝ x 4³⁄₁₆ in. This very well-made piece has G.I.R.S. authentication number C88-9. $1000

Collection of David G. & Barbara J. Shirley

L to R: POINTED-END PENDANT, perhaps salvaged from large artifact in early times, 2⅛ in. long.   C—$20
Large and good ANCHOR-TYPE PENDANT, made of a high grade yellowish slate. Perfect condition, from Ohio, about 5 in. long. C—$225
Fine RECTANGULAR PENDANT, made of a smooth-grained hardstone; may have been salvaged from larger gorget in early times.   C—$45

Private collection.

Trapezoidal pendant, tallied top, Ohio, tan hardstone. Size, ⅛ x 1½ x 3 in. G.I.R.S. authentication number C89-28. On left. $500

Trapezoidal pendant, on right, with Adena (one side) drilling, from DeKalb County, Indiana. Made of dark gray and yellowish-white hardstone, it is ⅛⁄₁₆ x 2¹⁄₁₆ x 5¹⁄₃₂ in. Ex-coll. Dougherty, it bears G.I.R.S. authentication number C88-23. $2000

Collection of David G. & Barbara J. Shirley

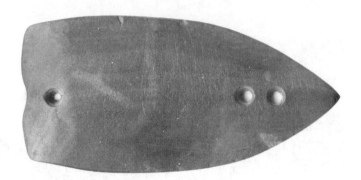

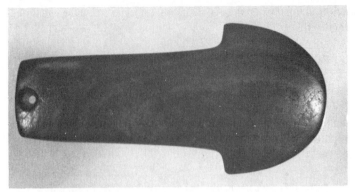

Sandal-sole gorget, Glacial Kame culture (Late Archaic), from Van Buren County, Michigan. Made of banded slate, the material is light red to gray-brown. Size, ³⁄₁₆ x 2⅛ x 4½ in. The artifact has prehistoric salvage or repair at the wide end. $400
Collection of David G. & Barbara J. Shirley

Anchor-type pendant, Early/Middle Woodland, from Franklin County, Ohio. Made of brown, black and tan banded slate, it measures 2⅛ x 4½ in. Ex-coll. Max Shipley. $900
Collection of David G. & Barbara J. Shirley

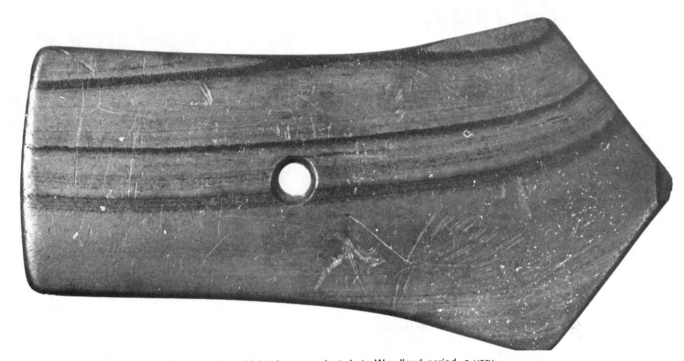

Pentagonal or shield-shape pendant, Late Woodland period, a very superior specimen. Made of banded glacial slate, it is 4⅞ in. high. It was found along the Old Portage Trail in Summit County, Ohio.
Museum quality

Bill & Margie Koup collection, Albuquerque, New Mexico; Bill Koup photograph

Anchor Pendant. Hardstone, greenish gray. 5⁵⁄₁₆ x 2 x ⅜''. G.I.R.S.
Allen Co., Ohio $2500

SLATE GORGETS

These artifacts typically have two holes, but variations have three or more. As with pendants, hardstone examples exist, but they are rare and high-priced. Most gorgets are long and thin. They are believed to have been ornaments, although how they were worn is a matter of individual belief. Some gorgets that average about 1½ in. in width, are thick and drilled, may have been Atl-atl weights. The gorget class pulls together some rather dissimilar types.

Elongated **two-hole expanded center gorget,** very well drilled, Midwestern Woodland period, and 5½ in. in length.
D—$115

Hardstone two-hole gorget, very well drilled, and from Illinois. It is 4⅛ in. long, just under 2 in. wide and only ⁵⁄₁₆ in. thick. Highly polished, holes symmetrical and equidistant from ends and sides. Granite-like stone with black, white and yellowish colors.
C—$725

Fine Hopewellian **reel-shaped gorget,** angular and very well balanced. Size, 4½ in. long and 3 in. wide, of attractive banded slate. Surface has a high polish; in perfect condition and from an old collection.
A—$400

Two-hole rectangular gorget, 1¾ in. by 3¼ in., clay-colored slate. One plow-mark across face, not deep.
C—$65

Nice **sandal-sole gorget,** a rare form, Glacial or Gravel-Kame period of Late Archaic. Bottom wider than top, which is 2 in.; piece is just over 6 in. in length. Good banded slate, and drilled in diagnostic pattern of 3 in. line holes, the last about ½ in. from top.
A—$500

Large slate **expanded-center gorget,** 6¼ in. long, 1¾ in. wide in center, very good overall form.
A-$425

Concavo-convex slate gorget, 4¼ in. long, 2¼ in. wide at ends. Drilled with two well-placed holes.
A—$350

Humped slate gorget, 4¼ in. long and 1¾ in. wide, drilled with two holes. Piece has good lines.
A—$200

Adena expanded-center gorget, holes equidistant from ends, drilled in Adena style from bottom side only. About 4 in. long, in perfect condition.
A—$135

Fine **elliptical gorget,** 5 in. long, about 3 in. wide at center. Woodland era; two holes equidistant from rounded ends.
C—$575

Very large **slate gorget,** a rare 3-hole sandal-sole type. It is 7¼ in. long and 2¾ in. wide at lower "instep" region. Symmetrical and well-finished.
A—$370

Cross-shaped slate gorget, two holes, 3 in. long and 1¾ in. wide. Projecting arm ends have a concave outline. Perfect condition.
A—$260

Key-hole type gorget, dark banded slate, central hole high up and near top which is irregular to a small degree. Sides and bottom with nicely rounded contours. Average size.
A—$175

Adena **oval-shaped gorget,** 4 in. long and 2¼ in. wide; well-drilled from a dark slate. Bands barely visible. D—$150

 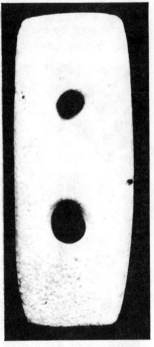

Unusual BAR GORGET, 2⁹⁄₁₆ in. long, and 1 in. wide. It is a humped-back type, made of galena and is covered with a thick white patina. Both obverse and reverse are shown. It evidences conical drilling and may be from the Adena culture, Woodland period. Found in Adams County, Illinois.
C—$100-$130
Photo courtesy John P. Grotte, Illinois.

STONE GORGET, 3¼ in. long 2 in. wide and ½ in. thick; it is made from a red stone material. Other artifacts from the same site indicate this may be a Mississippian type gorget. It was found in Tennessee.
C—$125-$175
Photo courtesy Jim Northcutt, Jr., Corinth, Mississippi.

SLATE GORGET, 3½ in. long and 2⅛ in. wide at center. Very well drilled with two holes; slate highly polished, and in good form. Item came from near Brantford, Ontario.
C—$125-$150
Photo courtesy Robert C. Calvert, London, Ontario, Canada.

SLATE OBJECT, drilled, 5¼ in. long and 1½ in. wide, ¼ in. thick. Piece is damaged at top end.   C—$20-$25

Photo courtesy Robert C. Calvert, London, Ontario, Canada.

Spineback gorget, Glacial Kame culture, gray and tan banded slate. A rare gorget form, it is 1 x 1¾ x 4¹⁄₁₆ in. It has been assigned G.I.R.S. authentication number 219. $500

Collection of David G. & Barbara J. Shirley

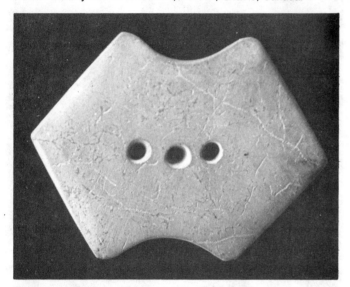

Rare three-hole gorget, made of polished limestone. It is 2⅝ x 3⅝ in. and is from Runnels County, TX. $275-$400

Grady McCrea collection, Miles, TX

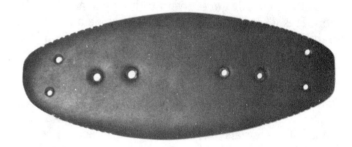

Eight-hole gorget, four in-line and two smaller pairs of extra holes, from Coryell County, Texas. This unusual piece is 2½ x 6½ in. $1200

L.M. Abbott, Jr. collection, Texas

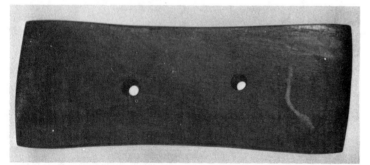

Rectangular two-hole gorget, from Hancock County, Ohio. It is made of banded slate in greenish-gray with darker banding. Size, ¼ x 2¼ x 6 in. It bears G.I.R.S. authentication number C89-24. $1000

Collection of David G. & Barbara J. Shirley

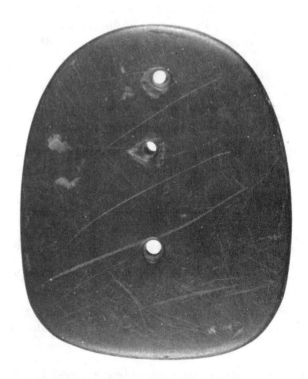

Three-hole pendant or gorget, black well-polished slate, 3 x 3⅝ in. Found in Ross County, Ohio, the piece may be Glacial Kame culture from the Late Archaic. $200-$275

Larry Garvin collection, Ohio

Spineback gorget, Glacial Kame culture, from Allen County, Ohio. It is gray banded slate with darker bands and size is ⅞ x 1⅜ x 4⅜ in. Pictured in *The Meuser Collection* (p. 74) it bears G.I.R.S. authentication number 221. $1000

Collection of David G. & Barbara J. Shirley

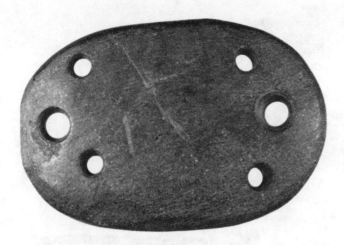

Spineback gorget, Glacial Kame (Late Archaic) culture, Sandusky County, Ohio. Material is banded slate in green, purple and black. Size is 1½ x 1¾ x 4¼ in., and the form is highly developed. Ex-colls. Diller, Ritchie and Driskill. $1500

Collection of David G. & Barbara J. Shirley

Gorget, six-holed, 2¼ x 3⅜ in. It is made from an unusual material, red hardstone with mica inclusions. This atypical piece is from Montgomery County, Ohio. $300

Larry Garvin collection, Ohio

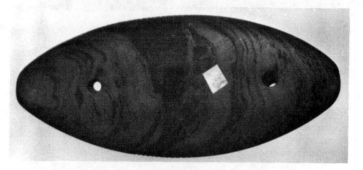

Humped or hump-type gorget, Glacial Kame (Late Archaic) culture, from Hardin County, Ohio. It is 4½ in. long and made from banded slate of the slipped or faulted variety (see change in pattern).

Museum quality

Bill & Margie Koup collection, Albuquerque, New Mexico; Bill Koup photograph

Elliptical gorget, Adena and Early Woodland period, with twelve tally marks on each side. From Allen County, Ohio, it is made of banded slate, gray with black bands. Size is ¼ x 2⅝ x 6 in. This fine piece of slate has G.I.R.S. authentication number C89-26. $2400

Collection of David G. & Barbara J. Shirley

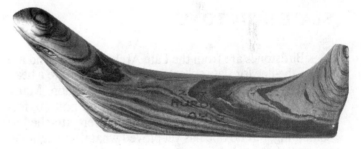

Eyed birdstone in green banded slate, fine lines, from Huron County, Ohio. Ex-coll. P. McNight, it is 5 in. long. Museum quality

Bill & Margie Koup collection, Albuquerque, New Mexico; Bill Koup photograph

Elliptical gorget, Adena or Early Woodland culture, from Knox County, Ohio. Made of greenish slate with darker bands, it measures ¼ x 2⁹⁄₁₆ x 6½ in. The large and well-finished artifact is ex-colls. Wehrle, Walters and Jardine. $1000

Collection of David G. & Barbara J. Shirley

SLATE GORGET, 2¾ in. long and 2 in. wide, ¼ in. thick. Found in Brant County, Ontario; made of well-banded slate and is nicely drilled.
C—$75-$100

Photo courtesy Robert C. Calvert, London, Ontario, Canada.

Superb and extremely high quality prehistoric gorgets, each 5¾ in. long.
Top, expanded-center Adena gorget, Franklin County, Indiana, green
banded slate.
Bottom, keeled gorget, Sandusky Co. Ohio. Ex-colls. Diller and Steere.
Both museum quality

Bill & Margie Koup collection, Albuquerque, New Mexico; Bill Koup
photograph

SLATE BIRDSTONES

Birdstones are from the Late Archaic period, and are top-of-the-line for slate collectors. Most "birds" have a head and beak, a flat-bottomed body, and a tail region. Many are drilled with two holes, front and rear on bottom, forming "L"-shaped holes. Obviously, they were attached to something, but no one has yet proved what that might be.

All that can be said today is that birdstones do resemble a bird setting a nest. Strangely, wings are never depicted in any way. Birdstones are found in a 500-mile range of Lake Erie, and many examples come from New York state and the Canadian provinces. A great many have been found in Ohio, Indiana, Illinois and Michigan.

Banded **slate birdstones**, 5¾ in. long, 1½ in. wide. Classic Glacial Kame elongated type, forward-slanted head and long beak. A—$1200

Slate birdstone, 4 in. long and 1½ in. wide, good shape, perfect condition. A—$900

Slate birdstone head, broken from body. Head is 1½ in. long; break area salvaged by grinding and base of neck has a slight groove around it, as if for thong attachment. C—$135

Slate birdstone, 4 in. long and 1½ in. wide, good lines. The piece has been restored. A—$185

Birdstone head, "popeye" type of green and black material. It is 1¼ in. long, and was salvaged in prehistoric times. The break is ground so that head sits firmly and erect. C—$200

Elongated **banded slate birdstone**, classic style, 5⅞ in. and 1½ in. wide at flared tail. Very graceful design and well-drilled. C—$1350

Slate birdstone, 4 in. long and 1¼ in. wide; a small-base type. A—$365

Quartzite birdstone, 4½ in. long and 2¼ in. wide. Piece has been restored. A—$150

Porphyry birdstone, popeye type, 4¼ in. long and 2⅛ in. wide, 2¾ in. high. Made of a mottled black and yellow material. C—$6000

BLACK SLATE BIRDSTONE, not drilled, and found at Point Peely, Ontario, Canada. It is 5¼ in. long and appears completely finished except for basal holes. Slight scrapes on one side, some damage to left side of head, minor. Very good lines to birdstone.
C—$1000-$1400

Photo courtesy Robert C. Calvert, London, Ontario, Canada.

SLATE BIRDSTONE, from near London, Ontario, Canada. Of banded material, piece is 4⅜ in. long. Birdstone has well-drilled base and is tally-marked on sides of neck, body and tail. Very small damaged area on left side, original. Incised mouths on birdstones are not common.
C—$1200-$1800

Photo courtesy Robert C. Calvert, London, Ontario, Canada.

SLATE BIRDSTONE, unusual form, and 6¼ in. in length. Found near Onondago, Ontario, near the Grand River. Like other birdstones, this is probably from Late Archaic times. The specimen is not drilled.
C—$1200-$1800

Photo courtesy Robert C. Calvert, London, Ontario, Canada.

SLATE BIRDSTONE, from Victoria County, Ontario, Canada. This is a fine popeyed specimen, and measures 4⅛ in. in length. Piece is drilled on bottom ridges and is in perfect condition.
C—$2500-$3800

Photo courtesy Robert C. Calvert, London, Ontario, Canada.

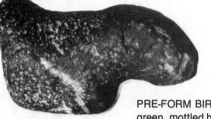

PRE-FORM BIRDSTONE made of a green, mottled hardstone and 3½ in. long and 1¾ in. high. Found near Komoka, Ontario, Canada. This piece evidences slight polishing.
C—$50-$100

Courtesy Robert C. Calvert, London, Ontario, Canada.

EFFIGY SLATES

While no one really knows how birdstones were used, neither is it known what effigy slates represent. They most resemble "lizards", or salamanders, but many forms are so highly stylized that not much more can be said. Some forms resemble animals like swimming beavers or otters; others look like a snake that has swallowed a large meal.

Effigies are rarely drilled. They have a flat bottom, a head region, jutting shoulders and generally taper into a tail region. Some were crudely made while others are superb specimens of the slate-workers' art.

In the opinion of the writer, these are Atl-atl weights from the Middle Archaic time-frame. The market value of better specimens is beginning to approach that of average-grade birdstones.

Banded slate effigy stone, Midwestern area, 5 in. long. Head squared off, shoulders very high, short neck region. Body and tail tapered very nicely; overall, well-made and polished piece.
A—$650

Slate effigy stone, nicely tapered and with abrupt expansion near head region. Piece is 4⅛ in. long, of a dark-colored and banded slate.
C—$525

Slate effigy figure, 5 in. long and 1½ in. wide. Piece has a wide, elongated body, small head and broad tail. More than a salamander, it resembles the profile of a beaver.
A—$175

BIRDSTONE, from near Sault St. Marie, Ontario, Canada. Piece is 3½ in. long and 2 in. high at head and tail. Hardstone material, undrilled, and is probably an unfinished specimen. Good form. C—$400-$700

Courtesy Robert C. Calvert, London, Ontario, Canada.

Slate lizard effigy, 4 in. long and 1½ in. wide, very rounded features including head, shoulders and short tail. Perfect condition, well-polished. A—$325

Slate beaver effigy, 4 in. long and 1½ in. wide. Rather an abstract depiction, rare form, fine condition. A—$360

Slate Effigy or lizard, 5 in. long and 1½ in. wide. Piece has squared-off head and tail ends, very narrow and jutting shoulders. No damage. An exceptionally well-made and attractive piece. A—$775

Slate effigy form, 4 in. long, 1¾ in. wide at shoulders. Blunt head, straight taper from shoulders to tail. Perfect condition. A—$165

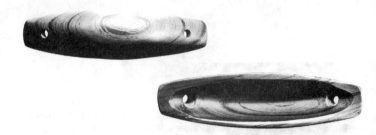

DRILLED SLATE BOATSTONE, top and bottom views. This boatstone is of the rounded type and is a near-perfect example of the type. In size, color and workmanship it would have few equals. Note the excellent cupping, typical of the type. This piece is 4½ in. long and 1¼ in. wide at center. Made of a green and black banded slate, it is from the Grand Rapids, Michigan area. C—$700-$1000

Courtesy Ferrel Anderson, photographer; Thomas Browner Collection; Davenport, Iowa.

PAINT PALETTE, 10½ in. in diameter, made of slate. Design is a repeated bird motif; this piece was found near Memphis, Tennessee, in 1837 and is late prehistoric, Mississippian era. C—$2000

S.E. Kernaghan photo; Marguerite Kernaghan Collection.

CEREMONIAL PICK made of slate, and 13¾ in. in length. It is well-polished and in good condition, from Brant County, Ontario. An unusual artifact type. C—$200-$300

Courtesy Robert C. Calvert, London, Ontario, Canada.

BOATSTONE: FLAT, UNCUPPED PRIMARY FORM. (Browner): "Boatstones are an Archaic cultural manifestation. Like bannerstones, they seem to have begun in the Southeastern states. From simple uncupped bars used as Atl-atl weights they evolved into intricately shaped and deeply cupped artifacts of unknown use. Boatstones continued into Mississippian times and some of the forms are incised and show rare symmetry and workmanship."
This piece is 3¾ in. long and is made from a brown sandstone. It is from Yell County, Arkansas. C—$200-$350

Courtesy Ferrel Anderson, photographer; Thomas Browner Collection; Davenport, Iowa.

OTHER BANDED SLATE ARTIFACTS

Slate tube, 3¼ in. long and 1¾ in. wide, drilled for entire length with one large hole. A—$185

Banded slate phallus, depicting male penis glans, 3‍5⁄16 in. high, resting on enlarged flat base. Realistic and colorful material, black bands on reddish background. Unknown time period. Surface find in western Ohio. C—$450

Slate bar amulet, 7¾ in. long and ¾ in. wide, with raised section, ridge-like, in center. Beautiful flowing lines, and high-quality slate. C—$575

Banded slate spud, (unusual flared-bit celtiform axe), 10¼ in. long, 3⅛ in. wide at blade tips. Dark green slate with reddish bands. D—$500

Banded slate tube or tubular pipe, 7¼ in. long, ¾ in. wide. Good lines; piece has been restored. A—$250

Slate bar-weight, notched in center, 3¾ in. long, 1 in. wide. A—$55

Slate pestle, bell-type, 6 in. high and 4 in. in basal diameter. A—$70

Slate pestle, long roller type, 19½ in. in length and 2½ in. in diameter.   A—$200

Slate axe, 8½ in. high and 4¾ in. wide.   A—$160

Slate pendant, 3¼ in. long and 1¾ in. wide, thin and rectangular, one hole at end. Piece interesting because one face is cross-hatched with incised lines.   C—$155

Slate lizard effigy, 4⅞ in. long, bulbous-body type, rounded "tail", tally-marks around shoulder ridge. Perfect condition, very nice banding.   C—$850

Spineback gorget, 4⅜ in. long, with single protruding knob between two drill-holes. Fine banding in specimen and highly polished surface.   C—$825

Animal-head effigy, 1⅞ in. long, unknown species, picked up on Illinois Archaic site.   C—$165

Suggested Reading

Townsend, Earl C. Jr., *Birdstones of the North American Indian;* Privately published, Indianapolis, Indiana, 1959

Shell ornaments, Pennsylvania and New York, ca. 1700s. Values depend on decoration, finesse and condition, with purple items being worth more than white due to rarity.

Top, talon or claw effigies, lizard effigy.	$25-$35 each
Middle, turtles and "ducks", in center.	$100-$300 each

Gary L. Fogelman collection, Pennsylvania

BOATSTONE; DEEP CUP TYPE (Browner): "This example represents the end of boatstone evolution. This specimen is notable in both its deep cup and its extremely thin walls. Minor chips at one edge detracts a bit, but does not harm overall value. Boatstones are usually made of banded slate. However, quartz, granite, sandstone, limestone and steatite were also used."
This piece is 2¾ in. long and 1⅞ in. wide. Made of brown sandstone, it is from Independence County, Arkansas.   C—$500-$750

Courtesy Ferrel Anderson, photographer; Thomas Browner Collection; Davenport, Iowa.

Fine SLATE TUBE, 3⅝ in. long, of green slate with bold black bands. Perfect condition; completely drilled and straight, from small to larger end. Old markings, "Forest, Hardin Co.". An Ohio piece, probably Archaic period.   C—$225

Private collection.

Bar amulet, Early Woodland, Butler County, Ohio. Made of rare hardstone, light green with brown spots, it measures ¹⁵⁄₁₆ x 1³⁄₁₆ x 3⅝ in. Ex-colls. Dr. Meuser and D. Driskill. It was assigned G.I.R.S. authentication number C89-30. $700

Collection of David G. & Barbara J. Shirley

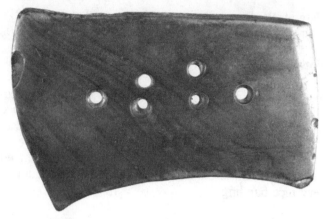

Bar amulet, Early Woodland, from Indiana. It is made of light gray banded slate with darker bands, and is ¾ x 1⁵⁄₃₂ x 3¹³⁄₁₆ in. The reverse ends are string-worn between the holes. Ex-coll. Parks, and with G.I.R.S. authentication number C88-6.

Collection of David G. & Barbara J. Shirley $800

Drilled slate artifact, possibly a reworked gorget or pendant. It is probably from Ohio, 2½ x 4 in., and is made of highly polished banded slate. $125-$150

Larry Garvin collection, Ohio

Bar amulet, Early Woodland and Red Ochre, Noble County, Indiana. It is gray banded slate with darker bands and measures ⅞ x ⁹⁄₁₆ x 3⅞ in. It is assigned G.I.R.S. authentication number C88-4. $600

Collection of David G. & Barbara J. Shirley

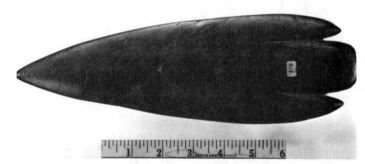

Bar amulet, Red Ochre Early Woodland, from Tiffin (Seneca County), Ohio. Made of gray banded slate with darker banding, it is ⅞ x 1¼ x 3¼ in. It bears G.I.R.S. authentication number C88-26.

Collection of David G. & Barbara J. Shirley $500

Slate blade, highly polished and well-shaped, from Maine. Material is gray slate with wide dark gray bands. This particular piece has been pictured in several early publications.   Museum quality

Collection of David G. & Barbara J. Shirley

Bar amulet, Early Woodland period, from St. Joseph County, Michigan. Made of gray slate with light and dark banding, it is ⅞ x ⅞ x 5¼ in. It carries G.I.R.S. authentication number C89-29. $1500

Collection of David G. & Barbara J. Shirley

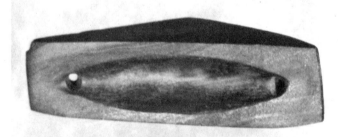

Boatstone, scooped and drilled, rare angular type, from Howard County, Indiana. Made of gray banded slate with darker bands, it was found by Arthur Hunt in 1934, and is ex-colls. Stubbe, Schmatz, Doming and Mear. $1000

Collection of David G. & Barbara J. Shirley

Bar amulet, Early Woodland, undrilled and made of black and white hardstone. From Portage County, Ohio, it is 1⅛ x 1⁵⁄₁₆ x 2¾ in. It is pictured in the Dr. Meuser book (p. 40) and *Ohio Slate Types* (p. 69). The artifact bears G.I.R.S. authentication number C89-31. $1500

Collection of David G. & Barbara J. Shirley

Stone and slate artifacts, various regions.
Far left, gorget, New York, slate $90
Top left, gorget, St. Joseph County, Michigan, banded slate, elliptical
type, 5½ in. $100
Top right, gorget, Adena, sandstone, Kentucky $75

Center, left to right:
Gorget, granite, Kingston, Massachusetts $60
Pendant, hematite, grooved, Ohio $25
Pendant, human effigy, salvaged, from Waterbury, Connecticut, rare$300
Bottom left to right:
Gorget, Adena boat-shaped (Hopewell type but with Adena cone-shaped
drilling, from bottom), Ohio $45

Pendant, Indiana, ex-coll. Parks $75

Pocotopaug Trading Post, South Windsor, Connecticut

Boatstone, Woodland period, very finely drilled and scooped (bottom view). Made of gray banded slate with darker bands, size is $^{15}/_{16}$ x 1 x 6$^{25}/_{32}$ in. This piece has G.I.R.S. authentication number 216. This is an exceptionally long and well-made boatstone. $3000

Collection of David G. & Barbara J. Shirley

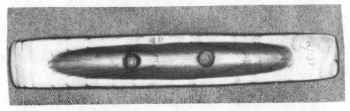

Bar amulet, Early Woodland, from Huron County, Ohio. Made of gray banded slate with darker bands, it is $^{11}/_{16}$ x ¾ x 7⅜ in. One of the finest bar amulets to come from the state, it is pictured in *Who's Who in Indian Relics No. 2* (p. 175). Ex-coll. Jack Walters, and with G.I.R.S. authentication number C88-3. $3000

Collection of David G. & Barbara J. Shirley

Plummets or plumb-bobs, Late Archaic and Woodland, top row left to right:
Sandstone, grooved, MS $100
Greenstone, drilled, LA $50
Brownstone, grooved, MS $125
Hematite, drilled, LA $50
Hematite, drilled, LA $30
2nd, left to right: Sandstone, MS $25
Polished sandstone, MS $15
Sandstone, cupped ends, MS $15
Grooved brownstone, LA $20
Grooved and polished, LA $35
Bottom, stemmed, MS; each $35

Wilfred A. Dick collection, Magnolia, Mississippi

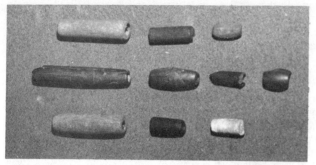

Redstone beads, elongated types, all drilled and polished. These came from the Poverty Point area of Louisiana. $15-$75 each

Wilfred A. Dick collection, Magnolia, Mississippi

Pentagonal or shield-shaped pendant, Late Hopewell, from Brown County, Ohio. Material is gray banded slate with darker banding and size is $2^{31}/_{64}$ x $4^{7}/_{16}$ in. It carries G.I.R.S. authentication number C88-13. This piece is nicely balanced. $700

Collection of David G. & Barbara J. Shirley

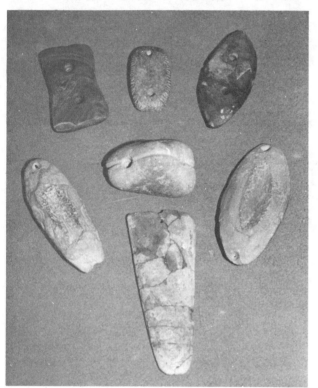

Drilled stone artifacts. Top row, left to right:

Greenstone gorget, MS	$125
Gray stone, tally-marked, MS	$175
Reddish-brown gorget, MS	$150
Middle, left to right: Boatstone	$35
Humped, lined drill-holes, MS	$125
Gray boatstone, two holes	$125
Bottom, clay pendant, MS	$125

Wilfred A. Dick collection, Magnolia, Mississippi

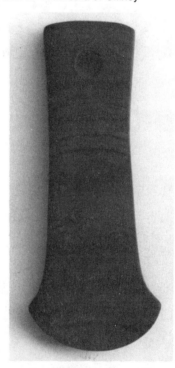

Anchor pendant, Woodland period, from Hardin County, Ohio. Material is gray banded slate with darker banding and size is $5/_{16}$ x $1\frac{3}{4}$ x $4\frac{1}{4}$ in. Ex-coll. Driskill #D-133.G.I.R.S. authentication number C88-8. This is a very attractive artifact. $700

Collection of David G. & Barbara J. Shirley

Trapezoidal pendant, Williams County, Ohio. Material is greenish-gray banded slate with darker banding. It is very thin and $2^{1}/_{32}$ x $5^{9}/_{32}$ in. This artistic piece has G.I.R.S. authentication number C88-10.$1000 plus

Collection of David G. & Barbara J. Shirley

Square Tower House, Mesa Verde National Park, Colorado. The existing four levels of the tower make it one of the highest in the Southwest. Other towers at other ruins may have competed, but they have largely crumbled with time.

Lar Hothem photo

Rock art, Indian Petroglyph State Park near Albuquerque, New Mexico. These two figures, pecked into the dark basalt rock, represent birds.

Lar Hothem photo

CHAPTER VIII

ARTIFACTS OF COPPER AND HEMATITE

Copper and hematite, both found in natural deposits, were much-used to make artifacts in prehistoric North America. They were, however, quite dissimilar and were worked in entirely different ways.

Copper was mined, dug from near the land surface, for thousands of years in the Lake Superior region, and copper artifacts are still being found today. Copper was formed by hammering the malleable material into new and useful shapes. This process — treating the metal almost like a plastic stone — was the third great tool-making method used in prehistoric North America.

Despite extensive copper use, and beginning with the Old Copper Culture (5000 BC) in Northcentral U.S., Amerinds above the Mexican-U.S. border did not melt of smelt copper. It was cold-worked. There is some evidence that Woodland and later-period groups heated the metal, but only so it could be pounded into thinner sheets and more varied forms. The small late-prehistoric cast bells (lost-wax process) of the Southwest have not been proven to have been made in the region.

The use of copper for tools, weapons, ornaments and ceremonial items spans more than 7000 years and the material was widely traded in early times. Among the groups which made important use of copper were the Middle Archaic peoples centered in what is today Wisconsin, the Glacial Kame peoples of 1500 BC, the Hopewell groups of pre-BC and post-AD years, Southeastern Amerinds of Mississippian times, and Northwest Coastal groups well into historic times. Other Amerinds valued copper and made artifacts from it.

Much copper was made into routine tools, but much was also reserved for specialty items and artistic creations. These range from beads to headdress ornaments and from finger rings and bracelets to panpipe whistle sets.

Collectors look for size in a copper piece, good condition, and an even color. Weight, and indication of solid copper, is a factor. Appearance is important. Rare artifacts, like a matched pair of earspools in good condition, would be especially desirable, also any copper with artistic forms or human figures.

There are some fraudulent prehistoric copper pieces around, but the early copper is difficult to fake convincingly. The forms — awls, points, celts — are easy enough to pound into shape. But two factors limit reproductions. One is corrosion or chemical erosion of the artifact itself.

Depending on whether the artifact was under water or beneath the earth, various mineral salts leach away copper parts, giving a characteristic pitted surface. Also, a colorful patina appears on the surface, this often a shade of dark green or brown. It is not easy to put the two together in a way that matches the appearance of an authentic specimen.

COPPER ARTIFACTS

Socketed copper blade, hafted by a wide base that has been pounded around to form an almost closed socket; overall length, 5 in. Lightly patinated and good condition.C—$175

Flat-stemmed copper blade, 5½ in. long, with stem the same thickness as blade, ³⁄₁₆ in. All parts in good condition.
C—$240

Copper rattail-hafted blade, blade-back straight, blade edge excurvate. Piece is 4 in. long, beautiful green patina. Said to have been found in shallow waters of a lake. Some corrosion on thin parts of blade but metal not weakened.
C—$145

Socketed copper blade, 6 in. long, about 2 in. wide at midlength. Center of black portion of socket base also has a small hole for a handle peg. Light patina, good condition.
C—$190

Copper celt, flared bit, fine shape. Piece is 3¾ in. long and 3 in. wide, with much patina.
G—$145

Copper chisel, Wisconsin, and 5¼ in. long, 1⅜ in. wide, ⅜ in. thick. Base shows some hammerstone battering. Very unusual, good condition.
D—$140

Copper beads from Midwestern late prehistoric site. Nine beads of similar small size, ¼ in. diameter. Unusual.
C—$95

Copper Adena bracelet, Woodland period, contains about 300 degrees of arc, tapered tips. About ⅜ in. thick at center. Scarce artifact from an admired culture.
C—$340

Curved copper semi-lunar knife, Wisconsin. It is 4½ in. long, has two upright tangs formerly secured to wooden handle, now gone. Blade averages ¼ in. thick.C—$225

Copper celt from Alpena, Michigan. It is red-brown with green patination and measures 1³⁄₁₆ x 3⁵⁄₁₆ in. This is a very good piece of prehistoric copper. $200

Collection of David G. & Barbara J. Shirley

Copper spud or adz from Wisconsin in Old Copper Culture, open-ended design. Note the stress fracture in the metal from use.

Courtesy E. Neiburger/Andent, Inc. $800

Opposite view of the copper spud or adz with stress fracture in the metal. The longitudinal ridge put in for strength runs the length of the piece.

Courtesy E. Neiburger/Andent, Inc. $800

Copper knife with solid haft, from Wisconsin, Old Copper Culture. It is just over 5 in. long. $350-$500

Courtesy E. Neiburger/Andent, Inc.

Copper rattail point, unusual in that it is also tanged and with shallow notches at sides of point. Piece 3 in. long. Tangs both slightly bent. Nice patina overall.   C—$95

Conical **copper point,** 2½ in. long; patinated.   D—$45

Copper chisel, northern Michigan, 1 in. wide at center, 4⅞ in. long. Medium corrosion, convex blade edge, flat poll, good lines.   D—$260

Duo-tipped copper awl, Michigan, 8⅛ in. long, ⅜ in. in diameter in center. Has medium corrosion, overall good condition.   C—$300

Copper celt, Minnesota, 7 in. long, 2¾ in. wide at bit, 1½ in. wide at squared poll top. Nice patina and good lines.   C—$355

Copper fish-hook, Wisconsin, 1½ in. long. Made of a thin roll of beaten copper, twisted and pounded into shape.   C—$30

Copper needle, Minnesota, 3⅛ in. long, bent and badly corroded.   C—$12

Copper celt, New York state, 3¾ in. long and ½ in. thick. Green patina, very regular lines.   C—$175

Copper celt, 4⅜ in. and 2⅛ in. wide. Found in 1969 in Wisconsin.   C—$320

Copper fish-hook, 1¼ in. long made from rolled and pounded copper strip. Good condition.   C—$23

Tapered-stem blade, 3½ in. long, lightly corroded. It is not known whether this form was knife or spear as blade edges are similar and excurvate.   D—$85

Historic period copper needle, from Apache site near Cajote, New Mexico, and ca. 1850.   D—$25

Contemporary **Northwest Coast chief's copper,** made and signed by Lelooska.   A—$700

Copper rat-tail type spear head, Old Copper Culture, eastcentral Wisconsin. The unusually long haft area is actually longer than the blade itself.

Courtesy E. Neiburger/Andent, Inc. $450-$650

117

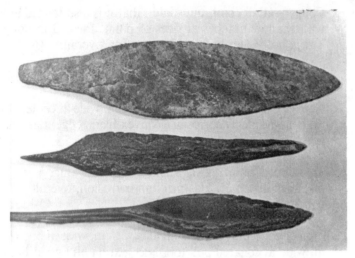

Three types of copper spear points or blades, Old Copper Culture, from Wisconsin. Top, flat blade. Middle, short-tail. Bottom, rat-tail.
Courtesy E. Neiburger/Andent, Inc.   Each $300-$550

Copper spud or adz blade, from northcentral Wisconsin. Note the closed-corner (see arrow) design of manufacture which provided greater strength. $700-$800
Courtesy E. Neiburger/Andent, Inc.

Curved copper knife (semi-luncate), surface-found in Wisconsin. It is Old Copper Culture, with hafting tang for handle.
Courtesy E. Neiburger/Andent, Inc. $400-$650

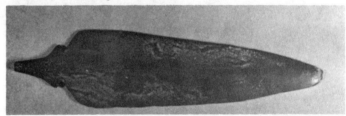

Copper spear point or blade from central Wisconsin, Old Copper Culture of the Late Archaic period. The hafting is very unusual, being a combination of notching and stemming. $500-$750
Courtesy E. Neiburger/Andent, Inc.

Copper celt, 6 in. long, from northeastern Wisconsin. It is Old Copper Culture and ca. 3000 BC. This artifact has a fine taper to the form.
Courtesy E. Neiburger/Andent, Inc. $450-$650

The reverse of copper spear point or blade from central Wisconsin showing unusual tang. $500-$750
Courtesy E. Neiburger/Andent, Inc.

Copper spud adz blade, from northern Wisconsin. The bent-side section of the artifact once had a wooden handle. $350-$550
Courtesy E. Neiburger/Andent, Inc.

Various copper artifacts. Top, spear or projectile point. $50
2nd row, copper pendants, some more detailed and elaborate.
                    Each $20-$100
3rd row, points and tubular beads, beads from Southeastern U.S.
Wilfred A. Dick collection, Magnolia, Mississippi   Each $10-$35

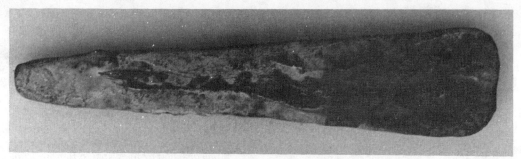

Copper celt, form Alpena, Michigan. It is reddish with green patination and measures 1½ x 6⅞ in. This is a fine early artifact. $400

Collection of David G. & Barbara J. Shirley

Catlinite pendant, found by Patricia McCrea. It has two holes drilled, one through the side and one through the top; 2¼ in. long. It is from Runnels County, Texas.   Museum quality

Grady McCrea collection, Miles, Texas

Copper open ring, possibly personal facial ornament, a personal find by the owner in Barron County, Wisconsin. It is delicate and fine, 1½ in. in diameter. $100

Dennis R. Lindblad collection, Chetek, Wisconsin

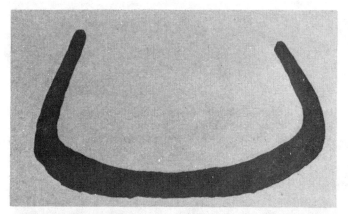

Reverse of above pendant

Copper crescent knife, probably from Middle to Late Archaic period, 1¾ x 3 in. wide. A personal find by the owner, it is from Barron County, Wisconsin. $125-$175

Dennis R. Lindblad collection, Chetek, Wisconsin

Rare artifacts made of clear crystal quartz.
Left, cone, Woodland period, 1⅛ x 2³⁄₁₆ in., Ross County, Ohio.$250-$400
Right, hammerstone, unknown period, Wyandot County, Ohio, 1½ x 2⅛ in. $150-$250

Private collection, Ohio

Copper spearpoint, rolled-shaft type, 3½ in. long. The blade edge is very sharp all around to the stem beginning. Very good condition. It was a personal find by the owner in Barron County, Wisconsin. $200

Dennis R. Lindblad collection, Chetek, Wisconsin

Double-notched / stemmed copper blade or point, very rare type and thought to be much earlier than the socketed blades with median ridges on both faces. It is ⅞ x 2¾ in. and a personal find by the owner in Barron County, Wisconsin. $175

Dennis R. Lindblad collection, Chetek, Wisconsin

Copper crescent handled knife. Old Copper culture of the Late Archaic period, from Barron County, Wisconsin. A personal find of the owner, it is 4½ in. wide and 5½ in. high. This design, with the one-piece closed handle, is quite rare. Very good condition. $500-$750

Dennis R. Lindblad collection, Chetek, Wisconsin

Copper knife with one-piece handle, a personal find by the owner in Barron County, Wisconsin. Old Copper culture, it is very good condition and 4¾ in. long. $185

Dennis R. Lindblad collection, Chetek, Wisconsin

Copper socketed spearpoint or pike, very heavy, very fine condition. It is ⁹⁄₁₆ in. wide at the base and 4 in. long, with a median ridge on one side. This was a personal find by the owner in Barron County, Wisconsin.

Dennis R. Lindblad collection, Chetek, Wisconsin $300

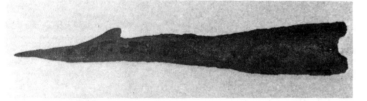

Socketed copper spearpoint or blade, with characteristic median ridge and very symmetrical shape; good condition. This 4¾ in. specimen was a personal find by the owner in Barron County, Wisconsin. $200

Dennis R. Lindblad collection, Chetek, Wisconsin

Copper harpoon, rolled shaft, with a very distinct barb and delicate tip. Old Copper culture, this item is 4 in. long. It was a personal find by the owner in Barron County, Wisconsin. $350

Dennis R. Lindblad collection, Chetek, Wisconsin

Copper knife blade with handle, Old Copper culture, a personal find by the owner in Barron County, Wisconsin. This fine piece is 4¾ in. long.

Dennis R. Lindblad collection, Chetek, Wisconsin $175

Double-pointed (?) copper awl, perforator or pike, unusual configuration, quite pointed on both ends. It is 5 in. long, and a personal find by the owner in Barron County, Wisconsin. $250-$350

Dennis R. Lindblad collection, Chetek, Wisconsin

Copper awl or perforator, very precisely made and with little sign of wear. It is 4⅜ in. long and a personal find by the owner in Barron County, Wisconsin. $125

Dennis R. Lindblad collection, Chetek, Wisconsin

Copper rat-tail point, very good condition, and a personal find by the owner. It is 2¾ in. long. Such artifacts may also have been knife blades.
Dennis R. Lindblad collection, Chetek, Wisconsin $125

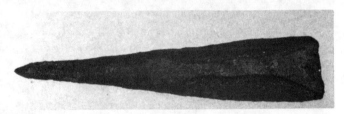

Socketed copper point, a personal find by the owner in Barron County, Wisconsin. It is 3⅛ in. long. $150

Dennis R. Lindblad collection, Chetek, Wisconsin

HEMATITE ARTIFACTS

Hematite, an iron ore, is colored steel gray to black and from dull to brilliant red. It has a double distinction, for it was used for both artifacts and paint in prehistoric times. Many cultures, including the Red Ochre peoples, valued powdered hematite or ochre in rituals. Occasionally paint cups are found with ochre traces still in them.

This hard material, from examination of unfinished pieces, was made into artifacts by the familiar peck-and-abrasion method. Hematite was widely used for both tools and strange artifacts that seem to have had no utility, like the Woodland-era cones that resemble tiny mounds.

Hematite was preferred for certain artifacts, like the plummets and some small adz-blades. And almost any artifact made of hard-stone is likely to have a counterpart, somewhere, in hematite. Some of the artifacts for certain reasons become exfoliated. That is, the surface peels and flakes away, becoming uneven.

Collectors look for good shape and pleasing lines. Size is of some importance, but hematite artifacts tend to be rather small due to weight. A high polish is admired, plus few or no rough areas remaining from the original nodule of ore.

At present fakes are not a serious problem, partly because hematite is a difficult material to work due to its hardness. Apparently, artifacts made today would not be a paying proposition.

Hematite cone, ¾ in. high and 1½ in. in diameter. A—$60

Red Hematite celt, 1⅝ in. long and 1⅝ in. wide, with polish on bit.   G—$40

Hematite plummet, 3⅛ in. long, drilled at small end, classic tear-drop shape. Polished overall, black color. D—$135

Hematite celt, Missouri, 3½ in. long.   G—$26

Hematite plummet, 2⅞ in. long, one end rounded and grooved, other end pointed. Slendar and well-polished.
C—$115

Hematite cone, 1¼ in. high and 1¼ in. in basal diameter.
A—$33

Hematite pendant, 3¼ in. long and 1½ in. wide at bottom. Well-made, with single large drill-hole at top center, rust-red color, highly polished.   C—$240

Hematite plummet, 2 in. high and 1 in. diameter. A—$42

Hematite gorget, rectangular form, two drill holes; piece is 3½ in. long, with highly polished surface, no damage.
C—$325

Hematite discoidal, 2½ in. in diameter and 1½ in. high. Very good color in this extremely well-made piece. G—$320

Hematite plummet, extra-large size. It is 3¼ in. high and 1 in. in diameter.   A—$155

Hematite birdstone, 2¼ in. long and 1½ in. high. A—$795

Hematite plummet, 1¾ in. high and ¾ in. diameter. A—$55

Hematite celt, 3¾ in. long and 1¾ in. wide.   A—$70

Artifacts made from other natural materials

Cannel coal gorget, 6½ in. long and 2¼ in. wide. Three-hole sandal-sole type, fine condition.   A—$550

Sheet-mica cut-out, ca. AD 500, Hopewellian and Midwestern. Piece depicts the canine tooth of a bear and is 1⅜ in. long. Base has a small drill-hole. Material probably imported from the Carolinas via early trade. A scarce piece, in that mica layer-flakes easily.   C—$140

Cannel coal disc, 2¼ in. in diameter, ⅛ in. in thickness, probably late prehistoric. Use unknown.   C—$8

Thin, curved **mica strips,** each with minute holes at one end. Seven pieces, each measuring 1⅛ in. long and resembling eagle or hawk claws. Rare decorative ornaments and from southern Ohio. C—$10 each

Cannel coal pendant, 2¼ in. long and about 1 in. wide, drilled at smaller end. D—$35

Meteoritic iron chisel, collected in state of Washington, and remaining section 3¼ in. long. Lower blade in good condition but back portion of piece broken in early times. Rare piece. C—$225

Jadeite blade, probably for woodworking adz, from West Coast of Canada, a 4⅜ in. long. Has typical concave adz blade and good condition. Rare material and probably very early. C—$600

Galena (lead ore) pendant, 2¼ in. long ¾ in. wide, and pale white color. Undrilled, so may also have been intended as a small gorget. C—$32

A young Ute warrior and his dog, with bow and iron-tipped arrows. Note the attractive necklace and full-length leggings. Picture taken in the Uintah Valley, on the eastern slope of the Wasatch Mountain, in Utah. Photo by John K. Hillers, 1873-1874.

Photo courtesy Utah State Historical Society, Collection of Smithsonian Institution

The Papago potter: Edward S. Curtis, photographer.

Photo courtesy National Photography Collection, Neg. #C-30076, Public Archives of Canada

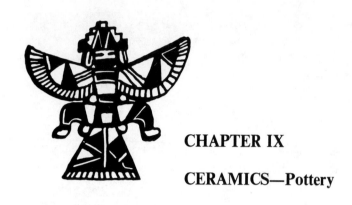

CHAPTER IX

CERAMICS—Pottery

(Considerable writing and material was contributed to this chapter by John W. Barry, P.O. Box 583, Davis, Ca. 95616, who is especially knowledgeable in the contemporary Pueblo pottery field. He contributed the entire pre-listings sections, also selections from his Indian Rock Arts catalog and suggestions for further reading. Used with permission).

INTRODUCTION

Reflections of native American art through the ceramic media equal and often surpass artistic expression through weavings, jewelry, and canvas. Traditional ceramics usually are executed with natural materials and methods employed for several centuries.

Recognizing that there are contemporary styles using contemporary materials and methods to create ceramic Indian art, the skill, creativity and inspiration of the artist are inherent in every piece of Pueblo pottery. These people have an apparent need, coupled with a natural artistry, to express beauty.

It is a natural sequence of events that there is an increasing awareness of this art form as we take shelter from the complexities of our society, examining values and searching for natural esthetics.

There are several excellent books on American Indian Pottery. For those interested, a list of references is included at the end of this article. The purpose of this chapter is to provide an overview of this art form.

Within the scope of our discussion, ceramics is defined as items crafted from clay by Native Americans. This includes numerous types, styles, colors, designs and shapes to include beakers, vases, bowls, bottles, scoops, mugs, plates, pitchers, animal and human figurines, jars and ladles, and effigy vessels.

Pottery collectors differ in what they collect as do collectors of any other art form. Some collections represent either prehistoric, historic or contemporary pottery. Some single out one pueblo; others may collect a certain style from one or several areas while still others may collect only miniatures, non-traditional pottery, or pottery produced by a single potter. The choice is great.

I suggest that you consider concentrating on a particular theme if you plan to become a serious collector; otherwise, choose a few pieces which compliment your decor. The objective is to pursue this art form in a manner which provides you the most enjoyment.

HISTORIC DEVELOPMENT AND CLASSIFICATION

Archaeologists and anthropologists (Martin et al 1947) estimate that pottery made its debut in North America 2500 years ago. Fine ceramics were made by the Hohokam people of the Southwest 200 BC, and by the Mogollon culture around the opening of the Christian era (Tanner 1968). Later Indian immigrants may have brought pottery types to North America, as suggested by similarities to some Asian types.

But pottery had already been established in the New World. Pottery is of immense importance to the archaeologist in classifying, dating, correlating cultures, and providing valuable clues to their rise and fall.

Pottery is a sensitive indicator of changes within a culture. It shows the influences and mixing of other cultures, and when found in site with burials or ceremonial chambers it provides the archaeologist opportunities to understand the user's life styles. A two-name system is used by archaeologists to describe distinctive pottery classes, such as Mesa Verde Black-on-White.

Prehistoric pottery. Classifying prehistoric pottery, particularly those pieces found east of the Mississippi River, is best accomplished by geographic area as there was simultaneous development in various geographical areas. For those interested in more of an in-depth study of the pottery produced by various cultures, books such as Martin, Quimbly and Colliers' book, *Indians Before Columbus,* should be reviewed.

Historic pottery. Historic pottery, chronologically, is pottery produced after the arrival of Coronado to the area of New Mexico in 1540. Some define historic pottery as that produced after 1600 AD, while others use 1700 AD.

Pueblo V: 1700 to Present. Pottery was produced by many of the Pueblos during the early part of the period, at the Pueblos of Acoma, Cochiti, Walpi, Sichomovi, Hano, Skungopovi, Shipaulovi, Mishongonovi, Isleta, Jemez, Laguna, Nambe', Picuris, Sandia, San Ildefonso, San Juan, Santa Ana, Santo Domingo, Zia, Taos, Pojoaque, Tesuque, and Zuni.

Pottery from this period reflects the most advanced of all pottery produced in North America. There were great varieties of types, styles, decoration, colors and designs. This and the contemporary expressions which are an extension of the Historic Period provide the most commonly collected and desirable pottery for the collector.

By 1900 AD pottery seemed destined to extinction. Except for ceremonial and very limited utilitarian use, native pottery was not in general use or needed by the Indian. The reason was the ready availability of cooking and eating ware from the Anglo Culture.

The 20th century has seen a dramatic revival of pottery and the emergence of new types and styles. Thanks to the efforts and encouragement of the traders, museums, and numerous interested individuals, pottery continues and even flourishes in parts of the Southwest. Pottery is now being made for market by all the inhabited pueblos of the Southwest.

Traditional pottery is now being made by the Cherokee and Catawba. Other pottery forms and styles are appearing on the market from tribes throughout the United States. For the most part, however, they are non-traditional in design or manufacture

CONTEMPORARY POTTERY

Visiting a potter at her home is a rewarding experience. Most potters are more than willing to visit and explain the process of making pottery. They usually have pots in various stages of production and depending upon your timing you may see a group of pots being removed from their primitive type firing pit. The potter will show you the clay, polishing stone, and pots awaiting delivery to customers.

It is advisable to make an appointment before your visit. Winter is the best time to visit and make your purchases. At that time you will not be competing with other tourists and various public shows and markets, which require a large inventory. Potters also will keep their better pieces for these shows. Some reservations require that you check in with the reservation officials or Pueblo governor's office before visiting potters within their boundaries.

Most Indian pottery produced today is made by Southwestern pueblos and rancheria people of Arizona. The Southwest pueblos which produce significant amounts of pottery include the Pueblos of Santa Clara, San Ildefonso, Zia, Cochiti, Jemez, Zuni, Acoma, and the Hopi (First Mesa). There is somewhat limited production at San Juan, Tesuque, Santo Domingo, San Lorenzo (Picuris), Taos, Laguna, Pojoaque, Isleta, Sandia, San Felipe, Santa Ana and Nambe.

The rancherias, including Maricopa, Yuma, Pima, and Papago, have either ceased making pottery or produce relatively small amounts. Generally the latter has not shared the popularity of Pueblo wares. The Navajo make a traditional working ware primarily for their own use; **however,** some Navajo pottery is sold to the public. Through Federal programs designed to provide employment to the Utes and Sioux, non-traditional kiln-fired ceramics with Indian motif are produced in limited quantities for the tourist market. With the popularity of Indian pottery more of the non-traditional types will undoubtedly appear on the market.

POTTERS — A PROFILE

There are many excellent ceramic artists today producing a great variety of pottery. Their excellence equals and may even surpass the accomplishments of well known Indian potters. They are producing traditional styles and patterns. Others are creating contemporary ceramics which express an unlimited imagination of style, media, and shape, such as the carved pots made by Joseph Lonewolf.

Young potters such as Laura Gachupin of Jemez Pueblo and Thelma Talachy of Pojoaque Pueblo are making outstanding examples of contemporary pottery with a balance of traditional designs and contemporary styles. Virginia Ebelacker at Santa Clara Pueblo specializes in traditional black storage jars. Her award-winning pieces are sought-after by museums and collectors.

Seferina Ortiz of Cochiti uses traditional methods to produce story tellers, figurines, and pots with lizards. Like the other potters she learned from her mother and finds a ready collector market for her pots. Minnie Vigil of Santa Clara is a prolific pottery who produces an outstanding variety of styles and colors. These potters have two traits in common — they are outstanding artists and are willing to share their enthusiasm of the art with you.

METHOD OF PRODUCTION

There were five basic methods used by North American Indians to make pottery. None employed a potters wheel or anything resembling a wheel.

1. **Coil method..** Rolls of clay are built upon a clay base in a spiral manner. The sides of the pot are developed by successive coils and the sides are smoothed by a piece of gourd, shell, or smooth stone. The Hopi and Rio Grande Pueblos use this method today.

2. **Coil method with Paddle and Anvil.** This method is similar to the coil method except that coils are rarely applied spirally. A paddle and anvil are used to thin and compress the seams. The rancheria and prehistoric people of the Middle and Lower Gila River district of Arizona used this technique.

3. **Paddle and Anvil Method.** No coils are used but the paddle and anvil were used as described above. Some Northern Plains Indians used this method.

4. **Modeling Method.** Eskimos probably used this method which consisted simply of modeling clay into the desired form by hand.

5. **Molded in Basket Method.** In this method a layer of clay was molded to the interior of the basket. During the firing process the basket is lost, producing a pot with indentations of the basket on the exterior. This is probably one of the first methods used to produce pottery in the Southwest.

There are two types of firing processes, commonly referred to as oxidation and reduction. In the oxidation process the fire, having access to air, burns hot and clean. In the reduction process the fire is cooler and fueled with animal manure to produce carbon.

Red ware and lighter colored pots are produced by the oxidation method while the popular black pots from Santa Clara and San Ildefonso are fired by the reduction process. Firing usually lasts for about three hours and may reach temperatures up to 1500 degress F.

A skillful potter can produce a small simple pot in about two hours, exclusive of drying and firing, which may take at least another 15 hours. Large pots require several weeks to complete, depending upon the amount of decoration and polishing.

Present day Pueblo pottery is made essentially in the same manner as prehistoric pottery. Women usually are the potters, although assistance is often provided by son and husband in decorating the pottery. In recent years several men have become known as outstanding ceramic artists, such as Tony Da, Carlos Dunlop and Joseph Lonewolf.

Maria Martinez's husband Julian was probably the first modern day male potter. He decorated many of Maria's pots. Pottery making is usually learned from mother or grandmother.

The type and source of clay, which dictates the color and use of the final product, varies widely among the pueblos. Clay collected from the Rio Grande Pueblo area usually turn red or orange when fired, while those west and north turn white to gray. Proper selection and preparation of the clay are essential to making a quality pot.

The pulverized clay is mixed with water and cured for several days. The clay must be uniformly moist. A base is formed free hand and coils of clay are used to build the side. Vessel walls are thinned usually by a gourd rind and the outer sides are polished with a smoothed river pebble. After the pot is allowed to dry it is decorated with vegetal or mineral paints. The process, although simply presented, requires skill, patience and experience.

SELECTING A PIECE OF POTTERY

Your initial reaction to a piece of pottery should guide your ultimate selection. If the piece is esthetically pleasing initially, in all probability it will remain so if it satisfies other secondary characteristics. Disregard price if possible, particularly if you are looking for collector pieces. A collector piece is one made by a famous potter, is usually unique and probably demands a high price.

First look for cracks. Cracks do occur during the firing and cooling process. Some are readily detectable while others are very inconspicuous. Be sure to examine the pottery interior. Prehistoric pottery usually has chips and cracks. Although these effect the price, they are not particularly objectionable because of the rarity of prehistoric pottery.

It is best to avoid any pot which has a crack or chip as it will always be of lesser value. Experienced collectors have their own method of testing for soundess. One common test is to tap the rim of the pot with your fingernail, as you would to evaluate a crystal wine glass. There should be a resonant sound and not a thud. Many pieces of pottery such as miniatures and figurines are not suitable to this test. Symmetry or overall evenness is important and the pot should sit tall, not lopsided.

Polished pottery such as Santa Clara Pueblo black ware should be smooth and even-textured. Polishing the bowl and on the bottom represents additional effort of the potter, usually not encountered in most pottery. The design should be symmetrical, lines relatively even, and designs balanced. Condition dictates prices of contemporary, historic, and prehistoric pottery. Note that when handling a pot always place one hand on the bottom.

Generally each pueblo or pottery-producing reservation has a style and technique which is culturally acceptable. What might be acceptable or even necessary to one may be entirely unacceptable to another.

An example would be black firemarks on Taos pottery which reflects higher firing temperatures necessary for utilitarian purposes. These would be unacceptable to fine Santa Clara redware. Round bottom Navajo pots also serve a purpose for open-fire cooking while decorative San Ildefonso pots with a round bottom would be unacceptable as a decorator or collectors item.

One cannot generalize about color. Many potters are experimenting with various color, media and combination. If you are a traditionalist, look for color, particularly in polychrome pieces, which represent the traditional style. Most pots are painted before firing which fixes the color. If the paint will rub off, reconsider your purchase.

Inexpensive pots from a few pueblos are painted after firing. These represent a style and it is your decision whether or not they have a place in your collection. These are not to be confused with some of the outstanding oil and acrylic painted pots from Zia made by Madinas which have appeared in recent years and are in demand by collectors.

Look for small pits on the surface. Some pots from Acoma and other pueblos have impurities and tempering materials essential to strengthening and bonding. Occasionally pitting may develop after firing. This is no reflection upon the skill of the potter; depending upon the severity, it may affect the pots' appeal and value.

Some of the traditional type pots from the pueblos of Zia, Taos, Picuris, Acoma and Santo Domingo are utilitarian while most pots from other pueblos are strictly decorative. Your dealer or the potter will discuss this with you.

Properly seasoned pots from Taos and Picuris are excellent for oven use. Although some Indians may use their native pottery for special purposes, cost usually dictates that the pot be displayed as a piece of art. There is a wide choice and the informed buyer will make fewer mistakes in his selection. If you are inexperienced, buy from a knowledgeable dealer or a recognized potter.

THE FUTURE

The future of all Indian arts and crafts is dependent upon the attitude, motivations and changing culture of the Indians. Pottery is no exception, although there are several fulltime potters making a living as ceramic artists. They are motivated by economic benefits as well as by a need for recognition of their accomplishments. As long as there is an appreciation of pottery it will continue to be produced.

Quality pottery by recognized potters will continue to appreciate in value. Historic and prehistoric pottery will become part of institutional collections and this will result in less pottery being available to private collectors. Styles will continue to change with the imagination of the artists. This creativity is essential to the future vitality of this art.

(J.W.B)

BROKEN SECTION OF POTTERY VESSEL, found near Calabogie, Ontario, Canada. A Canadian archaeologist has identified the section as "Black-necked" type, typical of the late Huron-Petun people of southern Ontario, Age: AD 1450—AD 1550.   C—$14
Photo courtesy Howard Popkie, Arnprior, Ontario, Canada.

EASTERN AND MISSISSIPPI WATERSHED PREHISTORIC POTTERY

Large **pottery bowl,** from Arkansas, 7 in. high and 7¼ in. in diameter. No restoration or cracks; piece has cross-hatched rim design.   G—$250

Mississippi culture **ceramic bowl,** 8 in. wide and 3½ in. high; rim has coiled baked clay resembling 3-strand rope twist. One major break has been skillfully restored. Except for rim decoration, a plain but well-made piece.D—$190

Round-bodied **Iroquois vessel,** 5 in. high, 5½ in. wide at mid-body. Reinforced upper rim decorated with incised lines. Gray-white in color, pot is in good condition.C—$365

Low **ceramic bowl,** Mississippi culture and from Louisiana, painted lines decorate the straight sides. Bowl is 8½ in. diameter, 3½ in. high. One section of the bowl bottom has been restored.   C—$170

Caddoan effigy bowl, 3 in. high and 8 in. wide. Piece has three raised head-like nodes on an outstanding polished and engraved friendship bowl. Lines filled with red pigment.   G—$900

Mississippi culture **ceramic vessel,** Tennessee, circular and with knobs on the rim. Piece is 9 in. diameter and 4 in. high, with a reinforced rim. No decorations.   C—$285

Grayware bowl, fine condition and 5 in. high and 7 in. in diameter. From Arkansas.   G—$70

Flare-top **ceramic vessel,** Louisiana, 13 in. high and 8½ in. in diameter. It has cord-marked decoration on the surface, is a brown-gray color. Round body and rim. No restorations.   D—$365

Ceramic effigy vessel, from southeastern U.S. and 8½ in. high. Human figure depicts kneeling man; some red paint remains on exterior. Vessel damaged and restored in base area, also in several sections of the rim. Figure is fine.   D—$500

Southern Cult pottery bottle, rare, 8½ in. high and 7 in. in diameter. Four human hands go around the bottle, in raised relief. No restoration, but some very minor rim and body damage.   G—$800

Quapaw ceramic "teapot", 8 in. high and 9¼ in. in diameter. Painted red, white and brown; in fine condition.   G—$1400

Pottery bowl, from Woodland site in Pennsylvania, thick shell-tempered piece 6 in. in diameter, the same in height. No decoration and no handles. Very early vessel, probably BC period.   C—$220

Fine ceramic, **frog effigy vessel,** 4 in. high and 7 in. long. Superb workstyle, finely detailed, and with a rattle head; no restoration.   G—$700

Caddoan **ceramic vessel,** from Arkansas, late prehistoric times. It stands 9 in. high and rounded base is 9½ in. in diameter. Deeply incised with swirling-circle pattern. Well-done, no damage and no restoration.   C—$800

Turkey effigy rattle bowl, 10 in. in diameter and 6½ in. high. From Mississippian mound-builder period.G—$500

Caddoan water bottle, 9¼ in. high and 6½ in. width. No designs, but piece has a fine slick black finish and fine balance, only very minor repair.   G—$350

127

Caddoan vessel with incised exterior, from Oklahoma. This large pot is 8 x 9 in. and very thin.   Unlisted

Private collection

SHELL-TEMPERED POT, from Hardin County, Tennessee, and probably from the Mississippian culture. Pot is 5 in. high and 5¾ in. across at top opening; circumference is 22 in.   Unlisted

Private collection

Caddo seed jar, late prehistoric, from Craighead County, Arkansas. This well-formed pot is 5 x 7 in.   Unlisted

Private collection

Compound bowl, grayware, Mississippi Valley. It is 4 in. high.   Unlisted

Private collection

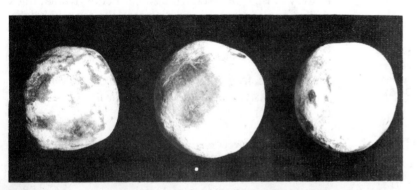

POTTERY BALLS, found with 16 others on the bank of the Tennessee River near Savannah, Tennessee. Each shows evidence of having been in a fire. Use uncertain; may have been heated and used as we use charcoal, or dropped in a vessel for heating and cooking. Each is about the size of a golf ball. Mississippian culture.   C—$3 each

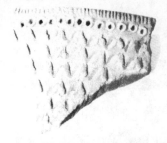

TWO POTTERY SHARDS, found near Pickwick Dam, Tennessee. They are rare for the area because of the thumbnail impression in darker piece and forefinger and thumbnail impression on the other. These are probably Mississippian in origin. The larger sherd is 5 in. long.   C—$4

Photo courtesy Jim Northcutt, Jr., Corinth, Mississippi.

Mound Place incised bottle, Mississippi period, in grayware. This beautiful piece is 9½ in. high and the decorating is very well-done.
Private collection   Unlisted

CERAMIC VESSEL, 4½ in. high and 8 in. diameter, plainware. Gray color, and found in Canada. Vessel is ca. AD 700-1100.   Unlisted

Photo courtesy Howard Popkie, Arnprior, Canada.

Piecrust bowl, tallied rim, Mississippian period. This grayware pot is 3⅛ in. high and 6½ in. in diameter.   Unlisted
Private collection

Mississippian bowl, piecrust or tallied rim, grayware, from Arkansas. It is 2¾ in. high and 6¾ in. in diameter.   Unlisted
Private collection

Cat-serpent effigy bowl, grayware, from Arkansas. It is 7 in. in diameter and 6¾ in high. A fine Mississippian-era ceramic, it is in top condition.
Private collection   Unlisted

Grayware frog effigy bowl, from Arkansas, 3 in. high and 5 in. diameter.
Private collection   Unlisted

Duck effigy bowl, grayware, from Arkansas. This interesting vessel is 7 in. high at the head and 6 in. in diameter.   Unlisted
Private collection

Medallion pot, grayware, from Mississippi County, Arkansas. This well-shaped ceramic is 5¼ in. high.   Unlisted
Private collection

Prehistoric grayware bowl, Arkansas, with very unusual designs. These are punctate zoomorphic figures in the pottery; an owl is visible, plus three other forms. This pot is 4½ in. high.   Unlisted
Private collection

Fluted pot or jar, ornate nandles, gadroon sides. Made of grayware, it is 6¼ in. in diameter and 4 in. high. From Lake County, Tennessee.
Private collection   Unlisted

Grouping of pottery trowels, used for shaping and smoothing pottery vessels. Made of tan or gray baked clay, the highest is 3½ in. All from Arkansas.   Unlisted

Private collection

Hooded humpback effigy jar, 5¼ in. high, grayware, and a well-executed ceramic. It is from the Mississippi Watershed region.   Unlisted

Private collection

Humped human effigy figure pot, from Arkansas, 7½ in. high. This female figure is done in tan and gray, and is in top condition.Unlisted

Private collection

Narrow-top bottle, prehistoric, Mississippi Valley, plainware or grayware. It is 6¾ in. high.   Unlisted

Private collection

Southeastern U.S. pottery, both from Arkansas and both Caddoan. Left, vase form, 4 in. in diameter and 4 in. high.
Right, jar or vase, 4½ in. in diameter, 4 in. high.

Private collection   Unlisted

Group of six **Caddoan miniature bottles,** averaging 2 in. in height. Some fine engraved examples, and sold as a group only.   G—$275

Square-bodied **Iroquois vessel,** New York, 7 in. high and 5½ in. wide at top. Top rim is decorated with incised ladder-like markings, while body has parallel lines. Gray-black color and no restoration.   D—$400

Mississippi culture **water bottle,** from Missouri, with some minor restoration. Piece is 7 in. high and 7 in. diameter, with a pedestal base.   G—$125

Mint condition **water bottle,** from Arkansas, 7 in. high and 6 in. in diameter. Good shape.   G—$120

Perforated disc base water bottle, found in Arkansas and 8 in. high and 6⅝ in. in diameter. Perfectly balanced and with some restoration to rim and base.   G—$235

Bird effigy vessel, 5 in. long, from Florida and ca. AD 500. Well-executed and originally hand painted features, now gone. An unusual piece and in fine condition. C—$650

Strap-handled pots, various decorations on the exteriors, all from Arkansas.   Unlisted
Private collection

Various pottery types, decorated examples on right and left, all from Arkansas.   Unlisted
Private collection

Southeastern U.S. prehistoric pottery. Left, Hodges engraved, Caddoan, 5¾ in. in diameter, 3½ in. high.
Right, Woodland, brushed exterior and pie-crust rim, 5 in. in diameter, 3¾ in. high.   Unlisted
Private collection

Pottery types, tall bottle at center, all from Arkansas.   Unlisted
Private collection

Prehistoric vase-bottle, Caddo, swirl design of red on white, from Arkansas.   Unlisted
Private collection

Prehistoric Southeastern pottery, Crocket Curvalinear, from Arkansas. It is 6½ in. in diameter and a pleasingly formed pot.   Unlisted
Private collection

132

Duck or snake effigy bowl, from Cross County, Arkansas. A scarce , vessel, it is 12¾ in. long. Unlisted
Private collection

Water bottle, prehistoric Southeastern U.S., incised concentric circles, from Arkansas. It is 8 in. high and a well-formed piece. Unlisted
Private collection

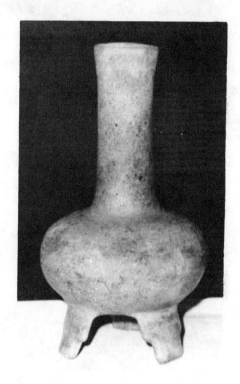

Effigy bowl, prehistoric Southeastern pottery, "Wounded Hawk" form. It is 7½ in. in diameter and 8¾ in. from crest to tail. This fine piece is from Arkansas. Unlisted
Private collection

Tripodal water bottle, extra-fine, with slab type stepped feet. It is from eastern Arkansas. Unlisted
Private collection

Southeastern U.S. prehistoric pottery.
Left, Campbell Compound jar over jar, 5¼ in. diameter, 4¾ in. high. Northeastern U.S. prehistoric pottery. Seneca (Iroquois) jar, sawtooth rim, 4½ in. diameter, 4¼ in. high. Unlisted
Private collection

133

Tripodal water bottle with bulbous feet and disc or platform type base. This is a unique piece because of the basal style; from Mississippi County, Arkansas. Unlisted
Private collection

Rounded bottle pot, shouldered, grayware or plainware. It is 7½ in. high. Unlisted
Private collection

Tripodal water bottle with bulbous feet, Mississippi County, Arkansas. This is a fairly scarce type. Unlisted
Private collection

Carinated bowl or bottle, grayware, prehistoric. It is 5 in. high and 6½ in. in diameter. Unlisted
Private collection

Stirrup bottle, Mississippi County, Arkansas. This work has excellent shape and finish. Unlisted
Private collection

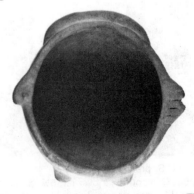

Fish effigy bowl, prehistoric, grayware, from Arkansas. This fine bowl is 5½ in. from nose to tail. Unlisted
Private collection

Late prehistoric Southeastern U.S. bowl, Caddoan, from Arkansas. It is Friendship Engraved, 7¾ in. in diameter. Unlisted
Private collection

Group of miniature pottery bowls, prehistoric, Mississippi Valley. These are made of tan or gray pottery. The duck effigy bowl, front, is 3½ in. in diameter. Unlisted
Private collection

Mississippian period ceramic jar, ca. AD 1000-1500, Barton / Parkin style. It is from Arkansas, 5 in. in diameter and 6 in. high. Unlisted
Private collection

Group of miniature bowls, prehistoric, from Arkansas. These are gray or tan in color; the front bowl is 2⅝ in. high. Unlisted
Private collection

Prehistoric pottery vessels, various shapes, all from Arkansas. Unlisted
Private collection

Large flared-rim bowl, very good condition, from Arkansas. Unlisted
Private collection

Bowl in the effigy of a sleeping goose, very scarce, from Pemiscot County, Missouri. Length from head to tail is 10½ in. and the bowl diameter is 9 in. It is in fine condition.   Unlisted
Private collection

Seed jar, prehistoric (late), from Clark County, Arkansas. It is 6 in. in diameter and 6¾ in. high.   Unlisted
Private collection

Prehistoric Southeastern pottery, Military Road vase, 10 in. high. This nicely flared pot is from Arkansas.   Unlisted
Private collection

136

Pottery bowls, 7 to 12 in. in diameter, two with reddish paint. All from
Arkansas.   Unlisted
Private collection

Southern U.S. pottery, mainly from Arkansas, miniature examples in
front row. The sun-disc effigy in front, 2nd from right, is from Louisiana.
                                                             Unlisted

Private collection

Prehistoric pottery.
Left, Caddo engraved vase, very light and thin, 6 x 6 in., from Oklahoma.
                                                             Unlisted
Right, Caddo engraved bowl, extremely light and thin, 5 x 6 in., from
Oklahoma.   Unlisted

Private collection

Outstanding effigy pottery. Deer bowl (AR); frog bowl (AR); human figure
(Mexico); human figure (AR); duck bowl (AR); large duck bowl (AR); dog
(Mexico); Sun effigy (LA); miniature bird bowl (AR); center bird bowl (LA).
Unlisted

Private collection

Prehistoric Southeastern pottery, both from Arkansas.
Left, Foster Trailed incised, 5 in. in diameter, restored.
Right, Foster Trailed incised, 5¾ in. in diameter.   Unlisted

Private collection

Late prehistoric pottery, both pieces from Arkansas.
Left, hunch-back human effigy, 3¾ in. high, Cross County.
Right, miniature water bottle, 3½ in. high, Bell plain design.

Private collection   Unlisted

Compound vessels, Mississippian era.
Left, rare; one side is buff, the other dark gray, 8 in. wide, from Pemiscot
County, MO.
Center, disc base, Mississippi County, AR, 7⅜ in. wide.
Right, Mississippi County, AR, 6½ in. wide and 3 in. high.

Unlisted

Private collection

138

WESTERN PREHISTORIC CERAMIC VESSELS

Anasazi/Pueblo III vessel, 12½ in. in diameter, exterior and interior decorated with geometric squares and alternating bands of white and red. Small portion of bowl rim has been expertly restored. Quite impressive piece. C—$795

Mimbres geometric design bowl, with usual kill-hole. Piece is 10 in. in diameter and 5 in. high. Restored. G—$550

Anasazi handled mug, Colorado, with geometric motif painted on sides. Ceramic piece stands 4½ in. high, and is in perfect condition. C—$300

Early **seed pot,** or storage vessel, from Colorado, and painted with varied motifs and Pueblo I or II period. It is 12½ in. high and 18½ in. in diameter. Unusual item, and in fine condition, no restoration. C—$900

Mimbres ceramic bowl, 11¾ in. in diameter, with checkerboard design in black and white on interior. Has small kill-hole in bottom, otherwise perfect condition. D—$600

Mimbres vessel, 9 in. in diameter and 3 in. high, red on white concentric rim bands with inner concentric bands. Star in center, and kill-hole. G—$700

Anasazi corrugated ceramic jar, 9 in. in height, some original damage to base but could be restored. C—$260

Salado ceramic jar, 7½ in. in diameter and 5 in. high. Geometric designs, excellent condition, and ca. AD 1200-AD 1450. G—$600

Chaco Canyon black on white **pitcher,** 4½ in. high and 4 in. in diameter. G—$325

Zuni ceramic bowl, prehistoric, with stylized horned toad (?) motif painted around interior. Piece is circular, 13¼ in. in diameter, and some damage to rim area. C—$565

Anasazi ceramic bowl, 13 in. in diameter, about 4 in. high. Semicircular designs painted inside, except for bottom. Rim is damaged in several places. D—$395

BLACK-ON-WHITE BOWL, 3½ in. high and 6 in. in diameter. This type is called a "seed pot" by collectors. It has a small crack on the rim but is in excellent condition. Anasazi culture, from San Juan County. Colorado, near Mesa Verde. Circa AD 1100-1300. C—$400

Photo courtesy Claude Britt, Jr., Many Farms, Arizona.

Coal Mine Mesa corrugated jar, 11 in. diameter and 14½ in. high. Some rim damage. G—$325

Handled ceramic pitcher, Anasazi, but looks almost modern. Piece is 10½ in. high, with expanded base. Bottom has circular streaks, top has lightning pattern. Some restoration to handle, but not major. D—$500

Jeddito pottery bowl, 8 in. in diameter and 3 in. high. Geometric painting inside and out, and in mint condition. This piece is ca. AD 1400. G—$425

Southwestern Indian large **ceramic spoon or scoop,** probably Hohokam, 9¼ in. long, and shallow. Decorative interior lines of yellow and brown. Handle cracked in places. C—$220

Fine **Casa Grande effigy bowl,** 4½ in. high and 7½ in. in diameter. Has bird-like head, and four legs which were broken off and smoothed. G—$440

Black on white bowl, 6 in. in diameter and 5 in. high. The piece has a stylized human effigy figure on the bottom, interior. Large chip missing from the rim. G—$500

Hohokam pottery vessel, 11½ in. in diameter, undecorated, good condition; top opening 7 in. in diameter. Base is fire-darkened and heat-cracked. C—$245

Four Mile Ruin bowl, 9 in. in diameter and 4 in. high. Polychrome, with geometric design. Painted inside and out; this is a restored piece. G—$700

Black on white pitcher, 3½ in. high and 4½ in. at base. Geometric designs, Tularosa type, good condition.G—$295

Salado ceramic, 7 in. in diameter and 5 in. high. Geometric designs, and ca. AD 1200-1450. G—$475

Mimbres bowl, 6 in. in diameter. Has a well-executed rabbit design, only usual minor deterioration. Ca. AD 1250. G—$1100

Casa Grande bowl, unusual square shape, mint condition. Piece is 2½ in. high and 4¼ in. diameter. Note: It had a miniature axe, a polished stone pendant and miniature bowl and shell ring all inside bowl when it was found. All included. G—$550

Zuni food bowl, 12 in. in diameter and 4 in. high. Painted geometric designs inside and out, and one small area of restoration on the bottom. G—$1150

Casa Grande culture **effigy ceramic,** 6 in. high and 5 in. wide. Human male, superb detail, excellent condition, and from New Mexico. G—$700

Mimbres bowl, 9 in. in diameter and 3½ in. high. Design is concentric rim bands with inner-spaced geometrics; with kill-hole. C—$800

Anasazi/Pueblo-III ceramic bowl, 14 in. in diameter, interior painted with swirls and zigzag lines, exterior similar. No damage, no restoration. G—$800

Chaco Canyon type black on white **pitcher,** 5½ in. high and 4 in. in basal diameter. Geometric design, and good condition. G—$300

Diegueno olla or storage vessel, Southwestern California, 13 in. high and 8 in. wide, mouth 4 in. wide. Restoration to rim and part of bottom. C—$325

Anasazi black on white **mug,** 5½ in. high and 6 in. in diameter. Has a rope-twist pottery handle, in excellent condition. Piece is ca. AD 950. G—$375

Mogollon polished brownware, 9 in. in diameter and same measure high. Piece has heavy restoration and is ca. AD 400-600. G—$265

Black on orange **ceramic bowl,** Bedehochi type. Zone geometric design, and 6½ in. in diameter, 3 in. high. G—$450

MESA VERDE LADLE or dipper, 10 in. long and with bowl 4½ in. diameter. Anasazi culture, from Mancos, San Juan County, Colorado. The handle is restored; otherwise in fine condition; this piece would be worth $300—$400, if not restored and perfect. Circa AD 1150. C—$265

Photo courtesy Claude Britt, Jr., Many Farms, Arizona.

Tularosa olla, black on white, very symmetrical and about 13 in. in diameter. It has pitting on one side and some wear to paint; otherwise, very good condition for this early and rare vessel form. $750

Alvin Lee Moreland collection, Corpus Christi, Texas

MESA VERDE MUG, 5 in. by 4½ in. and decorated with black mineral paint on a white background. Anasazi culture, from Yellow Jacket, Colorado, and ca. AD 1100—1300. C—$400

Photo courtesy Claude Britt, Jr., Many Farms, Arizona.

Pottery, prehistoric, Salt River redware from Arizona, 6 in. in diameter. It is ca. AD 800-1000 $150

Pocotopaug Trading Post, South Windsor, Connecticut

Pottery vessel, red designs on brown background, 9½ in. high and 11¾ in. in diameter. From Arizona, it is Hohokam culture and ca. 9th Century. $2500

Courtesy The Curio Shop, Anderson, California

Gila bowl, AD 1100-1300, from Arizona. Size is about 5 in. in diameter; it is red on the exterior and has a black on buff interior. Interesting design, and overall in mint condition. $400

Alvin Lee Moreland, Corpus Christi, Texas

141

Anasazi canteen, from Colorado, 6 in. wide at widest. Ca. AD 1100-1300, it has a fine design. There is a pressure crack and a minor rim chip.

Alvin Lee Moreland, Corpus Christi, Texas $550

Southwestern prehistoric pot, Anasazi, black on white interior with red exterior. It is from Arizona and 7 in. in diameter, ca. AD 1000-1250.
$400-$450

Pocotopaug Trading Post, South Windsor, CT

Prehistoric olla, Salado Redware, Anasazi. It is 6½ in. in diameter and 6 in. high. Ex-museum, it is ca. AD 1200-1400. $350

Morris' Art & Artifacts, Anaheim, California; Dawn Gober photograph

SAN ILDEFONSO JAR, 3½ in. high and 4½ in. in diameter. This Pueblo is the home of the famous potter Maria Martinez. Although Ildefonso pottery is quite heavy, not thin like the Zia and Acoma, prices of well-finished pieces are rather high. C—$600

Photo courtesy Harvey and Rose King, Muskogee, Oklahoma.

Southwestern prehistoric pot, zoomorphic decoration, brown and cream. Size is 3¾ in. high and 6¾ in. in diameter. This piece is very well-made and in top condition. $400-$600

Private collection

Southwestern pottery vessel, corrugated utility grayware. It was formed by pinching together the side-coils as they were layered up. Size, 3¾ in. in diameter, 3¼ in. high. AD 1000-1400. $200

Private collection

Prehistoric Southwestern pottery, black on white, Anasazi. From Arizona, it is 9 in. diameter and ca. AD 1000-1200. $200-$250

Pocotopaug Trading Post, South Windsor, CT

Southwestern prehistoric pottery, Anasazi, black and white interior, red exterior, 6¼ in. in diameter. It is ca. AD 1000-1200. $150-$175

Pocotopaug Trading Post, South Windsor, CT

Southwestern prehistoric pot, 2½ in. high and 5⅜ in. in diameter. It is black and cream on red, a well-made ceramic from Arizona.Unlisted

Private collection

Gila bowl, from Arizona, 7 in. in diameter. The exterior is red and the interior is a black on buff design, a geometric pinwheel. This pottery piece is cracked and glued in two places. $475

Alvin Lee Moreland, Corpus Christi, Texas

Southwestern prehistoric pottery, Mogollon, from the Gila River area of southeastern Arizona. Ca. AD 1000-1250, it is 7 in. in diameter.
                                                                    $175-$200

Pocotopaug Trading Post, South Windsor, CT

Prehistoric bowl, Mimbres, black on red, from the Mogollon Rim. It is 4 x 7 in., ex-museum and ca. AD 1100-1300 $500

Morris' Art & Artifacts, Anaheim, California; Dawn Gober photograph

HISTORIC CERAMICS

Hopi pottery vessel, mint condition, 4⅞ in. high and 5½ in. in diameter. Unsigned, and ca. 1920.   G—$400

Zia ceramic pot, 4½ in. high, 6 in. in diameter, with brown slip. Red and black painted bird designs; cracked and repaired, but with good appearance. Zia Pueblo, ca. 1940. Marked S.P. Medina.   G—$325

Acoma ceramic vessel, 4½ in. in diameter, stylized animal depicted, nice finish and good design.   C—$225

Hopi vase, Sikyatki revival style, and ca. 1935.   G—$285

San Ildefonso polychrome plate, 10 in. in diameter, 2 in. high. Ca. 1920.   G—$385

Miniature Acoma pot, with loop handle. Piece is 2½ in. high and 3½ in. wide. Has good paint and age.   G—$295

Zuni fetish bowl, depicting frog and water bugs. It is 9 in. across and 4 in. high, in good condition. Ca. 1930.   G—$135

Santa Clara bowl, with incised serpent design. Piece is 6½ in. in diameter and 5½ in. high Ca. 1940, and signed, Helen.   G—$650

Santa Clara wedding vase, 7 in. diameter and 8½ in. high. Good condition; ca. 1920.   G—$300

San Ildefonso ceramic, 12 in. in diameter and 11½ in. high; black on black water jar. It has minor rim chips and is ca. 1910.   G—$300

Acoma head pot, 9 in. high and 12 in. across. It has geometric designs, is in excellent condition, very thin-walled. Ca. 1920.   G—$475

Small basket-type **miniature Acoma pot,** 2½ in. high and 4 in. in diameter, and ca. 1930.   G—$625

Hopi ceramic bowl, reddish slip, 4 in. high and 8½ in. in diameter. Excellent condition, with red and black painted design. Ca. 1930.   G—$110

Historic **San Ildefonso bowl,** 11 in. across and 5 in. high. Polychrome bowl painted inside and out, geometric design. There is chip damage around lower exterior.   G—$650

Hopi jar, 4½ in. high and 6 in. in diameter. Not signed, but well done and ca. 1920's.   G—$225

Mojave pitcher, 5 in. high, and diamond painted design. Ca. 1940.   G—$130

Tesque rain god, 7 in. high, with figure sitting with hands over eyes and bowl in lap. Ca. 1920.   G—$155

Acoma pueblo pot, black and orange-red on tan, ca. 1890. In beautiful condition, this fine work is 11½ x 11½ in. $6500-$7000
Dennis R. Phillips / Fine American Indian Art, Chicago, IL

Pottery vessel, abstract bird decoration in red and black against white. This fine pot is 6 in. high and 8½ in. in diameter. It is from Acoma pueblo and was worked in the 1950s. $600
Courtesy The Curio Shop, Anderson, California

Pottery vessel, black and orange decorations on white with white interior. It is 6½ in. high and 9½ in. in diameter. This piece was made at Acoma pueblo in the 1950s. $600
Courtesy The Curio Shop, Anderson, California

Pottery, Acoma pueblo, 12 in. diameter and 12½ in. high, orange-red and black on white. This fine piece is ca. 1890.

$6500-$7000

Dennis R. Phillips / Fine American Indian Art, Chicago, IL

Pottery vessel, yellow and black designs with yellow interior, Acoma pueblo. It is 9 in. high and 9½ in. in diameter. This well-made pot is from the 1950s. $900

Courtesy The Curio Shop, Anderson, California

Pottery, high bowl, Acoma pueblo, 8 in. in height. It is red and black on cream with a red interior. Ca. 1890-1910. $350-$400

Pocotopaug Trading Post, South Windsor, CT

Pottery vessel, orange and black on white, 9½ in. high and 11 in. in diameter. It is from the 1940s and was made in Acoma pueblo. $750

Courtesy The Curio Shop, Anderson, California

Acoma pueblo pottery bowl, black, yellow-buff and orange-red against cream, ca. 1910. It is 8 in. high and 11 in. in diameter. $750

Private collection

Acoma pueblo pottery bowl, white and black, from the 1940s. It is 8 in. high and 10 in. in diameter. $425

Private collection

Acoma pueblo pot, red and black designs on creamy white, 11¼ in.
high and 12½ in. in diameter. This very fine piece is ca. 1900.
$7500

Dennis R. Phillips / Fine American Indian Art, Chicago, IL

Pottery vessel, insect motif in black, yellow and orange, 6 in. high and
7½ in. in diameter. It is from Acoma pueblo and was made in the 1930s.
$700

Courtesy The Curio Shop, Anderson, California

Pottery olla, Acoma, ca. 1920, size 9½ in. diameter and 7½ in. high.
Very symmetrical and the thin wall has a good ring tone. Colors are
orange with black and white designs. White slip shows some crazing,
otherwise in excellent condition. Ex-coll. Fruchtel.
$650

Sherman Holbert Collection, Fort Mille Lacs, Onamia, Minnesota

Pottery vessel, Acoma pueblo, New Mexico, black and orange on white,
with orange interior. This fine piece is 7 in. high and 8½ in. in diameter;
it was made in the 1950s.
$800

Courtesy The Curio Shop, Anderson, California

Pottery vessel, black design on white with orange interior, 8 in. high
and 9 in. in diameter. This is from Acoma pueblo and was made in the
1940s. This is a very artistic pot.
$1400

Courtesy The Curio Shop, Anderson, California

Historic Pueblo pot, Acoma, 7 in. high, black and orange-red on cream,
ca. 1920s.
$300

Pocotopaug Trading Post, South Windsor, CT

146

Pottery vessel, 7 in. high and 4½ in. in diameter. It has a five-color design and is from Acoma pueblo. It was made in the 1950s and has a pleasing color combination. $800

Courtesy The Curio Shop, Anderson, California

Pottery vessel, black deer with red heartlines against white, orange interior. This fine pot is from Acoma pueblo and 11½ in. high and 9 in. in diameter. It was made in the 1940s. $800

Courtesy The Curio Shop, Anderson, California

Zia pueblo bowl, animal motif, from the 1920s. It is 9 in. high and 10½ in. in diameter. Designs are black against a light tan ground; this is a fine early pot. $1650

Private collection

Pottery vessel, very well decorated in black and orange, from Zuni pueblo. It is 9¾ in. high and 11 in. in diameter. This fine work was made in the 1930s. $1800

Courtesy The Curio Shop, Anderson, California

Zia pueblo pottery polychrome bowl, 9½ in. high and 11 in. in diameter. It is ca. 1910 and a fine early pot in top condition.

$1200

Private collection

Zuni owl pottery, 12 in. high, brown and orange on white. $600

Courtesy Dr. Fred Belk, Corrales, New Mexico

Pottery bowl, Santa Clara pueblo, 4½ x 7¾ in. Ca. 1920s, this is a fine period piece, cream on red and highly polished. Condition is excellent, with only a very small interior rim chip. $225

Sherman Holbert Collection, Fort Mille Lacs, Onamia, Minnesota

Hopi bowl, unsigned, black and orange-red on tan-cream, 3 x 8 in. From the 1920s, it is in excellent condition. $245

Courtesy John Isaac, Albuquerque, New Mexico

Laguna pueblo pottery vase, orange-red and black against cream, from the 1960s. It is 8 in. high and 8 in. in diameter. $325

Private collection

Bowl or pot, Cochiti pueblo, black on cream white. It is a top-level work, approximately 11 x 14 in. in diameter, and ca. 1880. $8500

Dennis R. Phillips / Fine American Indian Art, Chicago, IL

Santo Domingo pueblo pot, black on tan-cream, ca. 1890. This top condition piece is 8½ in. in diameter and 9¼ in. high. $2500

Dennis R. Phillips / Fine American Indian Art, Chicago, IL

Pottery vessel, Isleta pueblo, New Mexico, 2¾ in. high and 5½ in. in diameter. It has orange and black designs on white and is of museum quality; a rare historic bowl from the 1880-90s. $1200

Courtesy The Curio Shop, Anderson, California

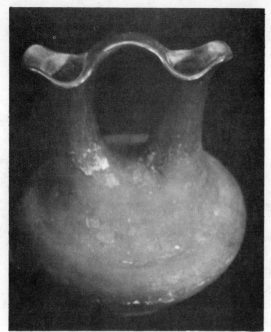

Redware wedding vase, very early San Ildefonso piece, 1870-1880s. It measures 10 x 14 in. and is in excellent condition.

$1250

Larry Lantz, First Mesa, South Bend, Indiana

Storage jar, large size, Zia pueblo, 17 in. high and 20 in. in diameter. This four-color polychrome pottery piece is ca. 1910 and quite rare and beautiful. $45,000

Courtesy Adobe Gallery, Albuquerque, New Mexico

Pueblo bowl, orange-brown and black on cream, 9 in. high and 13 in. in diameter. This fine piece is ca. 1925. $950

Courtesy John Isaac, Albuquerque, New Mexico

Olla, Laguna pueblo, four-color polychrome pot in pleasing design. It is 12 x 12 in. and ca. 1900. $9500

Courtesy Adobe Gallery, Albuquerque, New Mexico

Picuris pottery vase, 9 in. in diameter and 9½ in. high. It is tan-orange and from the early 1900s. $500

Private collection

Historic Pueblo pot or vase, orange-red and black on cream, 11 in. high, ca. 1920s. $250

Pocotopaug Trading Post, South Windsor, CT

Ceremonial plate, San Ildefonso pueblo, 9 in. in diameter. The design is red and black on tan, with the piece ca. 1890. There is some damage and restoration. $800

Courtesy John Isaac, Albuquerque, New Mexico

Pot, polished blackware, by Helen Shupa, Santa Clara pueblo. This fine piece, ca. 1985, is 6½ in. by 5½ in. high. $2500

Dennis R. Phillips / Fine American Indian Art, Chicago, IL

Zuni olla, deer with heartline, very fine condition, 16 in. wide. A top specimen in every way. $10,000

Courtesy Dr. Fred Belk, Corrales, New Mexico

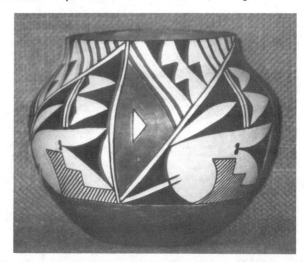

Polychrome pot in black and red-orange against white, Acoma. It is 5 x 5½ in., in perfect condition and made by Virginia Lowden ca. 1970. $450

Marguerite L. Kernaghan collection; photograph by Marguerite L. and Stewart W. Kernaghan, Bellvue, Colorado

Storyteller with ten children, Jemez pueblo. It is signed P.M.C., Jemez Pue., and is 5 x 6¼ x 7½ in. Ca. 1975. $450

Marguerite L. Kernaghan collection; photograph by Marguerite L. and Stewart W. Kernaghan, Bellvue, Colorado

CONTEMPORARY AND/OR SIGNED SOUTHWESTERN POTTERY

Small, well-made **Santo Domingo pottery vessel,** bird effigy, 2 in. high and 4 in. long.   G—$100

Miniature Acoma pot, with lighting designs.   A—$55

Acoma bowl, whiteware with brown flowers painted design, 3 in. high and 4½ in. in width. Piece has large coiled handles.   G—$105

Tesque **pottery effigy figure.**   A—$50

Santa Clara pottery vessel, 3½ in. high and 7½ in. in diameter, red and white, and in mint condition. G—$140

Acoma pottery vessel, 8 in. high and 9 in. in diameter, very thin and extremely fine shape.   G—$685

Santo Domingo pot, 11 in. across and 10 in. high, excellent condition, and with geometric checkerboard design.   G—$700

Hopi contemporary pot, 5 in. high and 6½ in. in diameter, with stylized bird design. Signed, Emily Komalestewa.   G—$300

Santo Domingo pot, made by Santana Melchor. A—$115

Miniature Acoma pot, made by B. Cerno.   A—$75

Santa Clara pot, made by Jo Ann.   A—$110

Ceramic plate, perfect condition and with feather design, by Maria and Popovi Da.   G—$3500

Hopi contemporary pot, 8½ in. in diameter and 8 in. high; designed with fine-lined center band with geometric neck. Signed, Ruby Shroulate.   G—$325

Hopi bowl, 3 in. high and 7 in. in diameter, very nice. Signed, Viola Howato.   G—$300

Santa Clara ceramic, 5½ in. in diameter, 4 in. high. Small black on black piece, with painted knife design. Signed, Minnie.   G—$295

Hopi pot, 7 in. in diameter and 6 in. high, showing fine geometric design. Signed, Rondina Huma.   G—$375

Hopi bowl, 3 in. high and 7¾ in. in diameter. Signed, Viola Howato, First Mesa, 1968.   G—$825

Santa Clara seed jar, 6 in. across and 5 in. high. Design is an incised bear paw. Signed, Minnie.   G—$325

San Ildefonso pot, made by Blue Corn.   A—$75

ZUNI POLYCHROME POT, 9½ in. high and 11 in. in diameter. These are no longer being made; ca. 1960.   C—$1200
William Sosa photo; Marguerite Kernaghan Collection.

Miniature Santa Clara pot, made by Little Snow. A—$75

Hopi cylinder-shape jar, 9 in. high and 5½ in. in diameter. Beautiful firing marks and design. Signed, by Sadi Adams, Flower-woman.   G—$360

Ceramic miniature, 2 in. high and 4 in. in diameter. Black on black design. Signed, Blue Corn.   G—$495

Acoma pot, 9 in. in diameter and 8½ in. high. Fine line work, with geometric wide band. Signed, R.S. G—$300

Ceramic bowl, 6 in. high and 8 in. in diameter, good design and black on black. By Maria and Santana.   G—$2000

Miniature Acoma pot, by B. Cerno.   A—$65

Acoma pot, 8½ in. across and 7 in. high, zone fine-line design. Signed, Ruby Shroulate.   G—$325

San Ildefonso pot, made by Florence Naranjo. A—$95

San Ildefonso ceramic bowl, 5 in. high and 8 in. diameter. Piece is black on black, feather design. By Blue Corn.   G—$1800

San Ildefonso pot, made by Linda.   A—$270

Acoma pot, 9 in. across and 7½ in. high. Band of fine-line work around center, geometric design on neck. Signed R. Shroulate.   G—$300

ZIA JAR, 7 in. in height and diameter. (HK: "Zia pottery has long been recognized as among the best pottery of the Southwest. This is due to precision firing, which produces a 'ring' when tapped, like our fine cut glass. GOOD Zia pottery will hold water, the only Pueblo pottery that will. The roadrunner, New Mexico's State Bird, is the typical decoration of the Zia. Their pottery is still being used in the kitchen of the Zia household.") Ca. 1973.   C—$500-$750

Photo courtesy Harvey and Rose King, Muskogee, Oklahoma.

SAN JUAN CARVED POLYCHROME BOWL, 3½ in. high and 5 in. in diameter. Ca. 1972.   C—$400-$500

Photo courtesy Harvey and Rose King, Muskogee, Oklahoma.

The following information is a special section on the pottery and artwork of the various Southwestern Pueblos. Those that currently produce contemporary (post-1950) ceramic wares are represented. The writer — for this New Edition — wishes to thank John W. Barry for special permission to use this material. Examples have been selected at random.

Mr. Barry operates INDIAN ROCK GALLERY (P.O. Box 583, Davis, California 95617-0583) and is especially knowledgeable in the field of contemporary Pueblo ceramics. His primary business is contemporary Pueblo pottery and he authored the important recent book, *American Indian Pottery,* which is listed following this section.

CONTEMPORARY PUEBLO POTTERY

Acoma Pueblo jar-bowl black on cream with deer design, by Lucy M. Lewis, 5¾ in. diameter, 1977.   G—$900

Acoma Pueblo wedding base, polychrome with stylized bird, by Marie Z. Chino, 8½ in. high, ca. 1970.   G—$1200

Acoma Pueblo olla, brown and tan on cream, by Juanita Keene, 10 in. diameter, 1979.   G—$650

Acoma Pueblo jar, polychrome with stylized birds, by Ethel Shields, 9 in. high, ca. 1960.   G—$500

Acoma Pueblo jar, fine-line design, black on white, 3½ in. high, ca. 1950.   G—$125

Acoma Pueblo miniature, hand molded, turtle, polychrome turtle shell on white, ca. 1977.   G—$15

Acoma Pueblo corrugated seed jar, white, by Stella Shutiva, 10 in. dia., 1979.   G—$1200

Acoma Pueblo canteen, polychrome, with Mimbres lizard design, by Emma Lewis, 5 in. in dia., ca. 1975.G—$550

Cochiti Pueblo Storyteller, polychrome, by Dorothy Trujillo, 7 in. high, 1979.   G—$395

Cochiti Pueblo owl, by Seferina Ortiz, 3 in. high, 1979.   G—$75

Cochiti Pueblo Storyteller, polychrome, signed "Felipa", 4 in. high.   G—$250

Hopi bowl, brown-black on buff, by James Huma, 4 in. dia., ca. 1970.   G—$250

Hopi jar, four-color on cream, by Frogwoman (Joy Navasie), 8 in. high, ca. 1978.   G—$1200

Hopi jar-bowl, red and black on tan, by Dextra Nampeyo, 5½ in. dia., 1978.   G—$1200

Hopi jar, black and red on orange-tan, by Verla Dewakuku, 7¾ in. dia., ca. 1970.   G—$495

Hopi jar-bowl, black on tan, 2⅝ in. high, ca. 1977.G—$65

Hopi seed jar, black on cream, 1¾ in. high, ca. 1977.   G—$75

TESQUE MINIATURE WEDDING VASE, 4 in. high and 4½ in. in diameter. Tesque pottery is not fired, but sun-dried and painted with gaudy showcard paints. Many were made as tourist curios. Ca. 1975.   C—$35

Photo courtesy Harvey and Rose King, Muskogee, Oklahoma.

Hopi jar, black on red, 5½ in. dia., ca. 1965. G—$200

Isleta Pueblo bell, polychrome, by Stella Teller, 4 in. dia., ca. 1975.   G—$60

Jemez Pueblo "Kiva" bowl, tan color, by Juanita Fraqua, 6½ in. dia., 1978.   G—$375

Jemez Pueblo owl, polychrome, by Maxine Toya, 3 in. high, 1978.   G—$250

Jemez Pueblo wedding vase, maize design, by Laura Gachupin, 10½ in. high, 1979.   G—$950

Jemez Pueblo miniature jar, black on red, 2 in. high, 1979.   G—$40

Jemez Pueblo bowl, poster paints, 2 in. high, ca. 1970.   G—$35

Jemez Pueblo jar, polychrome, by Bertha Gachupin, 4 in. dia., 1978.   G—$150

153

JEMEZ BOWL, 7½ in. high and 8½ in. diameter. Some of the pottery was sun-baked for the tourist trade. Ca. 1970.　C—$110-$175
Photo courtesy Harvey and Rose King, Muskogee, Oklahoma.

Nambe/Pojoaque Pueblo vase, polychrome, by Virginia Gutierrez, 7½ in. high, 1980.　G—$185

Pecos Revival Pueblo bowl, by Jemez pottery, modern with swastika interior design, 5 in. dia., 1979.　G—$225

Pojoaque Pueblo textured vase, polychrome, by Joe and Thelma Talachy, 1½ in. high, 1979.　G—$75

San Ildefonso Pueblo bowl, plain black polish, by Maria Poveka, 5 in. dia., 1979　G—$975

San Ildefonso Pueblo jar, by Carlos Dunlap, 4½ in. high, 1979.　G—$300

San Ildefonso Pueblo bowl, polychrome, by Blue Corn, 5⅜ in. dia., some spalling, 1974.　G—$950

San Ildefonso Pueblo vase, feather design, by Albert and Josephine Vigil, 5 in. high, 1977.　G—$425

San Juan Pueblo bowl, by Rosita de Herrera, 6 in. dia., 1976.　G—$395

Santa Clara Pueblo bowl, incised bird figure, by Art and Martha Cody (Haungooah), 2 in. high, 1975.　G—$750

Santa Clara Pueblo lidded jar, polished black-ware with bear paw imprint, by Anita Suazok, 7 in. high.G—$950

Santa Clara Pueblo plate, Eagle Dancer design, by Goldenrod, 2⅝ in., dia., 1980.　G—$425

Santa Clara Pueblo jar, black-ware with melon design, by Anita Suazo, 3 in. high, 1979.　G—$300

Santa Clara Pueblo carved vase, black-ware, by Mary Singer, 12½ in. high, 1979.　G—$1200

Santo Domingo Pueblo pitcher, double-lipped, by Santana Melchor, 11 in. dia., ca. 1960.　G—$950

Santo Domingo Pueblo jar, polychrome, with stylized bird, by Robert Tenorio, 9 in. high, 1979.　G—$600

Santo Domingo Pueblo bowl with handle, polychrome, by Robert Tenorio, 4 in. high, 1977.　G—$350

Taos Pueblo Mud-head figurine, by Alma L. Concha, 5½ in. high, ca. 1975.　G—$200

Tesque Pueblo "Rain god" figurine, tourist item, 6 in. high, ca. 1970.　G—$100

Ysleta-Tigua Pueblo wedding vase, polychrome, by Lucy F. Rodela, 12 in. high, 1979.　G—$150

Zia Pueblo olla, polychrome with pattern triple-replicated, by Sofia Medina, 12 in. high, ca. 1969.　G—$775

CHEROKEE JAR, 5¾ in. high and 5½ in. in diameter.　C—$175
Photo courtesy Harvey and Rose King, Muskogee, Oklahoma.

Zia Pueblo olla, polychrome, stylized red bird decorations in black, by Helen Gachupin, 8½ in. dia., 1979.G—$300

Zia Pueblo jar, polychrome, by Eusebia Shije, 5 in. dia., ca. 1969.　G—$250

Zia Pueblo bowl, acrylic painted dancing figure, by J.D. Medina, 10½ in. dia., 1979.　G—$2500

Zuni Pueblo jar, polychrome, by Jennie Laate, 4⅛ in. high, 1979.　G—$275

Zuni Pueblo olla, animal designs, polychrome, 9½ in. high ca. 1960.   G—$950

Pottery basket with twisted handles, 4½ in. by 5 in., and fine collector piece. Ca. 1965, black on black matte. By Lucaria Tofoya, Santa Clara Pueblo. Signed.   G—$125

Carved pottery bowl, 5¼ in. high, the same in diameter. Color, red on tan in carved area, good collector piece. By Helen Tapia, Santa Clara Pueblo. Signed   G—$210

Pottery dish, 5 in. in diameter, black on black and with feather design. By Ramona Tapia, Santa Clara Pueblo.   G—$100

Pottery dish, 1¾ in. high and 6¼ in. in diameter. Piece has design on rim and inside of clouds, raindrops, kiva steps and mountains. By Minnie Vigil, Santa Clara Pueblo. Signed.   G—$280

Miniature storage jar, 2¼ in. high and 2¾ in. in diameter, red, tan, and black with feather design. By Minnie Vigil, Santa Clara Pueblo.   G—$135

Pottery bowl, 4 in. high and 4½ in. in diameter. Piece is red, white and black, with traditional flower design. By Santa Melchor, Santo Domingo Pueblo. Signed.   G—$450

Pottery bowl, 4¼ in. in diameter and 3¼ in. high, black, red and pale red. Piece has flower and bird design. By Robert Tenerio, Santo Domingo Pueblo. Signed.G—$200

Wedding vase, 7 in. high and 4¾ in. in diameter. Piece has traditional Zia bird design. Sofia Medina, Zia Pueblo. Signed.   G—$350

Pottery bowl, 4½ in. in diameter, with bird design. Red, brown on white colors. By Dominguita H. Pino, Zia Pueblo. Signed.   G—$200

Pottery bowl, 5¼ in. in diameter. Outstanding traditional piece, red, brown and white. By Eusebia Shije, Zia Pueblo. Signed.   G—$250

Suggested Reading

Maxwell Museum of Anthropology, *Seven Families in Pueblo Pottery;* University of New Mexico Press, Albuquerque, New Mexico, 1974.

Hyde, Hazel, *Maria Making Pottery;* The Sunstone Press, Santa Fe, New Mexico, 1973.

Tanner, Clara Lee, *Prehistoric Southwestern Craft Arts;* University of Arizona Press, Tucson, Arizona, 1976.

Bunzel, Ruth J., *The Pueblo Potter, A Study of Creative Imagination in Primitive Art;* Dover Publications, New York, NY., 1972 edition.

Arizona Highways, (Special Edition) *Southwestern Pottery Today;* Arizona Highway Department, Phoenix, Arizona, May 1974.

Lambert, Margaret F., *Pueblo Indian Pottery;* Museum of New Mexico Press, Popular Series Pamphlet No. 5, Santa Fe, New Mexico, 1966.

Toulouse, Betty. *Pueblo Pottery of the New Mexico Indians.* Museum of New Mexico Press. 1977.

Martin, Paul S., George I. Quimby and Donald Collier, *Indians Before Columbus.* The University of Chicago Press, Chicago and London, 1947.

Harlow, Francis H. *Modern Pueblo Pottery.* Northland Press. Flagstaff, Arizona, 1977.

WATER-SERPENT (Avanyu) POT, 13 in. high and 11 in. diameter. Santa Clara Pueblo, by Belen Tapia.   C—$3000

Photo courtesy William Scoble. The Ansel Adams Gallery, Yosemite National Park, California.

Large SAN ILDEFONSO POT, 9½ in. high and 7½ in. diameter, black on black feather design. Pot was made and signed by Maria and Popovi Da, and received by present owner as a gift from Popovi Da in 1962.
C—$7000

Small SAN ILDEFONSO POT, (near Santa Fe, New Mexico), 2½ in. by 3½ in. Black on black design, made and signed by Maria and Santana, ca. 1958.
C—$350

Marguerite Kernaghan Collection; William A. Sosa, photo.

Pottery vessel, black designs on white with orange interior, Acoma pueblo. It is 7½ in. high and 7 in. in diameter, and from the 1970s.$500
Courtesy The Curio Shop, Anderson, California

Pottery vessel, orange and black designs on white, 9½ in. high and 10½ in. in diameter. It is from Acoma pueblo and was made in the 1960s.$800
Courtesy The Curio Shop, Anderson, California

Olla, Acoma pueblo, polychrome, with fluted rim. It is 9½ in. high and 11½ in. in diameter, ca. 1920s. $3500
Courtesy Adobe Gallery, Albuquerque, New Mexico

Pottery vessel, orange and black on white, orange interior. It is 7½ in. high and 9 in. in diameter, and from Acoma pueblo. It dates to the 1960s.
$900

Courtesy The Curio Shop, Anderson, California

Seed jar, Acoma pueblo, black-on-white. It is by Dorothy Torivio, 1 x 2½ in. This delightful miniature is ca. 1991. $250
Courtesy Adobe Gallery, Albuquerque, New Mexico

Seed bowl, Acoma, signed R. Concho, Acoma, NM. It is ca. 1979 with the Mimbres gila monster designs. Size is 3 x 5 in.; perfect condition.$600

Marguerite L. Kernaghan collection; photograph by Marguerite L. and Stewart W. Kernaghan, Bellvue, Colorado

Polychrome singer with five children and one dog, Acoma, signed Frances Torivio, Acoma, NM. It is 4 x 7 in. and ca. 1975. $450

Marguerite L. Kernaghan collection; photograph by Marguerite L. and Stewart W. Kernaghan, Bellvue, Colorado

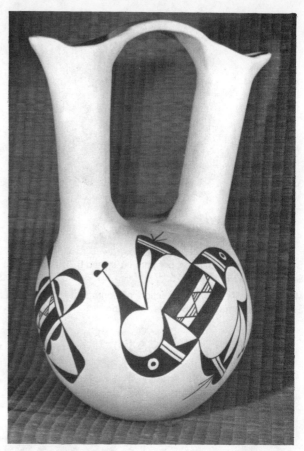

Pottery double-necked vase or pitcher, brown-black and orange designs on white. It is 14 in. high and 8 in. wide and was made in the 1970s. It is from Acoma pueblo. $1200

Courtesy The Curio Shop, Anderson, California

Olla, polychrome, Acoma pueblo, with heartline deer design. It is by Lucy Lewis, 5¼ x 6¼ in., ca. 1968. $2200

Courtesy Adobe Gallery, Albuquerque, New Mexico

Bowl, black-on-black with feather design, 3 x 5 in. This superb pot was purchased in Colorado in 1979 for $250, according to receipts of the previous owner. It was made by Adam and Santana, (Martinez), San Ildefonso pueblo. $550-$800

Hothem collection, Ohio

Storyteller with five children, polychrome, signed D. Trujillo, Cochiti, NM. Size is 5 x 7½ in., ca. 1975. $450

Marguerite L. Kernaghan collection; photograph by Marguerite L. and Stewart W. Kernaghan, Bellvue, Colorado

Mudhead storyteller with 13 children, Hopi, signed Norma Sakenima, Hopi, Hoteville, AZ. It is 6½ x 12 x 17 in. and ca. 1980. $750

Marguerite L. Kernaghan collection; photograph by Marguerite L. and Stewart W. Kernaghan, Bellvue, Colorado

Storyteller figurine, Santa Clara from Cochiti pueblo. It is by Louis and Virginia Naranjo, 6¼ in. high and ca. 1992. $895

Courtesy Adobe Gallery, Albuquerque, New Mexico

Drummer figure, Cochiti, made by Seferina Ortiz. The drum was made by her husband Guadalupe Ortiz, a famous drum maker. This figure received Second Place at the 1983 Santa Fe Indian Market. Made ca. 1980, this 5 x 10½ in. work has several turquoise sets. Museum quality

Marguerite L. Kernaghan collection; photograph by Marguerite L. and Stewart W. Kernaghan, Bellvue, Colorado

Bowl, black-on-black, by Maria Martinez and Popovi Da, ca. 1960. This is a fine example by famous potters, being 3¼ x 7 in.

$3500

Dennis R. Phillips / Fine American Indian Art, Chicago, IL

Maria Poveka (Martinez) polished blackware bowl, San Ildefonso pueblo, ca. 1950. A superb plain bowl, it is 3 x 9½ in. $3000

Dennis R. Phillips / Fine American Indian Art, Chicago, IL

Maria pot, by Maria and Popovi Da, San Ildefonso pueblo, black-on-black plate. It has gun-metal finish, is 2 in. deep and 11¼ in. in diameter, ca. 1960s. A superb piece. $9500

Courtesy Adobe Gallery, Albuquerque, New Mexico

Black-on-black bowl, by Marie Martinez / Santana, and ca. 1950. This beautiful piece is 6 in. in diameter. $1200

Dennis R. Phillips / Fine American Indian Art, Chicago, IL

Maria jar, Maria and Popovi Da, San Ildefonso pueblo, black-on-black. It is 7½ in. high and 9¼ in. in diameter, ca. 1970. A top-grade piece.
Courtesy Adobe Gallery, Albuquerque, New Mexico $7500

Black-on-black bowl made by Margaret Tafoya, ca. 1960. The beautiful ceramic work is in mint condition, and 9 in. in diameter. $3000

Courtesy John Isaac, Albuquerque, New Mexico

Contemporary Pueblo pottery, all left to right:
Acoma black and red on white $50
Jemez bowl, 6 in. diameter $100
Jemez small bowl $40
Acoma pottery owl $125

Pocotopaug Trading Post, South Windsor, CT

159

Recent stoneware effigy lidded container, gray-black designs on speckled tan. By Robert Tenorio, it is 8 in. in diameter. $150

Courtesy John Isaac, Albuquerque, New Mexico

Black-on-black vase, round base and squared top, 13 in. high. By Flora Naranjo, the vase is ca. 1975; condition is mint. $950

Courtesy John Isaac, Albuquerque, New Mexico

Seed jar, Hopi, polychrome, 3½ x 4½ in. It is by Dextra Quotsquiva Nampeyo, and ca. 1992. $1400

Courtesy Adobe Gallery, Albuquerque, New Mexico

Polychrome shaped vessel; it has only the firing hole in the bottom and no other opening. It is carved and decorated with seed beads, turquoise and coral, and is a very beautiful piece. Size is 3½ x 10½ in.

Museum quality

Marguerite L. Kernaghan collection; photograph by Marguerite L. and Stewart W. Kernaghan, Bellvue, Colorado

Pottery vase, Santa Clara pueblo, signed M. Tafoya. It has the bear-paw design and is 9 x 11 in. $795-$895

Larry Lantz, First Mesa, South Bend, Indiana

Polychrome pot, Jemez pueblo, signed R. Sandia, Jemez. This fine bowl is ca. 1984 and 4½ x 10¾ in. $550

Marguerite L. Kernaghan collection; photograph by Marguerite L. and Stewart W. Kernaghan, Bellvue, Colorado

Jar, polychrome, Hopi, by Elva Nampeyo. It is 11 in. high and 16 in. in diameter, ca. 1980s. $5000

Courtesy Adobe Gallery, Albuquerque, New Mexico

Polychrome bowl, Hopi, signed Melda Nampeyo, ca. 1985. This pottery piece is well-painted and a good collectible pot. $450

Marguerite L. Kernaghan collection; photograph by Marguerite L. and Stewart W. Kernaghan, Bellvue, Colorado

Santa Clara pueblo canteen by Margaret Tafoya, redware with bear-paw imprint, ca. 1960. This is a top-grade pottery piece. $3000

Dennis R. Phillips / Fine American Indian Art, Chicago, IL

Carved egg-shaped pot, Hopi, ca. 1988. The maker is C.R. Claw Nampeyo; perfect condition and 4 x 5¾ in. It has the Kokopelli design. $750

Marguerite L. Kernaghan collection; photograph by Marguerite L. and Stewart W. Kernaghan, Bellvue, Colorado

Carved pottery jar, Santa Clara pueblo, black, with Avanyu (water serpent) design, by Teresita Naranjo. It is 4 x 6½ in., ca. 1991. $2500

Courtesy Adobe Gallery, Albuquerque, New Mexico

161

Jar, fluted, contemporary example from Laguna pueblo. It is 13 x 13 in., by Andrew Padilla, ca. 1992. $895

Courtesy Adobe Gallery, Albuquerque, New Mexico

Seed jar, miniature, Santa Clara pueblo buff on red. It is by Delores Curran, 1¾ x 1¾ in., ca. 1980. $695

Courtesy Adobe Gallery, Albuquerque, New Mexico

White House ruins, Canyon de Chelly National Monument, Arizona. The photograph was taken from the valley or canyon floor. Lower buildings extended higher originally, though tree-trunk ladders may have been used to reach the upper level.

Lar Hothem photo

162

CHAPTER X

HISTORIC TRADE—
ERA COLLECTIBLES

The field of trade-era objects has two aspects. One is that the objects were made, for the most part, by Europeans for trade with the Indians. And, though whites did indeed use some of these items (axes, kettles and the like) themselves, the artifacts have been identified with Amerinds ever since.

In short — and for the only such chapter in this book — these are Indian collectibles not actually made by Indians.

Before, during and after the great fur trade of the 1700's and early 1800's, axes and other edged tools were popular. After the utilitarian objects were obtained, apparently the decorative items were sought. Trade silver and glass beads were much in demand, partially because they were well-made and attractive, but also because they were made of materials unknown to the Native Americans.

BASIC TRADE AXE FORMS

Most trade axes were of wrought (hand-forged) iron, made in the American Colonies, Canada and Europe. The iron head had a round or oval hafting "eye", a long, often back-slung blade, and an inlaid steel cutting edge. Inferior specimens sometimes lacked this last feature, being traded to unsuspecting recipients, making the axe both brittle and nearly useless. Trade axes were used throughout the 1700's and most of the 1800's, until factory-made examples became widely available.

Similar axe and tomahawk heads are being made today for the frontier afficionados, and can be mistaken for old and valuable pieces. A certain amount of pitting and scabbing should be on genuine specimens, and the lap-weld around the eye and flowing into the flat blade is usually visible. Value is much less if the steel cutting edge is missing.

Condition is important; a small, intact specimen is more to be desired than a larger piece with much serious rusting and large chips missing from the blade. To paraphrase a knowledgeable Midwestern collector, one should look for a good piece in good condition, at a good price.

A legible and traceable marker's stamp, town or state of origin, or a date will add to specimen value. All three make a very desirable, and rarely obtainable, combination. (Information in this paragraph, by the way, also pertains to the pipe-tomahawks). Many axeheads have been surface-finds, and will show the signs of having been weathered for many years.

TRADE-ERA AXE HEADS

Trade-iron axe head, round hafting eye, 6¾ in. long. Some corrosion, but average; from northern Illinois trading-post site, ca. 1830. G—$200

Metal trade axe, 5½ in. long and 2 in. wide, nice shape. It has a hole in the back portion, and was possibly used as a pipe. G—$185

Small squared **belt axe,** 4¼ in. high, and with oblong haft receptacle or eye. Cutting edge good, condition good. Probably late 1800's and found on an historic Indian site in Iowa. C—$135

Metal **trade axe,** good size, 7¾ in. long and 3½ in. wide, and ca. 1700. G—$195

Trade iron **axe head,** no haft or handle, 8 in. long and blade 5⅜ in. wide at cutting bit. Nicely hand-forged, light age pitting, and a solid piece. D—$210

Badly corroded trade **axe head,** from northern Ohio, 6¼ in. high. Undamaged, but heavy rust has eaten out portions of the lower blade and portions of the eye-strap. C—$75

(The following five listings, of metal axe and pipe-heads only, are courtesy of Bob Coddington, Illinois. Note that these are 1970 figures. In the writer's opinion, values would now be five or six times as high).

Tomahawk head of iron, with surface rust, recovered by means of a metal detector on site of old Ottawa or Huron village along bank of Thames River in Ontario, Canada. This piece was part of a cache of trade tomahawk heads in an old iron pot with a mixture of mud and beads. While rusted, this item must have been in new condition when cached, as it has the appearance of having never been used.

It has the steel insert on leading edge of blade. The location where this piece was recovered was not far from the site of "The Battle of the Thames" (1813) where the American General Harrison defeated the Shawnee Chief, Tecumseh and General Proctor of the British Army, in the War of 1812. It was in this engagement that Tecumseh lost his life. This piece is the "modern" type squaw hatchet.
(1970) C—$95

Iron pipe-tomahawk head. British-type bowl of either American or English manufacture. (1970) C—$225

Belt hatchet head, ca. 1780, found on Chippewa National Forest site, Old Leech Lake Indian Reservation, while digging a well. Steel insert in leading edge of blade. This type of squaw axe was popular as a trade commodity and was widely distributed by the Hudson Bay and X.Y. companies.
(1970) C—$200

Spontoon-type tomahawk head, of the squaw hatchet variety, of Trois Rivieves, or Chautiere, Quebec (Canada) manufacture. Piece is heavily rusted. Obtained from Six Nations (Iroquois) Reserve at Brantford, Ontario, and a very early French type. Ca. 1750. (1970) C—$280

Squaw hatchet head, of early trade variety. Recovered by Peter Cloud, a Chippewa Indian, on Squaw Point of Leech Lake, Minnesota, while plowing garden on site of Chief Flatmouth's old Pillager Chippewa village. From its conditon this piece was evidently discarded as being worn out, and of no further use. Ca. 1780. (1970) C—$75

THREE TRADE-ERA IRON AXES, with middle specimen about 6 in. long. Top and middle pieces have damaged blade edge; bottom piece, marked "ARIT" is heavily worn.

AXES: Left D—$145
Middle D—$145
Right D—$50

Historic TRADE AXE, about 8 in. long. Iron is somewhat battered and corroded around the upper haft portion, the eye. D—$100

Photo—Lar Hothem.

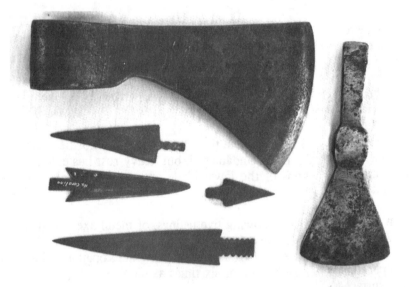

Trade iron and steel artifacts. Top center, trade axe, 6¼ in., from New York $150
Axe with extended poll, CT $85
Trade points, lower left examples, bottom 4½ in.
$10-$45 each

Pocotopaug Trading Post, South Windsor, CT

IRON AXE HEAD, 8¼ in. long and 4⅜ in. wide. Heavy blade is typical of belt axes of this type. The eye is rounded, showing evidence of flattening. The entire head is uniformly pitted and shows a fine brown patina. No doubt it was highly prized as tool and weapon. Touchmark has not yet been identified; piece is ca. late 1700's/early 1800's. C—$300-$425
Photo courtesy Sheridan P. Barnard, Franklin, Massachusetts.

IRON PIPE TOMAHAWK with 27 in. ash stem. A horse design is stamped on both sides of the blade. A human skull bone is tied to the stem-handle. Ca. 1870. Museum quality

Nedra Matteucci's Fenn Galleries, Santa Fe, New Mexico

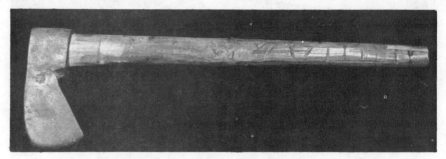

Belt axe, French, trade item from the late 1700s. It has a handforged iron head and original wooden handle; from Vincennes, Indiana. The presence of the handle makes this a rare piece. $695-$795

Larry Lantz, First Mesa, South Bend, Indiana

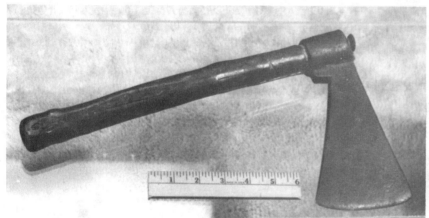

Trade iron axe head with very old handle, both in fine condition. $200-$300

Collection of David G. & Barbara J. Shirley

Trade axes, each with an original wooden handle. These are from Northeastern U.S., and are very scarce items. each, $300-$600

Philip L. Russo collection, Danbury, CT

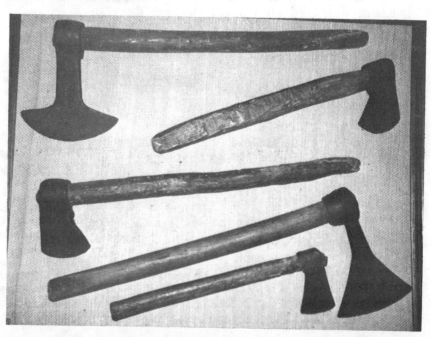

Trade axes, each with an original wooden handle, all from Northeastern U.S. Note the very different handle styles for each; all are probably hardwood.
each $300-$700
Philip L. Russo collection, Danbury, CT

HAFTED TRADE-ERA HEADS (complete)

(Information courtesy Bob Coddington, Illinois)
So-called **squaw hatchet** with very unusual haft, elaborately decorated with carvings of diamonds, stars, etc. Top of handle has thirteen carved five-point stars encased in "Vs" at each end. Ring in end of haft. This piece could possibly have belonged to a frontiersman (White) during the American Revolution, or a friendly Indian ally of the original Thirteen Colonies.   (1970) C—$350

Iron **squaw hatchet,** haft decorated with brass braid tassel, probably from tunic facings, or epaulet of British or French uniform tunic. Ca. 1760-1780.   (1970) C—$375

Squaw hatchet of iron, haft decorated with trade tacks and five large white bead sets, typical trade items. Ca. 1780.
(1970) C—$265

PIPE-TOMAHAWKS

Better specimens of the pipe-axe/tomahawk (best not to use the terms "pipe-hawk" or "hawk" around serious collectors) are considered a high-art form. Ranging from plain to fancy to presentation-grade — these with the original handle — they grace a limited number of collections.

Still, the writer is aware of several instances where good pipe-tomahawks were purchased at farm auctions for nominal sums, at two to ten percent of actual value. In the world of Amerind collectibles, such things happen:

It may not be possible to totally fake a complete pipe-tomahawk (considered by collectors to be pipes, not weapons) head and handle. Beyond the factors of metal-

working and the head, there is the problem of properly shaping and aging the wood handle-stem. More likely, and to beware of, is an oldish handle hafted to a good but mediocre head.

Usually the fit is not close, the wood is not a seasoned hardwood, and the whole is not a unit. The two sections just do not belong together. If the haft is supposed to be original, or at least of comparable age, both head and handle should evidence a believable amount of wear.

And conversely, an ornate handle will usually not accompany a very plain pipe-tomahawk head. Also don't be too impressed with the assertion that the piece belonged to famous Chief So-and-So, for this usually cannot be documented.

IRON PIPE AXE, haft 19½ in. long, blade 7⅝ in. high. It has a heavy forged blade of flaring design, while pipe bowl is crudely made and shows some repair. The maple haft appears to have been a later addition and shows multi-beaded cuffs and a horse hair suspension. The piece is typical of the Midwest-Great Lakes region; it is ca. early to mid 1800s. Note beaded strips on handle.   C—$1500-$2500

Photo courtesy Sheridan P. Barnard, Franklin, Massachusetts.

Pipe-tomahawk, ca. 1780. Head is 7¼ in. high, blade has 1⅞ in. cutting edge. Original or at least very old handle, 15¾ in. long. Fine condition.　　　　C—$1100

Spontoon-type pipe tomahawk head, no haft. Piece is 9½ in. long and 3½ in. wide. Spontoon-types have a spear-like blade instead of a curved blade.　　　G—$400

Rare spontoon-head pipe-tomahawk, no haft. Piece is 10¾ in. long, and seems to be all iron. Reported to have come from historic Indian site in Kansas.　　　C—$445

Trade tomahawk with hammer poll, 10 in. long and 3 in. wide. Found in New York, and ca. mid-18th Century.　　　G—$160

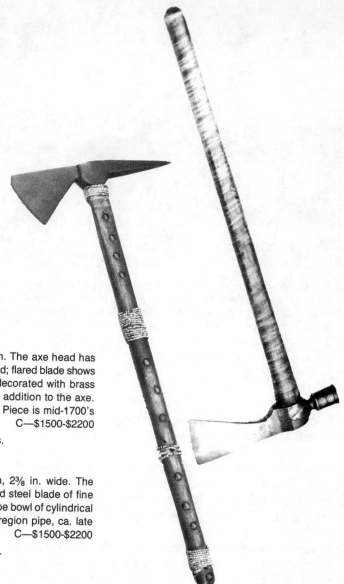

Left:
IRON SPIKE AXE, with haft 18 in. long, and blade 7½ in. high. The axe head has a long, straight spike of square cross-section, eye is wedge-shaped; flared blade shows definite notches on the edge. Haft is ovoid in cross-section, decorated with brass tacks; suspensions of hairpipe and beads appear to be a later addition to the axe. Style attributed to Western Great Lakes East to New England. Piece is mid-1700's to early 1800's.　　　C—$1500-$2200

Photo courtesy Sheridan P. Barnard, Franklin, Massachusetts.

Far Right:
STEEL PIPE AXE, haft 20½ in. long and blade 7¾ in. high, 2⅜ in. wide. The undecorated, drilled and cylindrical wooden handle has a flared steel blade of fine manufacture. The blade is attached with a flanged, engraved pipe bowl of cylindrical shape. Handle is a later addition to the head. This is a Plains region pipe, ca. late 1800's.　　　C—$1500-$2200

Photo courtesy Sheridan P. Barnard, Franklin, Massachusetts.

Brass pipe tomahawk, good and original head, with a later (but still old) undrilled handle. Stem-handle is file-burned and beaded.　　　D—$675

Pipe tomahawk, head only, and in good, sound condition.　　　D—$400

Brass pipe tomahawk, of later Reservation period. Original stem, but value reduced when an uninformed person sanded the wood.　　　D—$425

Pipe-tomahawk, presentation-grade. French or British and probably late 1700's. Piece is from western Pennsylvania, and head is 6½ in. high. Length, with handle, 17 in.; handle may be maple wood. Good condition, and blade has pewter inserts in shape of half moon and stars. C—$1500

Brass pipe-tomahawk with original handle. A genuine piece of fine style and quality.　　　G—$900

Iron tomahawk, cast blade with heart cut-out; handle is lead inlayed with bands and crosses. Ca. 1880-1890.　　　D—$400

Pipe-tomahawk, authentic early wooden handle, brass head with only minor battering damage at pipe poll. Attractive.　　　D—$825

Good **brass pipe-tomahawk,** guaranteed genuine and in excellent condition. Nice patina on brass, file-burned handle, partially beaded.　　　G—$750

Pipe tomahawk with old handle, iron head in good condition, has the steel insert. Plain but solid piece. D—$650

Pipe tomahawk, ca. 1790. Brass pipe tomahawk with original wood haft. Heavily worn. Leading edge formerly held dovetailed steel bit. Floral motif on bowl and blade. Length of haft 19½ in. and head is 5½ in.　　　G—$650

(The following listings in trade-iron section are courtesy Bob Coddington, Illinois. Values are 1970, and in the writer's opinion, are currently less than one-third fair market prices.)

167

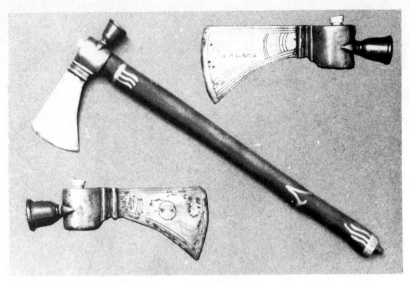

Cheek-cah-kose (Little Crane) presentation grade pipe tomahawk. Little Crane was a Chief of the Pottawattomie, with a village at the headwaters of the Tippecanoe River in northern Indiana. Three views: Left and right sides of head; and full view. Head is of engraved pewter, with a brass screw-out bowl. The blade is hallmarked (DV) over a coronet. Presentation pieces of this quality are rare. Ca. 1767.   C—$5000

Photo courtesy Bob Coddington, Illinois.

Typical early **trade iron pipe-tomahawk,** with curl at base of haft, very plain, ca. 1790.   (1970) C—$375

Massive British Broad-Arrow marked **iron pipe-tomahawk,** with superb inlays of pewter or silver on haft. Type presented to chiefs by British government for loyalty and friendship.   (1970) C—$600

Iron pipe-tomahawk with unusual flaring pipe bowl, slim narrow blade, with pewter-inlayed haft. Ca. 1780-1800.   (1970) C—$600

Pewter pipe-axe elaborately engraved with bleeding heart, leaves and scrimshaw on one side of blade. Large turtle, bow and what appears to be initials "L.H." and profuse engraving. Bowl is deeply and elaborately engraved. Handle is inlayed with pewter bands.   (1970) C—$650

Iron pipe-axe, small short handle with "wi ix" burned in haft. Example of the early French type, strap tomahawk, very old. Ca. 1695-1710, and heavily rusted.(1970) C—$335

Trade-type pipe-tomahawk of wrought iron, severely plain, scroll type mouthpiece, probably of British manufacture. Strap type with steel insert on leading edge of blade. Ca. 1770-1800.   (1970) C—$325

Excellent **French-type pewter pipe-tomahawk** of presentation quality with Trois Rivieves, Quebec (Canada) markings. Type presented to Canadian chiefs for loyalty. Ca. 1750, and with pewter inlays.   (1970) C—$600

Plains Indian artifacts, with pipe bag shown elsewhere. Top, pipe-tomahawk with a large steel head that is pierced with a diamond cut-out. The haft is decorated with brass tacks and file-branding with a suspension consisting of brass wire, brass beads, talons, teeth and an 1847 one-cent coin. Length, 26 in.; ca. 1860s-1870s.

Museum quality

Dave Hrachovy, Cedar Glen, California

Very fine presentation **pewter pipe-axe** with inscription dated 1797. Half-moon and star cut-out, acorn-shape pipe bowl. A wolf is engraved with leaves and star on one side of the blade. Handle has nice pewter inlays. From a Canadian collection.   (1970) C—$650

Brass pick-type spontoon tomahawk, "J.H." over sword. The pick is four-sided. Piece has a beautiful handle inlayed with silver and bone, overall an exquisite work of art. Ca. 1760.   (1970) C—$550

Women's dress, Shoshone, pony-beads with buckskin. This superb piece is from the mid-1880's. **$25,000**. *Courtesy Canfield Gallery, Santa Fe, New Mexico.*

Warshirt, Blackfoot, beaded and fringed. This superb hide artwork is ca. 1875 and in top condition. **$50,000**. *Courtesy Canfield Gallery, Santa Fe, New Mexico.*

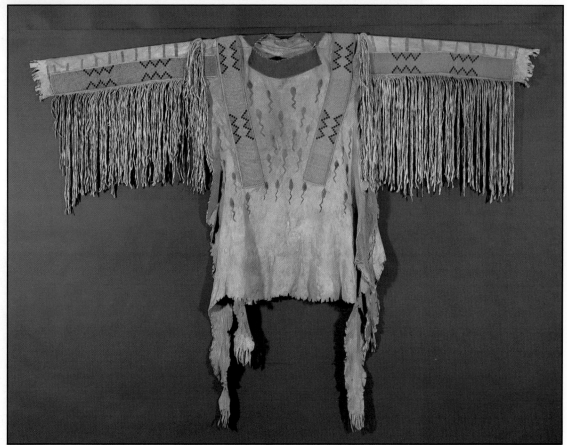

Warshirt, Northern Plains Indian, with colorful and intricate quillwork. This very rare piece is mid-1800's. **$75,000**. *Courtesy Canfield Gallery, Santa Fe, New Mexico.*

Pipe bag, Arapaho, 36" long. Nicely fringed and in bright and pleasing colors, this piece is from the late 1800's. **$6,000**. *Courtesy Canfield Gallery, Santa Fe, New Mexico.*

Women's leggings, Crow, beaded trade-cloth, from the late 1800's. The beading is in superb condition. **$3,000**. *Courtesy Canfield Gallery, Santa Fe, New Mexico.*

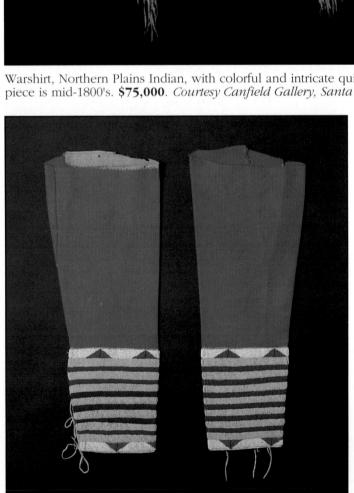

Beaded Decorative Sash, fringed, ½" wide and 45" long. Over a dozen different colored beads were used, and nearly 4,000 are in the sash. Good condition. **$55**. *Private collection.*

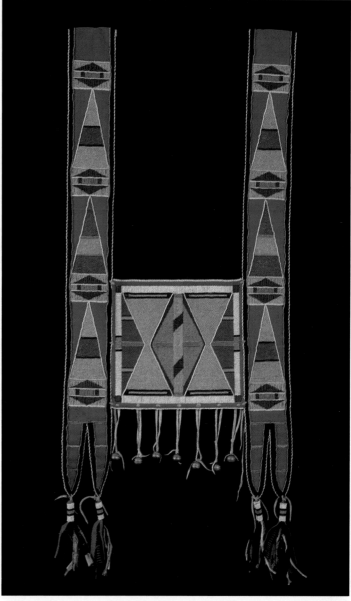

Medicine bundle case, Crow/Nez Perce, from the mid-1800's. It has fine geometric designs and exceptional fringing. **$7,500**. *Courtesy Canfield Gallery, Santa Fe, New Mexico.*

Martingale or horse collar, Crow, many bold colors, from the 1800's. This is a scarce and fine item. **$15,000**. *Courtesy Canfield Gallery, Santa Fe, New Mexico.*

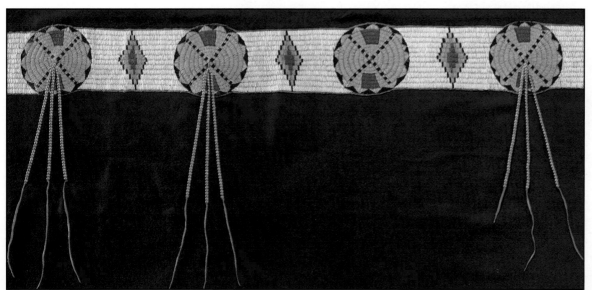

Cheyenne Beaded Blanket Strip, ca. 1870's. *Courtesy Morning Star Gallery, Santa Fe, New Mexico.*

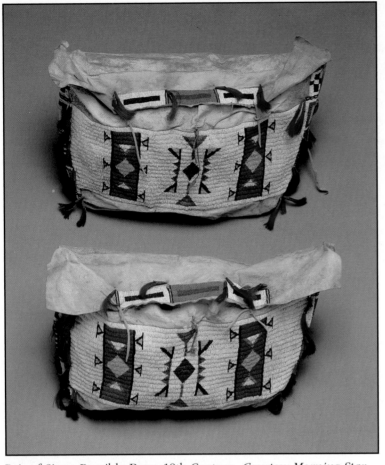

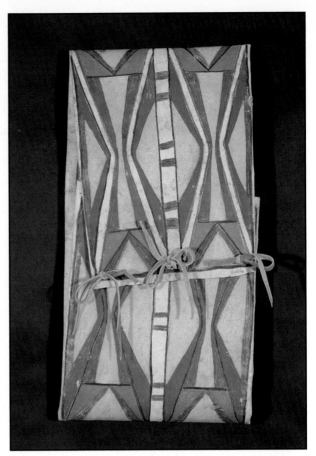

Pair of Sioux Possible Bags, 19th Century. *Courtesy Morning Star Gallery, Santa Fe, New Mexico.*

Parfleche, Plateau, from the late 1800's. Done in half a dozen colors, this fine piece measures 14" x 28". **$5,000.** *Courtesy Canfield Gallery, Santa Fe, New Mexico.*

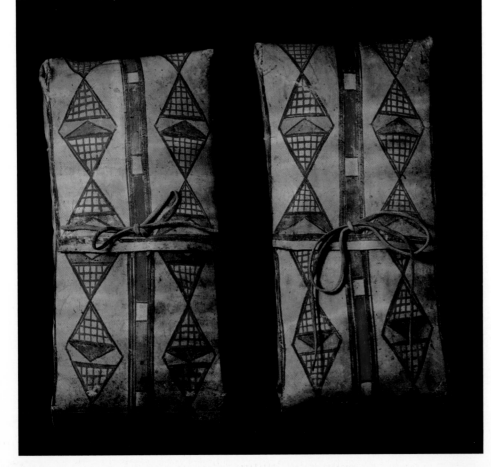

Parfleche, Plateau, each approximately 14" x 28". This pair is superbly matched and from the late 1800's. **$6,000.** *Courtesy Canfield Gallery, Santa Fe, New Mexico.*

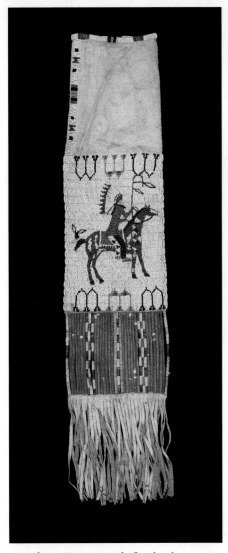

Pipe bag, Sioux, with finely done pictorial motif. This beautiful piece is 29" long and from the late 1800's. **$10,000**. *Courtesy Canfield Gallery, Santa Fe, New Mexico.*

Rifle Cases **(Top to Bottom):** Cheyenne, 1870's; Sioux, 1870's; Crow, 1870's. *Courtesy Morning Star Gallery, Santa Fe, New Mexico.*

Old Navajo dolls, ca 1940. Sizes, 6¾" x 7¼" and 10" tall. These evidence signs that they were played with frequently. They are trimmed with beads, metal belt, etc. **Small, $200 - 300. Large, #350 - 500.** *Courtesy Marguerite and Stewart Kernaghan Collection, Bellvue, Colorado.*

Great Lakes region beaded pin-cushion, 5½", corner to corner, type sold in Niagara Falls area, early 1900's - 1940's. **$50.** *Private Collection.*

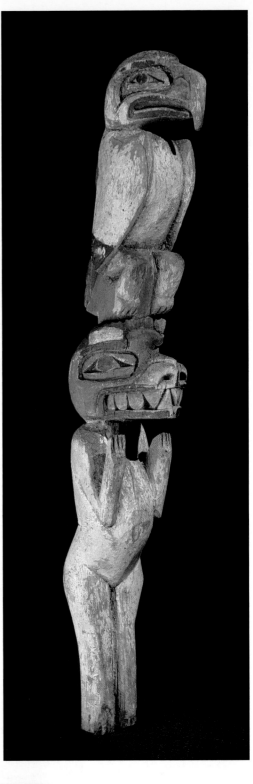

Tlingit Feast Ladle and Basket.
*Courtesy Morning Star Gallery,
Santa Fe, New Mexico.*

Apache Fiddle. *Courtesy
Morning Star Gallery,
Santa Fe, New Mexico.*

Kwakiutl Speaker's Staff.
*Courtesy Morning Star
Gallery, Santa Fe,
New Mexico.*

Solid-cast silver beaver,
trade-era, touchmarked
"TR", 2¾" long. From
Canada, ca. late 1700's.
$400. *Private Collection.*

Group of Apache Baskets.
Courtesy Morning Star Gallery, Santa Fe, New Mexico.

Footed basket, Papago, 4" x 7½" top diameter. **$45.** *Private Collection.*

Papago basket, Southwest, 3¾″ x 6½" top diameter. **$65.** *Private Collection.*

Papago basket, Southwest, 2¼ x 7⅛" top diameter. **$55.** *Private Collection.*

Papago basket, Southwest, worn, 4⅛″ x 10" top diameter. **$50.** *Private Collection.*

Basketry plaque, well-woven and old, South-western U.S., good age, average used condition, 12" in diameter. **$115.** *Private Collection.*

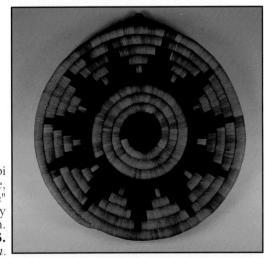

Hopi basketry plaque, Southwest, 9½" in diameter, very fine condition. **$45.** *Private Collection.*

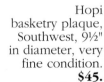

Group of Pueblo Pottery.
*Courtesy Morning Star Gallery,
Santa Fe, New Mexico.*

Ocoma Olla. *Courtesy Morning
Star Gallery, Santa Fe,
New Mexico.*

Zuni Olla. *Courtesy Morning Star Gallery, Santa Fe, New Mexico.*

Ceremonial pottery bowl, Zuni, diameter 12". This beautiful ceramic in top condition is from the late-1800's. **$12,000**. *Courtesy Canfield Gallery, Santa Fe, New Mexico.*

Dominquito S. Tomasita, 5½" x 7½" diameter, ca 1960's - 1970?. **$250.** *Indian Rock Arts, Davis, CA.*

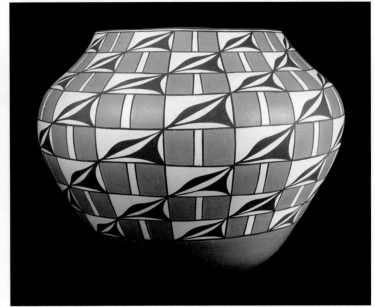

Laguna, 12½", ca 1989. **$700.** *Indian Rock Arts, Davis, CA.*

Acoma, 12" diameter, ca 1950's. **$700.** *Indian Rock Arts, Davis, CA.*

Laguna, 3" x 3¼" diameter, ca 1920, jar. **$150.** *Indian Rock Arts, Davis, CA.*

Acoma, 12" diameter, ca 1940's - 1970?. **$850.** *Indian Rock Arts, Davis, CA.*

Acoma, 10" diameter, ca 1984, Barbara & Joe
Cerno. **$1,500.** *Indian Rock Arts, Davis, CA.*

Zuni, 10½" diameter, ca 1989, by A. Peynetsa. **$450.** *Indian
Rock Arts, Davis, CA.*

Jemez, Lamra Guchipin, ca 1985. **$600.**
Indian Rock Arts, Davis, CA.

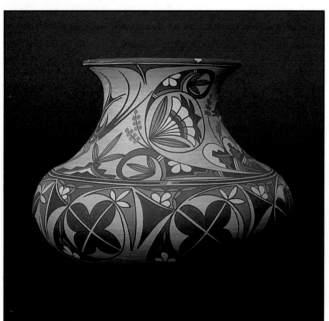

Jemez, Bertha Gachupin, seed jar, 6" diameter, ca 1987.
$295. *Indian Rock Arts, Davis, CA.*

Santa Clara, Lois Gutierrez, ca 1982.
$1,200. *Indian Rock Arts, Davis, CA.*

Tlingit Basket Group.
Courtesy Morning Star Gallery, Santa Fe, New Mexico.

Sandcast silver bracelet, recent, marked "N. TSO". **$110.** *Private Collection.*

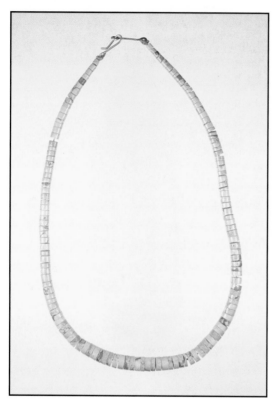

Turquoise necklace, graduated beads, old, 16" strand. **$150.** *Private Collection.*

Pendant, 3⅜", signed "REffie C. / Zuni". **$90.** *Private Collection.*

Navajo and Zuni Bracelets. Silver and Turquoise. *Courtesy Morning Star Gallery, Santa Fe, New Mexico.*

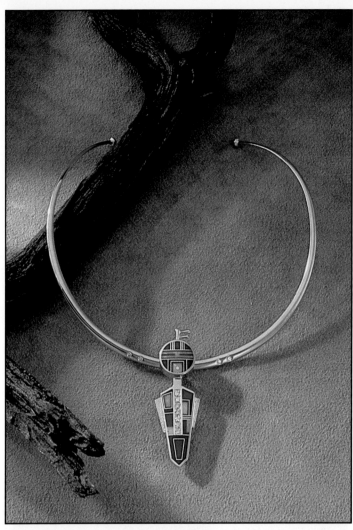

14K gold yei pendant
on red coral heishi and
matching bracelet.
Pieces are inlaid with
red and pink coral, lapis
and Chinese turquoise;
designed by Ray Tracey.
Necklace $7,500.
Bracelet $7,500.
*Courtesy Ray Tracey
Galleries, Santa Fe,
New Mexico.*

14K gold yei
pendant on collar.
Pendant is inlaid
with sugilite, opals
and embellished with
diamonds. Diamonds
also set in collar;
designed by Ray
Tracey. **$10,000**.
*Courtesy Ray Tracey
Galleries, Santa Fe,
New Mexico.*

14K Gold heartline
bear necklace inlaid
with lapis, Chinese
turquoise, red coral
and diamonds;
designed by Ray
Tracey. **$18,000**.
*Courtesy Ray Tracey
Galleries, Santa Fe,
New Mexico.*

14K gold yei pendent on seed
pearls, bracelet and earrings inlaid
with sugilite, opals and diamonds;
designed by Ray Tracey. **Pendant
on pearls $6,000; Bracelet $7,000;
Earrings $1,200**. *Courtesy Ray
Tracey Galleries, Santa Fe, New
Mexico.*

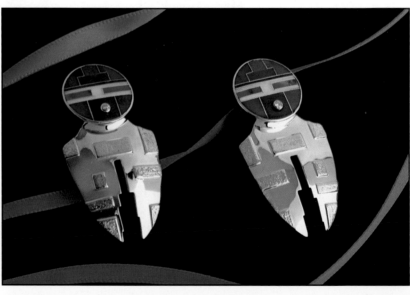

14K gold pendent, bracelet and earrings inlaid with sugilite,
pink coral, opals and diamonds; designed by Ray Tracey.
Pendant $7,000; Bracelet $8,000; Earrings $2,500.
Courtesy Ray Tracey Galleries, Santa Fe, New Mexico.

Sterling Silver yei
earrings inlaid with lapis
and opal; deigned by Ray
Tracey. **$450**.
*Courtesy Ray Tracey
Galleries, Santa Fe,
New Mexico.*

Three Stone Discoidals. **Left:** Perforated-center disc, 3⅛" in diameter, possibly from Ohio. **$300. Center:** Large disc, 4⅜" in diameter, from Illinois. **$650. Right:** Very unusual flint disc, 2¼" in diameter from Tennessee. **$550.** *Photo courtesy Summers Redick, Worthington, Ohio.*

Near-Ceremonial Class Stone Pestle, probably Northwest Coast region, prehistoric, of a highly polished dense black material. Piece is 6¾" long and 3½" across at base (larger) end. **$950.** *Photo courtesy Summers Redick, Worthington, Ohio.*

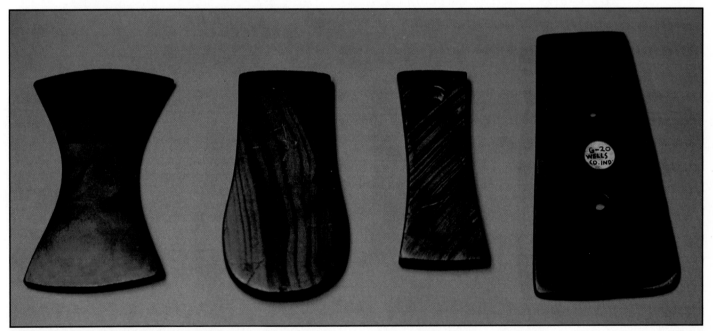

Four Slate Pieces Prehistoric, of different kinds of banded slate. **Left to Right:** A Bi-concave gorget, undrilled, 5" long, **$300**; A keyhole-type pendant 5" long, very symmetrical, **$400**; A bell shaped pendant 4½" long of very good work style, **$325**; A rectangular two-hole gorget from 6" long, withone large and one small end. *Photo courtesy Summers Redick, Worthington, Ohio.*

Polished Flint Spade, 10" long and 4¼" wide. In position photographed, top side is excurvate, bottom side flattish. Piece shows good use-polish. **$450.** *Photo courtesy Summers Redick, Worthington, Ohio.*

Calf Creek blade, about 2¼" long, found by owner in Sequoyah County, Oklahoma. These are Early Archaic, ca. 7000 BC. **$175**. *Courtesy James Bruner Collection, Oklahoma.*

Meserve, Dalton-related and Late Paleo/Early Archaic period, found in Haskell County, Oklahoma by owner. This piece is 3" long. **$200**. *Courtesy James Bruner Collection, Oklahoma.*

Dalton, 3½" long, Late Paleo/Early Archaic, found in Haskell County, Oklahoma by owner. Undamaged Daltons are not common. **$175**. *Courtesy James Bruner Collection, Oklahoma.*

Corner-tang knife, Late Archaic period, found in Muskogee County by owner. These are fairly scarce blades. Length, 3". **$200**. *Courtesy James Bruner Collection, Oklahoma.*

Dovetail Blade, over 4" long of translucent Flintridge material, white and rust-red. Very slight damage to tip, but fine form and superb chipping. **$350.** *Photo courtesy Mike Miller, Lancaster, Ohio.*

Fine Flint Blades of exceptional size and workstyle. **Left to Right:** A 4½" long beveled-edge type, **$300.** A 6" long Turkeytail, **$375.** A side-notched blade 4⅜" long,, **$250.**

Plainview, Late Paleo / Early Archaic, found by the owner in Haskell County, Oklahoma. Length, 3". **$150.** *James Bruner collection, Oklahoma.*

Two flint celts or adzes, one 8¼" long, the other 9¼" long. Of cream-brown flint, both are highly polished. **$300.** *Photo courtesy Summers Redick, Worhtington, Ohio.*

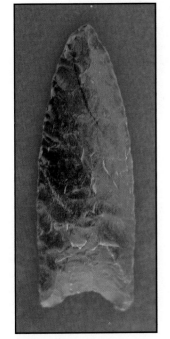

Plainview, 2¾" long, fine point or blade found in Haskell County, Oklahoma, by owner. **$175.** *James Bruner collection, Oklahoma.*

Selection of Guilford-Type Points, averaging 2¾" long. Of various types of chert and flint, all are from the North Carolina region. **$15 each.** *Photo courtesy Summers Redick, Worthington, Ohio.*

Typical point and blade types found by owner in eastern. Oklahoma **$ Unlisted.** *James Bruner collection, Oklahoma.*

Bone awls, all found in Haskell County, Oklahoma, by the owner. **Frame $80.** *James Bruner collection, Oklahoma.*

Fine frame of typical points and blades found in east-central Oklahoma by the owner. **$ Unlisted.** *James Bruner collection, Oklahoma.*

Great Lakes weaponry. Top, ball-headed club, polished hardwood, ca. 1760. $4500
Bottom, pipe-tomahawk, original handle, hand-forged head with steel blade, oak handle with silver inlays and carved horn mouthpiece. Rare piece, ca. 1780. $3000

Private collection; photo by John McLaughlin

Pipe-tomahawk with original handle, ca. 1860-1870, and a style often favored by Plains Indians. It has the handle decorated with beads and tacks. Head, 10½ in. high; handle, 25 in. long. $1500-$2200

Philip L. Russo collection, Danbury, CT

TRADE SILVER ORNAMENTS

Even before a man named Paul Revere invented a rolling press to flatten silver bars to a predetermined thinness, trade silver artifacts were very popular items. In addition to the flat pendants and brooches, crosses and gorgets of myriad forms, there were solid-cast and hollow-cast effigies.

Such forms ranged from turtles to beavers to the esoteric and much-admired "kissing otters", touching noses and swimming, seen from above. Hudson Bay Company contributed countless fine specimens, most of which went into the Northern reaches of the United States, the top fur-producing regions.

Trade silver copies are being made today from a metal called nickel silver, a combination of copper, nickel and zinc. It is cheaper and more durable than pure silver. Such copies are very good and they sell for a fraction of genuine trade silver.

Unfortunately, most are not marked as reproductions. Amerind trade silver may have a blackish tarnish and may be somewhat corroded. It should show some signs of one and a half to two centuries of age.

Double-bar cross, trade silver of typical thin sheet metal, 4½ in. high. The top has a small silver ring for suspension; piece was probably worn as a pendant. Good condition.   C—$300

Trade silver pendant, 1⅞ in. wide, 2¼ in. high, single suspension hole at top. Piece has star cut-outs and floral designs. Touch-marked by maker; probably Canadian. From the Great Lakes area.   C—$200

Double-bar cross, trade silver of typical thin sheet metal, 4½ in. high. The top has a small silver ring for suspension; piece was probably worn as a pendant. Good condition.   C—$225

Trade silver pendant, 1⅞ in. wide, 2¼ in. high, single suspension hole at top. Piece has star cut-outs and floral designs. Touch-marked by maker; probably Canadian. From the Great Lakes area.   C—$220

Trade silver brooch, with both suspension hole and back-pin. Piece is somewhat corroded, said to be an excavated find in Upper Michigan. About 2 in. high. Has a council-fire cut-out design.   C—$115

Trade silver finger ring, plain, but not common. It is ¹³⁄₁₆ in. in exterior diameter. Fair condition.   C—$95

Small **trade silver brooch,** has pin on back for attachment; 2⅛ in. high, with rounded triangular shape. It has masonic-symbol cut-out decorations. Touchmarked by maker.   C—$120

Large circular **trade silver brooch,** scalloped edge, 3⅛ in. in diameter, with touchmark of 1728 Canadian silversmith. Has pin at cut-out center; extremely good workmanship and condition, no corrosion.   C—$445

Trade silver headband, 6 in. in diameter, sheet silver, with heart and diamonds cut-outs. Perfect condition, slight pitting only, touch-marked.   C—$950

Trade silver cross, 3¼ in. long, holed for suspension and with decorative tool impressions. Thick-cast, touchmarked.   C—$240

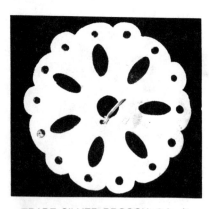

TRADE SILVER BROOCH, 2 in. in diameter, and with elliptical and circular cutouts, scalloped rim, and touchmarked "DE". Sheet silver, and perfect condition.   C—Above $250

Photo courtesy Bob Coddington, Illinois.

From left to right:
TRADE SILVER CROSS PENDANT, 1¼ in. high, drilled for suspension. Piece has incised lines on face.   C—$250

Photo courtesy Bob Coddington, Illinois.

TRADE SILVER CROSS, ⅞ in. in length. Piece has inscribed lines on face, with touchmark "DS" This was purchased with the original string of trade beads, not shown; price was for the entire necklace.   C—$350

Photo courtesy Bob Coddington, Illinois.

Small TRADE SILVER CROSS PENDANT, 1 in. high, and with circular loop for cord.   C—$250

Photo courtesy Bob Coddington, Illinois.

From left to right:

TRADE SILVER MASONIC EMBLEM, 1¼ in. high. Pin that held brooch is visible in center.   C—$150

Photo courtesy Bob Coddington, Illinois.

TRADE SILVER BROOCH, circular form and with cross-shaped cutouts; piece is ¾ in. in diameter, of sheet silver.   C—$125

Photo courtesy Bob Coddington, Illinois.

Hatchet-shaped TRADE SILVER BROOCH, 1¼ in. high.   C—$125

Photo courtesy Bob Coddington, Illinois.

Trade silver buttons, high-domed and backed. Very decorative and well-made.   each C—$25

Trade silver cross, double-bar type, 4¾ in. high. Piece is touch-marked.   C—$350

Trade silver beaver, 5½ in. long and solid-cast silver. Fine condition, professionally tested (not German silver) and weight is one pound. Touchmarked   C—$950

Trade silver beaver pendant, 2¾ in. long, solid-cast, touchmarked. Canadian or U.S. Colonies, Ca. 1780.   C—$375

Trade silver beavers, each 1¾ in. long, hollow-cast. Set of three, each is touchmarked and perfect condition.   C—$600

Trade silver cross, double-bar type, sheet silver, 5½ in. high. Excellent condition and touchmarked.   C—$400

Trade silver armbands, pair, sheet silver and 4¼ in. in diameter. Edges scrolled, otherwise plain. Fair condition.   C—$425

Trade silver crown / hat-band, Iroquois, ⅝ in. high and 24 in. around. This superb piece is Northern United States / Ontario, Canada, and ca. 1790. $750

Pat & Dave Summers, Native American Artifacts, Victor, New York

From left to right:

TRADE SILVER BEAVER PENDANT, solid-cast silver, 1½ in. long. Touchmarked on rounded back.   C—$250

Photo courtesy Bob Coddington, Illinois.

TRADE SILVER BEAVER, 1⅜ in. long, hollow-cast silver. Touchmarked "B" on back.   C—$260

Photo courtesy Bob Coddington, Illinois.

TRADE SILVER BEAVER PENDANT, solid-cast silver, 1¼ in. long.   C—$240

Photo courtesy Bob Coddington, Illinois.

From left to right:

TRADE SILVER BEAVER PENDANT, solid-cast silver, 1¼ in. long. C—Above $250

Photo courtesy Bob Coddington, Illinois.

TRADE SILVER TURTLE PENDANT, ¾ in. long, and solid-cast silver. C—Above $200

Photo courtesy Bob Coddington, Illinois.

TRADE SILVER TURTLE IMAGE, ¾ in. long and hollow-cast silver. Touchmarked on back.   C—Above $200

Photo courtesy Bob Coddington, Illinois.

Trade silver artifacts, early historic period. Top, cross, 4¾ in. high, engraved with beaver gnawing down a tree. $550
Bottom, brooch, 1⅞ in., with touchmark "CA". $225
Both items came from Monroe County, IL, and are very scarce.

Pocotopaug Trading Post, South Windsor, CT

Trade silver ornaments.
Left, nose ring, 1760-1820. $125
Top right, small English / Cayuga cross, ca. 1760. $185
Large "Council Fire" brooch, bottom left, ca. 1760-1820. $250
Bottom right, superb brooch, ca. 1760-1820. $300

Pat & Dave Summers, Native American Aritfacts, Victor, NY

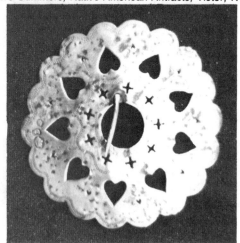

Trade silver brooch, Onondaga, British-made, with heart and cross designs. This exquisite piece is 3 in. across, ca. 1790, and has the maker's touchmarks. $220

Pat & Dave Summers, Native American Aritfacts, Victor, NY

Trade silver brooch, showing silver tongue used for fastening to clothing. The "DS" touchmark may be David Stroughton, who worked in Canada in the early 1800s. Size, about 1½ in. high. $75

Private collection

GLASS TRADE BEADS

The early trade-glass beads were usually medium to large in size. These are different from the countless tiny "seed" beads that were worked into designs on bark or fabric or leather. The "major" trade beads were worn in strands of a dozen to many hundred.

Such glass beads were largely made in Europe, especially the old glass-manufacturing towns of Italy. And the crafts people there made some wonderful products. Solid-colored, faceted, round, oblong, multi-colored — all found their way to North America. There was also heavy traffic into Africa, and many beads sold today as "American Indian" have actually come from Africa.

Glass beads are being reproduced, of course, so it is best to first check the seller's credentials. Good beads may show extensive wear around the hole-ends. Some may be chipped, with such edges not sharp. Single beads to the advanced collector may be worth from a few cents to $25 or $30 and more depending on rarity.

Fine strand of **old trade beads,** found on site near the Red River in Texas. They are at least late 1600's, and may have been traded by the Spanish. Strand is 20 in. long, graduated from small size to larger, and with heavy patina. G—$150

Cranberry red glass beads, 24 in. long strand. G—$75

Strand of **mille fiore trade beads.** A—$45

Blue glass beads, strand, with smaller striped beads interspersed, and length of 26 in. G—$80

Trade beads, strand 34 in. long, white milk glass in tube shape, with six shell spacers. From Oklahoma. G—$80

Strand of **cobalt blue globular beads** 28 in. long. G—$100

Strand of old **glass trade beads,** 20 in. long. Colors are pale red, yellow, blue and black. G—$45

Hudson Bay **white beads,** with Cornaline d'Aleppo red beads, and a length of 26 in. G—$110

Extremely long strand of **white milkglass trade beads,** tube shaped with average bead length of 1 in. (25 mm). Strand is 90 in. in length G—$125

Red "whiteheart" beads, with one section of blue beads, strand 27 in. long. G—$95

Pale red **round trade beads,** strand length 24 in. and ca. late 1800's. G—$100

Tile beads, various colors, strand 28 in. long. G—$95

Strand of pale **blue and white trade beads,** 20 in. in length. Beads have a heavy patina and are from site on the Tennessee River. G—$135

Strand of faceted **Russian blue beads,** 33 in. long.
G—$125

Strand of small **red glass beads,** 22 in. long; from northwest Oklahoma.
G—$90

Strand of **trade beads,** green glass beads with 13 amber glass beads, and 24 in. long.
G—$100

Strand of deep **cobalt-blue beads,** 24 in. long. They are round and all the same size; a beautiful strand. G—$115

Fine old **trade bead necklace,** with two large dentilium shells, large blue chevron beads and red "whiteheart" beads. Strand is 22 in. long.
G—$130

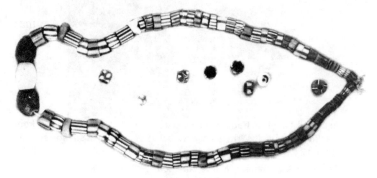

Large strand of Western U.S. TRADE BEADS, large blue beads to either side of central large white bead; said to have been screened from an historic Indian site.
C—$95

Private collection

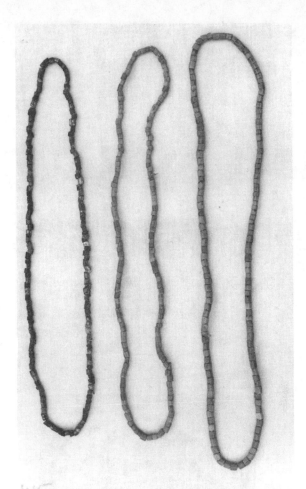

Trade beads, all Columbia River area, ca. 1850.
Left, Russian cobalt blue, faceted, heavy patina, 24 in. long. $150
Center, Russian light blue faceted, highly prized, The Dalles area, 26 in. long. $125
Right, Russian light blue faceted, The Dalles, highly prized, strand 28 in. long. $150

Morris' Art & Artifacts, Anaheim, California; Dawn Gober photograph

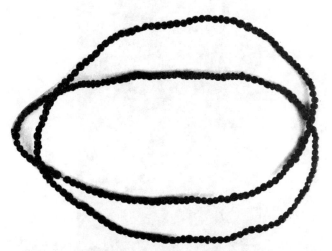

FRENCH TRADE BEADS, with 248 beads in the two strands. Beads average ⅛ in. diameter, and came from a Brant County site in Ontario. Such beads were used before 1650. Beads are red, blue, white and amber.
C—$115-$160

Photo courtesy Robert C. Calvert, London, Ontario, Canada.

Dutch trade beads from New York state, ca. 1640. These are scarce early beads.
$20, each

Lee Hallman collection, Telford, Pennsylvania

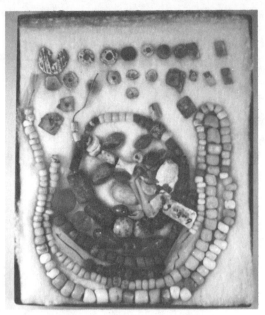

Beads and trade beads, all found in California. Group, $50

Lee Hallman collection, Telford, Pennsylvania

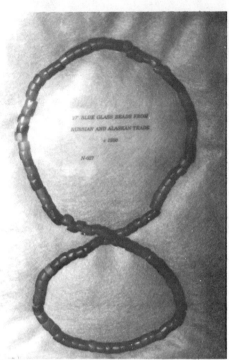

Russian Blue glass trade bead necklace, 27 in. long, ca. 1850. It is from Alaska and ex-coll. Wray. These attractive beads are in several shades of blue. $175

Pat & Dave Summers, Native American Artifacts, Victor, NY

Glass trade bead necklace, early Seneca Iroquois beads plus four shell disc beads, strand 32 in. long. From near West Bloomfield, NY, these are ca. 1610-1630 and ex-coll. Wray. $500

Pat & Dave Summers, Native American Artifacts, Victor, NY

Shell wampum necklace, 60 white shell beads and 63 red glass trade beads plus two shell discs. This rare Seneca adornment is from near Victor, NY, ca. 1675-1687, and ex-coll. Wray. $330

Pat & Dave Summers, Native American Artifacts, Victor, NY

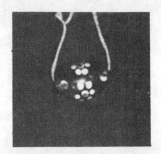

Trade beads, exceptional frame, 130 round drawn-glass Seneca beads in various colors. These were found in the 1930s on a pre-1687 site near Victor, NY. Ex-coll. Wray, of Rush, NY. $350

Pat & Dave Summers, Native American Artifacts, Victor, NY

Ambassador pressed glass polychrome bead, 34mm long, from the 1800s. This is a beautiful and relatively scarce bead.

$25

Wendy Wolfsen collection, Michigan

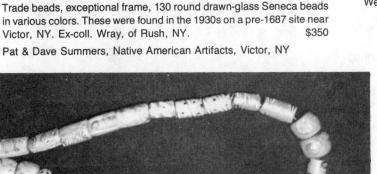

Yellow fancies beads, wound polychrome glass, 32 beads in the necklace. Smallest, 5mm, largest 10mm, longest 15mm. These are from the 1700s. $55

Wendy Wolfsen collection, Michigan

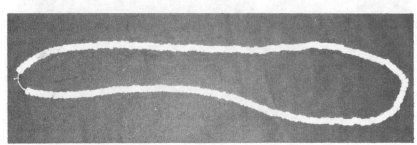

Gooseberry drawn glass beads, translucent with solid white stripes. This string has 26 beads, each 3mm in size. From the late 1700s. $35

Wendy Wolfsen collection, Michigan

Wound glass polychrome beads with red, blue and brown floral designs. Beads are 12mm; the necklace, from the early 1700s, has 51 beads.$50

Wendy Wolfsen collection, Michigan

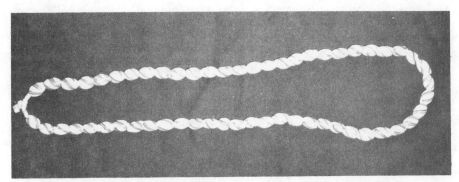

Wound glass polychrome glass beads with blue striped designs. The beads, from the 1700s are 12mm; the necklace has 57 beads. $50

Wendy Wolfsen collection, Michigan

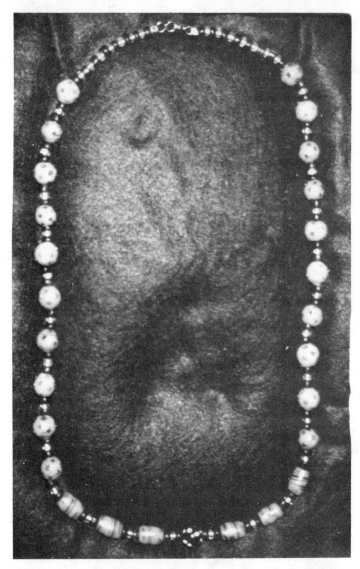

Necklace, Venetian glass beads, large yellow fancies 12mm diameter, small red beads 4mm. These beads are from the AD 1700-1800 period.
$80

Wendy Wolfsen collection, Michigan

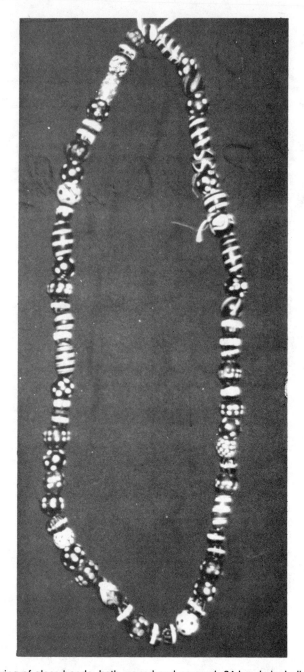

String of glass beads, both wound and pressed, 64 beads including: Fancy polychrome beads, eye beads, horn beads, pink pineapple bead, oval fancies, feather bead, etc. Size range is from 6 to 24mm, and they are from the 1700s. $100

Wendy Wolfsen collection, Michigan

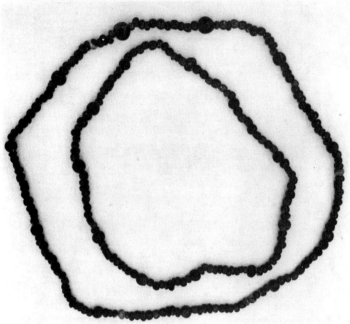

Trade beads, type Tia Commashuck meaning Chief of the Beads, not Indian Chief. These were traded by the Lewis and Clark expedition; these are ca. 1800-1850.

Smaller, 20-inch strand $75
Larger, 28-inch strand $125

Morris' Art & Artifacts, Anaheim, California; Dawn Gober photograph

OTHER TRADE-ERA COLLECTIBLES

Winchester **Indian rifle,** tack-decorated, with history attached via tag. Condition only fair; throat of stock rawhide-wrapped, may be split. Decorated with brass trade tacks.   A—$700

Indian Police rifle, caliber 45/70, and a Remington-Keene repeating rifle. Difficult to obtain today and a problem with fakes, due to premium prices. Guaranteed authentic and collected on a Dakota Reservation.   G—$1500

Old musket, average condition for metal, wood stock not good. Last decorated with brass tacks in Plains Indian style.   D—$650

Indian musket, old Barnett trade piece. Stock has minor repair that does not affect value; overall fair-good condition.   D—$2250

Cut-down trade musket, old and with brass tack decorations. From a Montana collection.   D—$400

Northwest trade gun, by Barnett. The earliest of the Barnett's marked 1805 and in original flintlock. Possibly saw service at the start of the Northwest Company or the American Fur Company, etc. Absolutely genuine; circle fox visible on stock.   G—$3200

Metal arrowpoint, 4½ in. long. A good old piece, and Cree type from South Dakota.   G—$35

Iron arrow point, Tesuque Pueblo, 18th or 19th Century,   D—$40

Brass arrowhead, from historic Indian site in New Jersey. Probably salvaged from White-made brass kettle or utensil. Piece is 1½ in. long and triangular-shaped with small stem.   C—$22

Taos Pueblo arrow, wooden shaft with blood-line and metal point. Sinew wrapped, good condition, 24 in. long.G—$85

Old **converted musket,** with old brass tacks showing Indian use, authentic.   G—$500

Rare **1866 Winchester carbine,** with all wood carved in various Northwest Coast designs.   A—$2700

Barnett trade musket in original percussion, late trade period. Once covered with brass tacks on wooden portions, many now removed.   D—$2400

Spear or lance point, fine hand-forged early piece. Excellent condition.   D—$150

Old brass trade pail, as traded or issued to the Indians. These were once common on reservations, but now are scarce.   D—$165

Gun barrel hide scraper, made from the barrel of a trade musket; hide-wrapped.   D—$155

Strike-a-light, hand-forged, and an excavated find.D—$45

177

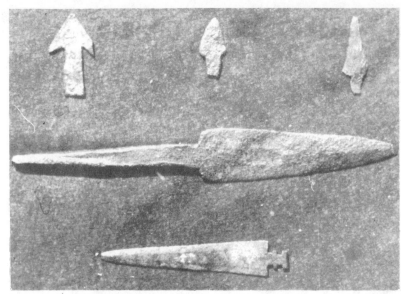

Metal TRADE-ERA PROJECTILE POINTS and large blade. Top three are Indian-made from barrel hoops. The long blade or spear was Indian-made from a file. Bottom point was a Comanchero trade item, with four basal notches. All from the historic period, 100 to 300 years old. Artifacts are from 1 in. to 7½ in. in length.   C—$15-$150

Photo courtesy Wayne Parker, Texas.

Sioux steel-tipped arrow.   G—$25

Three metal lance heads, different sizes and types. Average length is 5½ in. Sold as group of three.   G—$175

Trade-iron lance head, from Iowa. Piece is 9 in. long, and a maximum thickness about ⅜ in. Head is triangular and in good condition. Iron is slightly pitted.   C—$235

Copper trade token, from New Mexican trading post ruins.   D—$10

Russell Green River trade knife, 9½ in. long. Has an antler handle and old leather sheath.   G—$200

Skinning knife in old case, trade-steel and possibly made from an old file. Plains Indians, but sheath plain and deteriorated.   D—$155

Drilled Germanic coin pendant, found in central Ohio. Site has produced gunflints and brass points that were Indian-made from salvaged metal. Reverse of coins read, "12 Einen Reichs Thaler, A. 1771". Hole made with hot needle awl, as there is minute silver-melt on both sides of small hole.   C—$45

Hand-forged strike-a-light, good old excavated item. (Such pieces were the steel in flint and steel kits for fire-making).   G—$65

Historic Midwestern gunflint, ¾ in. long, native-chipped from Ohio flint, probably late 1700's. Found on Muskingum River site that has produced objects from that era. Uncommon.   G—$9

Steel strike-a-light, good condition.   D—$45

Trade iron hoe, 5¾ in. high and 5⅞ in. wide, with circular hafting hole partially forming hoe top. Some corrosion along rounded sides, but cutting edge very good.   C—$95

Iron fish-spear head, from Columbia River region, perhaps used during annual salmon run. Head is 7 in. long and 4½ in. wide. Each tine has a single barb. Apparently a trade piece.   C—$135

George Washington peace medal, the facing bust that has considerable mention in the peace medal book. Silver plated and guaranteed genuine.   G—$1200

Rectangular soapstone bullet mold, picked up near a South Dakota historic Indian site, with two cavities for round bullets. Probably early 1800's. Both halves are present; piece is 3½ in. long, 2⅛ in. wide.   C—$110

Spark-striker, "knuckle-duster" type made from an old steel file, and with ends upturned in an artistic fashion. Piece is 3¾ in. long, fine condition.   C—$75

Suggested Reading

Kuck, Robert, *Tomahawks Illustrated,* Brookside Enterprises, New Knoxville, Ohio 45871

Peterson, Harold, *American Indian Tomahawks,* Museum of the American Indian, Heye Foundation, 1971

Prucha, Francis P., *Indian Peace Medals In American History,* University of Nebraska Press

The Museum of the Fur Trade Quarterly, Rt. 2/Box 18, Chadron, Nebraska 69337; Charles E. Hanson, Jr., Editor/Director.

Peace medal, British, 1757, rare. $1000
Courtesy Dr. Fred Belk, Corrales, New Mexico

TRADE-ERA CLAY PIPES, human face or effigy variety. Such pipe bowls were made in molds, pressed into shape. The clay is kaolin, a white, yellow or gray material found in deposits in New England area and some Southeastern states.   C—$10 each
Private collection.

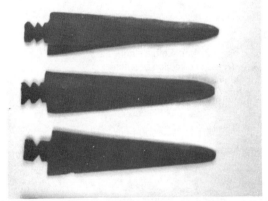

Barrel-strap iron points for arrow-heads, from the 1870s. $25, each
Lee Hallman collection, Telford, Pennsylvania

Trade-era iron, two axeheads, knife or spear with socketed handle and a harpoon head. $150-$300 each
Philip L. Russo collection, Danbury, CT

Iron arrowhead found in the Custer battlefield area. $25
Lee Hallman collection, Telford, Pennsylvania

Trade era spearpoint or knife, metal, from the 1700s.
Lee Hallman collection, Telford, Pennsylvania $100

Historic-era copper trade kettle, from northeastern Mississippi. Early copper and brass kettles are scarce items. $200
Wilfred A. Dick collection, Magnolia, Mississippi

TWO STEEL-BLADE KNIVES, with beaded sheath fitting blade to right. Left, a single-edge blade fashioned from a discarded saw blade; blade riveted to a section of antler forming a handle. Piece is Northern Plains Flathead, Montana. Ca. mid to late 1800's. Right, typical "butcher" type trade knife, with steel blade marked "Bozum", a wooden split handle and riveted brass hardware. The piece is Montana Sioux, and ca. mid to late 1800's.

C—$900 each

Photo courtesy Sheridan P. Barnard, Franklin, Massachusetts.

TRADE-ERA CLAY PIPES, plain variety, and common over Eastern U.S. historic sites.
D—$9 each

Private collection.

TRADE-ERA CLAY PIPES, some plain and some with effigy faces. Condition is average-good for most pipes were mold-made from a high-quality clay called kaolin. Ca. 1800.   C—$9 each

Lar Hothem photo.

180

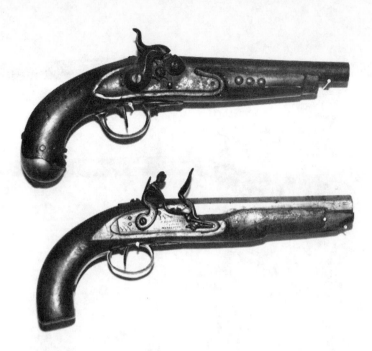

Indian pistols. Top, unmarked German or Austrian percussion that is tacked and shows much use. Ca. 1840s-1850s.
Bottom, "P POWELL & CO. / ST. LOUIS" marked flintlock with 56 caliber brass barrel marked "LONDON". Forearm is painted and gun has been well-used. This very rare pistol was probably a kit gun made of component parts for the early Missouri River trade. Ca. 1840s-1850s.
Both museum quality

Dave Hrachovy, Cedar Glen, California

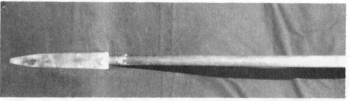

Plains lance, made of wood, brass, tacks and steel. The shaft is made from calvary flagpole and the tip is a Sheffield blade. It is 6 feet long and 19th century. $2000

Private collection, photo by John McLaughlin

GEORGE WASHINGTON PEACE MEDAL, 2½ in. in diameter. Item is made of pewter and dated 1789. This medal was not made by the U.S. government but by a fur trade company. This medal was much-coveted by the Indians.   Museum quality

Nedra Matteucci's Fenn Galleries, Santa Fe, New Mexico

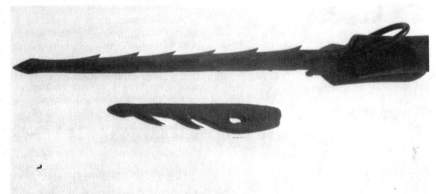

Trade-era artifacts, historic period.
Top, iron harpoon from Alaska, probably Russian.
Bottom, iron harpoon point, Alaska, once fitted to a wooden shaft. These are unusual artifacts.   Museum quality

Private collection

Indian-manufactured barrel-strap metal points.
Lee Hallman collection, Telford, PA
$35-$45

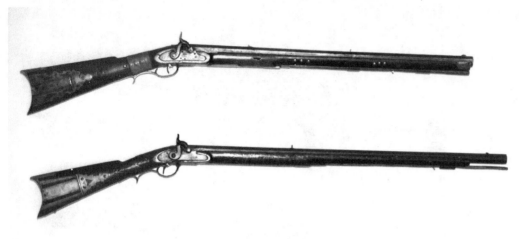

Indian guns, fur trade era. Top, "Warranted" marked on the lock of this 50 caliber full-stock Plains rifle which has a hide repair on the cracked wrist and was tacked by the Indian. Obtained in 1950 from the Goff Creek Lodge on the North Fork of the Shoshone River by Yellowstone Park in Wyoming. It was originally collected by John Goff, a well-known hunter at the turn of the century who was Teddy Roosevelt's guide on his bear and mountain lion hunts. Ca. 1830s-1840s.

Bottom, "J. FORDNEY / LANCASTER PA" marked Indian gun of 50 caliber. It is a full-stock percussion Plains rifle with brass tacks on the cheekrest. It is a contract gun made in 1837 for the American Fur Company. Ca. 1830s-1840s. Both museum quality

Dave Hrachovy, Cedar Glen, California

Indian guns, top, Folsom shown elsewhere. Bottom, "CONESTOGA RIFLE WORKS / LANCASTER, PA" marked Indian gun of 55 caliber. It is a full-stock percussion Plains rifle with a hide repair at the wrist and saddle wear showing Indian use. These guns were made by Leman for the Western trade. Ca. 1860s-1870s. $3000-$4000

Dave Hrachovy, Cedar Glen, California

Indian "carbines". Top, "PARKER FIELD & SON / 1860" marked Indian trade gun of 60 caliber, shortened barrel with cutdown stock into carbine size for horseback. Original flint with tacked stock and brass serpent sideplate. These guns were used by the Hudson Bay Company for the Indian trade, ca. 1860s. Bottom, Springfield percussion rifle marked "1864" and cut down into carbine size with shortened barrel and forearm. The gun is tacked and has much saddle wear; a hide wrap served as a barrel band. This piece was obtained from a North Dakota museum which had acquired it from an Indian family on the Standing Rock reservation. Ca. 1860s.

Both museum quality

Dave Hrachovy, Cedar Glen, California

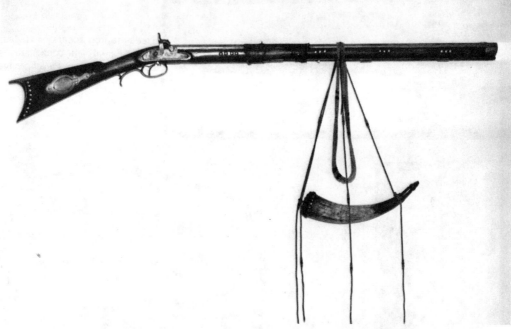

Indian gun and powder horn. Top, "HENRY FOLSOM & CO. / ST. LOUIS MO" marked Indian gun of 56 caliber. It is a full-stock percussion Plains rifle with brass tacks and a buffalo hide wrap denoting Indian usage. This is a very rare St. Louis gun collected in Montana by Arnold Marcus Chernoff. It is ca. 1860s-1870s.   Museum quality
Bottom, Plains Indian powder horn with beaded cord strap. The horn is brass-tacked and painted, and is 13 in. long. Ca. 1860s-1870s.
$2500-$3000

Dave Hrachovy, Cedar Glen, California

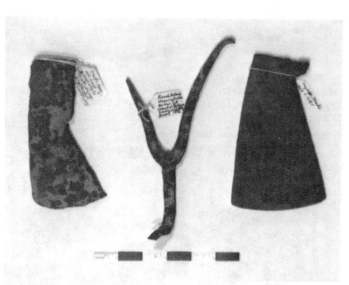

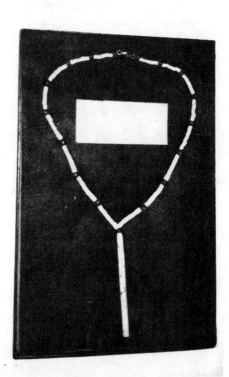

Trade iron items.
Left, axe-head, 6 in. long, New York state, ca. 1860.
$120
Center, 17th century French iron oar steering guide, 4¾ x 8½ in., Irondequoit Bay, NY
$100
Iron axe, Cayuga, three touch-marks, 4 x 6 in. From Cayuga Lake, NY, ca. 1680.
$60

Pat & Dave Summers, Native American Artifacts, Victor, NY

Wampum (white shell) and dark red glass beads from New York state. The small wampum beads are 7mm long, the glass beads are 8mm, the long shell bead 130mm. All are ca. 1660.
$400

Wendy Wolfsen collection, Michigan

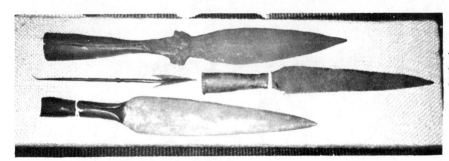

Trade-era iron spears or blades, socketed handles, three different blade configurations. Note also the barbed harpoon head. All are from the Northeastern U.S. $100-$450 each

Philip L. Russo collection, Danbury, CT

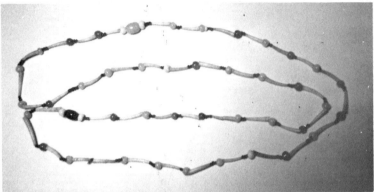

Bead strand, mixed types: Dentallium (shell) 25mm long, large Chinese beads 26mm, small Chinese 9mm, pre-white hearts, glass-wound, 3mm. Various time-periods. $125

Wendy Wolfsen collection, Michigan

Glass and shell beads: Large glass (wound) white, 5mm, small glass white 4mm, small pre-white hearts 4mm, large pre-white hearts 10mm, large shell bead 20mm, small shell beads 4mm. All are from California and ca. 1790-1810. $75

Wendy Wolfsen collection, Michigan.

Necklace, blue Russian faceted glass beads, drawn, graduated string. Beads: Smallest 4mm, largest 10mm, longest 23mm. These are ca. 1720s to 1800s. $150

Wendy Wolfsen collection, Michigan

Necklace, wound glass beads mainly in pale greens, bead diameter 6mm. These early beads, ca. 1700-1740, are from Hamilton County, Tennessee. $50

Wendy Wolfsen collection, Michigan

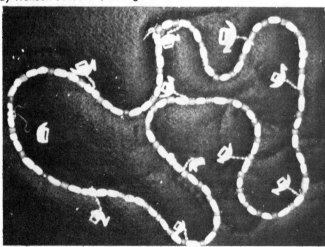

Necklace, drawn and wound glass trade beads with copper animals in sheet-metal cutouts. Large beads 15mm, seed beads 3mm, small beads 8mm, copper animals 31mm. This fine and rare necklace is early AD 1700s. $1000

Wendy Wolfsen collection, Michigan

Gunstock club, polished hardwood with steel knife-like blade, ca. 1840.$900
Private collection, photo by John McLaughlin

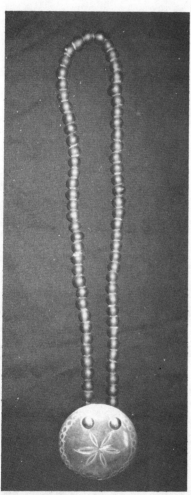

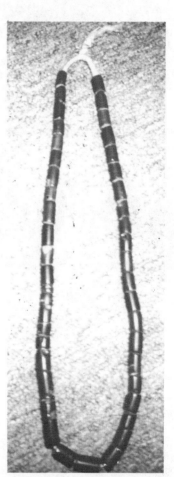

Translucent olive-colored glass beads with silver pendant. Beads, 9mm, pendant, 71mm. This necklace is late 1700s to early 1800s, and in beautiful condition. $300

Wendy Wolfsen collection, Michigan

Necklace, tubular drawn glass beads of the yellow heart design, bead length 14mm. This fine necklace is from the AD 1600s, with beads a rich reddish-amber color. $125

Wendy Wolfsen collection, Michigan

Indian woman and dog, with axe and firewood; picture taken in state of Washington, date unknown.

Photographer unknown; courtesy Photography Collection, Suzzallo Library, University of Washington

Indian woman weaving a basket. Note completed basket, two partially finished, and supply of spare weaving materials. Picture taken in state of Washington, ca. 1897-1899.

Photographer, Anders B. Wilse; courtesy Photography Collection, Suzzallo Library, University of Washington.

INDIAN WOMAN, and child in suspension-type wooden cradle. She is rocking the cradle with cord and foot. Note reed or fibre matting, basket, and woven tapestry in background. Picture taken at Neah Bay, Washington, ca. 1890.

Photographyer, Samuel Gay Morse; courtesy Photography Collection, Suzzallo Library, University of Washington

Indian woman, in state of Washington, seated before rough-plank dwelling, squatting on rough mat. Note small-mesh fishnet in background and fiber strands in hand, perhaps for basketry work. Ca. 1900-1905.

Photographer, Norman Edson; courtesy Photography Collection, Suzzallo Library, University of Washington

CHAPTER XI
BASKETS

(The writer wishes to thank Dick Weatherford, Washington State, for the introduction to this chapter on basketry, and for the books in the Suggested Reading section of it. Used with permission).

Like most of the great Aboriginal Art in existence today, the baskets of the Indians of North America were intended primarily for everyday use. The decorations applied and woven in, the curious shapes, whimsical lids, and hanging feathers and beads may look useless, but they all attest to the Indians' talent for making what is useful also pleasing to the eye and touch.

Baskets in collections today are, for the most part, only the very latest representations of the craft. Baskets, trays, woven mats and clothing, reed and stick toys and jewelry existed in prehistoric times all over the world, as surely as did the more durable arrowheads, spearpoints, pipes, pottery and other ceremonial rock and wood art.

But because textiles are more susceptible to disintegration with age and use, the vase majority of baskets, trays, and mats by which we judge the art as practiced by the Indians of North America have been made in the past 200 years, and most of those since 1880.

Collectors of baskets may judge the commercial value of an item by different standards. For some, age alone determines value. That is, any basket in any condition over, say, 150 years old is automatically rare and expensive. Others are more interested in the aesthetic properties: shape, coloring and patina, the use made of the fiber — how tightly the basket is coiled or woven — how carefully the shape and size of the coils and other elements are matched, and how well the decorative fiber matches the structure fiber.

Still others collect only baskets whose condition is near to new as possible. And, finally, there are those who collect for size only, or for decorative motifs, or for tribal area and type. All of these are reasons for collecting baskets, but not all of them determine commercial or market value per se.

For example, age alone is not a sufficient reason for a basket being valuable, especially if the basket, although quite old, is crudely made or heavily damaged or aesthetically unpleasing. Size also does not determine value, since a very large basket may bring a smaller price than a very small, finely woven and decorated piece.

Value is itself a relative term, and monetary value is only one factor to be considered in making up a collection. Sentimental association is as real to the collector as cash value, but sentimental value more often than not cannot be expressed to others and usually cannot be marketed.

For the serious collector, then, who wished to gather some baskets, regardless of their sentimental value or particular age, for the purposes of show, personal enjoyment, and, possibly, investment, there are some things to consider before buying.

The first rule of collecting anything is that the condition of each piece must be excellent. Baskets — like books, stained glass windows, arrowheads, beaded vests, Navajo rugs and other collectibles — must be in fine condition in order to bring and retain high prices. Baskets with broken edges, repairs, re-dying or painting over, missing parts, holes, etc., are simply not as valuable as perfect pieces, and they never will be, even if they are restored.

Having slightly damaged baskets in a collection does not necessarily diminish the value of the collection, but it doesn't help much either. Of course, some baskets are so rare as to put the lie to the absoluteness of the condition rule, but the exceptions are very few indeed.

Next to condition, the aesthetic qualities of a basket determine value. The qualities are difficult to explain in this short space, and they won't mean much to the collector who has not seen and studied a number of baskets. But aesthetic qualities include the fineness of the weaving and/or coiling, the regularity of the design and the degree to which it enhances the shape of the basket itself — as opposed to detracting from its shape by being too large or small or complex or simple to be comfortably accommodated on the piece.

One of the most pleasing qualities of North American Indian basketry is its sensory appeal. Good baskets feel and look and even smell natural; they are well-shaped and well-made. The genius of them is that they incorporate art in the utilitarian object, that they make what is useful also pleasing to touch and see. That quality is difficult to assess and describe. It is easier and appreciate sensorily, and that is one reason why many examples of baskets are pictured in this book.

Collectors who read this will note that I have not touched on such considerations as materials and tribal groups as determinants of market value. I agree that what a basket is made of and who made it have something to do with the value of it. But these values are more relative to the collector's own tastes, and they are first subject to the standards of condition and aesthetic quality mentioned above.

Certainly, a finely made Tlingit or Washoe basket brings more on the market than a small, plain, rather crude Pomo basket. But beginning collectors will not be able to make successful determinations of value without some more study. I suggest it is not wise to study, or even to buy, simply for tribal area or material.

One must see many types of baskets themselves, as well as pictures of them, in order to get a clear idea of their shapes, designs, and materials. Most larger state, city, and university museums have some baskets to see and compare. And the collector will want to frequent the auctions, antique shows and shops, Indian gallery showrooms and the like before making any selections.

I strongly suggest that the collector also read about baskets, how they are and were made, materials and methods of construction, designs, shapes, age, etc. The collector who relies purely upon rumor and the seller's word is very likely to be unhappy about some purchases.

It is always best to know, to be able to judge independently and with some authority the baskets one is likely to pay a good deal of money for. See Suggested Reading for a few selected major reference works for the collector. These will, in addition to this book, provide necessary information.

(D.W.)

The basket listings in this section have been set up in alphabetical form rather than the usual regional/chronological sequence. This has been done so that baskets by known Indian groups can be easily located.

While not all basket-making Indian groups are represented, these are some of the baskets likely to be encountered. Historic and recent baskets are included, plus many contemporary examples. A wide selection has purposefully been included here.

Apache shallow-bowl basket, with designs in stars and crosses. It is 14 in. in diameter, and condition is fair. D—$1125

Apache shallow-bowl basket, 18 in. in diameter, and in excellent condition. Designs of dogs, men and horses; two major breaks on rim which do not detract from value. C—$1350

Apache burden basket, 11½ in. high, typical construction with hard leather or rawhide bottom, plain, average condition and showing much wear. ca. 1920's. D—$600

Apache burden basket, contemporary, and 6½ in. across and 5 in. high. Geometric pattern, with tin cones hanging from buckskin straps. G—$125

Apache burden basket, contemporary, 8 in. across and 6 in. high. Geometric pattern; tin cones on buckskin straps. G—$225

Apache burden basket, contemporary, 12 in. across and 10½ in. high. With negative pattern, excellent condition, and tin cone danglers. G—$495

Apache grain barrel basket, 11 in. high and 10 in. in diameter. Geometric designs with eight human figures. Rim of basket shows some wear and repair, but generally in nice condition. Ca. before 1900. G—$600

Apache grain or seed container basket, 17 in. high. Has geometric designs in black, on tan background. Extra-fine overall condition. Ca. early 1900's C—$1500

Apache plaque basket, geometric design. Piece is 16 in. in diameter and 5 in. high. Nice stitch, good condition. G—$1000

Apache plaque basket, 22 in. in diameter and 6 in. high. Design: Twenty dog and men figures. One bad spot 3 in. from rim, and condition fair. G—$1800

Apache miniature basket, 5½ in. across and 1 in. high. Good condition, with radiating-star design. G—$325

Apache storage basket, with black chain-link and human figure decorative motif on side. Basket is 14½ in. in diameter. C—$700

Apache basketry tray, 10½ in. in diameter, and very old. Ca. late-1800's or 90's. C—$295

Apache wedding basket, 13 in. in diameter, and very old. D—$75

Apache water-bottle basket, (or "tus"), with coating of pitch to make it waterproof. Collected about 1935 and 17 in. in height. Good condition and not common. C—$1000

Apache water-bottle basket, with one of two horsehair handles remaining. Pitch missing in small sections. Piece is 13½ in. in height, and not well preserved. Old. C—$250

Apache water-bottle basket, with pine-patch covering. Contemporary. Has leather carrying straps; it is 5 in. across and 9 in. high. G—$135

Mescalero Apache lidded basket, 7 in. wide and 5 in. high. Good condition, and ca. 1900.   G—$360

Western Apache basket, 12 in. across and 2 in. high, with a moderate stitch. Whirlwind design in bottom and geometric design on exterior.   G—$315

Athabascan birchbark basket, and Washo basket, both one auction lot. Athabascan is 2¾ in. by 4 in., Washo is 1½ in. by 3½ in.   A—$130

Bannock/Shoshone berry basket, 8 in. by 8½ in. A—$110

Bannock basket, 8½ in. by 13 in.   A—$95

Bannock/Paiute gathering basket.   A—$70

Bella-Bella basket-covered jar.   A—$50

Bella-Coola cedar-bark basket, state of Washington, and 12¼ in. high. Decorated with entertwined cedar root strips, and of some age.   C—$110

Chehalis basket, 4½ in. by 9½ in.   A—$45

Chehalis basket, 4¼ in. by 6¼ in. Has woven designs of geometrics and crosses; in mint condition.   A—$250

Chemehuevi basket, 11½ in. across and 2 in. high, with a design of two geometric concentric bands. Piece has a moderate stitch; good condition.   G—$600

BURDEN BASKET: White River Apache, Arizona. Used as a utility basket by Indian women, carried on the back and supported by a strap from the person's forehead. Excellent condition; 18 in. wide and 10 in. high; ca. 1940.   Museum quality

Photo courtesy W.J. Crawford, The Americana Galleries, Phoenix, Arizona.

Papago basket, chocolate brown on tan ground. This piece is in very good condition, with a top diameter of 7¼ in. and height of 4¾ in. $55-$65

Private collection

CONTEMPORARY BASKETS, Left, Passamaquoddy lidded basket, 6¾ in. in diameter. Wood splint and sweetgrass.   C—$35

Right: PENOBSCOT LIDDED BASKET, 3½ in. in diameter.   D—$25

Photo courtesy American Indian World, Ltd., Denver, Colorado.

Chippewa birchbark basket, 4½ in. high and 9⅝ in. in diameter. Designs done in sweetgrass and quill. A—$70

Coushatta swampcane basket, collected in Louisiana in the 1950's. Size, 4⅜ in. in diameter.   C—$75

Hopi wedding basket, 10½ in. diameter, from the 1970s. It has black and red designs against yellow-tan. $150

Private collection

Coushatta basket tray, 6 in. diameter, and with two unusual handles. Made of coiled pine needles, small floral designs, slight damage to bottom. D—$50

Cowlitz lidded basket, 3 in. by 4¼ in. A—$145

Cowlitz basket, 10¾ in. by 14¼ in. A—$430

Fraser River basketry trays, two sold as one lot. A—$75

Fraser River basket, 7¼ in. by 9 in. by 7 in. A—$145

Hat creek basket-covered wine bottle, 10 in. high. It has lightning design in redbud weave. Good condition. G—$195

Hat Creek basket, 3½ in. by 6¼ in. A—$325

Havasupai basketry bowl, 7 in. across and 4 in. high. It has red analine dye swastika pattern, good condition. G—$595

Havasupai basket, coiled fiber, 11¾ in. diameter. Designs a series of small, connected triangles. C—$300

Havasupai basketry plaque, or plate, 12 in. in diameter. It has orange and black geometric "crepe paper" design. G—$425

Hoopa basketry hat, 3¾ in. high by 7¼ in. across, of close-twined weave. Fine condition. (Hupa) C—$350

Hopi coiled-bowl basket, 9¼ in. in diameter, faded floral designs. Basket overall in good condition. C—$200

Hopi coiled-bowl basket, 7 in. diameter, with geometric designs on sides. Average good condition, bottom somewhat deteriorated. D—$150

Hopi coiled-bowl basket, Second Mesa, 4 in. high and 4 in. in diameter. A—$45

Hopi wicker-bowl basket, 9 in. in diameter, excellent condition. Geometric designs on side. C—$220

Hopi corn-sifter basket, recent, with sturdy hoop around top. Wicker form is 15 in. in diameter, decorated with spiral designs radiating out from center. C—$160

Hopi miniature plaque, Second Mesa, contemporary. Has Polychrome star design, and is 4 in. across. G—$85

Hopi miniature bowl, 1½ in. across and 1½ in. high. Second Mesa contemporary, with geometric design. G—$90

Hopi miniature coil plaque, 3¼ in. in diameter. D—$30

Hopi miniature coil plaque, 2½ in. in diameter. D—$25

Hopi coiled plaque, old. Second Mesa, ca. 1930. Piece is 14½ in. across. D—$275

Hopi coiled tray, 14½ in. in diameter, Third Mesa. A—$110

Hopi basketry tray, 11 in. in diameter, Second Mesa. Has mythical figure as central design. C—$230

Hopi wickerwork tray, 17¼ in. in diameter; very regular designs in black. C—$310

Hupa cooking basket, 3⅛ in. by 5¼ in. A—$90

Hupa covered basket, 8 in. in diameter, with geometric designs in tan and cream colors. Some damage to one portion of bottom, not major. D—$145

Hupa basketry hat, 6⅝ in. in diameter. A—$155

Hupa basketry hat, 7 in. in diameter and 4 in. high. Made using half-stitch; piece has two geometric and concentric bands. G—$250

Hupa basketry mush bowl, 3½ in. high and 6 in. in diameter. Tan and light brown colors, nice design, perfect condition. Ca. 1900. G—$230

Karok basketry cradleboard, sit-down style. Piece is finely woven basketry, with sun shade in yellow quillwork. G—$400

Karok basketry mush bowl, reverse pattern. It is 5½ in. across and 3½ in. high. Good condition. G—$150

Karok oval-shape basket with inverted bottom. Half-twist polychrome design, measuring 10 in. long by 7 in. wide and 5 in. high. Good condition. G—$235

Klamath basket, 3½ in. by 6½ in. A—$40

Klamath trinket basket, 3 in. high, 4 in. in diameter. Simple design in brown colors, excellent condition. G—$125

Klamath gambling tray, 14 in. in diameter. Good condition, and ca. 1900. G—$495

Klikitat basket, 4 in. by 4½ in. A—$155

Klikitat gathering basket, with undulating and raised rim top. Basket is 11¼ in. high, medium-good condition. C—$230

Klikitat miniature basket. A—$50

Klikitat baskets, both miniature, sold as one lot. A—$110

Klikitat basketry trunk with lid, 14½ in. across, 15 in. high and 26½ in. long. It has polychrome geometric design, in nice condition. G—$950

Kuskokwim River basket, with yarn trim. Piece is 5½ in. by 6½ in. A—$55

Lilooet basket, 12½ in. by 16 in. and 14 in. high.A—$245

Lilooet basket, 8¼ in. by 10¼ in. and 12½ in. high.
A—$60

Maidu basketry bowl, 6 in. across and 3 in. high. In traditional Maidu pattern, average weave, good condition. Piece is ca. 1910. G—$330

Maidu miniature basket, 1¼ in. high, 1¾ in. in diameter. Very tight and regular weave, perfect condition.C—$195

Maidu basketry tray, 8½ in. in diameter. A—$100

Makah lidded basket, 4 in. across and 2 in. high. Geometric banded design in polychrome. G—$100

Makah basket, 7 in. in diameter, with zigzag designs on side. Slight fraying at one portion of rim. Tight weave.
D—$110

Makah basketry covered bottle, 12 in. high, good condition. G—$240

Makah basketry covered bottle, 12½ in. high, weaving with figure design. A—$145

Makah basketry covered bottle, one-half pint whiskey, and 6½ in. high. G—$165

Makah/Nootka basketry-covered bottle, 12¼ in. high.
A—$165

Makah jewel basket. A—$40

Makah/Nootka miniature baskets, two, sold as one lot.
A—$35

Makah basketed net float and small **basketry covered bottle,** sold as one lot. A—$110

Makah twisted-twine basket, 5 in. in diameter. C—$70

Mandan basket, wood splint, rare item and quite old. Piece is circular and 8 in. high. C—$400

Mission basket, very large, 18½ in. in diameter and 10 in. high. Minor rim damage, and ca. 1900. G—$850

Mission basket, from California, 20 in. across and 12 in. high. Has a six-point negative star in bottom. G—$245

Mission basket, bowl-shape, 6 in. in diameter and 2 in. high. Geometric design with star pattern on bottom. Average weave and condition. G—$200

Mission plaque, made of varigated juncus grass, average weave. It is 15 in. across by 2½ in. high. G—$310

Mission basketry tray, made by the California Mission Indians, and 12 in. across and 2½ in. high. Mint condition.
G—$700

Miwok basket, 12 in. high and 7 in. in diameter. Good condition, and ca. 1900. G—$575

Modoc hat, 6 in. by 11½ in. A—$195

Modoc hat, 7 in. in diameter. A—$135

Modoc basketry cap, diamond decorations, 6¼ in. in average diameter, and about 5 in. high. C—$250

Mohawk sweetgrass gift baskets, two, sold as one lot.
A—$45

Navajo wedding basket, 15 in. in diameter, tight weave, ca. 1860. D—$185

Navajo wedding basket, 13¼ in. in diameter. A—$245

Nootka basket, tan with black and brown designs depicting early seafaring scenes. Lidded, piece is 9 in. high, 15 in. in diameter. Perfect condition. C—$1600

Nootka basket, old, 2⅝ in. by 4⅛ in. A—$120

Nootka whaler's hat, 10½ in. by 10½ in. A—$495

Ojibwa wicker basket made of peeled willow, and collected in Minnesota. About 8 in. high. Not recent, but not of great age. C—$85

Splint collecting basket, Indian group unknown, New England area. Piece is 8 in. by 9 in. by 5 in. high. Wood well-woven, good condition. C—$135

Maine Indian birch-bark container, possibly a blueberry collecting basket. Piece is 9¼ in. wide and 14 in. long, with average wear. Old, and not common. C—$125

Penobscot white ash basket, ribbed and handled, 13 in. long and 7 in. wide. Recent. C—$95

Passamaquoddy "curlicue" basket, made of ultra-thin strips of brown ash. Round and 5 in. high. This type of "whatnot" basket often had a cover; if so, it is now missing.
C—$28

Passamaquoddy basket, Maine, splint-woven of brown ash. It stands 18¾ in. high, carved wood handles on opposite sides of top. Style is the familiar commercial fish-scale basket. Tightly woven and contemporary. C—$130

Paiute coiled-bowl basket, with beaded exterior. Piece is 4¾ in. in diameter. A few beads missing, but an exceptional work. C—$345

Paiute lidded basket, 5 in. high and 6½ in. across. Has polychrome geometric design. G—$310

Paiute basketry covered bottle, 10 in. high. Good condition, and ca. 1900. G—$190

Southern Paiute basketry hat. A—$130

Paiute hat, 8½ in. across and 5½ in. high. It has two geometric concentric bands. G—$290

Paiute seed jar, with in-and-out weave for design, a single concentric band. Piece is 8 in. high and 5½ in. in diameter. G—$140

Paiute basketry water jar, with pine pitch on outside. Has horse hair handles, and is 7½ in. high and 5½ in. across. Nice condition. G—$165

Panamint basket, 10½ in. across and 5 in. high. Design is two geometric concentric bands with rim ticking; there are 15 stitches to the inch, five coils to the inch. G—$900

Panamint basket, 10½ in. across, 4 in. high. Has reversing diamond pattern, with unusual start on bottom. Fair condition, with some rim damage. G—$595

Papago basket, 13 in. in diameter, 4½ in. high. Faint geometric designs on sides. C—$190

Papago lidded basket, 5 in. in diameter and 3½ in. high. Of bleached yucca and devil's claw, it has large butterflies on side and coyote tracks on lid. G—$190

Papago miniature basket, 1 in. high, 1½ in. in diameter, brown with white simple designs. C—$105

Papago oval basketry tray, 12 in. wide, 15 in. long and 3½ in. deep. Loose weave typical of Papago, and with brown design. Good condition. G—$150

Papago plaque, old, and 15 in. in diameter, 3½ in. high. Design is concentric squares from center. G—$285

Papago waste paper basket, contemporary, 10 in. diameter and 12 in. high. Design of dogs and men. G—$220

Pima basketry bowl, 16 in. in diameter and 5 in. high. Has salt and pepper design, and in fair condition. G—$525

Pima coiled-bowl basket, 6½ in. high, with geometric designs. In poor condition, has extensive damage. C—$55

Pima shallow-bowl basket, 17½ in. in diameter, with star design. Extra-good condition. D—$390

Modoc twined tray, the design woven with dyed porcupine quill. It is 18 in. in diameter and ca. 1880. $1200-$1500
Terry Schafer collection, Marietta, Ohio

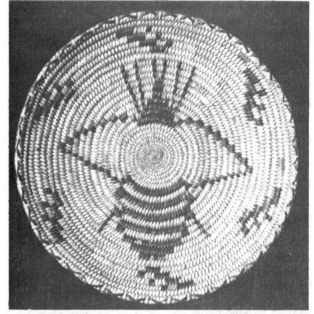

Papago coiled figural tray, woven with yucca and sumac root (red), very finely woven. It is 6½ in. in diameter and ca. 1930. $600-$800
Terry Schafer collection, Marietta, Ohio

Basketry jar, coiled, decorated with humans and saguaro cactus forms. This exquisite Pima work is 9½ x 8½ in. high. It is ca. 1920. $690
Pat & Dave Summers, Native American Artifacts, Victor, NY

194

Pima fretwork basket, 16 in. in diameter. In nice condition and old, early 1900's or before.   G—$380

Pima grain barrel, 12½ in. high and 11 in. in diameter. Has large open mouth and geometric design. Good condition.   G—$760

Pima lidded horsehair miniature basket, 1 in. in diameter and 1 in. high. Has a geometric design element.G—$70

Pima coiled plaque, 11 in. in diameter, with "maze" design on bottom. Average good condition.   C—$320

Pima miniature basketry plaque, 2⅜ in. in diameter. Very uniformly woven, and geometric design. Good condition.   C—$75

Pitt River basket, 8 in. across and 7½ in. high. Has geometric design interspaced with snow flakes.G—$395

Pitt River basket, 10 in. in diameter. In good condition, and ca. 1900.   G—$210

Pomo basket, 6 in. in diameter.   D—$155

Pomo basket, beaded, coil manufacture, and 9¼ in. in diameter. Two sizes of shell beads used to set off basic stepped-pyramid design.   C—$345

Pomo beaded boat-shaped basket, 4½ in. long, 3½ in. wide and 1½ in. high. Has green beaded background with red beads for geometric pattern. Fully beaded.   G—$660

Pomo feathered basket, from California, about 12 in. in diameter. Decorated with blue, green and white feathers. Condition good.   A—$295

Salish (Coastal) miniature baskets, two, sold as one lot.   A—$95

Salish (Coastal) basket, 5 in. by 7½ in.   A—$30

Satsop basket, twined, 7½ in. by 12 in.   A—$220

Seminole coiled basket, with coils of sweetgrass. Basket is 4 in. high, 6½ in. in diameter, and plain. Has flat cover, undecorated. Collected in the 1950's.   C—$85

Shasta miniature basket.   A—$70

Shasta basket, 3¼ in. by 5½ in.   A—$135

Shasta basket, 3 in. high and 6½ in. in diameter. Geometric designs, exceptionally good condition.   C—$150

Shoshone burden basket, 10 in. by 12½ in.   A—$135

Shoshone basket, 5 in. high in. in diameter, plain utility container, good condition.   C—$90

Siletz burden basket, 9 in. by 18 in.   A—$75

Skokomish berry basket, 6¾ in. by 8½ in.   A—$190

Skokomish basket, 5 in. by 7 in.   A—$65

Thompson River lidded basket, British Columbia, Canada, 4 in. by 4 in.   A—$155

Thompson River basketry trunk, with lid. Piece has imbricated diamond and cross designs. Dimensions are 15 in. across and 27 in. long and 15 in. high. Fair condition.   G—$1300

Tlingit basket, 6 in. in diameter and 4½ in. high. Geometric design, medium stitch, excellent condition.   G—$700

Tlingit basket with butterfly designs, 4 in. by 6¾ in.   A—$145

Tlingit basketry tray, 5¾ in. in diameter and 1¾ in. high.   A—$75

Tlingit basket, 5 in. in diameter and 6 in. high. Good condition and ca. 1880.   G—$620

Tlingit lidded basket 4½ in. by 6½ in.   A—$625

Tlingit basket, 5½ in. high and 6 in. across. Design of two concentric geometric bands; slight damage to piece.   G—$410

Tlingit basket, measuring 2½ in. by 3⅛ in.   A—$50

Tsimshian lidded basket, 4¾ in. by 7 in.   A—$60

Tulare basket, California, small base and flaring top, 9 in. high and 16½ in. in top diameter. Lightning decorations on exterior sides. Fair condition.   C—$1200

Tulare basket, very large, 21 in. in diameter and 11 in. high. Pattern is two bands of polychrome rattlesnake designs. Condition excellent.   G—$2600

Tulare basket, 7½ in. in diameter and 3½ in. high. Piece has serrated step pattern, polychrome, and squaw stitch. Condition good.   G—$280

Tulare basket with rattlesnake designs.   A—$165

Washo basket, oval shape, 2¾ in. by 6¼ in. and 4⅞ in. high.   A—$210

Washo basket, 7¼ in. in diameter, with banded exterior design. Has close weave, and is in good condition.C—$195

Washo basket, 7 in. in diameter and 4 in. high, with geometric design.   G—$145

YUROK BASKET, 9½ in. in diameter and 7 in. high. Design is diamonds and rectangles. Piece is in good condition and probably early 1900s. C—$325

Photo courtesy R. M. Weatherford, Washington

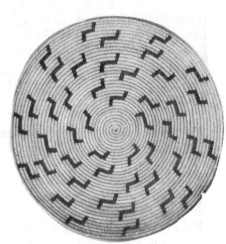

MAIDU BASKETRY PLATE, 14 in. diameter, from Northern California. Coiled, ca. 1900. C—$2500

Courtesy LaPerriere Collection, California

WOOD-SPLINT BASKET, recent, about 12 in. high and 15 in. in diameter. This could either be a Great Lakes area piece, but is more likely Cherokee-made ca. 1950. Note characteristic way each handle end is worked back through the wood, which is typical of Cherokee work. Collected in Ohio; bottom is square and top opening is round. Perfect condition. C—$145

Private collection

Left: HOOPA BASKET, Northern California, 10 in. diameter, ca. 1910. C—$700

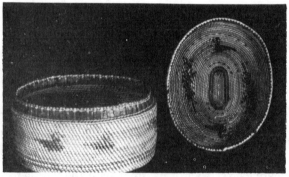

MAKAH LIDDED BASKET, Northwest Coast, 2½ in. high, fair condition, ca. 1930. C—$125

John Barry photo.

HUPA-YUROK BASKETRY HAT, from Northern California, 7½ in. top diameter. Twined, early 1900s. C—$170-$200

Courtesy LaPerriere Collection, California

MAKAH LIDDED BASKET, Northwest Coast, ca. 1940. C—$150

John Barry photo.

HOOPA BASKETRY HAT, 4 in. high, ca. 1910. C—$500

Bob LaPerriere photo.

HOOPA BASKET, 4 in. high, ca. 1910. C—$400

Bob LaPerriere photo.

Left: APACHE BASKET, 21 in. high, ca. 1910.   C—$5500

Photo courtesy John Barry.

Left: LIDDED BASKET, Yurok-Hupa-Karok group. Northern California. 6¾ in. top diameter. Twined, ca. 1910.   C—$750

Courtesy LaPerriere Collection, California

Right: HAVASUPAI PLAQUE, Arizona, 11¼ in. diameter. Materials are willow and devil's claw, 15 coils per inch, 13 stitches per inch. Coiled, representation of two women, men and dogs. By Karen Martinez, 1974.   C—$500

Courtesy LaPerriere Collection, California

KLAMATH BASKET, Southern Oregon, 6 in. top diameter. Twined, soft and flexible, early 1900s.   C—$300

Courtesy LaPerriere Collection, California

Left: WESTERN APACHE BASKET, 10 in. diameter, from Arizona, ca. 1930. Coiled, 5 coils per inch. 14 stitches per inch.   C—$500

Courtesy LaPerriere Collection, California

KLAMATH BASKET, Southern Oregon, 5 in. top diameter. Twined, with yellow porcupine-quill decorations, early 1900s.   C—$200

Courtesy LaPerriere Collection, California

Left: PAPAGO BASKET,   10   in. diameter   at   top. Southern   Arizona. Coiled, 6 stitches per inch,   contemporary.   C—$200

Courtesy LaPerriere Collection, California

Far   Left: LUMMI BASKETRY BOTTLE, from Bellingham,   Washington, fine condition, ca. 1930.   C—$400

John Barry photo.

Left: LUMMI BASKETRY BOTTLE, from Bellingham, Washington. Item 11½ in. high ca. 1930.   C—$350

Photo LaPerriere photo

Right: PAPAGO BASKET, 6¾ in. top diameter, southern Arizona. Coiled, 8 stitches per inch, zoomorphic designs, 1930s or earlier.   C—$200

Courtesy LaPerriere Collection, California

197

Left: PAPAGO BASKET, 6½ in. top diameter, 4 coils per inch, 8 stitches per inch. Coiled, southern Arizona, mid-1900s.   C—$150

Courtesy LaPerriere Collection, California.

Shasta twined tray, woven with beargrass and maidenhair fern stems. Ca. 1900, it is 16 in. in diameter and 2 in. high. A very attractive weaving.
$900-$1200

Terry Schafer collection, Marietta, Ohio

Papago basketry.
Center, large serving tray basket, 12 x 18 in., late 1800s to early 1900s period. $265
Right, bowl basket, 6 x 6 in., early 1900s. $145

Larry Lantz, First Mesa, South Bend, Indiana

Maidu feast basket, 8 x 14 in., brown diamonds on tan. In fine condition, this ca. 1895 work is a rare historic piece. $4000

Courtesy John Isaac, Albuquerque, New Mexico

Papago basketry bowl, different and larger view of basket shown elsewhere, 6 x 6 in. $145

Larry Lantz, First Mesa, South Bend, Indiana

Wicker bowl, Hopi Third Mesa, 9 in. in diameter, ca. 1930s.$75-$100
Pocotopaug Trading Post, South Windsor, CT

Washo basket, 10½ in. in diameter and 5½ in. high. Single-rod construction; design is a serrated concentric band.
G—$245

Yavapai olla, a fine example of the storage basket. A—$235

Yokuts burden basket. A—$155

Yurok basketry mortar skirt or grain-catching hopper.
A—$210

Yurok miniature tobacco basket, 2½ in. by 2¾ in. A—$85

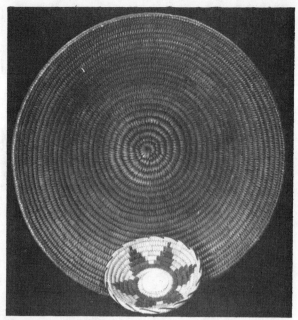

Southwestern Indian basketry.
Large center basket, Navajo-style wedding basket actually made by the Jicarilla Apache, 8 x 16 in. with faded old polychrome design. From the 1800s. $550-$650
Small center basket, Papago, 5 in. in diameter, star design bowl from the 1940s. $120

Larry Lantz, First Mesa, South Bend, Indiana

Olla basket, Apache, nicely executed diamond and triangle designs. This rare item is ca. 1880. $6500
Crown & Eagle Antiques, Inc., New Hope, Pennsylvania

Pima basket, dark brown against a light brown ground, 9 in. in diameter. It is from the 1930s. $350
Private collection

Penobscot quilled birch-bark round covered boxes, the designs done in natural and dyed porcupine quills (red, yellow, green and blue). They are sweetgrass-wound by thread on cover edge. Southeast Seaboard of Canada, ca. 1940s, 3 in. in diameter. $50, each
Frank Bergevin, Port of Call, Alexandria Bay, New York

Hopi wedding basket, 10½ in. in diameter, from the 1970s. It has black and red designs against yellow-tan.
Private collection $150

Southwestern woven basketry tray or plaque in various earth tones and a reddish center. This well-made work is 12¾ in. in diameter. $150-$200

Collection of David G. & Barbara J. Shirley

Papago basket, 12 in. long, with black human figures against a yellow-tan background. This is a well-made basket in mint condition. $500

Courtesy Dr. Fred Belk, Corrales, New Mexico

Pagago baskets, various sizes and designs, from the 1930s to the 1940s. $135-$250, each

Larry Lantz, First Mesa, South Bend, Indiana

Papago basket, 13½ in. diameter, 1950s. $500

Courtesy Tom Noeding

Wicker plaque, Hopi Third Mesa, whirlwind design, 12 in. in diameter. It is ca. 1930s. $175-$200

Pocotopaug Trading Post, South Windsor, CT

Basket, Chiricahua Apache, from the early 1900s. It is 5¾ x 15½ in. in diameter and is a coiled basket in dark red, orange and black decoration on an undyed background. Collected in the Southwest this large and attractive basket is in a fine state of repair. $600

Sherman Holbert Collection, Fort Mille Lacs, Onamia, Minnesota

Papago burden-basket, diamond-step design, ex-museum. It is 10 x 10 in. and a very well-made basket. Ca. 1880-1900. $375

Morris' Art & Artifacts, Anaheim, California; Dawn Gober photograph

Wedding tray, Navajo, pre-1930, size 3½ in. high and 12¼ in. in diameter. Possibly made by the Paiute, this coiled basket is in natural rust and brown. A fine example of a traditional ceremonial item. Ex-coll. Fruchtel. $275

Sherman Holbert Collection, Fort Mille Lacs, Onamia, Minnesota

Basket, vase or jar form, Pima, 8 in. high. This well-made example is ca. 1890-1910. $125-$150

Pocotopaug Trading Post, South Windsor, CT

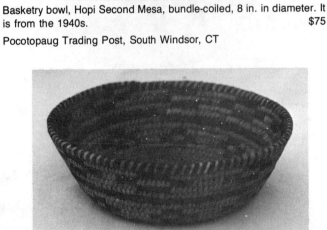

Basketry bowl, Hopi Second Mesa, bundle-coiled, 8 in. in diameter. It is from the 1940s. $75

Pocotopaug Trading Post, South Windsor, CT

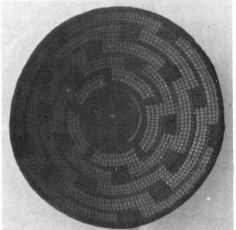

Basket, Pima, 7 in. in diameter, attractive design, ca. 1890-1910. $125-$150

Private collection

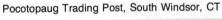

Basket, Papago, chocolate-brown designs on tan, 7 in. in diameter. It is ca. 1900-1920. $100-$125

Pocotopaug Trading Post, South Windsor, CT

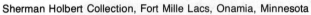

Pima basket, medium brown design on light brown or tan ground, perfect condition. Size, 3½ x 9½ in. $800-$1200

Marguerite L. Kernaghan collection; photograph by Marguerite L. and Stewart W. Kernaghan, Bellvue, Colorado

Figural basket, Papago, bird motif, 9 in. in diameter. It is ca. 1900-1910. $125-$150

Pocotopaug Trading Post, South Windsor, CT

Papago basket, medium wear on interior and exterior, yellow and caramel designs on tan background. Size is top diameter of 5⅝ in. and height is 2⅝ in. $35-$45

Private collection

Wicker plaque, Hopi Third Mesa, 12 in. in diameter, black and tan-yellow central design and inner rim of green and red. Ca. 1940s. $175-$200

Pocotopaug Trading Post, South Windsor, CT

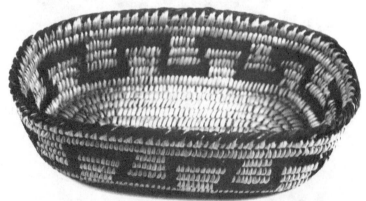

Papago basket, brown designs on light tan ground. Oblong, size is 3 x 5⅜ x 1⅜ in. high. Condition is excellent. $45-$55

Private collection

Southwestern basketry. Left, Hopi Second Mesa, bundle-coil, 6 in. in diameter, 1910-1920. $100-$125
Right, Papago, 5 in. in diameter, ca. 1940-1950. $50-$65
Pocotopaug Trading Post, South Windsor, CT

Wedding tray, Navajo, basketry in several subtle colors, 14 in. in diameter. This fine example is ca. 1910-1920. $275-$300
Pocotopaug Trading Post, South Windsor, CT

CANADIAN INDIAN BASKETS

It should be noted that some of the baskets already listed are also Canadian in origin. The names sometimes represent a basket making region rather than a specific Indian group. Among such baskets are Frazer River and Thompson River in British Columbia in Western Canada.

Plaited wood-strip basket, 14 in. in diameter and 8½ in. high. From Vancouver Island; work is good and serviceable. Probably a gathering basket for roots or shore seafoods. No decoration, fair condition. C—$95

Ash-splint basket, alternating dark and light brown colors, 16½ in. high, 11½ in. wide at rounded shoulders. Collected in Southeastern Canada. Basket design is from square at the bottom to round opening at top, with nice merge. Ca. 1900. C—$145

Small nondescript basket, wood splint, from Central Canada, and 3⅞ in. in diameter. Original colors of separate plaits were red and black, now faded. No cover. Good condition. C—$40

Historic-period basket, from Canada just above the Montana border. Piece is 7½ in. in diameter, and from an old collection. Material is a kind of reed, species unidentified. No decorative work. Basket is in good condition. C—$170

MISCELLANEOUS BASKETS

Northwest Coast basketry hat, 13½ in. in lower diameter, flat crown, and 9 in. high. For rain protection, this basketry hat has a very tight weave. Unusual. C—$650

Miniature sweetgrass basket, Eastern Woodlands, 3 in. in diameter, with cover. D—$35

Miniature sweetgrass basket, Eastern Woodlands, 2 in. in diameter, with cover. D—$30

Northern California basketry mortar skirt, 9½ in. high. It is 14 in. across the open top, and 4 in. across open bottom. Whole is shaped like a funnel, and the shield kept the pounded meal from flying from the mortar and being lost or mixed with grit. Historic; with diamond and lightning design. C—$815

Basketry head ring, used between top of head and carrying pot for steady transport of water vessel, etc. About 4½ in. in diameter, open center, about 1 in. thick. From Southwestern U.S., and old. C—$110

Southwestern prehistoric basket, 8½ in. in diameter, 4¾ in. high, gray-brown color. Basket has a medium-tight weave, no remaining decoration. Found during excavation of a dry cave in New Mexico. Reed used, but is now very brittle. C—$365

Cone-shaped California burden basket, 17 in. high; would have been used with the forehead strap or tumpline. Tribe unknown. A plain piece, showing average and acceptable wear.   C—$1400

Southwestern Oregon basketry cooking pot, circular, with extremely tight weave. Stepped pyramid designs, reinforced rim. Used with water, meat and roots; hot rocks were dropped in to boil the water and cook the food. Item is 11 in. high, 13½ in. diameter. Historic; damage to bottom.   C—$400

Suggested Reading

James, George W., *Indian Basketry;* San Francisco, 1902 (reprinted)

Mason, Otis T., *Aboriginal American Basketry: Studies In A Textile Art Without Machinery;* published in the Annual Report of the U.S. National Museum for 1902, and by Doubleday, Page, New York 1904 (3 Volumes)

Miles, Charles, and Bovis, Pierre; *American Indian and Eskimo Basketry: A Key To Identification,* San Francisco, 1969 (reprinted)

Iroquois (Mohawk) ash-splint basket, "strawberry" form, covered and edged with sweetgrass. Ca. 1940s, it is 3½ x 5¼ in. $80
Frank Bergevin, Port of Call, Alexandria Bay, NY

Klamath basket, stripe design of dark brown against light yellowish brown, from southern Oregon. It is 5 x 9 x 13 in., ex-museum, and ca. 1920. $350

Morris' Art & Artifacts, Anaheim, California; Dawn Gober photograph

River cane basket, Cherokee, large size, from the 1940s. $295

Larry Lantz, First Mesa, South Bend, Indiana

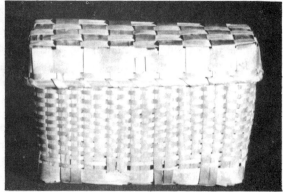

Splint basket of black ash, plaited, Mohawk, nicely stamped with red and blue designs. The basket is 7 x 12 x 7½ in. high. Late 1800s, New York state. $90

Pat & Dave Summers, Native American Artifacts, Victor, NY

Yokuts basket, human figure motif, 7 in. high and 10 in. in diameter. Design is dark brown on tan and this is a fine work, possibly from the 1920s. $1200

Private collection

Tlingit baskets, Northwest Coast, all made of spruce root and bear-grass.
Left, 7 in. high, ca. 1920s. $100-$125
Center, grizzly bear in false embroidery, 10½ in. high, ca. 1880-1900. $350-$400
Right, 7½ in. high, ca. 1920s. $125-$150
Pocotopaug Trading Post, South Windsor, CT

Basketry water bottle, Paiute, still showing traces of pine pitch coating.
Ex-museum, it is 10 in. in diameter and 13 in. high. Ca. 1880. $275
Morris' Art & Artifacts, Anaheim, California; Dawn Gober photograph

Splint basket, Mohawk, 7½ in. in diameter. This well-made work is ca.
1880-1900. $75
Pocotopaug Trading Post, South Windsor, CT

Lidded basket, Penobscot, splint and sweetgrass. It is 8 in. in diameter
and ca. 1920-1940. $50-$75
Pocotopaug Trading Post, South Windsor, CT

Handkerchief basket, Penobscot, 9 in. square, unusual lid or top. Ca.
1920s. $40-$50
Pocotopaug Trading Post, South Windsor, CT

Basketry vase, Penobscot, splint and sweetgrass, 8 in. high. In fine condition, it is ca. 1920-1940. $75
Pocotopaug Trading Post, South Windsor, CT

Twined hat, Karok, perfect condition. Design is black and brown against a cream ground. Size is 3½ x 6½ in.; ca. 1900. $400-$650

Marguerite L. Kernaghan collection; photograph by Marguerite L. and Stewart W. Kernaghan, Bellvue, Colorado

Beehive basket, Northeastern Woodlands, splint and sweetgrass. It is 8½ in. in diameter and ca. 1920s. $100-$125

Pocotopaug Trading Post, South Windsor, CT

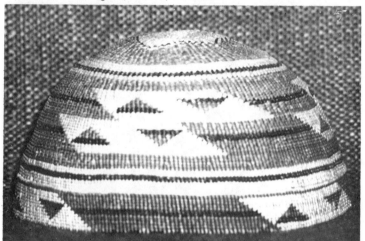

Twined hat, high-crowned, Yurok. In perfect condition, it is 7 x 10¼ in. and ca. 1920. $700-$1200

Marguerite L. Kernaghan collection; photograph by Marguerite L. and Stewart W. Kernaghan, Bellvue, Colorado

Sewing basket, Penobscot, 7½ in. in diameter. It is a well-made example, ca. 1920s. $50-$75

Pocotopaug Trading Post, South Windsor, CT

Twined hat, Hupa, perfect condition. The design is maroon, black and cream against a cream background. It is 3¼ x 6 in. and ca. 1900. $400-$650

Marguerite L. Kernaghan collection; photograph by Marguerite L. and Stewart W. Kernaghan, Bellvue, Colorado

Birch-bark basket, Micmac-Abenaki, maker Jim Rouix. It is recent-contemporary, and ca. 1980. Size of this pleasing piece is 5 x 5¾ in. $100

Marguerite L. Kernaghan collection; photograph by Marguerite L. and Stewart W. Kernaghan, Bellvue, Colorado

Shasta basket, step design, from northern California. Ex-museum, it is 5 in. in diameter and 4 in. high. Ca. 1920. $200

Morris' Art & Artifacts, Anaheim, California; Dawn Gober photograph

Strawberry basket, Iroquois, so-named because of basket shape and design. It is 5½ in. in diameter, decorated with curlicues. Ca. 1910-1930.
$65-$80

Pocotopaug Trading Post, South Windsor, CT

Lidded box, basketry, Makah, 5 in. in diameter. This delicate work is ca. 1890-1900. $100-$125

Pocotopaug Trading Post, South Windsor, CT

Close-up and different view of the Cherokee basket shown elsewhere. It has the government authorization tag from a North Carolina reservation and the weaver's name. Exceptional basket with documentation.
$325

Larry Lantz, First Mesa, South Bend, Indiana

Lidded basketry box, Nootka, 4¼ in. in diameter. This is a well-made Northwestern Coast artwork, ca. 1920s. $125-$175

Pocotopaug Trading Post, South Windsor, CT

207

Indian basket, split white oak, late 1800s, Chickasaw, from Mississippi.
$100

Wilfred A. Dick collection, Magnolia, Mississippi

Splint basket, Pequot, lidded, 14 in. diameter and 12 in. high. Nicely stamped, it is ca. 1860-1880. $250-$300

Pocotopaug Trading Post, South Windsor, CT

Lidded box, basketry, from the Yukon River area, Alaska. This fine piece is 4½ in. long and ca. 1920-1930. $100-$125

Pocotopaug Trading Post, South Windsor, CT

Splint basket, Pequot, potato-stamped, 8 in. square. This excellent piece is ca. 1880s. $125-$150

Pocotopaug Trading Post, South Windsor, CT

Picnic basket or carrying basket, Salish, 7 x 10 x 14 in. It has an imbricated butterfly design in black on yellow-tan. Ca. 1910-1925. $250-$300

Pocotopaug Trading Post, South Windsor, CT

Basket, Tlingit, designs in cedar bark and bear-grass. This pleasing piece is 6 in. high, ca. 1920s. $250-$350

Pocotopaug Trading Post, South Windsor, CT

MAKAH LIDDED BASKET, Northwest Coast, 4⅝ in. high, ca. 1940.
C—$200

John Barry photo.

MAKAH LIDDED BASKET, fair condition, 2¼ in. high, ca. 1940.
C—$75

John Barry photo.

MAIDU BASKET, coiled bowl, 4 in. high, ca. 1910. Bob LaPerriere photo.
C—$900

MAIDU BASKETS, both 3½ in. diameters, Northern California. Miniatures, coiled, dark material redbud, early 1900s. Top specimen with stain.

Top, C—$200
Bottom, C—$300

Courtesy LaPerriere Collection, California.

MAIDU BASKET, 7 in. width, 6 coils per inch, 13 stitches per inch, Northern California. Coiled, dark material redbud, ca. 1890. C—$1000

Courtesy LaPerriere Collection, California.

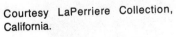

HUPA-YUROK BASKETRY HAT, from Northern California, 7½ in. top diameter. Twined, early 1900s.
C—$170-$200

Courtesy LaPerriere Collection, California.

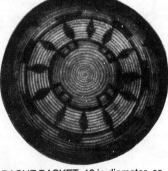

APACHE BASKET, 10 in diameter, ca. 1910.
C—$550

John Barry photo.

WASHO BASKET, 6 in. wide diameter, 4 in. high. Northern California. Coiled plain black fern design (Mt. Brake). 7 coils per inch, 15 stitches per inch, ca. 1890.
C—$800

Courtesy LaPerriere Collection, California.

KLAMATH BASKET, Northern California, 4 in. high, ca. 1910.
C—$375

Bob LaPerriere photo

WASHO SINGLE-ROD COIL BASKET, Northern California, 6 in. top diameter. Coiled 6 coils per inch. 10 stitches per inch, uncertain age.
C—$300

MODOC BOWL BASKET, 8¼ in. diameter. Northern California, ca. 1910.   C—$400

Bob LaPerriere photo

YUROK BASKET, by Geneva M. Maltz, Northern California, 2 in. high, ca. 1974.   C—$150

John Barry photo.

TLINGIT BASKETED BOTTLE, (probably Tlingit).
Southern Alaska, 3 in. bottle height plug 2½ in. wooden totem. Twined, inkwell, carved stopper with paint. Ca. 1910.   C—$800

Courtesy LaPerriere Collection, California

EASTERN MONO COOKING BASKET, Northern California, 14 in. top diameter. Coiled 12 stitches per inch, 7 coils per inch. Black zig-zag design. ca. 1900.   C—$2000

Courtesy LaPerriere Collection, California.

NOOTKA-MAKAH BASKETRY BOTTLE, from Vancouver, Washington state. Twined. 11½ in. high, early 1900s.   C—$500

Courtesy LaPerriere Collection, California

Far left: PIT RIVER BURDEN BASKET, small size, 7 in. high. Twined. Shasta area of Northern California, uncertain age.
C—$350

Courtesy LaPerriere Collection, California.

Left: BASKET, probably Shastan Group, Northern California, 17 in. in height and top diameter. Large burden basket, somewhat crude, some rim repairs, possibly early 1900s.   C—$2500

Courtesy LaPerriere Collection, California.

KLIKITAT BASKET, age uncertain, from British Columbia or Washington state. Top diameter 5¼ in., 3 in., high. Coiled, 6 stitches per inch.   C—$150

Courtesy LaPerriere Collection, California.

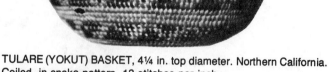

TULARE (YOKUT) BASKET, 4¼ in. top diameter. Northern California. Coiled, in snake pattern, 13 stitches per inch.

C—$300

Courtesy LaPerriere Collection, California.

Left: TLINGIT BASKET, 6 in. high, Southern Alaska. Twined, early 1900. This specimen with tear damage.
Torn condition. C—$300
In perfect condition C—$400

Courtesy LaPerriere Collection, California

Left: HAT CREEK BASKET, Shasta area of Northern California, 6½ in. wide. Twined, about early 1900s. C—$350

Courtesy LaPerriere Collection, California

Left: HOPI BASKETRY PLAQUE, 11 in. diameter. Northeastern Arizona. Coiled, pre-1940; from Second Mesa, this is the old type, thick, with more subtle colors. C—$300

Courtesy LaPerriere Collection, California

Above:
SALISH BASKET, British Columbia or Washington state, 8 in. top diameter. Imbricated design, coiled, 4 coils per inch. Ca. 1910. C—$250

Courtesy LaPerriere Collection, California

Right: POMO BASKET, age uncertain, Northern California, 2 in. top diameter. Coiled, 10 coils per inch, 23 stitches per inch. With war-canoe design. C—$500

Courtesy LaPerriere Collection, California

ESKIMO BASKET, 13 in. high, Alaska, ca. 1960. C—$400

Courtesy LaPerriere Collection, California

NAVAJO WEDDING BASKET, usually not made by Navajos, Northeastern Arizona, 9 in. diameter. Coiled, and contemporary. C—$150

Courtesy LaPerriere Collection, California

SHOSHONE BASKET, Southeastern California. From East of Sierras, probably Inyo County. Coiled, lightning design, 14 stitches per inch. Stabilized, pre-1900. C—$1800

Courtesy LaPerriere Collection, California

211

Covered box, Algonquian, birch-bark, northwest Quebec, ca.1950. It has a bear design with florals on front, sides and back. At 12 x 14 x 24 in., it is unusually large. $650

Frank Bergevin, Port of Call, Alexandria Bay, NY

Iroquois (Mohawk) ash-splint basket, potato-stamp designs in green and red on one strip. Size, 4 x 13 x 15½ in. $200

Frank Bergevin, Port of Call, Alexandria Bay, NY

Iroquois (Mohawk) ash-splint basket, potato-stamped, early 1900s. It is natural ash with strips of painted green ash, stamps in faint red. Size, 11 x 17 x 17 in. $325

Frank Bergevin, Port of Call, Alexandria Bay, NY

Set of three Iroquois (Mohawk) woven ash-splint and grass-covered baskets. All are early 1900s, with right basket marked "1904". $35-$50 each

Frank Bergevin, Port of Call, Alexandria Bay, NY

Twined hat, Yurok, perfect condition. It is 3½ x 6¼ in. and ca. 1900. $400-$650

Marguerite L. Kernaghan collection; photograph by Marguerite L. and Stewart W. Kernaghan, Bellvue, Colorado

Twined hat, Yurok, perfect condition. It is 3½ x 7½ in. and ca. 1920. $350-$600

Marguerite L. Kernaghan collection; photo by Marguerite L. and Stewart W. Kernaghan, Bellvue, Colorado

Unusual view of Cliff Palace Ruins, Mesa Verde National Park, Colorado.
Seen at top right, it is obvious how difficult it is to reach the site and
how easy it was to defend.

Lar Hothem photo

(Upper right in photo)

213

CHAPTER XII

BEADWORK AND QUILLWORK

American Indians are widely recognized to have done the world's finest decorative work with beads and quills. Quills were used in the Eastern Woodland regions and the Rocky Mountains and parts of Canada. The Plains Indians and many other groups favored beads. Quills and beads were sometimes used on the same item.

Porcupine quills were processed and dyed before use; the beads were ready-made trade goods. While generalizations regarding Amerind objects are somewhat difficult, there are basic design differences. In the Eastern Third of the country, bead or quillwork designs were often floral patterns, rounded designs. Western areas had more geometric patterns, angular designs.

The Indian appreciation for things of beauty meant that even everyday objects were sometimes decorated. Ceremonial items, like the fine pipe bags, were often heavily beaded in pleasing color combinations. In this chapter are some collecting areas in which bead or quillwork are especially important.

Value factors include the item decorated, with a complete work (example, bandolier bag) more admired than a part of an original piece (example, pipe bag panel). The complexity of the design counts considerably, involving both the design and the quantity of beads. A typical beadwork design employs many thousand small beads.

Fully beaded items, such as fetishes, are generally higher priced than a partially beaded object of the same size and type. The percentage of beads missing or quills lost or damaged is of great importance in arriving at a value.

The condition of the leather or trade cloth to which beads or quills are secured is to be regarded; a supple, quality leather is much better than poorly tanned and cracked leather. Indian-tanned leather is generally desired over commercial leather.

PIPE BAGS—FULLY OR PARTIALLY BEADED

Sioux pipe bag, old and of fine quality, large size and good condition.   G—$700

Cheyenne pipe bag, 22½ in. long with very nice beaded exterior over soft leather. Fringed and beaded tassels add another 7 in. to length. Good condition.   D—$920

Sioux pipe bag, 7 in. wide and 35 in. long, including fringe. Quillwork is fifty percent missing but beadwork is excellent and in geometric design with various colors of beads on white background.   G—$995

Cheyenne pipe bag, partially beaded, fully fringed. A—$360

Cree pipe bag, done on fine Indian-tanned leather. No quillwork, usual for this type; beaded panel at bottom is 6 in. by 6 in. One side shows floral design and other side shows tea cup and flowers beaded on white background. Old, and in nearly perfect condition.   G—$675

Sioux (?) pipe bag, quillwork and beadwork missing a considerable percentage of units.   D—$460

Sioux pipe bag, 12 in. long with fringe extra. The beaded panel at bottom is 4 in. by 7 in. and in excellent condition. Probably pre-1890.   G—$345

Sioux pipe bags, private collection, per each:C—$800-$1500

Sioux pipe bag with full drop that is nicely quilled.D—$925

Cheyenne pipe bag, well beaded and quilled, good condition.   D—$675

Sioux pipe bag, rebuilt. Old beadwork panels with new buckskin top, quillwork and fringe. Good designs and colors.   G—$595

Sioux pipe bag, beaded, and with unusual parfleche bottom. A—$495

Plains Indian pipe bag, fringed and quilled, good condition. D—$795

Cheyenne pipe bag, old and of very large size for a Cheyenne. Typical designs with fringed, quilled, drop. Piece has slight damage. G—$900

Cree pipe bag. No quillwork as is common on this style bag, but beaded panel on both sides and in stylized flowers. Vari-colored beads on white background. Piece is 7 in. wide and 28 in. long including fringe. Almost perfect condition. G—$875

Ladies pipe bag, Chippewa (Ojibwa), with applique stitching on both sides. This fine piece is from the 1880s. $650

Larry Lantz, First Mesa, South Bend, Indiana

ARAPHO PIPE BAG, standard size, with fringed bottom. Lower sections very well beaded in red, white, black and buff colors. Excellent condition, and ca. 1890. D—$1495

Photo courtesy Crazy Crow Trading Post, Denison, Texas.

Sioux BEADED PIPE BAG, 36 in. long, good design, well-beaded, and ca. 1870-80. D—$1500

Photo courtesy Winona Trading Post, Santa Fe—Pierre & Sylvia Bovis.

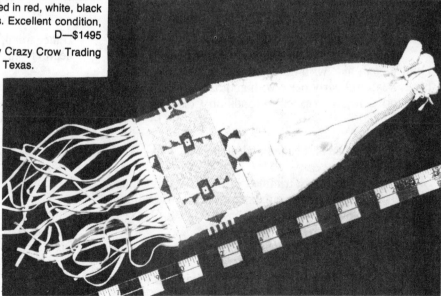

Pipe bag, Sioux, from South Dakota. It is sinew-sewn and brain-tanned, ca. 1880-1890, with rectangular panel beaded in red, white and two shades of blue. This is a fine bag. $895

Larry Lantz, First Mesa, South Bend, Indiana

215

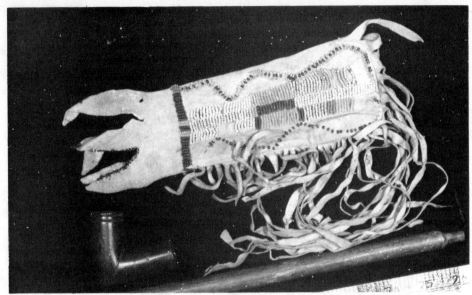

Sioux miniature pipe bag with Catlinite "L"-shaped pipe and original cylindrical stem 13 in. long. The complete set is from Mandan, North Dakota, and ca. 1870s.

Pipe and stem	$645
Pipe bag	$285

Larry Lantz, First Mesa, South Bend, Indiana

Beaded and quilled pipe bag, Sioux, 25 in. long. It is brain-tanned, ca. 1880-1890s, in excellent condition. Beadwork is geometric against a green ground. $1850

Larry Lantz, First Mesa, South Bend, Indiana

QUILLWORK

(Additional quillwork listings are in the **Clothing** chapter)

Plains Indian hair roach, nicely quilled, with horsehair.
D—$255

Quilled coat, hide with floral quilled designs on front and back. Beautiful early piece with about twenty percent of quillwork gone but in excellent condition. Colors are bright.
G—$1450

Cheyenne armbands, beaded and quilled. A—$120

Sioux quilled armbands, trimmed with ermine fur. Quilled danglers, and pair 12 in. in circumference. Good condition, and ca. 1900. G—$155

Hair ties, pair, nicely quilled. D—$100

Hair ties, quilled pair, with brightly colored fluffs and tin cone danglers. G—$55

Sioux quilled cuffs with American flag designs, good quality and condition. Pre-1900 items. G—$465

Dance wand, Plains Indian with wooden handle and quilled head, 14 in. long. Recent. C—$50

Quilled cradle, Arapaho. Top fully quilled in natural and purple quills. Quilled strips down side to cloth base; replaced boards but was done correctly. A beautiful example, and ca. 1870. G—$2900

Hair drop, very old, with trade beads and quillwork.
D—$180

Quilled pouch, 7 in. circular size. Front fully quilled, with quills dyed red, green and orange. Collected in 1930's from Big Sorrell Horse, a Blackfoot Indian in Montana. Piece is excellent, early and rare. G—$900

Quilled basket, Eastern Woodlands, 3⅛ in. in diameter, with fitted, original cover. Interior is birchbark, the whole covered with dyed porcupine quills, brown background. Probably early 1900's. Good condition. C—$145

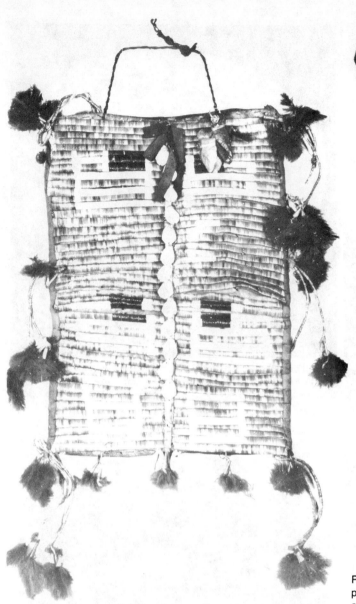

QUILLED BREASTPLATE with American flag motif, 21 in. long. Piece is ca. 1885.   Museum quality

Nedra Matteucci's Fenn Galleries, Santa Fe, New Mexico

QUILLED BIRCH BARK BOX, 5 in. on a side and 2¼ in. high. Flower designs done in dyed and natural quills (dyed, red and green); dried grass edging, with sides done in natural quills. Collected at Wisconsin Dells, Wisconsin. This is a Chippewa box, from the early 1900s.C—$375

Photo courtesy Bill Post Collection.

Quilled moccasins, Great Lakes and early, ca. 1790. These adult-size moccasins are quilled and ribboned on brown hide. $4500

Private collection; photo by John McLaughlin

QUILLED HORSE MANE HAIR PIECE, 14 in. long. The quills and hair are dyed red; tin cone jangles hang on the quilled leather. Ca. 1870.   Museum quality

Nedra Matteucci's Fenn Galleries, Santa Fe, New Mexico

Quilled birchbark lidded box, Woodlands region. It has a colorful floral design in blue-green, pinkish-red and yellow; size is 4 x 9¼ in. in diameter. Ex-coll. Casterline. $490

Pat & Dave Summers, Native American Artifacts, Victor, NY

Quilled birchbark lidded box, with alphabet sampler letters. This charming piece is 3½ x 4¼ in. in diameter, from Canada ca. 1930. Ex-coll. Casterline. $125

Pat & Dave Summers, Native American Artifacts, Victor, New York

Plaque, Chippewa, Great Lakes area, quilled florals on birchbark with grass border. It is 7 in. in diameter and ca. 1940s.

$50-$75

Pocotopaug Trading Post, South Windsor, CT

Baby carrier, Sioux, quilled, with elk done in quillwork. Materials are quills, cloth and hide. This fine work is ca. 1880.

$4000

Private collection, photo by John McLaughlin

BEADED AWL CASES

Awl case, fine fully beaded example, Cheyenne, with white, green and blue beadwork. Old horsehair dangles with tin cones. Piece is 8 in. long and ca. 1900.　　G—$275

Awl case, Sioux, fully beaded, with beaded drops; extra-fine condition, and old.　　D—$155

Awl case, Apache, beaded in geometric designs with tiny seed beads. Larger beads and tin-cone dangles; 14 in. long and in good condition.　　D—$310

Awl case, 12 in. long, with circular design done in blue, yellow and red beads. Sound condition and pre-1900 item.　　G—$145

Awl case, nicely beaded Plains Indian piece.　　A—$95

Awl case, with bone awl. Wooden top, and fully beaded; 9 in. long plus fringe.　　G—$220

BEADED CARRIERS—VARIOUS TYPES

Beaded bag, probably Nez Perce, 9 in. wide and 12½ in. long; all frontal beading intact. Simple star-like designs, two small and one large. Leather is dry but could be treated.　　C—$395

Beaded bag, 8 in. by 9 in. and a beautiful item. Bag has a blue background with roses and leaves design, with many early cut-glass beads. Excellent condition.　　G—$210

Beaded pouch, Sioux, and similar to a strike-a-light bag.　　G—$135

Beaded bag, Plains Indian, 6 in. by 8¼ in. Well-beaded on one side; good condition.　　D—$360

Beaded bag, Woodland Indian style and 6 in. by 6 in. Beadwork is done on black velvet as was usual; floral design with all beadwork intact. Top rim of bag shows some wear.　　G—$200

Bandolier bag, Chippewa, a large bag with typical floral designs on velvet. Good condition.　　G—$1000

Paint bag, a rare Sioux item. It is 12½ in. long, nearly full-beaded and with beaded fringes. A pouch-type container, it still has interior traces of ochre or powdered hematite. Beads are red, yellow and green.　　C—$800

Bandolier bag, Menominee, 38 in. long and 11 in. wide. Fully beaded and in very good condition. Ca. 1880.　　G—$995

Horseshoe-shaped pouch, classic Sioux, fully beaded and fringed. Piece is ca. 1885.　　C—$800

Leather bag, Woodlands Indian and beaded front in typical floral pattern. Possibly Ottawa in origin, it is 6¼ in. high. The pouch is fully fringed on all sides except top, which is closed by a beaded flap.　　C—$500

Wall bag, Sioux (?), fully beaded and with tin cone jangles. Nice condition, and piece is 12 in. long, ca. 1910.　G—$225

Belt pouch, with beaded eagle design.　　A—$110

Pitt River bag, triangular design. It has the highest quality loomed bead work and of the type done only by Indians on the Pitt River, Oregon. Specimen has an amber background with blue and white geometric designs, with beaded handle. Piece is 10 in. by 10 in. and ca. 1930.　　G—$350

Beaded bag, blue background with Nez Perce woman beaded as design. Well-done piece, 11 in. by 12 in., and scarce pictorial bag. Excellent condition.　　G—$320

Beaded tobacco bag, average condition.　　D—$330

Beaded bag, Woodland floral patterns, 6½ in. long. Beaded front and back on black trade-cloth velvet. Good condition, and collected in the Great Lakes area.　　C—$325

Beaded bag, Iroquois, beaded both sides on velveteen with red cloth binding. Piece is 6½ in. by 7½ in. and a good specimen. Ca. 1920.　　G—$210

Strike-a-light bag, Sioux, for flint and steel. Beaded one side, with carrying strap; piece is 3½ in. by 6 in. in good condition.　　C—$295

Beaded bag, Apache, buckskin with typical bead fringe and geometric designs.　　G—$195

Plateau bag, fully beaded using glass beads. Floral design; bag is 11 in. high and 9 in. wide.　　G—$235

Carry-all bag, Woodlands Indian, rounded bottom and lower edge of closing flap. Piece is 11 in. high and 11½ in. wide. Beadwork design on black velvet. Had carrying strap, now missing. Very good condition, very few beads gone.　　C—$420

Beaded bag, Caddo, fully beaded including flap and handle. Buckskin with cloth lining, and 5½ in. by 6 in. Piece has an unusual looped bead fringe. Ca. 1890. G—$225

Beaded belt pouch, Plateau area.　　A—$100

Strike-a-light bag, beaded in Plains Indian style.D—$195

Beaded bag, 9 in. by 10 in., zipper top with handles. Beads used to make bag are 40 to 50 years old. Gray background with stylized floral designs; excellent condition.G—$230

Medicine bag, Plains Indian, worn around the neck. Rare item, and ca. 1880.   D—$210

Tobacco bag, bead designs of standing Indian, and American flag. Slight damage.   G—$295

Beaded container, Apache, 8 in. wide and 5 in. high, black on buff designs.   C—$145

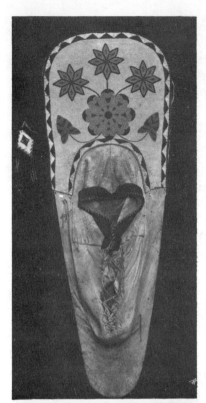

Baby-carrier, Nez Perce, wood frame with hide, cloth and bead-work. This is an ultra-fine example, ca. 1890. $6500

Private collection, photo by John McLaughlin

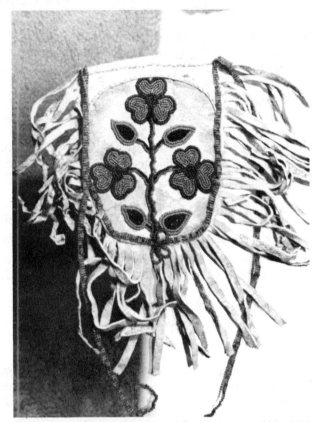

Small beaded bag, Eastern Woodlands / Great Lakes area, fringed sides. The floral motif is done in red, white, blue, green and black.$250-$325

Collection of David G. & Barbara J. Shirley

Beadwork; top left, Iroquois bag, floral motif both sides, ca. 1890.$185
Top right, Chippewa loom-beaded bag, 5 x 6½ in., butterfly and floral pattern. $385
Bottom left, Plateau bag, 7 x 11 in., 1890s, stylized eagle. $225
Iroquois beaded bag, 6½ x 7½ in., floral motif both sides, 1880s, fine work. $385

Larry Lantz, First Mesa, South Bend, Indiana

Baby-carrier, Ottawa, painted wood, cloth and beadwork. This exceptional piece is ca. 1880. $2500

Private collection; photo by John McLaughlin

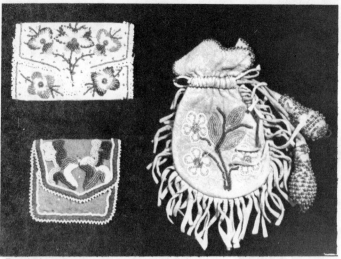

Beaded containers.
Top left, Iroquois (Oneida) needle case, 3 x 4½ in., late 1800s, bird and floral motif.　　　　　　　　　　$275
Bottom left, Northwest Coast (Tlingit) charm bag, 3 x 3 in., seed beads on green trade cloth, ca. 1875.　　　　$350
Right, Chippewa circular bag, late 1800s, brain-tanned, beaded both sides, beaded pompom draw-pulls.　　$285

Larry Lantz, First Mesa, South Bend, Indiana

Beaded bags. Left, tobacco bag, Chippewa, seed beads in abstract design, 6 x 7½ in., from Hayward, Wisconsin. It is late 1800s. $175
Right, shown elsewhere in book　　　　$225

Larry Lantz, First Mesa, South Bend, Indiana

Beaded bags.
Left, wall-pocket bag, Winnebago, black velveteen front, sugar sacking on back, 7 x 22½ in. Seed beads are in abstract floral design, ca. 1880s.　　　　　　　　　　$895
Right, Plateau bag, Yakima, 10 x 11 in. It is contour-beaded in red, blue and lime green, ca. 1880s.　　　　$850

Larry Lantz, First Mesa, South Bend, Indiana

Bandolier bag, Chippewa, ca. 1880-1910. It is 16½ x 36 in., and has exceptionally colorful beadwork. This piece has been restored and stabilized to preserve a rare piece of primitive art.　　$1950

Sherman Holbert Collection, Fort Mille Lacs, Onamia, Minnesota

Bandolier bag, Pottawatomi style, ca. 1860-1870. It is 17 x 41 in. and a truly great example of mid-1800 Indian bead art. Applique floral beadwork accents and separates the nearly flawless choke cherry pattern loom work of the tabs and strap. This is a giant bag compared with most loomed bandoliers.　　$3450

Sherman Holbert Collection, Fort Mille Lacs, Onamia, Minnesota

Woman's bag, Chippewa, late 1800s. Made of brain-tanned hide, it is 6 x 6 in. and has a beaded looped handle with seed beads in fishnet pattern on both sides. A fine piece. $595

Larry Lantz, First Mesa, South Bend, Indiana

Baby carrier, Ute, done in wood and hide, decorated with paint and beading. It is ca. 1880. $3500

Private collection, photo by John McLaughlin

Drawstring bag, Chippewa, floral beading in reds, white, green and blue. It is 4 in. high and ca. 1880-1890. $125

Pocotopaug Trading Post, South Windsor, CT

Pocket, Iroquois, Great Lakes area beadwork ca. 1885-1895, 4 x 4½ in. The fine beading is done on black and red cloth. $100

Pocotopaug Trading Post, South Windsor, CT

Sheath, Crow, hide with beadwork. This may be a whetstone case, ca. 1890. $800

Private collection, photo by John McLaughlin

Bag or purse, Micmac, drawstring top, Great Lakes region. This is a very fine example of a scarce item with colorful beading. It is 7½ x 11 in., ca. 1840-1860. $500

Pocotopaug Trading Post, South Windsor, CT

Wallet, Seneca, Great Lakes area beading, item 2½ x 4 in. Beads are in seven different colors, item ca. 1860-1870. $75

Pocotopaug Trading Post, South Windsor, CT

Bag or pocket, Iroquois, very colorful and attractive beading on black with red fringes, 5 x 6 in., ca. 1850-1860. $275

Pocotopaug Trading Post, South Windsor, CT

Pocket or bag, Iroquois, colorful floral design with red cloth edging and white beads in looped fringes. Ca. 1880-1890, it is 5 in. wide. $75

Pocotopaug Trading Post, South Windsor, CT

223

Bag, Iroquois, Great Lakes area beadwork, colorful floral designs. It is ca.1875-1885 and 6 x 7 in. $150-$200
Pocotopaug Trading Post, South Windsor, CT

Bag or pocket, Osage, heavily beaded, 6¾ x 8 in. It is from Kansas and ca. 1860-1880. $150
Pocotopaug Trading Post, South Windsor, CT

Pocket or bag, Iroquois, Great Lakes area, cross motif against red cloth, 3 x 4 in. It is ca. 1860-1870. $60
Pocotopaug Trading Post, South Windsor, CT

Bandolier bag, Great Lakes region, floral designs in beadwork over cloth. Ca. 1880.   Museum quality
Morning Star Gallery, Santa Fe, New Mexico

224

APACHE BEADED BAG, 7½ in. long. Piece has tin cone jangles, and is ca. 1880.
Museum Quality

Nedra Matteucci's Fenn Galleries, Santa Fe, New Mexico

BEADED BOTTLES

Beaded bottle, done by the Paiute Indians after they ceased doing basket work. Extra-large specimen, and 28 in. tall. White background with variety of geometric designs. Perfect condition. G—$695

Beaded bottle, very small 2¼ in. high and ¾ in. wide. With top, specimen is done on yellow beaded background with black and green geometric designs. Perfect. G—$95

Beaded bottle, 18 in. high. It has a zigzag pattern done in red, white, blue and black beads, very attractive. G—$420

Beaded bottle, 5 in. high. Beaded on small perfume bottle. Fully beaded including bottom with early crystal beads with red and blue geometric designs. G—$145

Plains Indian fetish, 6½ in. long, lizard form, but more nearly resembles a horned toad. Beaded design on top, beaded strip around edges, limbs and tail. C—$445

Beaded turtle umbilical fetish, for twins; two turtles are fastened together. Sioux Indian and extremely rare. G—$735

Lizard fetish, 6 in. long and 2 in. wide. A Sioux piece, it has blue beads on greasy-yellow background and two horsehair dangles on each end. One seam coming apart but easily repaired. Excellent condition and ca. 1890. G—$345

Turtle fetish, 4 in. by 2½ in. Multi-colored beadwork on commerical leather, done on reservation in the 1920's. A few beads missing but in excellent condition. G—$115

Turtle umbilical fetish, a Sioux beaded piece, old and in good condition. G—$310

225

Nez Perce beaded bottle, fully beaded in green, blue, white and red seed beads over leather covering bottle and stopper. It is 5½ in. high and ca. 1880s. $125

Frank Bergevin, Port of Call, Alexandria Bay, NY

MISCELLANEOUS BEADED AND QUILLED PIECES

Chippewa beaded panel, floral designs done on velvet and possibly originally a pillow cover. Old and fine condition. G—$235

Crow beaded panel, red trade cloth and 12 in. by 12 in. Floral motif; considerable moth damage and some beads missing. G—$110

Beaded necklace, probably Ottawa. Piece is 18 in. long, ¾ in. wide at sides and back, 2 in. wide at lower portion. Small beads in red, green and yellow, the whole very well done and unusual. C—$320

Beaded cigarette case, Chippewa, and contemporary. D—$25

Sioux cuffs, fully beaded, and 5 in. by 10 in. Piece has light blue background with red, blue and yellow geometric designs. Excellent condition, and 4 in. fringes on edges. Ca. 1930's. G—$225

Beaded blanket strip, Northern Cheyenne, and flag designs. A—$795

Crow belt, standard Crow stitch and colors in lavender, blue, yellow and red. Belt is 39 in. long and 2¾ in. wide. It is on harness leather and has brass tacks. Some beadwork is loose and some missing but in generally good condition. Pre-1890. G—$235

Athabascan beaded hair ties. A—$18

Beaded watch fob, Plains Indian and ca. 1920. D—$30

Beaded belt, fully beaded and Sioux. Piece is 28 in. long and 2 in. wide, fine condition. G—$325

Beaded sash, Woodland loom-beaded specimen. D—$130

Contour beadwork, four fine and old pieces, sold as one lot. A—$110

Choker, made by blackfoot Indians sometime prior to 1930 when it was collected. Choker fully beaded and 14 in. long and ¾ in. wide. An original scalp may be hanging from this choker, making it a very rare piece. G—$310

Arm bands, full beadwork over rawhide on these Sioux items. D—$145

Beaded cuffs, pair, Yakima. A—$110

Beaded strip, Cheyenne, and 25 in. long and 1¾ in. wide. Sinew-sewn beadwork in excellent condition. Ca. 1900. G—$255

Beaded head band, Sioux, 20 in. long with beads sewn on buckskin. Ends have ties. G—$60

Beaded bag front, rest of bag gone. Beadwork is excellent and complete. Piece is 5 in. by 5½ in. and done in old cut-glass beads, depicting bird motif. A good basis for a new pipe bag. G—$45

Beaded dress yoke, Apache. A—$35

Beaded arm bands, pair, Ponca, fully beaded on trade cloth and ca. 1890. D—$150

Bugle bead vest, very old. A—$600

Baby bonnet, Sioux, fully beaded and nice condition. G—$525

Beaded belt, 33 in. long and 2¾ in. wide. Fully beaded with overlaid stitch — not loomed. White background, geometric designs in red, yellow, blue and green beads, backed with cloth. Not too old but in excellent condition. G—$225

Loom-beaded belt, Northern Plateau area. A—$65

Beaded strip or belt, 46 in. long and 3 in. wide. Sinew sewn on buckskin in yellow, blue and red. G—$320

Wrist cuffs, beaded pair, Plains Indian. D—$105

Frame of seed beads, 8 in. by 12 in. and with multi-colored seed beads in floral motif, on trade cloth. D—$60

Beaded pillow, Chippewa, 6½ in. square. Has floral bead-work designs with beaded edging in seven colors. Quite unusual. D—$90

Beaded armbands, Flathead Indian. A—$38

Beaded headband, Sioux, beads on buckskin and ca. 1900. D—$60

Armbands, Blackfoot, 10½ in. long and 1 in. wide quilled dangles. Collected in Montana in 1932, but are much older. Pair. G—$145

Beaded headband, loom-beaded Cree, ca. 1885. D—$65

Pin cushion, Chippewa, 8 in. long. Piece has floral design in very small (18/0) beads, red, dark green, blue, pink and yellow. G—$95

Headband, Sioux, beaded with string hair-drops. D—$125

Beaded belt, Indian group unknown, 30 in. long and 3 in. wide. Loomed work; white background with seven deer woven into the design. G—$260

Suggested Reading

Whiteford, Andrew H.; *North American Indian Arts,* Golden Press, New York, 1970

Duncan, Kate C., *Northern Athapaskan Art: A Beadwork Tradition,* University of Washington Press, Seattle, 1989

Beaded bag, 2½ x 4 in., the beading done in brown, green and white on one side and brown, blue, black and white on the opposite side. The leather is Indian-tanned. $150-$200

Collection of David G. & Barbara J. Shirley

Woman's purse, Sioux, fully beaded, 4 x 8 in., Ca. 1880. $1000

Freya's Collectibles, Banff, Alberta, Canada

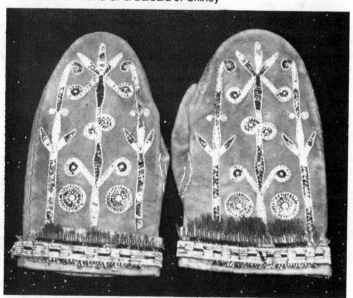

Quilled hide mittens, Eastern Great Lakes, Huron (?), with porcupine quills, tin cones and dyed animal hair. Ca. 1750. $5000

Private collection, photo by John McLaughlin

227

Beaded sash, Winnebago, early 1900s. It is 1¼ x 68 in., with blue beading on a white ground. $195

Larry Lantz, First Mesa, South Bend, Indiana

Loom-beaded sash, Winnebago, very early 1900s. It is beaded in green and yellow against white and is very heavy. This fine piece is 90 in. long. $750

Larry Lantz, First Mesa, South Bend, Indiana

Cap, beaded brimless Iroquois in classic form, blue velvet and colored glass beads. It is 3 x 7¼ in. in diameter, Six Nations, Canada, and ca. 1870. $500

Pat & Dave Summers, Native American Artifacts, Victor, NY

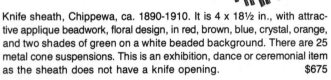

Quilled birchbark boxes, Mohawk, contemporary, container with beaver design 7 in. long. These are well-made and nicely decorated. $60-$150 each

Pocotopaug Trading Post, South Windsor, CT

Knife sheath, Chippewa, ca. 1890-1910. It is 4 x 18½ in., with attractive applique beadwork, floral design, in red, brown, blue, crystal, orange, and two shades of green on a white beaded background. There are 25 metal cone suspensions. This is an exhibition, dance or ceremonial item as the sheath does not have a knife opening. $675

Sherman Holbert Collection, Fort Mille Lacs, Onamia, Minnesota

228

Apron (dance costume), Chippewa, Leech Lake Reservation, Minnesota. Ca. 1920s, it is 18 x 20 in. and black velveteen beaded in a floral pattern of red, white, blue, green and yellow seed beeds. Edging is yarn with pink piping. $175

Sherman Holbert Collection, Fort Mille Lacs, Onamia, Minnesota.

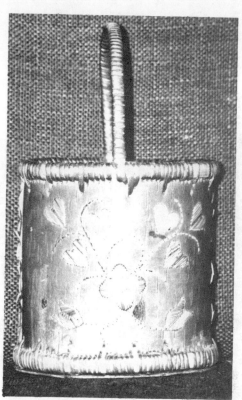

Quilled birch-bark basket, basswood handle, quilled floral and hearts design. Good condition, the box is 6 x 7 x 7 in., Chippewa, and ca. 1900. $125-$200

Marguerite L. Kernaghan collection; photograph by Marguerite L. and Stewart W. Kernaghan, Bellvue, Colorado

Knife case, Chippewa, hide, wood, cloth and floral beadwork. It is 14 in. long and ca. 1900. $1200

Private collection, photo by John McLaughlin

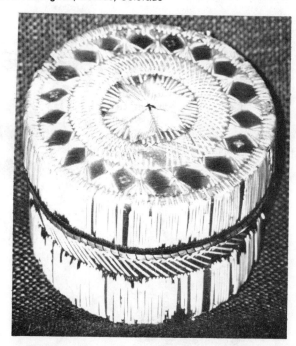

Quilled birchbark box, Chippewa, many quills missing. This 3¾ x 5¾ in. box is ca. 1900. $125-$200

Marguerite L. Kernaghan collection; photograph by Marguerite L. and Stewart W. Kernaghan, Bellvue, Colorado

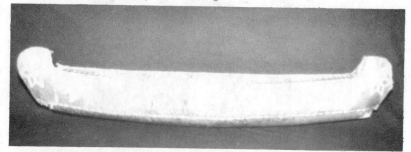

Model canoe, birchbark, with porcupine quill designs. It is a large 42 in. long, ca. 1910, and ex-coll. Casterline. $650

Pat & Dave Summers, Native American Artifacts, Victor, NY.

Small Delaware BEADED PURSE, 6 in. in diameter, with nicely balanced floral design on front. About 100 years old, it is ca. 1870-80.   D—$325

Photo courtesy Winona Trading Post, Santa Fe—Pierre & Sylvia Bovis.

Fine Sioux BEADED SADDLE BLANKET, leather and 25 in. wide, 46 in. long. Excellent designs, well-balanced piece, ca. 1880.   D—$2000

Photo courtesy Winona Trading Post, Santa Fe—Pierre & Sylvia Bovis.

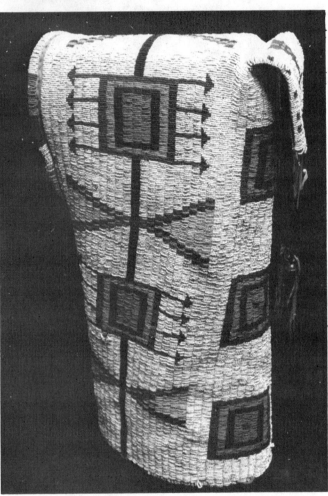

Winnebago BEADED BANDOLIER BAG, 36 in. long and 18 in. wide, beaded floral motifs. Note the superb condition of this excellent example of Indian art, ca. 1880.   D—$1600

Photo courtesy Winona Trading Post, Santa Fe—Pierre & Sylvia Bovis.

Baby-carrier, fully-beaded, in hide, metal, cloth, beads and bells. This Sioux artwork is ca. 1875. $4000

Private collection; photo by John McLaughlin

BEADED PURSE, 5 in. long, not counting strap. Tourist item, Southwestern states and possibly Apache work. Ca. 1950.   C—$45

Private collection

Beaded purse, Woodlands, with ribbon handle and lovely floral beading on both sides. This piece is 5 in. square and ca. 1875. $125

Pat & Dave Summers, Native American Artifacts, Victor, NY

Baby-carrier, Cheyenne, done on hide with cloth, beads and bells. This fine piece is ca. 1880. $3000-$4000

Private collection; photo by John McLaughlin

Plateau bag, beaded, Nez Perce, 10 x 12 in., floral pattern, from the 1890s. Fine condition. $395

Larry Lantz, First Mesa, South Bend, Indiana

Beaded bags.
Left, woman's possible bag, Sioux, beaded border and twisted beaded handle, 4½ x 6 in., 1890s. $245
Right, woman's bag, Oglala Sioux, brain-tanned, beaded both sides, 8 x 8 in. $250

Larry Lantz, First Mesa, South Bend, Indiana

Beaded purse with ribbon handle, fine floral beading on both sides, Iroquois. This excellent work is 7 in. square, from Quebec, Canada, and ca. 1880. $490

Pat & Dave Summers, Native American Artifacts, Victor, NY

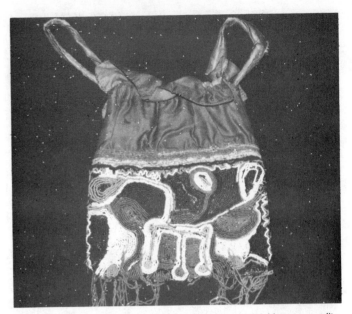

Pocket, Iroquois, Great Lakes area beadwork ca. 1885-1895, beading done on black and red cloth. It is 3½ x 4 in. $75

Pocotopaug Trading Post, South Windsor, CT

Lady's bag, Seminole, silk, cloth and beadwork, ca. 1850. Museum quality

Private collection, photo by John McLaughlin

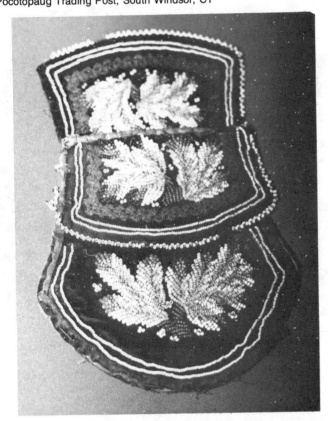

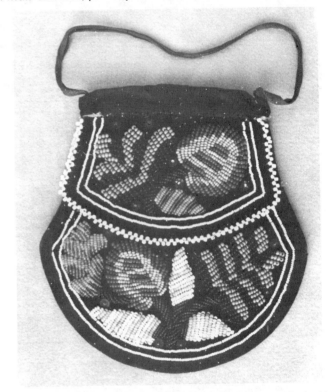

Bag, Iroquois, very attractive beading in many colors against black with red edging. It is ca. 1875-1885. $150-$200

Pocotopaug Trading Post, South Windsor, Connecticut

Beaded purse, early Tuscarora, with floral design on both sides. This 7½ in. square purse is from the Tuscarora reservation and ca. 1865. $275

Pat & Dave Summers, Native American Artifacts, Victor, NY

Knife case, Seminole, alligator hide, buckskin and beads. This unusual and fine piece is ca. 1860. Museum quality

Private collection, photo by John McLaughlin

232

Plains items.
Baby carrier, Cheyenne, with umbilical fetish. It is wood, cloth, hide, beads, tacks and paint, ca. 1870. $5000
Lower left, fetish, Nez Perce, beaded fringes.   Unlisted

Private collection, photo by John McLaughlin

Baby carrier, Kiowa, consisting of wood, tacks, hide, cloth and bead-work. This high-quality piece is ca. 1890. $10,000

Private collection, photo by John McLaughlin

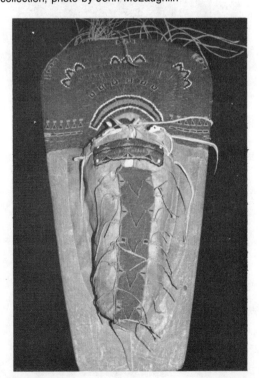

Baby carrier, Ute, wood and hide, decorated with paint and beading. This excellent work is ca. 1880. $3500
Private collection, photo by John McLaughlin

Bandolier bag, British Columbia, Canada, bag size 6 x 9 in. Done with bird, geometric and floral designs against red, it is ca. 1930s.$175-$250
Pocotopaug Trading Post, South Windsor, CT

233

Bandolier bags, finely decorated and in superb condition, both ca. 1870.
$3000 each

Private collection; photo by John McLaughlin

Beaded octopus bag, Tlingit, contemporary, 22 in. long. $1200

Freya's Collectibles, Banff, Alberta, Canada

Bandolier bag, Ojibwa, very fine beadwork throughout, 26 x 48 in. It
is ca. 1890. $5500

Freya's Collectibles, Banff, Alberta, Canada

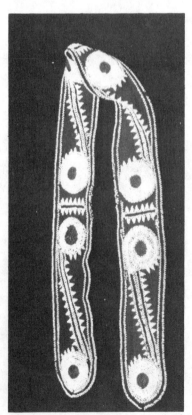

Sash, Choctaw, red stroud, black braid and interesting beadwork design.
Ca. 1850. $1200

Private collection, photo by John McLaughlin

Sash, Seminole, wool cloth, red yarn, ribbon and beads, ca. 1850. $3000
Private collection, photo by John McLaughlin

Sash, Creek or Cherokee, yarn with beads in diamond design. Ca. 1850.
$2000

Private collection, photo by John McLaughlin

Winnebago beaded sashes.
Top, 38 in. long with ties, red, green, yellow and black on white, early 1900s. $125
Bottom, 36 in. long, red, green and brown against white, 1890s. $175
Larry Lantz, First Mesa, South Bend, Indiana

Cloth panel with tassels, beaded floral design, Woodlands region. This pristine and well-done piece is 14 x 21½ in. and ca. 1890. Highest quality.
$1000

Pat & Dave Summers, Native American Artifacts, Victor, New York

Garrison cap, men's size, beaded in many colors. This outstanding Iroquois work is in pristine condition and is 11½ in. long. It is ca. 1850-1870 and from Ontario, Canada. $650

Pat & Dave Summers, Native American Artifacts, Victor, New York

Glengary hat, Iroquois, multi-colored beads on black with red ribbon trim and ties. This is a fine early piece, and unusual. $300

Michael F. Slasinski, Saginaw, Michigan

Cuffs, fully beaded, Winnebago. The beads are loomed and mounted on leather, well-worn but beads in place. Size each is 3¼ x 10½ in., and period is ca. 1910-1920. $600-$900 pair

Marguerite L. Kernaghan collection; photograph by Marguerite L. and Stewart W. Kernaghan, Bellvue, Colorado

Whimsies, Iroquois, Great Lakes area beadwork. Left, pillow dated 1924, 6 x 6 in. $60
Right, shoe form with delicate beading. $45

Pocotopaug Trading Post, South Windsor, CT

CHAPTER XIII
PIPES

Pipe forms began in the Archaic time-frame, and various types were made throughout North America. Generally pipes were made from a select material, a hardstone that was both compact and colorful.

The form, in principle, is simple. A pipe has an enclosed area that contains the smoking material — tobacco as we know it was not used widely until historic times — and a smaller, intersecting hole through which the smoke was drawn. Pipes range from large to small, effigy to plain, with workstyle from passable to superb.

Pipes are classified according to shape — tube, elbow, elongated, platform, and so forth. Some are mere bowls, while others are complete with stems and incised decorations. Earlier pipes tend to be simple; later forms are more elaborate. Many specimens took a great deal of time and skill to make and are avidly sought by collectors today. and are avidly sought by collectors today.

For this discussion, pipes can be divided into two large collecting fields. As with many other Amerind collectibles, these are before (prehistoric) and after, White-contact times (historic period). Prehistoric pipes tend to be the most varied in form, the most geographically divergent.

Historic Plains Indian style pipes are much more similar for the times. There is a certain sameness of size, design and material, with Minnesota red pipestone (also called Catlinite) the common stone. Such pipes were also popular in the Great Lakes area and other regions.

Value considerations for prehistoric pipes include material from which the pipe is made, with harder substances ranked higher than loose-grained stone. Polish is important, as are size and work-style. All drilling should be complete and well-done. Some tube-type pipes combine the two in a single elongated hole.

Effigy pipes usually command higher prices than ordinary pipes, and depictions of the human figure are especially valued. The rare Hopewellian effigy pipes — often mini-sculptures of birds or animals — can be worth in excess of $2000.

Historic times had many White-made pipes. They ranged from the rare Russian lead stem-and-bowl pipe of the far Northwest to numerous baked-clay and porcelain pipes of White mold-manufacture. The pipe-tomahawks of Eastern regions (covered elsewhere) are yet another example. The big collector item, however, is the Indian-made Plains-style pipe.

The typical Plains Indian Catlinite smoking instrument had a high, rounded bowl and a stem-receptacle of similar porportions. In profile, the two form either an "L"-shaped or an inverted "T"-shape. Some pipe forms were two-piece, with stem connecting the receptacle. And the stem, in turn, was either of wood or Catlinite.

Better pipes were stored and transported in the beaded and/or quilled pipe-bags, and were used on special occasions. The current value range for Plains-style pipes is $500-$3000, and more for extra-fine specimens. Most pipe heads are about the same size, so this is not usually a big value factor.

Overall workmanship is important, plus surface polish and completed and accurate drilling. Twisted-wood or paneled-wood stems are more desired than plain wooden stems, and Catlinite stems are very much sought-after. Pipes that can definitely be associated with an actual (and famous) Indian leader are definitely in the minority, and should be thoroughly documented.

It is pointed out that contemporary Catlinite pipes are being made by American Indians at the Pipestone National Monument in Minnesota. These are modern reproductions that much resemble Plains-style historic specimens; they sell in a range of $50-$200, and, with wood stem, are from 12 in. to 30 in. in length.

PREHISTORIC STONE PIPES

Sandstone tube pipe, 4½ in. long and 1¼ in. in diameter. A well-made piece, fully drilled the length.   A—$110

Caddo long-stem pipe, 9 in. long. Piece, from Arkansas, has minor stem breaks, but repaired; no bowl damage. Nice item.   G—$275

Hardstone tube pipe, 10¼ in. long, 1¼ in. in diameter near center. Made of black compact stone, highly polished on surface. Larger end evidences some battering, but nothing major.   D—$675

Bowl-type pipe, 1½ in. long, 1½ in. high, and made of Ohio pipestone.   A—$75

Round bowl-type pipe, made of compact light sandstone. Large hole ½ in. in diameter with smaller hole for stem. Pipe, with rounded bottom, is 1¾ in. high.   C—$95

Diegueno Indian **soapstone tube pipe,** 5 in. long and 1 in. across at smoking end. Drilled entire length, small to larger hole, no damage.   C—$370

Cylindrical banded-slate pipe bowl, flat bottomed. Bowl is 2⅛ in. high, exterior highly polished, good banding.D—$150

Wine-glass type pipe, Washington state, 4½ in. long and ⅞ in. wide at end. Polished stone resembling steatite, well-carved, perfect condition.   D—$440

Sandstone effigy pipe, 4 in. high and 3¼ in. wide. A crane-like bird is depicted, with beak touching ground, and bowl on back. Restored.   A—$370

Green soapstone or **steatite pipe,** from Virginia, bowl at one end of a flat base. Piece is 5⅜ in. long. Some damage to expanded rim of bowl, now expertly restored.C—$495

Platform-type pipe, steatite, 4 in. long and 1½ in. high, nicely polished.   A—$220

Raised-bowl pipe, with flat stem extending for 3¾ in. Height, 1½ in. Stem is just over 1 in. wide, with raised ridge along top center.   A—$600

Effigy platform pipe, pipestone, 3 in. long and 1¾ in. high, depicting a bird. Piece done in Hopewellian fashion. Head is restored.   A—$375

Steatite elbow-type pipe, 2½ in. long and 1½ in. high, very well polished.   A—$155

Sandstone effigy pipe, 3 in. high and 2 in. long, depicting a human figure with arms around the bowl. Piece is broken but not seriously.   A—$290

Steatite pipe, large bowl 4¼ in. high and with smaller stem about 2¾ in. long. Highly polished.   D—$415

Tubular pipe, pipestone, 7 in. long and 1¼ in. wide, with fully drilled, tapering hole. A very well-made piece, though broken and restored.   A—$800

Granite effigy pipe, 3½ in. high, 1½ in. wide. Bird figure with bowl on the back.   A—$320

Sandstone pipe made to represent a sitting frog or toad. Pipe has large smoking hole in middle of the back, stands 2 in. high. Good condition, and a well-made piece. Intensive wear around top of bowl.   C—$210

Hopewellian **platform-type pipe,** sandstone, very nicely carved and proportioned, 4¾ in. long. Piece is unfinished, having never been drilled for bowl or stem.   C—$255

Steatite pipe, tubular form, 1¼ in. in diameter and 3½ in. long. Ends lightly scarred, all minor, surface highly poslished.   D—$115

Sandstone pipe, barrel type. 2¼ in. high. Late prehistoric, Midwest. Some damage to top of bowl.   C—$95

Slate pipe, tubular form, 4¼ in. long and 1⅛ in. in diameter. Good banded material, high polish, drilled completely through, no damage.   C—$260

Stone pipe, elbow type, 3½ in. long and 1⅞ in. high. Squared edges, rather heavy in appearance, well-polished surface. One chip from mouthpiece area, but minor.   C—$240

Pipe, Northwest Coast "wineglass" tubular variety. Pipe is 2⅞ in. long, ⅞ in. in diameter at larger end, hole drilled the length. Smaller "bottom" mouthpiece end had hole drilled in corner, possibly for securing thong. D—$370

Steatite bird-effigy pipe, with sitting bird facing pipe bowl; 4¼ in. long. Small scratches on surface, none deep. Unusual; unknown time period, but prehistoric. Effigy well-carved.   C—$1050

Sandstone pipe, elbow-type, 2¾ in. long, 1¼ in. high. Plain, but well-made. From Oklahoma, and prehistoric. Surface still rough.   D—$75

Pipestone pipe, platform type, concave platform base, plain bowl. Piece is 4⅛ in. long, perfect condition, highly polished.   C—$1350

"L"-shaped pipe of greenish pipestone, 2⅛ in. long. Bowl has two incised lines around top near rim.   C—$170

Platform-type pipe of limestone, 3½ in. long and 1¾ in. high.   A—$175

Disc-bowl pipe, Illinois, made of gray-white material. Has a short rounded stem and is 1¾ in. high, 2½ in. long.   C—$350

Effigy pipe of sandstone, 5 in. long and 3 in. high, possibly representing a sitting bird with squat body and raised head.   A—$800

Iroquois pipe, pipestone, 5 in. long and 2 in. high. Bowl and stem form right angle; top of bowl has a widened, flat rim. The piece has been restored.   A—$175

Elbow-type pipe, North Carolina, expanded bowl set at right angles to squared base. Material a yellowish compact stone. Piece is 3 in. long.   C—$440

Large **platform-type pipe,** 4⅞ in. long, 3¼ in. high. Made of a polished dark brown stone, no damage. Well-polished; bowl fully drilled and stem partially drilled.   C—$700

Granite elbow-type pipe, 4 in. long and 2½ in. high.   A—$165

Iroquois pipe, long-stem type, 4½ in. long and 2 in. high. Round bowl, tubular stem, made of pipestone. This piece has restoration.   A—$175

Tubular pipe, state of Washington, of a type called "wineglass". One end flares abruptly, other end tapers to rounded and expanded mouthpiece. Piece is 5⅛ in. long, of a compact black stone. Slight damage to rim of smoking bowl, but minor.   C—$540

Elbow-type stone pipe, made of a fine-grain yellowish siltstone, and 3½ in. long, 1¾ in. high. Well-made and with good polish.   C—$395

Quartzite barrel-type pipe, 2 in. high and 1¾ in. in diameter, with hole for stem in center which connects with smoking compartment.   A—$195

EFFIGY CLAY PIPE, 5 in. long and 3¼ in. high at top of effigy head. Effigy types of artifacts tend to be more valued than plain types; this is a Canadian piece.   C—$225

Photo courtesy Robert C. Calvert, London, Ontario, Canada.

CLAY PIPE, 4 in. long and 2½ in. high, from Brant County, Ontario, Canada. This is a sturdy and well-made piece, late prehistoric or early historic.   C—$40-$50

Photo courtesy Robert Calvert, London, Ontario, Canada.

STONE EFFIGY PIPE, platform type, 3 in. high and 1¼ in. wide. Probably Woodland; pipe bowl top made in image of a turtle in its shell, a common Midwestern Hopewellian motif. From Canada, Lake Huron region. (Condition uncertain.)   C—$300-$600

STONE PIPE, made of banded slate, and an unfinished item. Pipe is 2¼ in. long and is drilled at both bowl and stem ends. Bowl top has a curious set of lines around bowl, which could have been centering guide for drilling, or just decoration, or a symbol representing the four directions.   C—$75-$125

Photo courtesy Robert C. Calvert, London, Ontario, Canada.

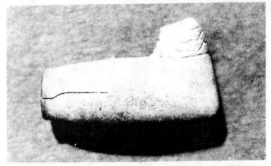

STONE ELBOW PIPE, excavated from a Texas Panhandle Pueblo site near Spearman. It is made from a material that is very fine-grained; a charred smoking substance is still inside the bowl. Bowl top has incised markings; pipe is 2 in. length, and probably dates AD 900—1300.   C—$175

Photo courtesy Wayne Parker, Texas.

CLAY PIPE, 3⅛ in. long and 1¾ in. high, and 1½ in. diagonally across pipe bowl. This is a Canadian piece and may be Neutral or Attawandoron in origin.   C—$95

STONE PIPE, prehistoric, unusual squared and elongated form. Larger end has pipe bowl, with connecting hole for stem in center of bottom side. Smaller end has two drill-holes connecting in "L" configuration. Smaller end is additionally grooved, and there are several deep grooves on topside—which would have been pipe front when in use. Unusual, and tally-notched. Piece is 2½ in. long.   C—$225-$275

Photo courtesy Robert C. Calvert, London, Ontario, Canada.

CLAY PIPE, 3½ in. long and 2¼ in. high and found near Hyde Park, London, Ontario, Canada. A well-shaped and sturdy late-prehistoric or early historic pipe.   C—$125

Photo courtesy Robert Calvert, London, Ontario, Canada.

Hopewell (Middle Woodland) platform type pipe, 1½ in. high and 2⅝ in. long. Material is a dark close-grained stone, possibly steatite. It is from the Scioto River area, Pike County, Ohio.

Museum quality

Larry Garvin collection, Ohio

Pipe, (bean type), a well-shaped pipe made of steatite nicely polished. It is from Stokes County, North Carolina. $800

Rodney M. Peck collection, Harrisburg, North Carolina

Prehistoric pipes.
Left, pottery elbow-type pipe, from Arkansas. $135
Pottery bird-head effigy pipe, Louisiana (shown elsewhere). $100
Small polished stone pipe. $75

Wilfred A. Dick collection, Magnolia, Mississippi

Tubular pipe, probably Adena and Early Woodland, material a tan-colored quartzite. Size, 1¼ x 2⅝ in.; from Hardin County, Ohio, this pipe has fine lines and a high polish. Unusual material for the type, and a plus for the piece. $750-$1000

Private collection, Ohio

Prehistoric pipes.
Left, bird-head pottery pipe, from Louisiana, different view.

Bottom left, Caddo pottery pipe, Arkansas. $100
Right, stone tubular pipe, the earliest type, Mississippi. $150
     $150

Wilfred A. Dick collection, Magnolia, Mississippi

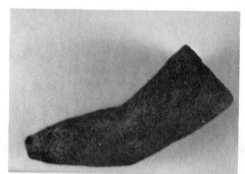

Bent-tube pipe, found in Lancaster County, Pennsylvania. $125

Lee Hallman collection, Telford, Pennsylvania

Prehistoric pipes, various regions.
Top left, alate form (winged), steatite, 8½ in., from North Carolina.$2500
Tube pipe, steatite, 5 in., California $500
Tube pipe, Ohio pipestone, 4 in. $225
Elbow pipe, steatite, 2½ in. long, Virginia $150

Pocotopaug Trading Post, South Windsor, CT

INDIAN-MADE HISTORIC PIPES

Red pipestone pipe, made in the form of a pipe-tomahawk, 19½ in. long. Plains Indian and probably late 1800's.   C—$450

T-shape Catlinite pipe, bowl 3¼ in. high and overall length 22½ in. Round stem with carved and painted design.   G—$510

Catlinite pipe head, Plains Indian, with redstone head 4¼ in. high and 6 in. long. Well-carved and nicely polished. Probably late 1800's.   C—$325

Catlinite pipe, old, with stem of pipestone also.A—$310

Red pipestone pipe, head 7 in. long and with 18½ in. wood stem.   D—$520

Catlinite pipe and stem, early period, both showing great age and use.   G—$410

Pipe, Catlinite, 9 in. long and 4 in. high, a classic speicmen of the Plains Indian style. Carved and polished; Northern Plains region, and mid-1800's.   G—$420

Pipe, with original pipe bag; Sioux, and pre-1900.A—$1000

Tube pipe, historic Chumash Indian, of green steatite.   A—$165

Pipe bowl, 4 in. long, 3½ in. high. Ornately sculpted Catlinite pipe bowl in unusually elaborate design. Surface worn to a fine patina. Northern Plains and mid-1800's.   G—$520

Eskimo pipe, with Siberian influence. Carved from wood, with inlayed pewter decorations.   A—$875

Pipe bowl, 10 in. long and 4 in. high. Catlinite pipe bag, with pierced-design "fin" between end and bowl. Cheyenne, and ca. 1900.   G—$410

Catlinite pipe and stem, with early spiral-carved stem. Top quality piece and in very nice condition.   G—$525

Sioux Catlinite pipe, with head 3 in. high and 8 in. long, with carved snake. The twisted wood stem is 15 in. in length. Piece is ca. 1920.   G—$410

Sioux Catlinite pipe, 3 in. high and 7 in. long. Carved squirrel facing the bowl. Wooden stem is 17 in. long. This piece is ca. 1920.   G—$345

Blackfoot pipe, Reservation-collected in the early 1900's. Bowl is black and carved in Blackfoot design; wooden stem, with old collection. Excellent condition.   G—$550

L-shaped Catlinite pipe, with short wooden stem. Head is 1¼ in. high and wooden stem is 6 in. long. Old label reads. "Kiowa, from Missouri River".   G—$260

Catlinite Sioux pipe, finest workmanship and condition. Pipe bowl and lower portions are inlayed with lead or pewter.   C—$945

Sioux Catlinite pipe, bowl 6 in. long and 3 in. high in the form of an eagle claw with cone. Wooden stem is 17 in. long. Ca. 1920.   G—$460

Sioux Catlinite pipe with quilled stem. Collected prior to 1900 and formerly in a major collection, Oklahoma. An early and fine piece.   G—$800

Sioux Catlinite pipe, bowl 4 in. high and 8 in. long, with solid Catlinite stem 17 in. long. Ca. 1880.   G—$530

Hupa soapstone tube pipe, California, ca. 1890.D—$75

Catlinite pipe, Western Plains Indian, bowl 3 in. high and 5 in. overall, with wood stem an additional 17¾ in. Bowl is cracked at base, but line is barely visible.   D—$520

Suggested Reading

Bierer, Bert W., *Indian Artifacts in the Southeast: A Sketchbook;* privately published, Columbia, South Carolina, 1977.

Hart, Gordon, *Hart's Prehistoric Pipe Rack,* privately published, Indiana, 1978

Catlinite pipe bowl, Hunkpapa Sioux, 4½ x 8½ in. This ex-museum piece has clan markings on the stem and is ca. 1880. $400

Morris' Art & Artifacts, Anaheim, California; Dawn Gober photograph

Great Lakes region pipes, Catlinite and pewter, ca. 1800. Top right, human head and animal head. $3500
Bottom left, human head and animal, fenestrated lower platform. $5000

Private collection; photo by John McLaughlin

PIPE, 31 in. long. Catlinite pipe bowl and wood stem ornamented with brass tacks and wrapped with plaited quilling. Northern Plains area, and pre-1900. Museum Quality
Photo courtesy Kenneth R. Canfield, Plains Indian Art, Kansas City, Missouri.

FRENCH TRADE PIPE, historic, from Ontario, Canada. Piece is 2 in. high and 2 in. long, quite well made and in fine condition.   C—$85

Photo courtesy Robert C. Calvert, London, Ontario, Canada.

Red Catlinite "SQUAW PIPE" with an intricately carved stem and bowl, each a separate piece. Pipe is about 7 in. long, including the spiral-carved stem.   D—$475

Photo courtesy Crazy Crow Trading Post, Denison, Texas.

Historic-era pipe, Plains style with long base and high bowl at one end, black steatite with pewter inlays. This is a large pipe, 3³⁄₁₆ x 7⁵⁄₁₆ in., from Sandusky County, Ohio, where it may have been traded in. This is a very well-made example with solid inlays and high material polish.
                    $1000-$1500

Private collection, Ohio

242

Bear effigy pipe, gray steatite, from southern Tennessee.   Museum quality
Private collection

Catlinite pipe, Ottawa, ca. 1840-60. This "L"-shaped pipe has two engraved bands at the ends of the stem and bowl and three projections at lower front. It is from northern Michigan. (Shown elsewhere).$295

Larry Lantz, First Mesa, South Bend, Indiana

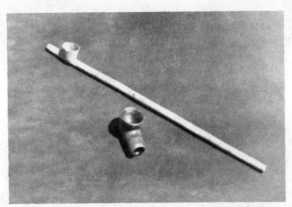

Caddo pipes, Mississippian period. Top, extra-long example at 9 in., with bowl thimble-size; from southwest Arkansas. This is a very fragile piece. $200-$300
Bottom, short-stem pipe, dark color, southwest Arkansas. $65-$100
Private collection

Clay pipe, prehistoric and in repaired condition. This pre-Iroquois smoking instrument is 4½ in. long. $190

Pat & Dave Summers, Native American Artifacts, Victor, NY

Pottery pipes, Mississippian era.
Left three, Mississippi County, Arkansas, fine conditions.$65-$125, each.
Right, pipe from Desha County, Arkansas. $125 plus
Private collection

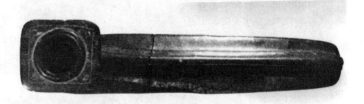

Platform pipe, Hamilton Culture (AD 600-700), from Hamilton County, Tennessee. It is made from dark gray steatite, with a quartz vein. Size, 2 x 10¾ in. This is a museum-quality piece. $10,000-$12,000

Rodney M. Peck collection, Harrisburg, North Carolina

Catlinite pipe bowl and stem, Plains Indian, an exquisite piece. It is 25 in. long and from the late 1800s. $2000

Pat & Dave Summers, Native American Artifacts, Victor, NY

Contemporary curley maple effigy pipe, highly polished, from Traverse City, Michigan. Made in the 1950s, the pipe is 16¼ in. long. $150

Michael F. Slasinski, Saginaw, Michigan

Catlinite (Minnesota red pipestone) pipe with beaded wooden stem, Northern Sioux. The bowl is 4½ x 8 in. and the stem is 20½ in. long. It is ca. 1900 and the stem portion is ex-coll. Casterline. $750

Pat & Dave Summers, Native American Artifacts, Victor, NY

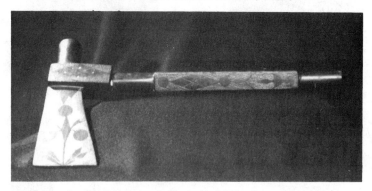

Catlinite pipe-tomahawk pipe, incised with floral and geometric designs. This excellent Sioux piece is 7½ in. high and 13¼ in. long. Ca. 1890-1900. $800

Pat & Dave Summers, Native American Artifacts, Victor, NY

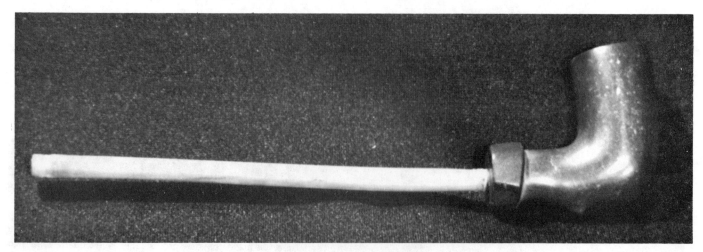

Catlinite pipe bowl with contemporary reed stem, bowl 1⅞ x 2⅛ in. This graceful knobbed and faceted pipe is ca. 1860-1870. $250

Pat & Dave Summers, Native American Artifacts, Victor, NY

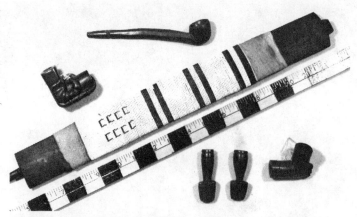

Catlinite pipes, various origins. These are Sioux, Chippewa, Fox and Ottawa, and all are from ca. 1850-1890s. Note the original Sioux beaded ash stem with horse-track designs.

Pipes, each $95-$450
Stem alone $395

Larry Lantz, First Mesa, South Bend, Indiana

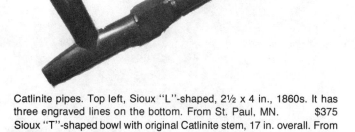

Catlinite pipes. Top left, Sioux ''L''-shaped, 2½ x 4 in., 1860s. It has three engraved lines on the bottom. From St. Paul, MN. $375
Sioux ''T''-shaped bowl with original Catlinite stem, 17 in. overall. From South Dakota, scarce. $895-$995

Larry Lantz, First Mesa, South Bend, Indiana

Catlinite pipe, Sioux, classic form from Dane County, Wisconsin. This fine, large pipe is late 1800s. $650

Larry Lantz, First Mesa, South Bend, Indiana

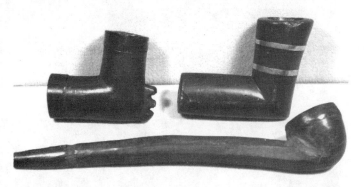

Catlinite pipes. Top left, Ottawa ''L''-shaped, 2 x 2½ in., 1840-1860. Note engraved rings on stem and bowl; from Michigan. $295
Top right, Sioux ''L''-shaped, with lead or pewter inlaid lines on bowl, 1850-60, North Dakota. $285
Bottom, shown elsewhere in book, Chippewa Voyager-type pipe, 6½ in. long, solid Catlinite, with seven engraved lines on bowl. $185

Larry Lantz, First Mesa, South Bend, Indiana

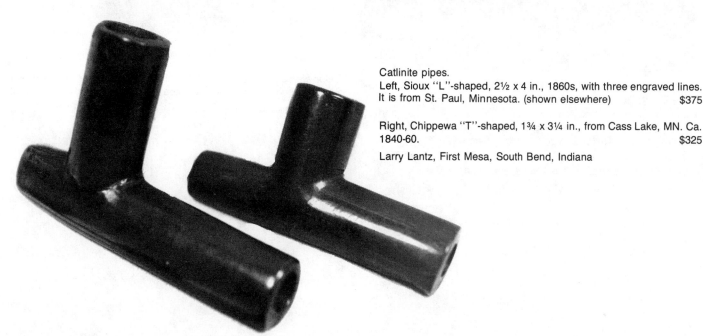

Catlinite pipes.
Left, Sioux ''L''-shaped, 2½ x 4 in., 1860s, with three engraved lines. It is from St. Paul, Minnesota. (shown elsewhere) $375

Right, Chippewa ''T''-shaped, 1¾ x 3¼ in., from Cass Lake, MN. Ca. 1840-60. $325

Larry Lantz, First Mesa, South Bend, Indiana

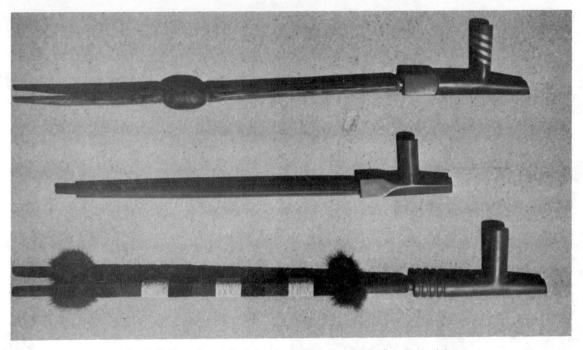

Plains Indian (Sioux) Catlinite pipes with wooden handles, both plain and decorated with fur and beads. Lengths, 22½ to 30 in. long. They are in perfect condition. $500-$1200 each

Marguerite L. Kernaghan collection; photograph by Marguerite L. and Stewart W. Kernaghan, Bellvue, Colorado

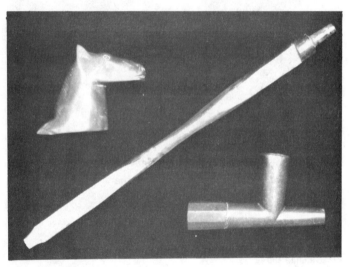

Catlinite artifacts.
Top left, Sioux, horsehead, 2¾ x 3½ in., 1890s, probably an unfinished pipe. It is from North Dakota. $165
Center and right, 12 in. original ash stem, carved so that flat surfaces occur on all four sides; also, ''T''-shaped pipe, 1½ x 4½ in.
Pipe and stem $765

Larry Lantz, First Mesa, South Bend, Indiana

Cup-type pipe bowl, mottled reddish granite, from northern Alabama. Hollow reed stems were often used with bowls like this. $150

Private collection

Paiute Indians, on the Kaibab Plateau, near the Grand Canyon of the Colorado, in northern Arizona. Photo by John K. Hillers, Powell Expedition, 1871-1875. The Indians here are playing the game of "Ni-aung-pi-kai", or "Kill the Bone".

Photo courtesy Utah State Historical Society, Collection of Smithsonian Institution.

CHAPTER XIV

CLOTHING, MOCCASINS AND LEATHERWORK

As with all natural and renderd materials to be worked, historic and recent Amerinds excelled in clothing and footwear. The leather was well-tanned and supple. Any decorations — beads, quills, paint — was put on with innate taste and practiced skill.

The sums being paid for such items, as evidenced by this chapter, are one indication of the esteem in which such work is now held. Faked pieces have thus far not been much of a problem, due to the complexity of matching both materials and artistic designs. Stone, in some cases, is easier to market than leather.

Articles most in demand appear to be complete and decorated dresses, skirts, vests and leggings, hopefully with documentation, usually without. If old and good, these are museum-quality items. Designs should be pleasing, the leather whole, and almost all beads and quills in place. Paint should still be somewhat bold, designs still visible. Leather fringes should be mostly intact and the item itself of some size.

For moccasins, Eastern examples tend to be soft-soled and floral-decorated. Moccasins can show some wear, but should not be holed on the bottoms or ripped badly.

Sides and top should be in good condition, with most bead and quill designs intact. Generally, the more beads or quills the greater the value, whether the piece is historic or recent. And note that items collected before about 1950 tend to be premium-priced.

WOMEN'S CLOTHING

Small girl's dress, 15 in. wide and 20 in. long, in Plains Indian design. Base is blue cloth with leather fringe and cowrie shell design; excellent condition and dresses this small are unusual. A pre-1900 piece.   G—$455

Buckskin dress, medium-size, Plains Indian, fawn color and fringed. Some bead decorations.   D—$795

Woman's dress, made of satin in bright purple color and with hundreds of metal dangles hanging from dress. Excellent condition and a Plateau piece. Ca. 1940's. G—$300

Woman's dress, for tall person, shoulder sections well-beaded, and overall made of doeskin. Superb condition and probably late 1880's; beading excellent, all fringes present. Typical Plains Indian beadwork designs in red, white and blue.   D—$2500

Woman's dress, single unit, dark brown and 41 in. long. Beadwork strips, in good condition.   D—$800

Woman's dress, small size and Nez Perce. On green cloth, yoke is nicely beaded with blue, black and red beads. Many cowrie shell decorations. Excellent condition, and probably from the 1920's.   G—$700

Woman's dress, Navajo, skirt and blouse, red and blue designs in weave; combined length of pair 53 in. long. Worn but good condition.   D—$675

Leather vest, woman's size, geometric beadwork designs, some damage to back but beadwork in good condition.   C—$395

Woman's vest, light-colored thin leather, beads and quillwork, old but in good condition.   A—$400

Woman's leggings, 7 in. by 12 in., fully beaded with yellow, red, green and purple beads. Very decorative set; Plateau origin and ca. 1930's.   G—$335

Woman's leggings, Plains Indian, good beadwork in good condition.   D—$525

Woman's leggings, Sioux, beautiful designs and colors. Sinew-sewn on buckskin and in excellent condition. Tag included suggests they belonged to the wife of a famous Lower Brule Sioux chief.   G—$1100

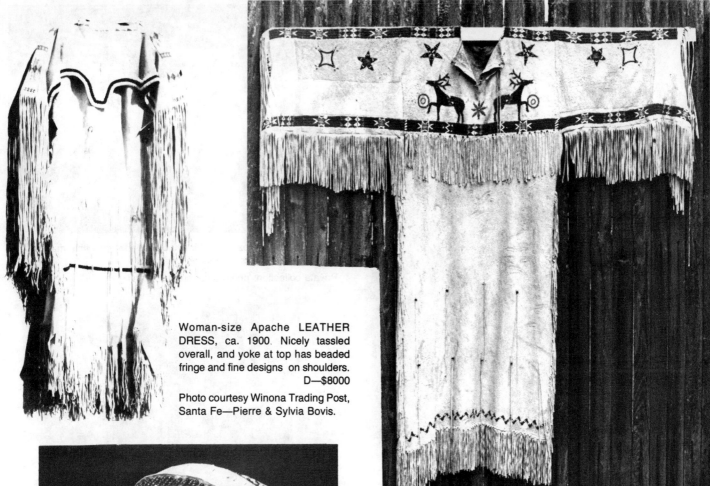

Woman-size Apache LEATHER DRESS, ca. 1900. Nicely tassled overall, and yoke at top has beaded fringe and fine designs on shoulders. D—$8000

Photo courtesy Winona Trading Post, Santa Fe—Pierre & Sylvia Bovis.

Dress, Sioux, Elk Dreamers Society, early 20th century. It is 52½ in. across and 55 in. long including fringes. A fine and well-made dress. $3500

Crown & Eagle Antiques, Inc., New Hope, PA

Wedding headdress, Umatilla, pony beads, hide, dentallium shells and Chinese coins, ca. 1880. Generally, these sell for $1000-$4000. $1500

Private collection; photo by John McLaughlin

MEN'S CLOTHING

Man's outfit, quilled, and Blackfoot. Set includes a war shirt, pair of gauntlets, rifle case and knife sheath. Quills are red, yellow, green, purple and natural, woven on hide. Outstanding and like-new condition. Ca. 1910-20.G—$5500

Woodlands jacket, 26 in. long, of leather; piece has beaded cuffs, front, and design on back. Fringes along underside of sleeves, and probably ca. 1930's. A—$625

"War shirt", probably Sioux, beaded front and back, but poor to fair condition overall. Piece was badly stored for a number of years and sections of beadwork are lost. About 75% of beadwork remains. Back design better than front. C—$500

Boy's jacket, Crow, floral beadwork and outlined. Jacket is lined, and made of buckskin with very fine beadwork. Good condition and ca. 1880. G—$750

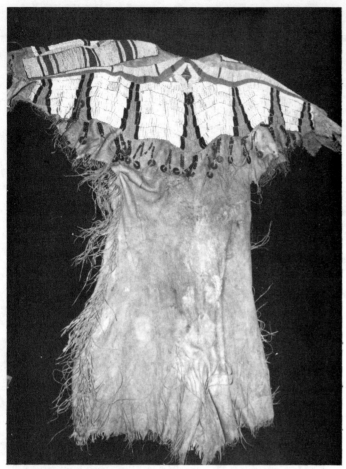

Woman's dress, Nez Perce, hide with pony beads, trade beads and Chinese coins. With finely beaded shoulder panels this is a very fine piece and ca. 1860. $9000

Private collection; photo by John McLaughlin

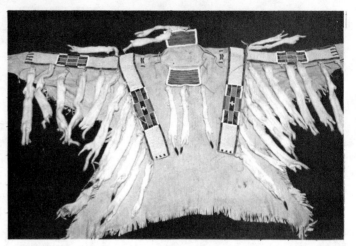

Ceremonial shirt, Nez Perce, hide and beaded strips with ermine drops. This superb piece is ca. 1900. $15,000

Private collection; photo by John McLaughlin

Vest, Sioux, men's size 38/40, ca. 1880-1890. Sinew-sewn and beaded on Indian leather and lined with cloth. Designs are American flags front and back, and bead colors are white background with blue, green, metallic gold and red white-hearts. Purchased by the original collector in South Dakota in 1920, it is ex-coll. Luongo. A superb period piece. $4500

Sherman Holbert Collection, Fort Mille Lacs, Onamia, Minnesota

Woodland vest, ca. 1900, excellent example on heavy late 1800s type wool vest. Beadwork is in many colors, near-mint condition. Vest 21¼ x 25½ in. $750

Sherman Holbert Collection, Fort Mille Lacs, Onamia, Minnesota

Leather vest, sleeveless, 18¼ in. from top to bottom. Beaded in floral designs at bottom and middle of front flaps. Piece was collected in northeastern Pennsylvania and is ca. 1920's.
D—$695

Man's vest done on commerical leather and lined in old cloth. Arrows and circles beaded front and back, in orange, yellow and bright blue colors. Medium-size, and ca. 1920-30's.
G—$300

Leggings, beaded on old blanket material. Beaded panels at bottom and measuring 7 in. by 12 in. Old blanket shows ribbon work on edges and slight moth damage; beadwork nearly perfect. Crow Indian, and ca. 1885. G—$1150

Man's leggings and vest, matched outfit, Plains Indian style. Well beaded the both, and ca. late 1880's. D—$1500

Leggings, 24 in. long, 7 in. wide, with short fringes on outer sides. Cheyenne. A—$400

Leggings, Ponca or Oto Indian. They are black trade cloth with tan cloth trim on bottom. All trim is outlined in light blue beads with many white stars beaded on cloth. Beautiful fine yellow fringe on edge of leggings. Ca. 1910.
G—$725

Men's beaded vest, Flathead, five colors against a white ground. In superb condition, this piece is ca. 1890. $975

Freya's Collectibles, Banff, Alberta, Canada

Vest, Chippewa, ca. 1890-1910. It is mens' size 34 and black velvet lined with cotton; nine buttons are abalone with metal back. Beading depicts flowers, leaves and vines, and in colors of old rose, gold, blue, pink, crystal, several of green, several shades of yellow. Very good condition, and an artistic vest. $1500

Sherman Holbert Collection, Fort Mille Lacs, Onamia, MN

Vest, Santee Sioux, mens' size 36/38, ca. 1870-1890. Buffalo hide was used for the front, tapestry style cloth for back. Front has beaded designs of birds and flowers, with beads in red, three shades of blue, amber, yellow, white, black, green, mauve and orange. Both sinew and thread were used for sewing, all hand-stitched. $1475

Sherman Holbert Collection, Fort Mille Lacs, Onamia, Minnesota

Pictorial vest, Sioux, figures on white beading, top condition. This rare vest is ca. 1890. $7500

Crown & Eagle Antiques, Inc., New Hope, PA

MAN-SIZE SIOUX LEGGINGS, ca. 1880, and with fine beadwork designs. D—$1300

Photo courtesy Winona Trading Post, Santa Fe—Pierre & Sylvia Bovis

GAUNTLETS

Moose hide gauntlets, Nez Perce Indian, 7 in. long. Decorated with cut-glass beads and with beaded floral-design panels on backs. Large, excellent condition and ca. 1930's. G—$375

Gauntlets, pair, woman's size. Partially beaded on cuffs, of Indian-tanned leather and cloth-lined. G—$165

Gauntlets, pair, 17 in. overall length with 6 in. fringe. Blackfoot, early, and man-size. Stylized floral designs beaded on cuffs; fingers have deteriorated and pair should be set behind glass to preserve the pieces. G—$250

Gauntlets, pair, Indian-tanned leather. Simple horseshoe designs beaded on cuff. Medium-size, in excellent condition. G—$175

Gauntlets, large and beautiful pair from Northern Plains region. Pair lined with fur; trade cloth, ca. 1870. D—$275

Gauntlets or gloves, Plateau, ca. 1920-1930, pair, 16 in. long. Made from Indian-tanned leather, floral beading on cuff fronts only. Bead colors are green, ruby, white, blue, yellow, metallic gray and metallic blue. Beading is in perfect condition. $350

Sherman Holbert Collection, Fort Mille Lacs, Onamia, MN

RELATED INDIAN APPAREL

Man's belt, of thick black commercial leather. Plains Indian, 35 in. long, with geometric designs in beadwork. Collected in Montana and in excellent condition. Possibly ca. 1900. C—$350

Two Sioux **arm bands,** both different, sold as one lot. A—$75

Very rare **wolf skin medicine cap,** and piece was in a University collection. Hair mostly present but some deterioration from age. An original Blackfoot item, ca. 1800. G—$325

252

Hair roach, done with porcupine guard hairs and red-dyed horsehair. Piece has a yarn and leather base; old and symmetrical.   G—$285

Man's belt, 42 in. long and 2½ in. wide. Beadwork on one side, geometric designs, fair condition and Blackfoot in origin.   D—$275

Nez Perce **dance apron.**   A—$50

Rectangular cape, red and blue cloth, 36 in. long and 19 in. wide. Piece has two loom-beaded strips 1¼ in. wide and 10 in. long. Attached are hawk bells, small mirrors and brass cone jingles. Very unusual item.   G—$215

Sioux **cuffs,** fair condition and workstyle.   D—$240

Dew claw medicine piece, made from the hide of a deer leg. Museum quality, decorated with mirrors and brass tacks. Sioux, and very early.   G—$500

Man's hair drop, beaded, Plains Indian style. D—$285

Woman's **beaded collar,** worn around neck and across shoulders. Shell beads cover the outside; done in several designs in glass beads. Fringed.   D—$285

Woodlands **apron,** design on velvet backing; tree and flowering plants done in beadwork.   C—$450

Headband, beaded Plains Indian type, 1⅛ in. wide and in good condition.   D—$195

Penobscot **fur hat,** ca. 1900.   D—$45

Infant's cap, northern Plains region, possibly antelope hide; completely covered on outside with tiny seed beads. Piece is 4½ in. in diameter, in good condition; an unusual item.   D—$600

Dance apron, Ponca-Oto, intricate seed bead design on black velveteen. Size, 15 x 16 in.; this is rare Prairie beadwork, ca. 1885. $425
Larry Lantz, First Mesa, South Bend, Indiana

Sash, Winnebago, 5½ x 96 in. This finger-woven sash is carefully and coarsely woven of colorful commercial yarns in light and dark blues and red. A near-perfect example of old multi-strand braid weaving, this fine piece is ca. 1950. $165
Sherman Holbert Collection, Fort Mille Lacs, Onamia, Minnesota

Sioux man's BEADED LEGGING STRIPS, 29 in. long and 3 in. wide, and all excellent condition. Ca. 1880.   D—$900
Photo courtesy Winona Trading Post, Santa Fe—Pierre & Sylvia Bovis.

Right:
Smoking cap, probably Seneca or Onodaga, New York state. Ca. 1870 or before, it is 4¼ x 11¾ in. It is beaded in a pattern of a green vine with fruits or flowers in many colors. The saw-tooth beaded border is in blue trimmed with white. Ex-coll. Fruchtel. $525
Sherman Holbert Collection, Fort Mille Lacs, Onamia, MN

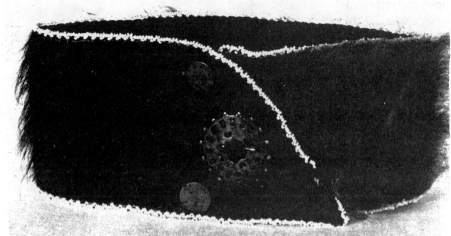

Turban, Osage, bear-belly fur edged with trade beads and lined with fabric and embellished with silver decoration. It is 4 in. high and late 1800s.
Museum quality

James Reid, LTD, Santa Fe, New Mexico

Shirt, Ute, Intermontane, 19th century. It is hide, stroud, German silver buckles, silk ribbons and paint. This rare item is quite attractive.$4000

Private collection; photo by John McLaughlin

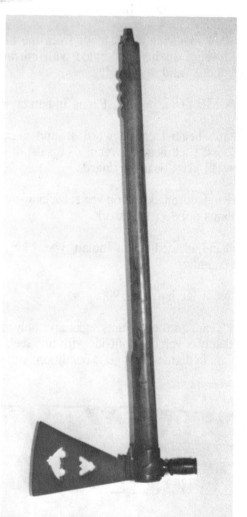

Glengarry cap, Iroquois, Great Lakes beadwork in floral motif, many bead colors. This fine piece is ca. 1870-1880. $350

Pocotopaug Trading Post, South Windsor, CT

Pipe-tomahawk, Plains Indian with a large steel head with blade pierced with bat and fly design cut-outs. The plain wood haft has four raised projections near the mouth-piece. This high-grade piece was collected by Arnold Marcus Chernoff. It is ca. 1860s-1870s.
Museum quality

Dave Hrachovy, Cedar Glen, California

MOCCASINS-Adult Size

Cree moccasins, 8 in. long, with quillwork on hide. Simple floral design and in excellent condition; ca. 1900.G—$210

Quilled and beaded **Sioux moccasins,** man's size.D—$395

Plains Indian beaded **moccasins,** beaded tops, rawhide bottoms. Very old and in good condition.   A—$450

Sioux **"ceremonial moccasins",** entirely beaded in geometric designs including soles. Adult sizes, good condition, almost all beadwork intact.   C—$700

Fully beaded **Sioux moccasins,** good early designs, and sinew-sewn on buckskin with rawhide soles.   C—$310

Cheyenne moccasins, very nicely beaded.   D—$350

Taos Pueblo moccasins, beadwork on toes, originally painted in yellow ochre.   D—$340

Arapaho moccasins, fully beaded, and 10½ in. long. Extremely fine condition with beaded cuffs; have "trail dusters" and red cloth bindings, sinew-sewn and beaded. Ca. 1910.   G—$460

Quilled **moccasins,** fine early designs, very old.A—$500

Deerskin **moccasins,** Woodlands Indian, upper parts covered with fine beadwork. Overall reddish leather, and ca. late 1880's.   D—$400

Blackfoot moccasins, man-size, partially beaded in blue, lavender and amber beads, classic style for this group. Collected on the Blackfoot reservation in the 1930's G—$450

Sioux beaded moccasins, good design.   A—$295

Sioux moccasins, man-size, light blue background with green and yellow designs. Excellent condition, and ca. 1910.   G—$415

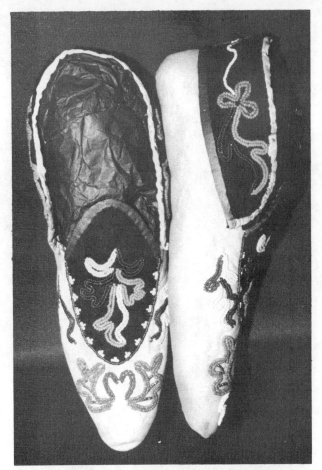

Men's moccasins, Tlingit, very nicely beaded in multiple colors, ca. 1880.
Freya's Collectibles, Banff, Alberta, Canada $1200

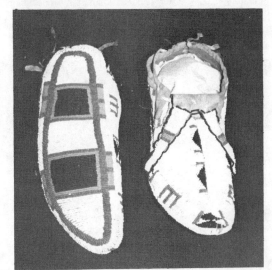

Ceremonial moccasins, Blackfoot, fully beaded in blue, yellow and red against a white background. Ca. 1880. $2000

Freya's Collectibles, Banff, Alberta, Canada

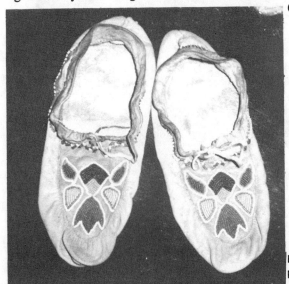

Beaded moccasins, light brown brain-tanned leather, Chippewa. This pair is from Michigan, year 1870. $350

Michael F. Slasinski, Saginaw, Michigan

255

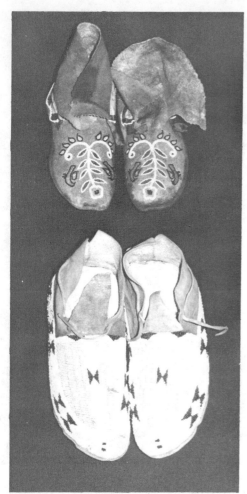

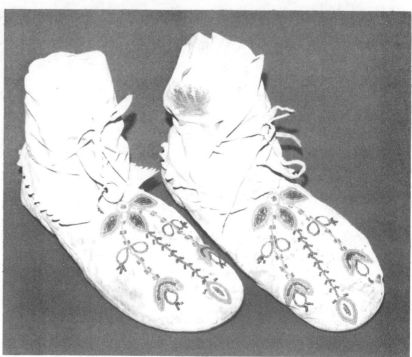

Early Metis men's moccasins with soft soles, delicate beadwork design, year 1865. $600

Freya's Collectibles, Banff, Alberta, Canada

Plains Indian moccasins, pairs. Top, Blackfoot men's moccasins, 1865. $650

Bottom, Arapahoe men's moccasins, 1880. $850

Freya's Collectibles, Banff, Alberta, Canada

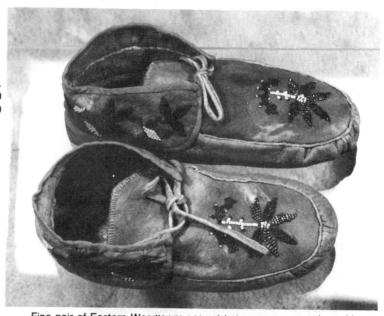

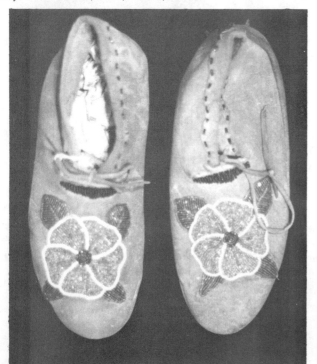

Fine pair of Eastern Woodlands / Great Lakes area moccasins, with beaded tops and ankle-flaps. Condition is very good for age.

Collection of David G. & Barbara J. Shirley $275-375

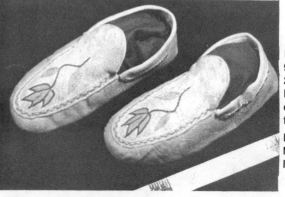

Moccasins, Cree, 9½ in. long, early 20th century. Decoration is thread embroidered in florals. $165

Larry Lantz, First Mesa, South Bend, Indiana

Moccasins, Athabascan, 11 in. long, early 1900s. They are seed-beaded in floral designs on smoked moosehide. $295

Larry Lantz, First Mesa, South Bend, Indiana

256

Moccasins, Mille Lacs Reservation Chippewa, 10 in. long. This contemporary pair is made of Indian smoke-tanned leather and beadwork is translucent green and gold and solid red and brown.

$145

Sherman Holbert Collection, Fort Mille Lacs, Onamia, MN

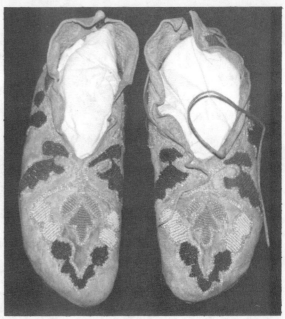

Moccasins, Osage, adult size, leather with beadwork in floral design and seven colors. Ca. 1920. $500

Private collection; photo by John McLaughlin

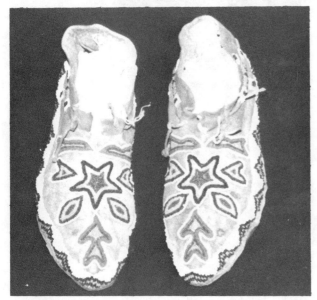

Moccasins, Ute, mens size, hide with beading in six colors. Ca. 1870.
$1500

Private collection; photo by John McLaughlin

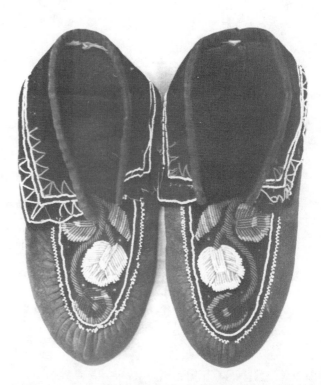

Moccasins, Iroquois, floral beading done in six basic colors against black, including two shades each of white, yellow, blue and reddish. Ca. 1860-1870. Very nice pair. $400

Pocotopaug Trading Post, South Windsor, CT

Moccasins, various groups and periods.
Top left, Canadian Chippewa, ca. 1920s-1930s, 11½ in. long, moosehide. $225
Top right, Shoshone, ca. 1940-1950, Indian-tanned leather, seven colors of beads in cascade pattern. $245
Bottom left, Hudson Bay Eskimo, ca. 1950, child's size in sealskin and rabbit, fine condition, attractive. $95
Bottom center, Dogrib-Canada, ca. 1930s, brain-tanned moosehide, floral beading. $95
Bottom right, Cree Indian, ca. 1920-1940, Indian-tanned moosehide, beading in two sizes and many colors, 11 in. long.
                                                                    $225

Sherman Holbert Collection, Fort Mille Lacs, Onamia, MN

MOCCASINS-Child's Size

Baby moccasins, 5 in. overall length and 2 in. wide. Toes partially beaded; Indian-tanned leather.   C—$95

Plains Indian baby moccasins, single specimen, 4¼ in. long. Top area beaded, bottom worn through; very nice beadwork design and that section in good condition.C—$30-45

Blackfoot baby moccasins, beaded pair.   A—$115

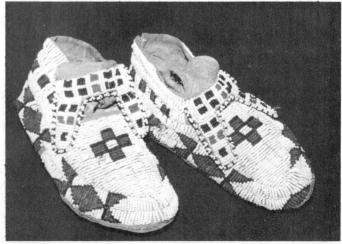

Assiniboin boys' moccasins with beaded tongues, beads red, blue and green against a white ground. These are year 1890. $600

Freya's Collectibles, Banff, Alberta, Canada

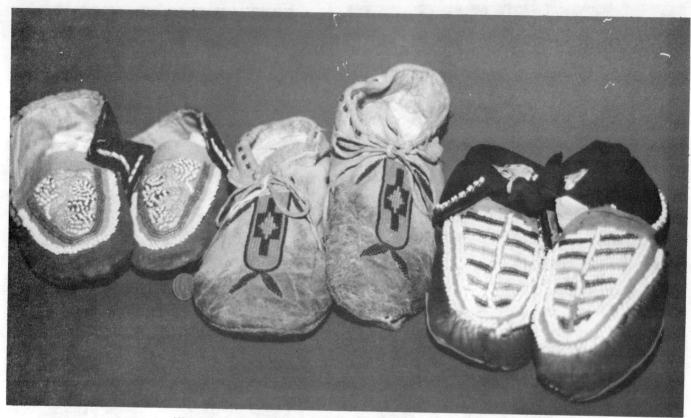

Woodlands moccasins. Left, Iroquois, beaded, 9½ in., ca. 1900.$250
Center, very nice Cree beaded leather, Manitoba, Canada, ca. 1920.$225
Right, colorful beaded leather, Quebec, Canada, 8 in. long, ca. 1890.
$200

Pat & Dave Summers, Native American Artifacts, Victor, NY

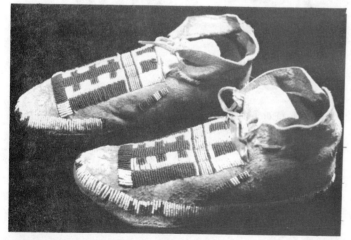

Moccasins, man's Southern Arapaho, 10 in. long, lazy stitch sewing with seed beads, late 1800s. An exceptional pair. $1100

Larry Lantz, First Mesa, South Bend, Indiana

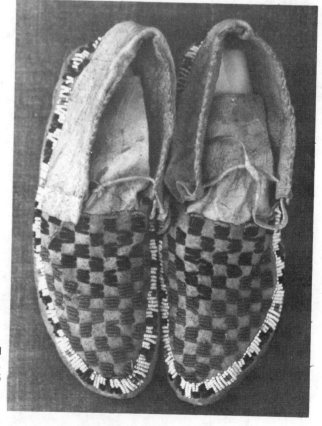

Moccasins, Cheyenne, beadwork done in checkerboard pattern of red and green with red, white, black and green around edges. Ca. 1870s.
$425

Pocotopaug Trading Post, South Windsor, CT

259

Moccasins, high-top, Sioux, 9½ in. long. Beaded panels are in several colors against white; late 1800s. $595

Larry Lantz, First Mesa, South Bend, Indiana

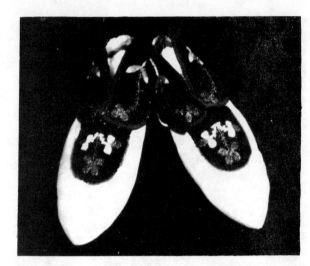

Huron MOCCASINS, 9½ in. long. Smoked buckskin with black cloth flaps and toe panels, beaded floral designs. Like-new condition, and ca. 1890. D—$375

Photo courtesy Crazy Crow Trading Post, Denison, TX

Oglalla Sioux WOMEN'S BOOTS, sinew sewn and fully beaded front and sides. The high tops make this pair a distinctive collector item; ca. 1920-25. D—$850

Photo courtesy Crazy Crow Trading Post, Denison, TX

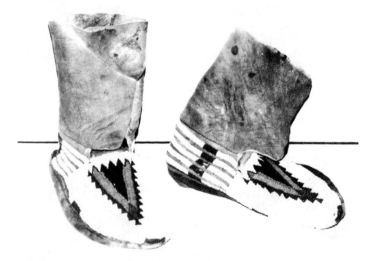

Pair of Nez Perce BEADED MAN'S MOCCASINS, ca. 1880, excellent condition and with fine beadwork overall. D—$900

Photo courtesy Winona Trading Post, Santa Fe—Pierre & Sylvia Bovis

CHILD'S MOCCASINS, 6½ in. long. Orange quillwork bands and an outline strip of pale blue beadwork. Northern Plains area, ca. 1880. G—$550

Photo courtesy Kenneth R. Canfield, Plains Indian Art, Kansas City, MO

RELATED INDIAN FOOTGEAR

Apache boots, pair, 27½ in. long. They have beaded crosses on the toes with small beaded band on tops.   G—$375

Three Plains Indian **beaded moccasins,** left foot only, and in man, woman and child sizes. Possibly, and for reasons unknown, three pairs were divided and marketed. Early 1900's fine beadwork, and excellent condition. All evidence similar handwork and may have been made by same person.   C—$375

Pair of **Cheyenne moccasins,** beaded.   A—$145

Southern Cheyenne or Kiowa boots, 15 in. high. Decorated with seed beads in strips, on yellow ochred hide. Excellent condition and ca. 1870-80.   G—$1200

Pair of **Cree beaded moccasins.**   A—$75

Pair of Tlingit **moccasin tops.**   A—$65

Moccasins, Eskimo or sub-Arctic, sealskin with rabbit trim, near-original condition, ca. 1940s. $150-$200
Pocotopaug Trading Post, South Windsor, CT

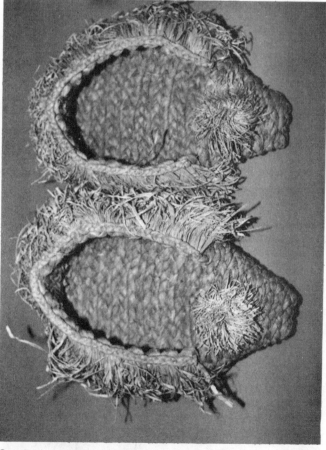

Corn-husk moccasins, yellow-tan in color, year 1952. They are Iroquois, from New York state. $150
Michael F. Slasinski, Saginaw, Michigan

Sandal, Basketmaker II period, from near Pruitt, New Mexico. Such very perishable items from prehistoric times are rare. $100-$150
Marguerite L. Kernaghan collection; photograph by Marguerite L. and Stewart W. Kernaghan, Bellvue, Colorado

261

LEATHERWORK COLLECTIBLES

Plains Indian saddle bags, matched pair, made of rawhide and fringed. C—$2200

Small **parfleche envelope,** 5 in. by 9 in. in standard design and excellent condition. Marked "Pendleton, Oregon" and dated 1930. G—$145

Leather **carrying bag,** Plains Indian and early. D—$495

Southern Plains pipe bag, 27 in. long, nicely glass-beaded, leather fringes, late 1880's. D—$675

Apache **carrying pouch** of shaped hide, 7 in. long. D—$160

Plains Indian lariat or lasso, with eye or slip-loop at one end, knotted at other. Still coiled and rawhide is hard. Estimated length is 23 feet. Very slight mouse-nibble damage, barely noticeable. Lariat averages ⅜ in. in diameter. Private collector values the piece at $15 per foot. Braided. C—$350

Matching pair of painted parfleche envelopes, 12 in. high and 26 in. long. Very nice designs painted; in excellent condition. Pairs are hard to obtain; good art pieces and very collectible. G—$800

Carrying bag, partially decorated front and back in geometric beadwork, late 1800's. Bag is 3 in. by 13 in. by 15 in., worn but good condition. Leather. D—$295

Strike-a-light bag, 5 in. by 3½ in. wide, northern Plains region. Leather with beadwork designs on one side. C—$280

Hair roach of deerhide and porcupine quills, very well preserved and an attractive piece. Ca. early 1900's. D—$150

Parfleche box, 6 in. by 9 in. by 14 in. All painted designs, early reservation period, nice condition. G—$345

Set of Plains Indian **leather dance bell straps,** which attached to outer sides of legs. Early 1900's, good bells. D—$135

Parfleche envelope, 8 in. by 7 in., with flexible leather wrap that closed front. Faint painted design. Plains Indian. A—$225

Dew claw necklace as used by the Sioux and many other tribes. All carved dew claws with trade beads, and pre-1900. G—$395

Chippewa shoulder bag, 12 in. by 15 in. and with 2½ in. wide carrying strap. Floral designs done in red, green and white beads, and bag with beaded tassels. G—$1350

Awl case, leather with beadwork, some beads missing. Piece is 9 in. long. D—$120

Miniature pipe bag, probably late 1800's. Deerskin, beaded designs on side, nicely fringed, and 10½ in. long. D—$220

Parfleche knife sheath with painted designs and tacks. Sioux, and old. G—$210

Dew claw bag, made from the leg skin of an elk. Old piece and in very good condition. G—$395

Flint and steel or **strike-a-light bag,** possibly Apache, with small hawk bells. Size, 3½ in. by 6½ in. and likely late 1800's. C—$365

SADDLEBAGS, 10 in. wide and unfolded length 62 in. Set of classic Apache saddlebags with rawhide cutouts over red tradecloth. This set is ca. 1890. G—$1800

Photo courtesy Kenneth R. Canfield, Plains Indian Art, Kansas City, Missouri.

Bow and quiver case with bow, Cheyenne, beaded and quilled. This top-grade piece is ca. 1875. $6500

Crown & Eagle Antiques, Inc., New Hope, Pennsylvania

Ermine (winter weasel) ceremonial bundle, Blackfoot, late 1800s. It has red and dark blue ribbons and brass tack eyes. Length, 14½ in.
Museum quality

Michael F. Slasinski, Saginaw, Michigan

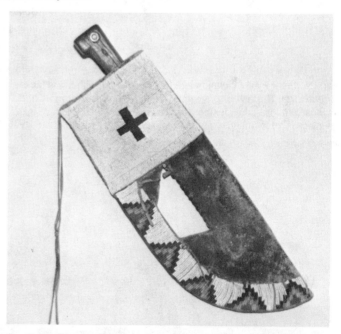

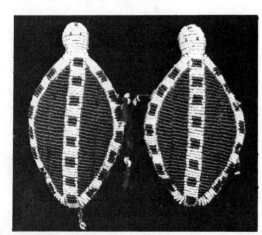

Amulets, turtle effigy, Sioux. This matching pair has green, red, blue and white beading. Ca. 1800s. Museum quality

Morning Star Gallery, Santa Fe, NM

Beaded knife case, Blackfoot, from the late 1800s. It has Indian-tanned leather with belt cut-out, and the blade is made from an old file with a wood handle. Length is 14½ in. for this 1870s-1880s piece.
$4000-$5000

Dave Hrachovy, Cedar Glen, California

Sioux arrow, point, shaft and fletching complete, 1870s. $125
Lee Hallman collection, Telford, Pennsylvania

Cheyenne - Pawnee arrow, just over 2 ft. long, ca. 1860s-1870s.$150
Lee Hallman collection, Telford, Pennsylvania

Gros Ventre Sioux arrow, metal tip, ca. 1860s-1870s $150
Lee Hallman collection, Telford, Pennsylvania

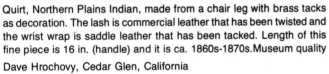

Southwestern U.S. arrow, painted in fletching area, ca. 1880s. $125
Lee Hallman collection, Telford, Pennsylvania

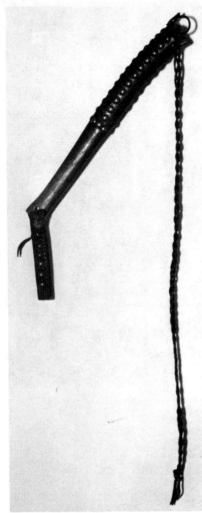

Quirt, Northern Plains Indian, made from a chair leg with brass tacks as decoration. The lash is commercial leather that has been twisted and the wrist wrap is saddle leather that has been tacked. Length of this fine piece is 16 in. (handle) and it is ca. 1860s-1870s.Museum quality

Dave Hrochovy, Cedar Glen, California

Sioux war club, stone head and wrapped handle, ca. 1880s. $250
Lee Hallman collection, Telford, Pennsylvania

Warclub, stone head with decorations and wrapped wooden handle. This piece is from the 1800s, and an excellent example of a Plains Indian weapon. $350-$550

Private collection

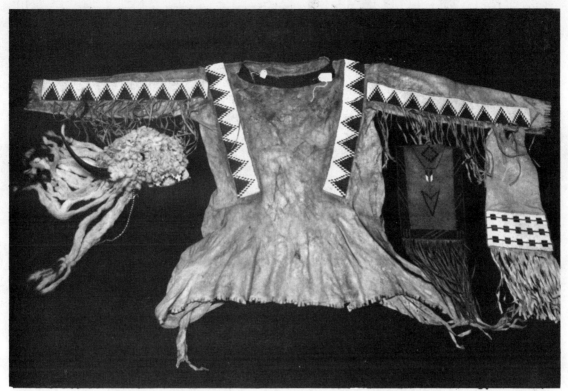

Blackfoot material. Left, horned headdress, trade cloth, ermine, buffalo
horns and beads, ca. 1890. $3000
Center, ceremonial shirt, hide, beads, trade cloth and ochre paint, ca.
1880. $7500
Right, mirror bag (rectangular), hide and beads, ca. 1890. $1200
Far right, pipe bag, hide and beaded both sides, ca. 1880. $2000

Private collection; photo by John McLaughlin

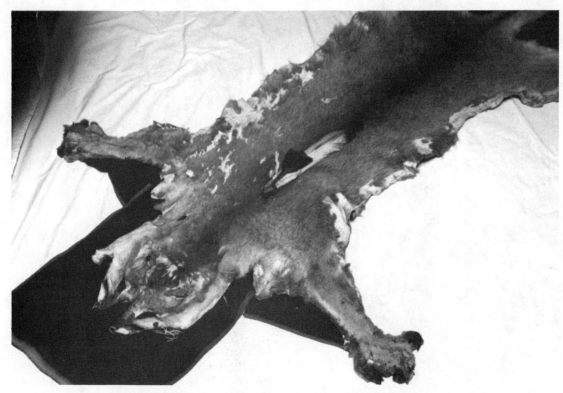

Saddle blanket, Crow, made of mountain lion pelt, cloth and feathers.
This unusual and rare item is ca. 1870. $5000

Private collection; photo by John McLaughlin

Child's fringed jacket, extensive beadwork, Crow Indian. This very high-quality piece is ca. 1870. $6500

Freya's Collectibles, Banff, Alberta, Canada

Coat, Santee Sioux, mens' size 40/42. It is made from buffalo calf hide, and decorated with blue, red, white and yellow beads depicting flowers, vines, leaves, stars and horses. Rawhide ties instead of buttons and fringed sleeves and shoulders, the piece is ca. 1880. A fine old Plains item. $4950

Sherman Holbert Collection, Fort Mille Lacs, Onamia, Minnesota

Small Eastern Woodlands / Great Lakes fringed bag with drawstring top and quillwork on side. Quills are dyed red, orange and white. $250-$325

Collection of David G. & Barbara J. Shirley

Shield-cover, Cheyenne, painted hide with feather, ca. 1860. $3000

Private collection, photo by John McLaughlin

266

The listings that follow have been selected because they are highly unusual or significantly different to warrant presentation. All were selected from Kenneth R. Canfield's Plains Indian Art Catalogues Nos. 1 and 2.

Following is an excerpt from Catalogue No. 1, written by Mr. Canfield. It allows a fleeting glimpse of artistic inspiration in the Plains Indian past. Used with permission.

"The American Great Plains is an awesome sweep of land and sky bounded by mountains and long sinuous rivers. The Northern Plains were dominated by the tribes of the Teton (or western) Sioux, who called themselves collectively the Dakota, and to a lesser degree by the Blackfeet, Crow, Gros Ventre, Assiniboin and Plains Cree. In the south were Kiowa and Comanche. Cheyenne, Arapaho and Pawnee ranged along the western margins of the grasslands. On the east lived Osage, Iowa, Oto, Mesquakie and Mandan.

"They differed widely by tribe — linguistically and ethnically — but they had much in common socially and culturally. The Northern Cheyenne and Sioux lived in such proximity that their artistic production overlaps.

"The plains tribes shared a way of life imposed upon them by the vast, harsh world in which they lived, a landscape of dazzling color and light, of violent contrast and great distance. Theirs was an environment of blinding white snow, of depths of blue sky, of the carmine red of lifeblood, of the endless green seas of grass on ochre plains.

"Death was always at hand, but they lived serenely at one with the universe. It seems hardly surprising that a sense of vivid intensity and wonder and magic should communicate itself to the view through the still living art of the Plains Indians."

NOTE: Values listed are ca.1975. Current values would be 2 to 6 times as high.

PLAINS INDIAN ART (Courtesy Kenneth R. Canfield)

Whetstone case, 5 in. long. Hide container ornamented with blue and white beadwork front and back. Sioux, from South Dakota, and pre-1890. G—$35

Man's warshirt, 38 in. long. Painted buckskin with beaded strips on shoulders and sleeves and beaded rosettes front and back. Ten winter-pelt weasel skins attached. Beaded geometric designs in orange, black and pale blue on a white background. Collected in Canada; Blackfeet (Piegan), from Alberta. Piece is ca. 1910. G—$2600

Carved wooden flute, 21½ in. long. Cedar flute incised in a spiral pattern. Lead soundplate surmounted by a wooden sound block carved in the shape of a horse and stained with red ochre. Paper tag affixed to sound block. Eastern Sioux, from the Northern Plains area, and mid-1880's. G—$495

Quillwork pipe bag, 28 in. long with fringes. Deerskin tobacco bag embroidered with red and yellow dyed porcupine quills, front and back. Quilled suspensions with tin cone and feather attachments. Old tag attached reads "Quilled pipe bag 1875". Northern Plains, and mid-1870's. G—$1560

Woman's boots, 25 in. long. Hard-soled boots of soft yellow dyed deerskin, with fringing at the tops. Narrow lines of beadwork in white, red and blue encircle the tops and ankles and frame the front flaps, which are studded with double rows or German silver buttons. Kiowa, Southern Plains area, ca.1875. G—$780

Ration ticket pouch, 4 in. long. Beaded bag with triangular figures of brown, yellow and light blue on a lavender field; flap and thong drawstring. Carry-strap of woven pale blue beadwork. Southern Plains regions, and pre-1900. G—$155

Tepee liner, with entire canvas 85 in. by 142 in. and area of ornamentation 55 in. by 92 in. Heavy canvas tepee liner ornamented in the traditional linear pattern with predominately orange bands of beadwork, interspersed with red yarn tufts. Along the top are 14 beaded medallions to which are attached cornhusk-wrapped suspensions, each terminating in a loop and deer-hoofs. Collected by Reese Kincaid about 1900 from the Nightwalker family. Cheyenne, from Oklahoma, and ca. 1900. G—$3500

Cornhusk belt, 37 in. long and 6 in. wide. "Cornhusk" — actually woven hemp fibers — on leather, with geometric designs imbricated in yarn. Three brass buckles, lined with calico. Nez Perce, Plateau area, and pre-1900. G—$625

Quilled breastplate, 10 in. wide and 16 in. long. Ornate breastplate of hide strips wrapped in predominately bright red quillwork in a geometric pattern. Ribbon, feather and tin-cone attachments. Sioux, Northern Plains region, and ca. 1890's. G—$1750

Pipe, 29 in. in length. Catlinite pipe bowl with wooden stem, wound with braided quilling and feathers. Provenance: Lawson Collection, Philbrook Art Center, Tulsa. Collected by Roberta Lawson, acquired by the museum in 1946. Deaccessioned in a trade in 1976. Sioux, Northern Plains area, and mid-1880's. G—$885

Pipe tamper, 11 in. long. Wooden pipe tamper carved of ash, the end shaped like a human foot, wrapped in braided red and white quillwork. Northern Plains region, and ca. 1910. G—$140

Baby leggings, 6 in. wide and 9 in. high. Diminutive pair of buckskin leggings, outlines with a band of geometric beaded figures on a blue field, edges trimmed with faceted metallic beads. An old tag attached reads "Paul Good Bear, Cheyenne". Cheyenne, Plains region, and ca. 1900. G—$145

Pair of child's dolls, large doll 13 in. high, smaller doll 11½ in. high. Pair of dolls made of buckskin and trade cloth, animal hair and yarn. Decorated with beading and blue and red paint. The smaller doll is painted with an eagle front and back on its buckskin shirt. The large doll has a crescent moon front and back, and a cross and falling star pattern under the shirt flaps. The painted images are similar to those found on Ghost Dance costumes of the period. Northern Plains area, and ca.1895.   G—$440 pair

Toy canoe, 42 in. long and 10 in. wide. Child's toy canoe, a detailed replica of full-size craft. Birchbark sealed with pitch, cedar planking, pine thwarts, tied with cedar root and fastened with wood pegs. (Compare no. 33 in Norman Feder's catalogue of the Jarvis collection of Eastern Plains Indian art in the Brooklyn Museum.) Ojibwa, and pre-1900.
G—$325

Mide bag, 46 in. long. Otter skin medicine bag of the Mide society, used to hold sacred objects for curing rites. Beaded panels of ribbon-edged velvet. The otter retains its claws, skull and teeth, and has one coat-button eye. Red-dyed feathers have been inserted into the nose. An old brass thimble is attached to one claw. Great Lakes area, and ca. 1870.
G—$825

Ghost Dance vest, 21 in. long. Man's vest beaded in pictographic style using blue, green, greasy yellow and transparent red beads. Front and back are four Ghost Dance-style crows executed in dark blue faceted beads. On the back are three zoomorphic forms with forked tails, perhaps lizards or dragonflies. On the front are geometric figures, composed of stepped triangles, and eight crosses. Sioux, ca. 1890.   G—$1950

Hairbrush, 12 in. long. Porcupine tail hair brush, with buckskin-wrapped and fringed handle. Bead detailing in transparent red, dark blue and lavender. A strip of quill-wrapped rawhide runs the length of the brush. Sioux (?), ca. 1890.   G—$295

Peyote rattle, 15 in. long, not including fringe. Gourd rattle on a wooden shaft, stitched with multicolored beadwork. Extensive use of small, faceted beads. Feather tip and cord fringe. Oklahoma, ca. 1930.   G—$210

Dance wand, 18 in. long. Quirt-style dance piece, red painted handle with brass tacks, braided rawhide suspension. Sioux, and ca. 1910.   G—$165

Loop necklace, of mandrel-wound white tradebeads, strung on thongs between rawhide strips. Six red beads, one at center of each strand; top strand broken and retied. Attachments include a cluster of deer-hoof janglers, a medicine bag of rough cloth stained dark and a long tassel of red-dyed horsehair partly wrapped in hide and with a wrapping of seed beads. Crow (?), and early 1880's.G—$775

Peyote bag, 5½ in. long. Metallic faceted beads around edge and at center of four-point star. Southern Plains region, ca. 1900.   G—$145

Breastplate, 21 in. in length. Large man's breastplate composed of bone hairpins, brass beads, rawhide spacers and thongs. Provenance: Abourezk collection, Mission, S.D. Sioux, and from the 1890's.   G—$1000

Tab bag, 12 in. long. Yellow-painted buckskin bag with beaded patterns of stepped triangles on a white background. Pendant from the bag is a long hide tab with two narrow strips of diagonal black and white beading. Southern Plains area, ca. 1900.   G—$255

Awl case, 39 in. long with trailers, Large, elaborate woman's awl case with long beaded trailers. Tin-cone and breath-feather attachments. Southern Plains region, and ca. 1900.
G—$525

Cape or yoke, 37 in. wide. Fringed buckskin edged in cowrie shells and trade beads. (Beaded in geometric patterns as described by Father Peter J. Powell in the Chicago Art Institute catalogue, The Native American Heritage.) Beaded in rose, blue, green and greasy yellow on a deep blue field. Sioux (?), and ca. 1880.   G—$1450

Bag, 5 in. long. Partly beaded with tiny faceted glass and brass beads. Lined with cotton cloth. Santee (?), and ca. 1895.   G—$140

Suggested Reading

(By the Editors), *The American Heritage Book of Indians,* McGraw Hill Book Company dist.; American Heritage Publishing Co., Inc. 1961

Koch, Ronald P., *Dress Clothing of the Plains Indians,* University of Oklahoma

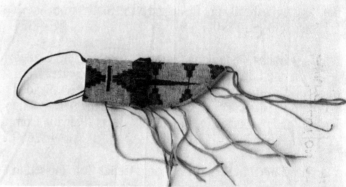

Knife sheath, Southern Cheyenne, fully beaded, fringed, with row of tin cones. Ex-museum, 10 in. long, ca. 1880. $275

Morris' Art & Artifacts, Anaheim, California; Dawn Gober photograph

Knife sheath, White Mountain Apache, fully beaded, three rows of tin cones, fringed, 9 in. long. It is ex-museum and ca. 1880. $275

Morris Art & Artifacts, Anaheim, California; Dawn Gober photograph

Skull-crusher, Oglala Sioux, handle wrapped with rawhide and 24 in. long. Ex-museum, it is ca. 1880. $225

Morris' Art & Artifacts, Anaheim, California; Dawn Gober photograph

PLAINS SHIELD, with paper-stuffed heron head tied on. The top half is painted in rainbow designs of red, black, green and yellow. Item is Northern Plains and pre-1880.

Museum quality

Nedra Matteucci's Fenn Galleries, Santa Fe, New Mexico

BUFFALO HIDE SHIELD, ¼ in. thick and 16½ in. in diameter. Green hand painted on center of shield with red dot in the hand. A Plains Indian piece, some Plains tribes pictured hand on shield, war shirt or pony to denote an enemy killed in combat, old red cloth sewn around the bottom edge and decorated with dentalium shells, old ribbed type, all sinewsewn. Remains of bird sinew sewn on edge, probably the owner's good luck charm or fetish. Ca. 1880. C—$1900

Photo courtesy Bill Post Collection.

Blackfoot parfleche, child's size, with painted geometric designs. In excellent condition, this is a 19th Century piece. $900

Courtesy Dr. Fred Belk, Corrales, New Mexico

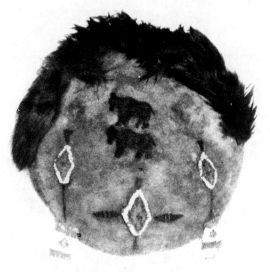

BEAR CULT SHIELD, 16 in. in diameter. Probably Cheyenne or Assiniboin, Montana. Piece has arm straps, 2 bears painted in black with humps, probably grizzley. Has 2 beaded diamonds and beaded tabs. Made of hide shrunk by heat process to ¼ in. to 5/16 in. thick. Bear hair trim across top of shield. Ca. 1860-70. $1950

Photo courtesy Bill Post Collection

BRAIDED SCALP-TANNED SKIN on beaded leather back; this is a leather medicine bag. The two feathers are from the golden eagle. Circa 1870.   Museum quality

Nedra Matteucci's Fenn Galleries, Santa Fe, New Mexico

270

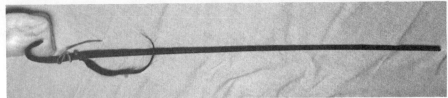

Coup-stick, Plains Indian, 3 ft. long and with finely carved birdhead. It has small brass tack eyes and is completed with leather and hair. Ca. 1870. $600

Private collection, photo by John McLaughlin

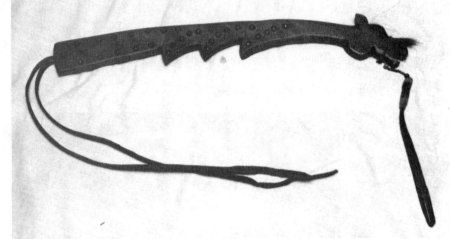

Quirt, Arapaho, done in horse effigy. It is wood with brass tacks, leather, horsehair and beads. Ca. 1900 for this fine piece. $2000

Private collection, photo by John McLaughlin

Bandolier bag, Arapaho, made of hide, cloth and beads. This very well beaded piece is ca. 1870. $800

Private collection, photo by John McLaughlin

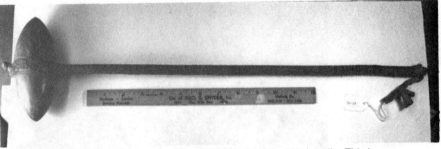

Sioux Ghost Dance war club, with muslin fabric on the handle. This is ca. 1890. $300

Lee Hallman collection, Telford, PA

Arrow, complete with point and guiding feathers, possibly Cheyenne, 1860s. $125

Lee Hallman collection, Telford, PA

Sioux arrow, point, shaft and fletching complete, 1870s. $125

Lee Hallman collection, Telford, PA

Boy's vest, Sioux, 17 x 20 in., fully beaded and fringed in red. Ca. 1880. $2000

Freya's Collectibles, Banff, Alberta, Canada

271

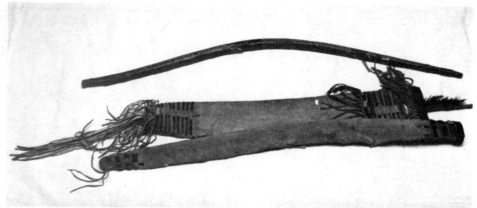

Bow and arrows with bow-case and quiver, Blackfoot. Materials are hide, cloth, beads, wood, feathers, snakeskin and paint. This rare outfit is ca. 1870. $7000

Private collection, photo by John McLaughlin

Left:
Tobacco bag, Crow, beaded on both sides and nicely fringed. It is 14½ in. long and 1880-1890. $2250

Larry Lantz, First Mesa, South Bend, Indiana

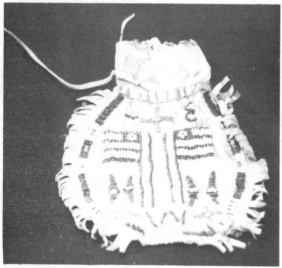

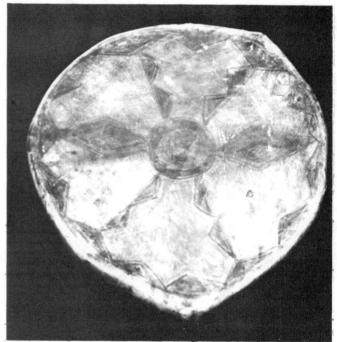

Dance shield, Northern Plains Indian, buffalo hide composition, from the 1800s. It has designs in red, yellow and blue and is 16 in. in diameter. This is a dramatic piece. $1800

Pat & Dave Summers, Native American Artifacts, Victor, NY

Beaded leather pouch, Plains Indian, beaded both sides. It is 6 x 6½ in. and a colorful item in top condition. It is from the 1800s.

$500

Pat & Dave Summers, Native American Artifacts, Victor, NY

"Pemmican pounder" or tent hammer, stone head with rawhide and wrap-around handle. Sioux, from the Dakotas. $165

Private collection

Parfleche container, Sioux, folded size 12 x 26 in. Unused condition, painted in bright blue and orange, with green patterns. It is made of heavy rawhide with hair removed, Indian leather ties. In very good condition, age is uncertain. $300

Sherman Holbert Collection, Fort Mille Lacs, Onamia, MN

Plains Indian drum and drumstick, 9½ in. in diameter. It is painted in yellow and red, and is ca. 1880s. $500

Private collection

Sioux breast-plate, bone hairpipes, brass, glass beads, antler crown, harness leather, rawhide, sinew-wrapped feathers, hawkbells. This is a contemporary piece, 10 x 18 in., from the Pine Ridge Reservation, South Dakota. $175

Morris' Art & Artifacts, Anaheim, California; Dawn Gober photograph

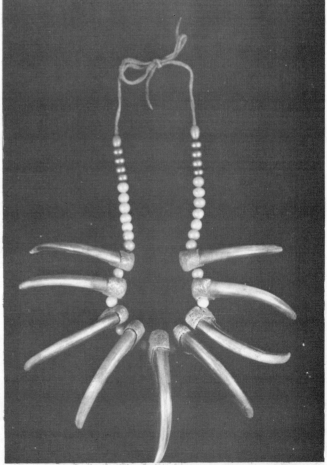

Saddle-bag, Plateau, probably ca. 1880s. Size, 14 x 100 in. long. On Indian-tanned elk hide decorated with old blanket material and some felt. This is a rare and beautiful piece of Indian costume horsetrapping, with slight damage and use-marks. $2500

Sherman Holbert Collection, Fort Mille Lacs, Onamia, MN

Bear-claw necklace, Northern Plains, with blue beads and brass beads. Ca. 1870. Museum quality

Morning Star Gallery, Santa Fe, New Mexico

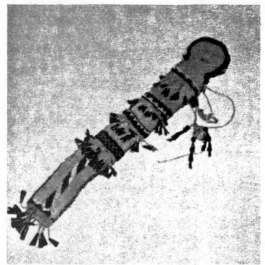

Awl case, Apache, beaded leather with tin cones, very good condition. This 2 x 15 in. piece is ca. 1880. Museum quality

James Reid, LTD, Santa Fe, New Mexico

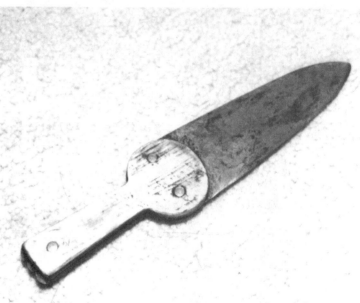

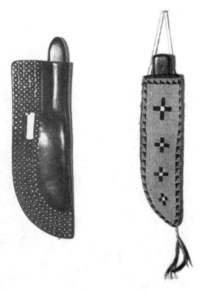

Plains sheath-knives. Left, saddle leather case with belt cut-out and decorated with brass tacks. Length, 12 in., ca. 1870s. $2500-3000 Right, buffalo hide beaded knife case with a tin cone and horsehair drop. Probably Sioux, Ca. 1870s, length 10 in. $2000-2500

Dave Hrachovy, Cedar Glen, California

Dag knife, Plateau area, this piece also known as the beaver-tail, dagger or stabber, with a double-edged blade. The handle is made of two pieces of mountain sheep horn, held together with copper rivets. Three brass tacks decorate the butt of the handle. Length, 9 in. and ca. 1830s-1840s. Quite rare. $6500-$7500

Dave Hrachovy, Cedar Glen, California

Plains Indian knives, typical group. Blades were obtained from traders, frontier blacksmiths or home-made from old files, etc. Indian-made handles are of wood, bone or antler with some being wire or hide-wrapped. Lengths are 9 to 13 in., ca. the 1800s. $100-$300 each

Quirt, Cheyenne, the wood carved in the "saw-tooth" style and with inside of teeth painted. Lash is of commercial leather with a fringed tanned hide tie. Wrist strap is tanned hide and beaded in a saw-tooth pattern and with tin cone drop. Handle length is 18 in. and the exceptional piece is ca. 1860s-1870s. Museum quality

Dave Hrachovy, Cedar Glen, California

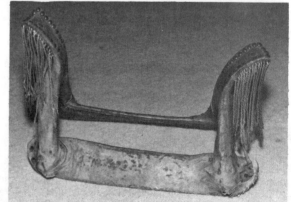

Saddle, Plains Indian hide-covered wood decorated with brass tacks and with painted, twisted fringe. The pommel and cantle are also painted. Length, 19 in. and ca. 1870s. $3000-$3500

Dave Hrachovy, Cedar Glen, California

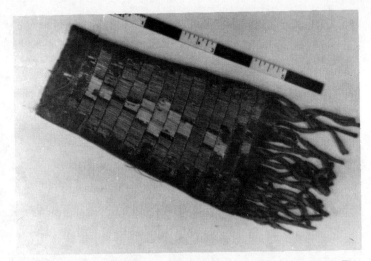

Zippered purse, Plains and possibly Sioux, very nicely beaded, 5 in. long. Ca. 1930s. $125-$175

Pocotopaug Trading Post, South Windsor, CT

Quilled flap, Plains, decorated on leather with red and yellow quillwork. This interesting old piece is ex-coll. Casterline. $125

Pat & Dave Summers, Native American Artifacts, Victor, New York

Pipe bag, Cheyenne, beaded, quilled and fringed antelope hide. It has a beaded bar design panel and "X" motif quilled panel. The hide fringe is decoratd with tin cones and horsehair. Length 32 in., ca. 1860s.

Museum quality

Dave Hrachovy, Cedar Glen, California

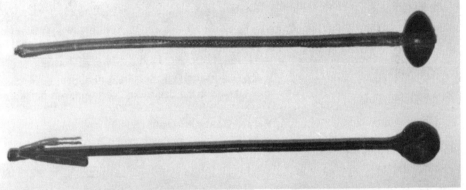

War-clubs, stone-headed with long hide-covered wooden hafts for use on horseback. These were typical weapons of the mid to late 1800s Plains Indians. The round-headed club has a beaded wrist strap of tanned hide. Lengths, 31 and 32 in. respectively. $750-$1000, each

Dave Hrachovy, Cedar Glen, California

Bow case and quiver with bow and arrows. Plains Indian case with two hide compartments of buffalo leather hung on a wide strap with fringe suspensions. Pony beads decorate the mouth of the quiver and bow has quill wrapping on the exposed end. This early "user" was collected from the Sioux of Sitting Bull's group at the Standing Rock Reservation. Arrows, 27 in.; bow, 51 in. long. Set is ca. 1840s-1860s. Museum quality

Dave Hrachovy, Cedar Glen, California

275

Newspaper Rock, Indian Creek State Park, Utah. One of the most famous rock art sites in the Southwest, most work was probably done by the Fremont culture, ca. AD 900-1200.

Randall Olsen photograph

The famous hogan, the earth-covered dwelling of the Navajo Indians. Note the one woman grinding material with a mano and stone metate, also the Navajo blanket to the right of hogan doorway. Dwellings like these were common into the early 1900's, photo ca. 1930.

Photo courtesy of Utah State Historical Society, Collection of Smithsonian Institution.

CHAPTER XV

WOODEN COLLECTIBLES

The great number of hafted stone woodworking tools from forested and coastal regions of prehistoric North America suggest wooden art and artifacts were once common. Certainly specialized chipped artifacts were also employed to carve wood into useful and pleasing objects. Almost all of such objects have been lost to time, bacteria — and the present.

The average person, asked to name early American Indian wood items, might mention some well-known examples. These might be prehistoric bows and arrows, or historic Northwest Coast totem poles or Iroquois false-face masks, or a few other memorable examples. With the exception of wood preserved by arid conditions in the Southwest and by permafrost in the far North, very few of such cultural creations survive.

Hundreds of wooden dugout watercraft have been found in the United States and Canada, and recoveries began to be made as soon as Europeans arrived. By far the largest number have come from the Eastern U.S., in an area ranging from New England to Florida. Most were sunk in swamps or lakes and became entirely or partially buried in mud and silt. When recovered under scientific conditions, special chemicals are used to preserve the wood.

Following is a very brief listing of early watercraft discoveries, along with some information on each find.

Case	Location	Date Found	Dimensions	Estimated Age
1 & 2	Ontario, Canada (Lakes?) *Two* dugouts	Unk.	Unk.	2000 years
3	Northwestern Ohio (Lake)	Late 1976 1976	22½ ft. Long, 3¼ ft. wide	2000-3000 years years
4	Southwestern state (River)	1970 (?)	Not large	Unk.
5	Manhattan, New York (Landfill)	1906	Broken half of dugout was 7 ft. long, 3 ft. wide	Unk.
6	Tennessee (River)	1797(?)	Unk.	Pre-1797
7	Michigan (Lake)	1971	17 ft. in length	300 years old; possibly earlier
8	Georgia (River)	Early 1977	24 ft. long	250 years
9	Florida (Lake)	1977/78 (?)	19 ft. long	200 years (sides burned)

Leaving the prehistoric and unknown regions, there are many wood collectibles from historic and recent times. The more desirable items have age as well as beauty, and are mainly from the 1700's into the early 1900's.

The wood should preferably be a heavy hardwood, with some surface patina due to age. Marks of manufacture, generally from White-supplied iron and steel tools, can be visible but not prominant to the point of distraction. Splitting and splintering should be at the absolute minimum, and wood rot or decay is a serious value negative. Some stain is permitted, especially with items like pemmican-pounders, for these are use-signs.

Many wood artifacts were further decorated with quilling (early) or beading (later), brass tacks or paint. This chapter consists of all-wood collectibles or Indian items that have a major part made of wood.

PREHISTORIC WOOD ITEMS

Southwestern **wooden rabbit-stick,** a slightly flat and curved stick about 23 in. long. These were thrown to bring down small game; sticks did not return, like the boomerang, but were retrieved on foot. C—$175

Oregon **Atl-atl,** 16¾ in. long and recovered from a dry cave. One end is thicker for handgrip, opposite end has antler or ivory hook for lance-butt and a shallow groove for the shaft connects the two. Pale evidence of paint remains. Piece is in fair condition. Rare. C—$495

Wood **digging stick,** Montana, 39 in. long and with lower end heavier and sharpened to a point. It may have been fire-hardened. Bark peeled from entire length; used for grubbing out roots. C—$40

Section of arrowshaft, 9 in. long, and a portion somewhere between missing front and back. Flint tools used for shaft smoothing, and marks still show on surface. C—$35

HISTORIC WOOD ITEMS

Central California **cradleboard,** full size, and decorated with sun shade with yarn ties. G—$495

Papago **carved wood club,** potato-masher type, and 1800's. D—$110

Carved wood Northwest Coast **Salish-Shaker power stick,** with deer toes and cover. This piece was made when the Shaker church was influential in the area. A—$1500

Ree Indian **wood-handled crooked knife,** 8¼ in. long, from a site in northern South Dakota. Handle has a small knife blade set at lower end, with working edge 1⅜ in. long. Not a common item, and old. C—$225

Cedar **canoe baler,** Northwest Coastal group. A—$95

Late historic Chippewa **wooden food container** or trencher, old and unusual. Rectangular, 5 in. deep, 13¼ in. long and 7 in. wide. Carved from hardwood, possibly maple. Wood sides and bottom average ⅝ in. thick, with some small age-cracks at ends. Smaller ends have a thickened projection to serve as handles. C—$495

Plains cane or **dance wand,** 19½ in. long, wood; top has tied feathers, base is hide-wrapped. Appears very old. D—$195

Sioux cane or **dance stick,** a natural wood formation carved and painted in the shape of a smiling snake. Colorful and a primitive art piece of exceptional note. G—$575

Cherokee **stick-ball racket,** 27 in. long, wood with rawhide lace. G—$80

Haida (NW Coast) **food trencher,** rectangular form, 15 in., 9½ in. wide. Ends up-curved, sides down-curved, and piece well-made of spruce (?) wood. Exterior once painted; an old item. C—$1500

Northwest Coast **spoon,** Kwakuitl, 14 in. long, curved wood. A—$155

Canoe paddle, possibly middle-1880's, Eastern Woodlands group. All wood, with even, flowing lines, well-carved. Upper handle region has some light incising in a simple pattern. Fine condition and not a common piece. C—$500

Navajo wood **battan weaving tool,** ca. 1880. D—$35

Lacross stick, probably Canadian Indian, just over 35 in. long. Hitting end has a laced rawhide flattish cup, handle end has thong-wrapped section for non-slip use. Excellent condition. C—$195

Sioux **beamer** or hide-scraping tool, 14½ in. long. It has a two-handed wood handle with metal blade insert. Wood is beautifully grained. G—$170

Central California **cradleboard,** full-size, with yarn decorated design on the sun shade. Piece has doeskin straps. G—$365

Ball-headed wood club, Woodland region, from Great Lakes area. It is carved from a single piece of wood, possibly oak burl, and is 22½ in. long. Plain, business-like piece. C—$895

Eastern Sioux **fertility wooden statue,** 14 in. high. Good condition and rare; piece could be older than ca. 1900. G—$1700

Sioux **cradleboard,** original wood frame and 24 in. long. Leather over wood, with beadwork designs. C—$695

Ball-headed war club, turn of the Century period; head has stone inset. Cross-hatching decoration on the handle, and good condition. G—$900

Pair of rather plain **wood stirrups,** both with portions of original rawhide fastenings at top. Northern Plains regions, simply carved, nicely matched. C—$250

Plains style **fleshing tool,** with metal blade edge; from Taos Pueblo and probably from the 1800's. D—$125

Wooden bowl, made from hardwood log, 7 in. wide and 20½ in. long. Good condition. Undecorated. C—$350

Blackfoot **fleshing tool,** wooden handle with sinew-wrapped metal blade, unusual shape to handle. Piece is 15 in. long. G—$165

Wood **stirring spoon,** California, 14 in. long, with well-carved handle. Early historic and from one of the interior desert groups. C—$145

Sioux, **willow back rest,** zone-painted, with incised tripod legs.   G—$800

Sioux **fleshing tool,** wood with metal side blade, ca. 1850.   D—$110

Ball-type wooden club, 20 in. long, with diameter of ball 4¼ in. May be Chippewa, but uncertain. Some incised lines on handle; an old and good piece.   D—$700

Wood and leather **cradleboard,** 21 in. high, and a basic wood-slat frame. Whole is somewhat deteriorated due to lack of attention in the past; a late 1800's item, and some beadwork remaining on leather portions, which is brittle.   C—$420

Four **Northwest Coast carvings:** Rattle, Adz, Potlatch bowl, and Shaman's spirit bent-box with lid. All are finely carved.   C—$1350 the four

Mask, Northwest United States, made of carved wood and horn. This is a nice old piece, quite unusual. $300
Wilfred A. Dick collection, Magnolia, Mississippi

Spoon, carved wood, Great Lakes region and Huron. It has a fine bird-effigy handle and is ca. 1870. $350
Private collection, photo by John McLaughlin

Feast bowl, Kwakitul, from Albertsville, British Columbia, Canada. It was collected in the 1920s and measures 10 in. high and 19 in. long. With dorsal-fin lid, body is old green stained color, abalone eyes and ivory teeth and side spots. The painted decorations are in red and white. A fine Northwest Coast item. $1175
Sherman Holbert Collection. Fort Mille Lacs, Onamia, MN

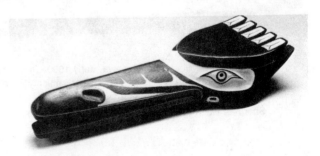

Mask, forehead, Kwakiutl, Northwest Coast. First collected in the 1920s it is 7 in. wide and 21¼ in. long. Carefully made, it has a remote attachment so the wearer can open and close the bill of the cormorant effigy during a dance ceremony. Carefully carved and painted black, red and white. An important Northwest Coast piece. $895
Sherman Holbert Collection, Fort Mille Lacs, Onamia, MN

Burden-carrier, wood and bark, Iroquois. This very fine piece is from the 1800s and ex-coll. Casterline. $400
Pat & Dave Summers, Native American Artifacts, Victor, NY

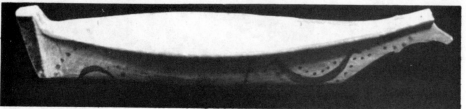

Toy cedar-wood canoe, Salish, from the late 1800s. It is 18 in. long and nicely painted. An old label reads "Made by Neah Bay Indians, Neah Bay, Washington". $350

Larry Lantz, First Mesa, South Bend, Indiana

Rare Atl-atl or lance-throwing stick from King Isle, Alaska. It was dated by the previous owner as being from the 1830s.

Museum quality

Private collection

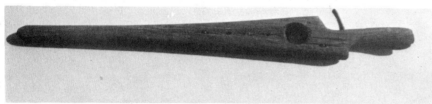

Another view of the wooden lance-thrower from Alaska showing finger-positioning peg. Atl-atls from North America are very scarce and tend to come from the Southwest or the Far North.   Museum quality

Private collection

Ball-headed club, one-piece burl wood, a mint Seneca Iroquois artifact. This very rare item is 26½ in. long and has a fine natural patina overall. It is from the 1800s. $1900

Pat & Dave Summers, Native American Artifacts, Victor, NY

Sugar spoon, Mille Lacs Chippewa, early 1900s. It is 39 in. long and used with large iron kettles for stirring nearly finished maple sugar. Old and well-used but in very good condition. $125

Sherman Holbert Collection, Fort Mille Lacs, Onamia, MN

Right:
Club, Sioux, horse-leg effigy form, wood and tacks with file blade. Ca. 1870. $1000

Private collection, photo by John McLaughlin

Birchbark basket, base larger than top, Northeastern Woodlands, 8 x 11 in. It is a ca. 1940s. $125-$175

Pocotopaug Trading Post, South Windsor, CT

Birchbark basket, squared base and rounded top, Northeastern Woodlands, 7½ in. in diameter. It is ca. 1940s. $45-$60

Pocotopaug Trading Post, South Windsor, CT

Wooden bowls, Great Lakes region. Left, brown wood, ca. 1860. $1000-$1500

Right, Winnebago, yellow-blond wood, ca. 1880. $150

Private collection, photo by John McLaughlin

Birchbark basket, Northeastern Woodlands, rectangular base and oblong top, 8 x 12 in. It is ca. 1840-1860. $175-$200

Pocotopaug Trading Post, South Windsor, CT

RECENT WOOD ITEMS (1900-1970)

Canadian Indian **meat drying rack,** unusual item. It consists of 8 peeled-bark wands secured to 3 crosspieces; the former are 40 in. long, the latter about 35 in. and thicker. Collected years ago North of Lake Erie and probably early 1900's. May have been used to dry or smoke freshwater fish. C—$185

Northwest Coast **wood totem,** Raven effigy, old. D—$145

Northwest Coast **war club.** A—$155

Tlingit (NW Coast) **paddle-spoon,** shaped like a miniature dugout canoe paddle, and 14½ in. long. (The more ornate forms were undoubtedly reserved for special occasions. Paddle-spoons were used to eat a Northwest Coast delicacy called "sopalalli" or "soap-berry", a mixture of berries and cold water frothed with oil from the olachen or candlefish). Very good condition; relief carving on straight wide lower portion may represent a mountain goat. C—$420

Wooden bow, 46½ in. long, narrowed and thicker at center. Believed to be from Plateau area, perfect, painted in faint black and red designs. This Century, early, probably pre-tourist times. Well done piece. C—$295

Northwest Coast **paddle-spoon,** undecorated, 13¾ in. long. Fair condition with cracking. C—$155

Northwest Coast **miniature canoe,** a copy of the high-prowed sea-going dugouts; piece is 3¾ in. wide and 19 in. long. Well-constructed of thin wood strips and held together with sinew through small holes. C—$350

Paiute **cradle board,** made of wicker and covered with partially beaded hide. Large and well-designed; some wicker missing. Made in the 1930's or 40's.   G—$700

Wooden **Iroquois mask,** False-Face society, about life-size or larger and with long horsetail hair. Shell eyes, red feathers and with black details. Not older than 1900; may be considerably later.   C—$595

Dance wand, Plains Indian, about 16 in. long. Knob head end has false scalp-lock of long hair, possibly bison beard, and with faded painted lines along shaft. Unusual.C—$225

Chippewa **maple sugar spoon.**   A—$65

Pair of Northwest Coast **carved miniature paddles,** 18 in. long. They have good stylized carving and are ca. 1930.   G—$200

Iroquois **wooden mask,** about 12 in. high and with exaggerated and twisted features. Ca. 1900.   C—$615

Eastern Woodlands Indian **lidded birchbark sugar box,** probably used for maple sugar storage. It is 9½ in. by 11 in. and 7 in. high. Ca. 1930's.   C—$155

Plains Indian **wooden-frame loom,** late period, probably for weaving of sashes. Piece is about 1½ ft. long, and 5 in. wide, with some original thread ties remaining.C—$180

Northwest Coast **raven rattle,** 14 in. long by 4½ in. in diameter. Piece is ca. 1930.   G—$1750

CHIPPEWA COURTING FLUTE, 1½ in. in diameter and 15 in. long. This is a courting object and has double chambers, carved bird head on end, and traces of red and green paint. Decorated with old hide and fringe; piece is 1890.   C—$495

Photo courtesy Bill Post Collection.

WOODEN KWAKIUTL PORTRAIT MASK, Northwest Coast carving, 9 in. high. This is a recent piece, and face is painted in black and red. Made by Calvin Hunt, ca. 1965.   C—$300-$450

Photo courtesy R.M. Weatherford, Columbus, Ohio.

THREADING SNOWSHOES, Mackenzie River, North West Territories, ca. 1920s.

Photo courtesy National Photography Collection, Neg. #C-38174. Public Archives of Canada.

Woodland Indian carved trail marker, Ottawa, Michigan, year 1923. It has painted blue highlights and represents a man, a woman, and an owl.   Museum quality

Michael F. Slasinski, Saginaw, Michigan

Birchbark canoe, scraped hearts and floral design, Cree Indian. Made in the 1920s, it is from Canada and quite large at 22½ in. long. $150

Michael F. Slasinski, Saginaw, Michigan

"Buffalo" mask, Cherokee, made in the 1950s. Made of painted wood, it is from North Carolina. Size is 7 x 12½ in. $110

Michael F. Slasinski, Saginaw, Michigan

Iroquois False Face mask from New York state, year 1920. Face is red-brown, with horsehair. Size, 6 x 11 in. This is a rare early artifact. $2000

Michael F. Slasinski, Saginaw, Michigan

Birchbark canoe, 33¼ x 148 in. This is a rare one-man or hunter's canoe made by Na-Ah-Qua-Geseg, Mille Lacs Chippewa. Ca. 1959, it is the only canoe ever offered for sale by the maker. Ex-colls. Johnson and Kouba. This is a museum quality item with historic significance. $2000

Sherman Holbert Collection, Fort Mille Lacs, Onamia, MN

CONTEMPORARY WOOD ITEMS

Navajo **cradleboard,** 36 in. long.   G—$175

Northwest Coast **carved halibut hook,** done by Tsungani.
                                                A—$195

Signed Northwest Coast **wood houseboard.**   A—$165

Apache **cradleboard,** 36 in. long.   G—$220

Northwest Coast **carved paddle,** 15½ in. long. Piece has painted killer-whale design, signed, John Bennall, Haida.
                                                G—$150

Iroquois False Face mask, from Brantford, Ontario, Canada. The face is barn red, hair is white, and eye-plates are copper. Size, 6 x 12 in., year 1989.
$125

Michael F. Slasinski, Saginaw, MI

Iroquois False Face mask, from Brantford, Ontario, Canada. It is ox-blood red with copper eyes, size 7 x 11 in. Year, 1991. $125

Michael F. Slasinski, Saginaw, Michigan

Water bucket, 11 x 13 in. high plus handle. Made by Bebe Earth, Chippewa, Mille Lacs Reservation, it is ca. 1986. It has reinforced double rim, and sealed with spruce pitch; used for carrying water or maple sap.$125

Sherman Holbert Collection, Fort Mille Lacs, Onamia, MN

Great Lakes region baskets. Left, Mille Lacs Chippewa, 19 x 22 in., birchbark, excellent work.$225
Left center, Mille Lacs Chippewa, rare large basket made by Maggie Kegg, basswood bark. $145
Right center, birchbark, Maggie Kegg, Mille Lacs Chippewa, excellent condition. $225
Right, decorated birchbark basket made by Rose Wind, acquired in 1987. $195

Sherman Holbert Collection, Fort Mille Lacs, Onamia, MN

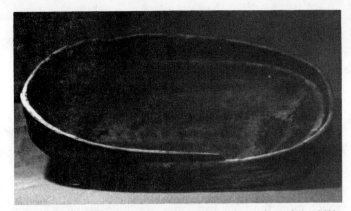

Wooden bowl, prehistoric, with rim. This extremely rare item, 9½ x 14¼ in., was found frozen in ice near Shismaref, Alaska. $650

Pat & Dave Summers, Native American Artifacts, Victor, NY

Carved wooden pipe stem, very well done and in top condition.$500-$600

Collection of David G. & Barbara J. Shirley

Baby-board, Mohawk, carved wood with painted designs, ca. 1870.$3000

Private collection; photo by John McLaughlin

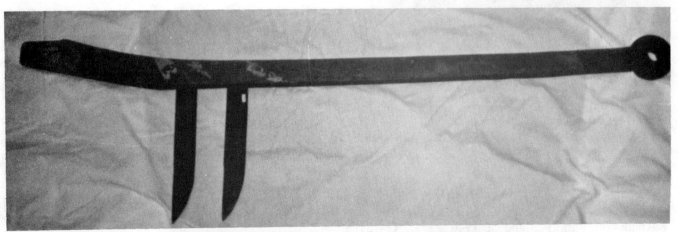

Club, Sioux, horse effigy, with wood, tacks, paint and inset knife blades.
It is ca. 1870. $1500

Private collection, photo by John McLaughlin

CHAPTER XVI

KACHINAS, DOLLS, TOYS, AND MUSICAL ITEMS

Hopi Kachinas are difficult to explain easily, for they are much more than doll-like forms. Kachinas depict Kachina dancers, which in turn represent spirits and forces important to the traditional and modern Hopi lifeway. Even inanimate objects may have such powers.

The Kachina dolls — and there are about 300 different characters that appear regularly and some 200 that appear occasionally — served to instruct Hopi children. Often superbly carved from cottonwood, Kachinas of the late 1880's and early 1900's soon became collector items.

Eventually original supplies were depleted, but demand continued and a new collecting field developed. Today no assemblage of Southwestern Indian works is considered representative without a Kachina or two.

Kachina figures vary in size from a few inches to several feet. Value factors include size and material, with hand-carved wood — some with moveable arms and legs — a favorite. Modern copies are mady by non-Indians in plaster and plastic and ceramics. For Indian made Kachinas, the skill of the maker counts for a great deal, and usually the more handwork the higher the value. Beyond the basic figure, Kachinas may be painted, and clothed and wear various ornaments, carry different symbols.

Two important sub-areas for collecting are the old, pre-tourist Kachinas and those made by well-known contemporary Indian artists. The best way to get a good Kachina at a good price is to know your source.

WARRIOR KACHINA or Ewiro Kachina (Hopi name), 22 in. high and width front to back 12½ in.   Unsigned.   G—$1100

Photo courtesy William Scoble, The Ansel Adams Gallery, Yosemite National Park, California.

KACHINAS

Kachina doll, 9 in. high and ca. 1940's.   G—$185

Hopi "Owl" Kachina, 7 in. high.   G—$145

"Hummingbird" Kachina, 8½ in. high and ca. 1940's.   G—$310

Two old Kachinas, ca. 1920, sold as one lot.   A—$180

Hopi "Ogre" Kachina, 7 in. high.   G—$170

Kachina doll, 16 in. high, in the form of a wolf with bow and arrow, in "Strongbow" form. Made by Fred Kubota; well-painted.   G—$380

Kachina doll, 8 in. high, and ca. 1940's.   G—$180

Kachina doll, 9½ in. high, ca. 1940's.   G—$210

Hopi "Mouse Warrior" Kachina, 14 in. high and well carved. Signed "N. Seltewa".   G—$350

Kachina doll, 7 in. high and ca. 1940's.   G—$180

"Mana" Kachina doll, 9 in. high and ca. 1940's.G—$195

"Mud-head" Kachinas, set of four on a base.   A—$210

"Mouse Warrior" Kachina, 8 in. high and signed, "S. Jackson".   G—$190

Kachina made by Willie Tewaquaptewa, 8 in. high, with painted features. This fine piece is in extremely fine condition for age, ca. 1940.

Courtesy John Isaac, Albuquerque, New Mexico $850

Clown Kachina, by Clarence Cleveland, height 10 to 12 in. The Eastern Cowboys, Scottsdale, Arizona $425-$650,

Hopi Kachina, superb Tsitoto Helmet Mask figure of cottonwood, in several well-done colors. It is 19 in. high, from Arizona, and ca. 1940.

Pat & Dave Summers, Native American Artifacts, Victor, NY $800

Sun Kachina, by Tino Youvella, 12½ in. high. $600
The Eastern Cowboys, Scottsdale, Arizona

White Buffalo Kachina, by Earl Yowytewa, 10 in. high. $395
The Eastern Cowboys, Scottsdale, Arizona

Eagle Kachina, by Coolidge Roy Jr., 9 in. high. $485
The Eastern Cowboys, Scottsdale, Arizona

Owl Kachina, by Preston Ami,
9 in. high. $485

The Eastern Cowboys,
Scottsdale, Arizona

Eagle Kachina, by Ron Duwyenie, 9 in. high. $485
The Eastern Cowboys, Scottsdale, Arizona

Butterfly Maiden Kachina, Hopi Maker Henry Shelton. This was done
on special order for Marguerite L. Kernaghan and is autographed. Size,
6 x 15½ in.   Museum quality

Marguerite L. Kernaghan collection; photograph by Marguerite L. and
Stewart W. Kernaghan, Bellvue, Colorado

Route 66 doll dating to the 1930s, early tourist item, in white, yellow, red and black paint. The interesting example is 7 in. high. $95

Courtesy John Isaac, Albuquerque, NM

Kachina, old, Hopi, no action shown. Done in six colors, size is 3 x 11¼ in.
$450-$750

Marguerite L. Kernaghan collection; photograph by Marguerite L. and Stewart W. Kernaghan, Bellvue, Colorado

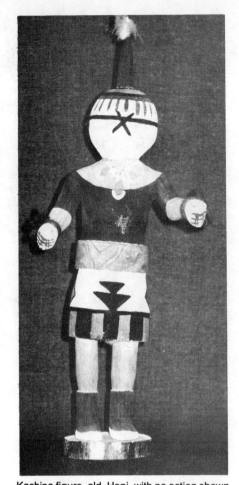

Kachina figure, old, Hopi, with no action shown. Done in seven colors, it is 5½ x 14 in.$450-$750

Marguerite L. Kernaghan collection; photograph by Marguerite L. and Stewart W. Kernaghan, Bellvue, Colorado

Chowilawa Kachina, done in seven colors. This figure was made by Jerry Lalapo and is 7½ x 11½ in.$400-$700

Marguerite L. Kernaghan collection; photograph by Marguerite L. and Stewart W. Kernaghan, Bellvue, Colorado

Mastoff Kachina, Hopi maker Raymond Parkett. This large figure is 8 x 16½ in. $500-$900

Marguerite L. Kernaghan collection; photograph by Marguerite L. and Stewart W. Kernaghan, Bellvue, Colorado

Hopi Kachinas, early dolls of the pre-1920 period. Prices for such early works vary greatly. $950-$2500

John C. Hill Antique Indian Art, Scottsdale, Arizona

Hopi Kachinas ca. 1940s. On the left is Ho'ote and on the right is a rare Red Buffalo Kachina. Both figures are in very fine condition.
$900-$1200, each

John C. Hill Antique Indian Art, Scottsdale, Arizona

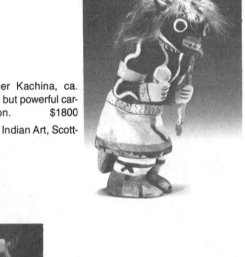

Hopi Buffalo Dancer Kachina, ca. 1920. This is a small but powerful carving, in top condition. $1800

John C. Hill Antique Indian Art, Scottsdale, Arizona

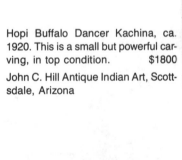

Hopi Buffalo Kachina, ca. 1940s, by Jimmy K. He was one of the first artists to sign his work (JK). $1500

John C. Hill Antique Indian Art, Scottsdale, Arizona

Hopi Butterfly Maiden or Palik Mana, ca. 1950s, by Jimmy K. This form is one of the most popular Kachinas, and this is a fine example. $2400

John C. Hill Antique Indian Art, Scottsdale, Arizona

Hopi Kachina, red, cream, yellow, blue and black, 8 in. high. It dates to the 1940s and is in fine condition. $450

Courtesy John Isaac, Albuquerque, New Mexico

Pang or Mountain Sheep Kachina, Hopi. This Kachina is about 55 years old and has a later base added about 1940. The figure appears in bands in an ordinary Kachina dance and has power over rain and spasms. This example is 16 in. tall. $900-$1500

Marguerite L. Kernaghan collection; photo by Marguerite L. and Stewart W. Kernaghan, Bellvue, Colorado

Konin Supai Kachina, Hopi, who appears in a regular Kachina dance and is a representation of the Hopi's neighbors to the west, the Havasupai Indians. The maker is Alfred Hitez and size is 6 x 9 in. $350-$600

Marguerite L. Kernaghan collection; photo by Marguerite L. and Stewart W. Kernaghan, Bellvue, Colorado

Hopi Kachinas.
Left, giant Kachina, 16 in. high, by Bill Scwiemaenewa. $750
Right, star Kachina, 15 in. high, by Leo Lacapa. $895
Both are made of cottonwood root.

Courtesy John W. Barry, California

291

Mudhead Clown Kachina carrying a Mudhead Clown (Koyemsi), Hopi.
They appear in mixed or regular dances and sometimes a group appears in a dance of their own. Comic-characters, they enliven serious
ceremonies. They are the only Kachina allowed to do whatever they want.
This fine piece was made by Robert Kayguoptewa and size is 5 x 12¾
in. $500-$850

Marguerite L. Kernaghan collection; photograph by Marguerite L. and
Stewart W. Kernaghan, Bellvue, Colorado

Rattle Kachina (AYA), Hopi. The name is derived from the mask which
resembles a Hopi rattle. He comes in pairs and rarely one at a time.
He carries yucca whips which he uses on a runner that does not win
a race. This figure was made by Carl Sulu and is 7 x 11 in.$400-$700

Marguerite L. Kernaghan collection; photo by Marguerite L. and Stewart
W. Kernaghan, Bellvue, Colorado

Left-handed Kachina (SUY-ANG-E-IF), Hopi. This Kachina carries his
bow in his right hand and all hunting gear is reversed. He appears as
a warrior in the Powamu ceremony. Size is 7½ x 14 in. $500-$900

Marguerite L. Kernaghan collection; photograph by Marguerite L. and
Stewart W. Kernaghan, Bellvue, Colorado

Kachina, Mong or Chief Kachina (wuwuyomo), Hopi. It is spoken of as "Old man kachina" because he is so ancient. Always appears in groups of four with the Pachavu Manas whom they lead into the villages. They appear in the Third Mesa extended form of the Powamu, the Palolokong Ceremony. The maker is Gilbert Naseyouma; size is 4½ x 14½ in. $500-$900

Marguerite L. Kernaghan collection; photograph by Marguerite L. and Stewart W. Kernaghan, Bellvue, Colorado

Chasing Star Kachina, Hopi, done in red, black, yellow and white. It was made by Ernest Chapella, First Mesa. Size is 6¾ x 12¼ in. $400-$700

Marguerite L. Kernaghan collection; photograph by Marguerite L. and Stewart W. Kernaghan, Bellvue, Colorado

NON-KACHINA DOLLS

"Koshare" doll, with figure holding baby. Piece is 15 in. high and signed, "Regina Naha".   G—$500

Cachiti "Storyteller" doll, with nine babies. Doll is 8 in. high and ca. 1960.   G—$615

Iemez "Storyteller" doll, and six babies. Piece is 7 in. high, and signed, "Toledo".   G—$310

INDIAN DOLLS

Indian doll, 13 in. high and from Western U.S., dressed in fringed moccasins, leather skirt. Wood face, non-moveable arms and legs, good condition. Ca. 1930's.   D—$185

Comtemporary **Navajo dolls,** pair, man 8 in. high and woman 7½ in. high. Modern items done by Navajos and dressed in authentic costumes; all handmade.   G—$85

Old **Indian doll,** 11 in. high, with beaded hair. Face made of old paper or corn husk; figure wrapped in part of an old blanket.   G—$285

Doll moccasins, fully beaded and just over 1 in. long. Pair.   C—$65

Old Pacific Plateau **beaded doll.**   A—$70

Navajo doll, probably Indian child's "companion", depicting woman in ceremonial dress. Doll is 10½ in. high and ca. 1910.   C—$250

Sioux pair of **man and woman dolls,** matched set 11 in. high. The dolls have human hair and are ca. 1900.   C—$725

Plains Indian doll, 9 in. high and with wood base. This was made for the old tourist trade; hide face with yarn hair and hide dress that is nicely beaded. Piece has partially beaded cradle on back, with child.   G—$165

Apache gun-dance dolls, averaging 10 in. high. The set of five is hand-carved.   D—$180

Commanche beaded doll with Plains bonnet and ca. 1880-90.   D—$110

Doll moccasins, pair of Sioux family beaded items, old and of good quality.   G—$160

Snohomish **basketry dolls,** man and woman, both 8 in. high.   A—$180

Child's play or **toy cradleboard,** late 1800's, and 11 in. high. Leather, partially beaded on wood frame. Good condition and rather scarce item.   C—$320

Miniature cradleboard with doll, 14 in. long and 5½ in. wide. Of old tan buckskin, piece has a fully beaded top section 5 in. wide and 6 in. long.   G—$480

White Buffalo Dancer, Hopi; this is not a Kachina as he has no mask. Nicely made and decorated, this 6 x 12 in. figure was made by Murray Harvey, Polacca, Arizona. $400-$750

Marguerite L. Kernaghan collection; photograph by Marguerite L. and Stewart W. Kernaghan, Bellvue, Colorado

Corn-husk doll, Iroquois, red wooden false face, rabbit fur hair, 5 in. high. It is from Brantford, Ontario, Canada, and year 1988.

$75

Michael F. Slasinski, Saginaw, Michigan

Hano Clown (Koshare), Hopi maker Murray Harvey. Size is 4¾ x 12 in. $400-$700

Marguerite L. Kernaghan collection; photograph by Marguerite L. and Stewart W. Kernaghan, Bellvue, Colorado

Sioux **pair of buckskin dolls,** both 11 in. high. Female has buckskin face and male has black face made of dried apple. Clothing has beaded decorations; good condition, and ca. 1920.   G—$365

Doll, Canadian Indian made, contemporary, carved from wood with a thin leather dress. Painted features, and 9 in. high.   C—$85

Iroquois corn husk doll, 8 in. high and 3½ in. wide. From false face society; good early tourist piece and with some beadwork; well-carved on a wood base.   G—$145

Seneca doll, collected in Eastern Canada, and probably from the 1940's. Corn husk body with thin cotton dress stained brown. Piece is about 10 in. high.   C—$90

Sioux child's tipi, old, with pictograph drawings and tin cone dangles. Much faded and shows considerable age; completely assembled with poles.   G—$440

Fraser River **miniature cradle,** 5½ in. by 13 in. A—$200

Carved doll in cradle, item 18 in. high and 7½ in. wide. Cradleboard in authentic style; doll has well-carved wood face. Done by LaLooska.   G—$485

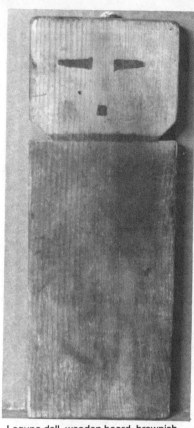

Laguna doll, wooden board, brownish body and tan-yellow face, features in blue-green. In used condition, the doll is 9 in. high. $120

Courtesy John Isaac, Albuquerque, NM

Hand-made doll, Navajo, 16 in. tall and in traditional costume. It is early 20th Century with beadwork and ceremonial accessories. $195

Larry Lantz, First Mesa, South Bend, Indiana

Doll, Apache, with cut hide poncho and skirt, high-top moccasins, cloth body and head. With tin cone drops, 14½ in. tall. Ca. 1880.
                                    Museum quality
Morning Star Gallery, Santa Fe, NM

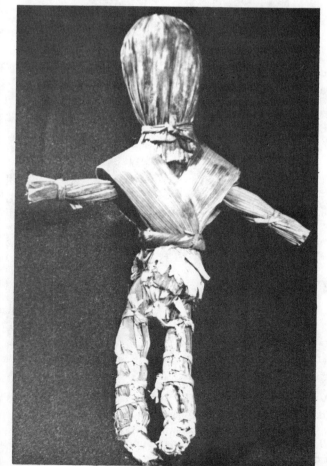

Cornhusk doll, faceless, very old. This Iroquois figure is 11 in. high and an interesting early piece. $100

Pat & Dave Summers, Native American Artifacts, Victor, NY

Doll, Cheyenne, beaded and fringed hide dress, with boots and buffalo hair.
                                    Museum quality
Morning Star Gallery, Santa Fe, New Mexico

295

Doll carrier, Crow, wood, hide, cloth and beads. This very well made piece is ca. 1890. $4000-$6000

Private collection, photo by John McLaughlin

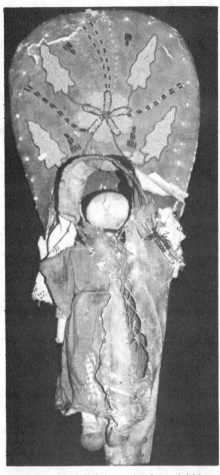

Doll, Flathead, hide, beaded dress fringe, red leggings. This superb piece is 16½ in. tall and ca. 1880s.   Museum quality

Morning Star Gallery, Santa Fe, NM

Doll carrier, Plateau, with doll. It is made of wood, hide and cloth, with beadwork. Ca. 1880. $900

Private collection, photo by John McLaughlin

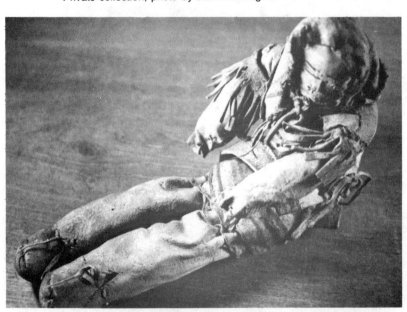

Doll carrier, Great Lakes region, with cornhusk doll, wood, cloth, yarn and beads. This interesting item is ca. 1900. $400

Private collection, photo by John McLaughlin

Indian doll, from near Eagle, Alaska, collected in the early 1900s. It has a cloth body and face with thread-sewn features and finely tanned clothing. Size, length 15 in. This is a rare item. $750

Private collection

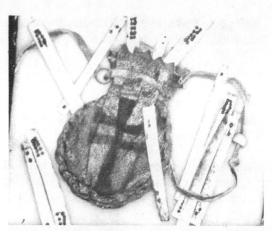

Apache game, hide bag with red decorations, drawstring top. The bone strips have various markings in black and are the playing pieces. A rare set. $900-$1500

Marguerite L. Kernaghan collection; photograph by Marguerite L. and Stewart W. Kernaghan, Bellvue, Colorado

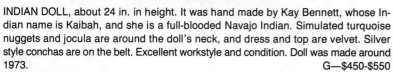

INDIAN DOLL, about 24 in. in height. It was hand made by Kay Bennett, whose Indian name is Kaibah, and she is a full-blooded Navajo Indian. Simulated turquoise nuggets and jocula are around the doll's neck, and dress and top are velvet. Silver style conchas are on the belt. Excellent workstyle and condition. Doll was made around 1973. G—$450-$550

Courtesy Hugo Poisson, photographer; Edmunds of Yarmouth, Inc.; West Yarmouth, Massachusetts.

Drum, Pueblo, red horse painted on top, black triangles on sides with yellow and red panels. This exceptional drum is ca. 1920-1940. Museum quality

Morning Star Gallery, Santa Fe, New Mexico

TOYS AND GAMES

Kiowa toy cradle with slat, 15 in. high. Made up of stained hide and partial beading. C—$700

Beaded buckskin **toy tipi,** Santee Sioux, an old item and in good condition. G—$550

Miniature travois, 17 in. long, Plains Indian and old. Two poles and small hide platform; unusual item. C—$145

Miniature Hupa cradle, 3¾ in. by 8½ in. A—$65

Miniature cradle, Paiute style, 14 in. long and 5 in. wide. Has wicker base, covered with hide and partially beaded. Piece is ca. 1930. G—$115

Child's toy travois, Sioux, in very fine condition. G—$180

Two **miniature Hupa cradles,** sold as one lot. A—$95

MUSICAL ITEMS — DRUMS

Drum, double-headed, painted with buffalo and eagle; a Pueblo piece and ca. 1890. D—$325

297

Plains-type drum, 14 in. in diameter, made of hide stretched on wood. Painted figure on hide. Old.　　　G—$335

Cree single-head drum, painted head, ca. 1920.D—$180

Drum, California Indian type, 6 in. high and 7 in. diameter. Hide stretched over wood, both ends covered and wood is painted. Good condition.　　　G—$210

Sioux drum, done on square box and 14 in. square. Painted with deer on one side and star on the other; stretched hide covers ends. Good sound and comes with early beater.　　　G—$240

Sioux drum, rawhide covered and laced wood drum, painted designs on ends, with beater.　　　G—$260

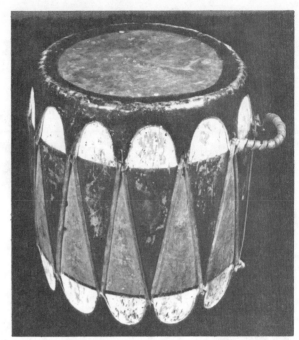

Drum, Pueblo, sides painted in red and green triangles. Ca. 1920-1940.
Museum quality

Morning Star Gallery, Santa Fe, New Mexico

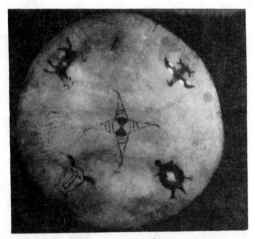

Cree Indian HAND DRUM, 16 in. in diameter. It has a very old hand-hewn wooden frame, and with painted zoomorphic designs on drumhead. Leather has a very small slit; a more modern drum-beater is included.　　　D—$350
Photo courtesy Crazy Crow Trading Post, Denison, Texas.

Drum, Sioux, hide and wood with painted background and animal figures. It is 19th century.　　　$4000
Private collection, photo by John McLaughlin

Drum, Pueblo, sides painted in pale plum and green, 7 in. in diameter and 10 in. high. It is ca. 1920-1940.　　　Museum quality
Morning Star Gallery, Santa Fe, New Mexico

Sioux hoop drum, 13 in. in diameter, hide covered single face, and piece has some age.　　　D—$195

Tourist-type drum, 10 in. in diameter, hide stretched over wood frame. Figure painted on hide, trimmed with feathers, and ca. 1940's.　　　G—$185

Indian drum, 11½ in. in diameter, some age.　　A—$60

Sioux hand-held drum, wood hoop type and hide covered. Drum is 11 in. in diameter.　　　G—$115

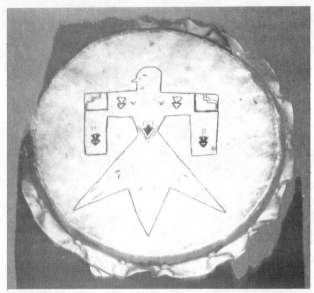

Dance drum, single-head, from the Iroquois on the Cayuga Reservation. With Thunderbird design, diameter is 10¼ in.; ca. 1920. $350-$600

Marguerite L. Kernaghan collection; photograph by Marguerite L. and Stewart W. Kernaghan, Bellvue, Colorado

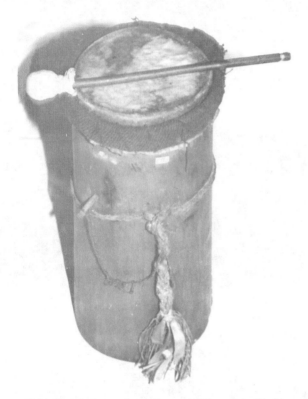

Drum, Mide, Great Lakes region, with wood, hide, paint, silk ribbon and cloth plus sweetgrass. It is 19th century. $1000

Private collection, photo by John McLaughlin

Plains-type drum, 16 in. in diameter and 3 in. thick, with beater. Hide stretched on wooden hoop; no design but pleasing tone.   G—$230

RATTLES

Hopi gourd rattle, painted black on white with swastika symbol.   D—$115

Peyote gourd rattle, recent, with red, white and blue beadwork; ebony handle has a buckskin figure.   D—$165

Medicine rattle, type sold by Northern Cheyenne Indians in Montana. Has a small leather ball on the end with horsehair; handle wrapped in rawhide. Made by Marion King.   G—$80

Plains rattle, 10 in. long and 3½ in. wide, and done with hide that has been made into the entire rattle. Has a light green painted design; 19th Century.   G—$210

Medicine rattle, Southwest type, a black leather hoop 4½ in. in diameter, with attached handle. Authentic. G—$240

Commanche rawhide rattle with horsetail decoration. Ca. 1890.   D—$185

Elk hoof rattle, part of medicine bundle, extra-fine condition.   G—$300

Bird-bone rasp, 9 in. long, from New Mexico.   D—$90

Peyote fan, Peyote style with gourd rattle. Seed bead design on wooden handle. Dyed hair on one end and woven leather fringe on the other.   G—$340

Plains Indian "bullroarer", a 9¾ in. flattened of wood with hole in smaller end. Item was whirled around the user on a cord, making a humming roar. Painted, but faded.   C—$75

Left: Larger CEREMONIAL RATTLE, companion piece to item on right. It is 5 in. in diameter with overall length 15 in. Pictured on rattle face is the Mide-related supernatural character Misshipeshu, otherwise known as the Underwater Panther, with a supernatural bird. Ca. 1895.   C—$400

Photo courtesy Bill Post Collection.

Right: Small CEREMONIAL RATTLE, Mide-wiwin Grand Medicine Society, Chippewa (Ojibway), 4 in. in diameter and 14 in. long. From Leech Lake, Minnesota; 5 small green turtles are on rattle face and edged in red color. All hide including sinew-sewn handle. Ca. 1895.   C—$400

Photo courtesy Bill Post collection

Bark rattle, Iroquois, 4½ x 13 in. This fine example is ca. 1900 and from New York state. $170

Pat & Dave Summers, Native American Artifacts, Victor, NY

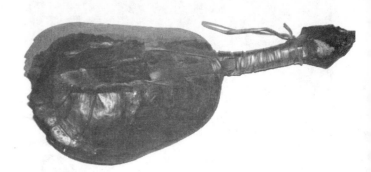

Turtle rattle, Iroquois, 16 in. long. It is made of wood with turtle shell, head and leather, with pebbles. It is 19th century. $1000

Private collection, photo by John McLaughlin

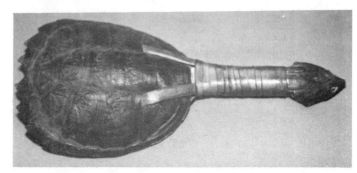

Contemporary snapping turtle rattle, Mohawk, from Ontario, Canada. This interesting piece is 14 in. long. $400

Michael F. Slasinski, Saginaw, Michigan

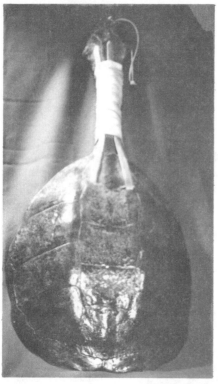

Turtle rattle, Iroquois, with leather handle winding. This large rattle is 27½ in. long. It is a contemporary piece, from New York state. $475

Pat & Dave Summers, Native American Artifacts, Victor, NY

Wooden bird-effigy rattle, Northwest Coast, Haida. Ca. early 1900s it is from Canada and is in perfect condition. $650-$1000

Marguerite L. Kernaghan collection; photograph by Marguerite L. and Stewart W. Kernaghan, Bellvue, Colorado

FLUTES & WHISTLES

Sioux love flute, 21 in. long, well carved and decorated, in good condition. Ca. 1920. G—$245

Small **Sioux flute,** sinew wrapped. G—$235

Bone flute, Plains Indian. A—$175

Sioux Grass Dance whistle, fine early piece with carved open-mouthed bird head. G—$330

Mogollon bird-whistle, red pottery, New Mexico.D—$90

CHAPTER XVII

WEAVINGS: BLANKETS AND RUGS

American Indian weavings are probably the warmest-looking and most useful of Amerind contemporary arts and crafts to live with. You can look at them, walk on them, sleep under them. Most of the older blankets are quite valuable as collector items, but modern rugs of good quality can be obtained at reasonable prices.

Weaving in North America has ranged from Northwest Coast spruce root mats to Plains robes made of rabbitskin strips. Today, the Navajo weavings are best known. They are certainly one of the Big Four of contemporary Amerind collectibles: Baskets, Blankets & Rugs, Jewelry and Pottery.

For the record, Pueblo blankets were made for centuries, but the Hopi Indians (here, the men often weave) now do most of the work. The Navajo Indians used natural cotton but then began to raise sheep for the wool.

The wool is chipped, cleaned and carded before it is spun on a whirling, handheld wooden spindle. Weft thread may be spun twice, while warp thread, which must be tight and strong, may be spun three times. If the wool is to be dyed, this step takes place; the dry wool is then rolled into balls, ready for the weaver.

The Navajo woman, the weaver, generally dyes only enough wool for the intended rug. This is for economy, but also so that any one dye color will match in the same rug and not be a different shade. Rugs, and the blankets before them, are woven on an upright loom which the Navajos may have developed and refined themselves. The warp threads (except for some historic Chief's blankets, where it is opposite) run up and down on the loom, or the length of the rug when it is completed.

Warp yarn is important, and experts say a wool warp is generally better than a cotton warp. It is more durable, making an all-wool rug, and the two age nicely together.

The weft threads run horizontally on the verticle loom, or the width of the finished rug. These are the design elements, formed by different weft colors. Any pattern will then be formed by the weft yarn. Without getting into a discussion of the actual weaving and tools used, it is enough to say that a good rug takes many hundred hours to make, and considerable degrees of experience of skill.

There are three colors of wool that might be in any one rug or late blanket, and they are sometimes combined to form different colors in the same rug.

1. **Natural:** Whitish, brown, gray and reddish black. Blackish wool is often dyed to make a solid black.

2. **Vegetal:** Dyed wool, the dye made from plant stems, roots, bark, etc. There are currently some 135 slightly different vegetal-dye colors. The best of these rugs are said to come from the Klagetoh region.

3. **Commercial:** (synthetic) Called "aniline" dyes, these were widely used in the last quarter of the 1800's and are still popular today.

Here are some of the historic Navajo blanket types, mostly from the 1850-1900 period. It is good to understand that these blankets were made for the Navajo's own wearing use and for trade.

The Chief's blanket was "exported" to other tribes and were so well-made that only an important person was said to be able to afford them. The best Navajo blankets — especially the complex double-faced blanket with different patterns on both sides using two distinct wefts — could hold water for awhile without seepage.

Shoulder blankets—ca. 1850 and later, men and women's sizes, simple stripes.

Striped blankets—Wearing blankets common among the Navajos until 1900's.

Banded blankets—"Fancier" striped varieties with additional designs between stripes.

Chief's blankets—Three varieties or "Phases" recognized, ca. 1850-1895.

1st Phase: Stripes of blackish color, red, white and blue

2nd Phase: Some red stripes divided into blocks; some blocks no longer joined by red. Greens sometimes used; designs within blocks.

3rd Phase: Some stripes have large diamond patterns, with the diamonds on the corners, the four sides, plus one in the center, nine in all. Multi-colored. Diamonds later became larger square crosses in some cases. Original 1st Phase stripes now only a small part of background.

Serape/Poncho-style blankets—Early and late periods, ca. 1860's-1880's. Diamond patterns, natural dyes. Some had a slit woven at center to go over the head.

Eye-Dazzler blankets—Ca. 1880-1910. Aniline or commercial dyes used. Blankets had a multitude of designs, especially zigzag lines and smaller, "busy" patterns. Examples had as many as nine different colors.

Other important blankets include **pictorial, wedge-weave child's blankets,** and the smaller **saddle throws. Bayeta blankets** were woven, when flannel-like red English blankets were unraveled and the yarn used in Navajo blankets. The period ca. 1850-1870 is considered to be the Classic Period, the golden age of Navajo blankets.

The last major Navajo blanket made a genuine break from the past. It is the **transitional blanket,** made in many eccentric patterns, some very well done. Ca. 1885-1900, some resembled earlier forms, others reverted to natural and vegetal colors. One significance is that these weavings are the last of the Navajo blankets before the changeover to rugs.

Before the turn of this century, quality White-made machine-woven blankets faltered and the White Indian traders decided to try something different.

With the completion of the railroads and many Eastern travelers in Navajo lands, a new demand arose for blankets. But it was for blankets used as rugs and tapestries, or floor coverings and wall hangings.

The Indians were encouraged to weave with heavier yarns, and in new sizes with new designs. Except for experiences like the "pound" rugs — when traders bought weavings according to weight, not quality — the enterprises have been highly successful.

Today, there are a dozen or so major Navajo weaving areas, each of which produces distinctive rug styles. The early blankets are commonly classed according to pattern. Today's rugs, except for the Yei rug or blanket and pictorials were named after the regions where they have been made for many years. But there has been so much departure from traditional and blending of patterns that these identify more rug style than a place style.

Here are some of the better-known contemporary Navajo blanket types.

Burntwater—Central panel in geometric style and a broad geometric border. Vegetal dyes.

Crystal—Simple and elegant patterns, vegetal dyes; these rugs have a certain "modern" look that is quite pleasing.

Ganado—Four-colored rugs; two natural (white, gray) and two aniline (red and enhanced black) colors are used.

Pictorial—Rugs woven with patterns of identifiable objects, people, animals, plants, feathers, etc.

Pine Springs—Designs are similar to Wide Ruins, but more vivid and with contrasting colors; earth tones.

Storm pattern—Symbolic dark geometric forms at the four corners, separated by broad white lightning designs.

Teec Nos Pos—Geometric designs in multi-colored shades, boldly outlined. Aniline dyes.

Two Grey Hills—Geometric basic designs, natural wools used; they are combined, also, to produce buff and gray.

Wide Ruins—Patterns closely follow those of late-Classic wearing blankets; horizontal bands, geometric designs with some bands.

Yei weavings—Yei figures copied from sacred sandpaintings (part of healing ceremonies). Light in weight compared with other contemporary rugs. These are often hung.

As of 1993, there has been an upsurge in prices for high-quality Navajo rugs. This has been due to a renewed interest in weaving arts, this based on a much larger number of collectors competing for a relatively few good rugs. Too, while rug-making has long been considered a craft, many of the pieces have come to be seen as fine art, again with appreciated prices. As cases in point, a $2000 rug in 1990 might go for $5000-$6000 today, and a $10,000 rug then might reach above $30,000 today.

OLDER BLANKETS

Navajo saddle blanket, 3 ft. 5 in. by 5 ft. 11 in., diamond patterns in red, natural-wool tufts as fringes. Several small burn holes in this specimen.   D—$800

Wearing blanket, 4 ft. 10 in. by 6 ft. 4 in., diagonal cut line. Homespun yarns, vegetal dye, good condition. Blanket is ca. 1885.   G—$2800

Serape-style blanket, Navajo, commercial (aniline) dyes, 4 ft. 3 in. by 6 ft. 1 in. Blanket made in four colors, in extra-good condition. Ca. 1800's.   C—$3900

Eye-dazzler blanket, size unknown, cotton wrap. Large blanket with damage that is repairable. Ca. 1890.G—$1300

Serape-style blanket, 6 ft. 3 in. by 4 ft. in., striped designs. Condition fair, with normal wear that shows. Late 1800's.   C—$2500

Transitional blanket, 50½ in. by 63½ in.   A—$200

Navajo blanket with red and rust designs, fawn-colored background. Minor moth damage; piece is 3 ft. 1 in. by 5 ft. 7 in.   C—$950

Transitional blanket, 4 ft. 6 in. by 7 ft. Design is serrated diamond showing heavy wear. Piece is ca. 1890.G—$1700

Navajo blanket, handspun wool with commerical dyes. Size is 5 ft. by 6 ft. 5 in. Excellent condition as blanket was stored for years. Wedge-weave pattern.   C—$2550

Zuni blanket, man's shawl style, 3 ft. 8 in. by 7 ft. 1 in. Multi-colored vegetal dyes; woven by men only, a rare piece in good condition. Blanket is pre-1920.   G—$5900

Chimayo blanket measuring 4 ft. 4 in. by 6 ft. 10 in.   A—$400

Saddle blanket, Navajo, 2 ft. 3½ in. by 3 ft. 1 in. Small size, good condition.   A—$300

Indian **blanket fragment,** section cut from old handwoven blanket. Red background, black designs. Piece is 19 in. long, 13 in. wide, with edges sewn to keep from fraying. All four sides decorated with horsehair. Unusual piece, unknown work.   C—$175

Navajo **saddle blanket,** 3 ft. 7 in. by 4 ft. 8 in., gray and black designs. Natural wool, fair condition.   D—$550

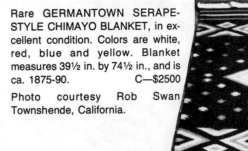

Rare GERMANTOWN SERAPE-STYLE CHIMAYO BLANKET, in excellent condition. Colors are white, red, blue and yellow. Blanket measures 39½ in. by 74½ in., and is ca. 1875-90.   C—$2500

Photo courtesy Rob Swan Townshende, California.

CHILD'S BLANKET of Merino sheep wool, which is like Angora. Rare, and condition excellent. Blanket, red, gray, white and black, is 30 in. by 50½ in. Ca. 1875-90.   C—$2500

Photo courtesy Rob Swan Townshende, California.

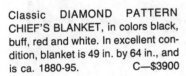

SERAPE-STYLE WOMAN'S BLANKET, early coarse weave. Black-bordered orange stripes on a cream background. It is 43½ in. by 64½ in. in very good condition. About Bosque Redondo.   C—$2500

Photo courtesy Rob Swan Townshende, California.

Classic DIAMOND PATTERN CHIEF'S BLANKET, in colors black, buff, red and white. In excellent condition, blanket is 49 in. by 64 in., and is ca. 1880-95.   C—$3900

Photo courtesy Rob Swan Townshende, California.

DIAMOND PATTERN BLANKET, medium-coarse weave, in colors red, white, black and gray. Excellent condition, and ca. 1895-1910.   C—$1200

Photo courtesy Rob Swan Townshende, California.

Classic DIAMOND PATTERN BLANKET, in colors red diamonds in white background and white diamonds in red background, brown borders. Eye-dazzler patterns, and excellent condition. Blanket is 39½ in. by 81½ in. It is ca. 1885-90.   C—$4000

Photo courtesy Rob Swan Townshende, California.

TRANSITIONAL DIAMOND PATTERN BLANKET, tight weave, in white, orangeish, and brown. Fair condition, and 47 in. by 62 in. Ca. 1890-1900.   C—$1500

Photo courtesy Rob Swan Townshende, California.

Rug, Navajo, ca. 1980 and 24½ x 30½ in. Pattern is a Teec Nos Pos dazzler in both hand-spun and commercial yarns and in natural color and natural and aniline dyes. The center stars are brilliant red with brown centers, bordered with alternating black, white, gray and brown.$390

Sherman Holbert Collection, Fort Mille Lacs, Onamia, MN

Saddle blanket, Navajo, very old. It measures 25½ x 44¼ in. and is black on yellow-tan. $150

Pat & Dave Summers, Native American Artifacts, Victor, NY

Rug, Navajo, optical illusion pattern. Contemporary, it is 27 x 54 in. and has natural grays and white, the black dye-enhanced to accent the contrast. Unusual and well-done design. $450

Sherman Holbert Collection, Fort Mille Lacs, Onamia, MN

Ganado rug, red, gray, black and white wools, with a strong and well-executed design. In impeccable condition, this 47 x 69 in. piece is ca. 1970.   Museum quality

James Reid, LTD, Santa Fe, New Mexico

304

Indian on horseback, pulling crossed-stick travois with traveling bundle; photo taken in Montana, unknown date, probably late 1800s.

Photographer Roland Reed; Courtesy Photography Collection, Suzzallo Library, University of Washington.

RECENT AND CONTEMPORARY RUGS

Teec Nos Pos rug, 50 in. by 90 in. Pristine condition, vibrant colors, and a rare piece. Ca. 1920.　　C—$8000

Navajo rug, diamond designs in many colors, 3½ ft. by about 6 ft., rust-red background with zigzag bands.
　　　　　　　　　　　　　　　　　　　C—$1700

Throw rug, Gallup (?), 17 in. by 39 in. Patterns in black, gray and white, excellent condition.　　G—$160

Pictorial rug, 48 in. by 66 in., and all natural wool colors. Weave is medium, and twenty feathers are woven into patterns. Item has a few minor stains and is about 1920's or 30's.　　　　　　　　　　　　　　G—$1150

Yei rug, 52 in. by 72 in. Pattern is five yeis surrounded by Rainbow God. Rug has "lazy lines" and comes with appraisal papers. Piece is about 50 years old. C—$2700

Navajo rug, 43 in. by 67 in., in good but worn condition.
　　　　　　　　　　　　　　　　　　　C—$1700

Navajo rug, moderated Klegetoh pattern, 5 ft. by 7 ft. Contemporary, and medium weave.　　G—$2500

Two Grey Hills rug, 30 in. by 35 in. Standard pattern, colors in tan, brown, black, gray and white. Rug has a tight weave and intricate pattern.　　G—$1100

Navajo **Tree of Life tapestry weaving,** from Shiprock, New Mexico. This rug type copies sandpainting designs.
　　　　　　　　　　　　　　　　　　　A—$1300

Navajo rug, Yeibichai dancers and head man. Rug is superfine, and 4 ft. 8 in. by 6 ft. Very tightly woven and in fine condition. Ca. early 1900.　　G—$3900

Two Grey Hills rug, 39 in. by 47 in. Colors gray, white, brown and black, and in good condition. Ca. 1950.
　　　　　　　　　　　　　　　　　　　G—$1600

Early **Navajo rug,** 33 in. by 58 in., with fine, tight weave. Good colors and designs; rug has slight stains on one side.
　　　　　　　　　　　　　　　　　　　G—$500

Wide Ruins rug, tapestry weaving style, 33 in. by 39 in., all natural wools and vegetal dyes.   A—$350

Navajo Sandpainting rug, 48 in. by 51 in., with very fine weave and in excellent condition. Ca. 1950's. G—$2600

Yei rug, 3 ft. by 5 ft., white background with five Yei figures. Good condition and ca. 1940.   C—$1300

Early **Navajo rug,** small size, good weave.   A—$425

Germantown rug, 24 in. by 31 in. Red with multi-color Eye-Dazzler pattern. Fringe on bottom intact; excellent condition. Ca. 1900.   G—$1100

Very old **Navajo rug,** 36 in. by 60 in. A high quality rug, but dirty and in need of repair. Poor condition. G—$100

Navajo rug, 3 ft. by 5½ ft., double-diamond pattern with geometric border. Medium-good condition, ca. 1930.   G—$550

Small **Germantown rug,** 22 in. square. Pattern in green and white on red background. Nice condition and ca. 1900.   G—$400

Yei rug, 35 in. by 53 in., multi-colored with brown background. Ca. 1950.   G—$1325

Pine Springs rug, 34 in. by 39½ in., natural wools and vegetal dyes.   A—$125

Teec Nos Pos rug, 42 in. by 64 in. Deep red predominates, with black, gray, white and orange colors. Very good design and in excellent condition. Ca. 1910-20.   G—$1250

Two Gray Hills rug, 49 in. by 73 in., colors are gray, white and black. Good condition, and ca. 1910.   G—$2000

Banded rug, 3 ft. 9 in. by 6 ft. 5 in., natural grays and whites, aniline reds and greens. Pattern may be derived from old wearing blankets. Contemporary.   D—$1700

Navajo rug, 31 in. by 56 in., vegetal dyed. Pattern is double-diamond with outlined design. Nice weave, and contemporary.   G—$725

Tapestry rug, Sandpainting designs, 53 in. by 72 in., and multi-colored. Gray background, extremely fine weave, a rare piece. Ca. 1960.   G—$10,500

Navajo rug, 5 ft. wide and 7 ft. long, diamond pattern in gray, white, red and black. Good condition.   G—$2200

Teec Nos Pos rug, 41 in. by 68 in., diamond pattern. Colors are red, black and gray and rug has a good, tight weave. Item is 40 to 50 years old.   G—$1650

Navajo rug, 58 in. by 83 in., very large and colorful with red and white swastikas. In good, sound usable condition.   G—$1350

Navajo rug, Klagetoh area, sunrise pattern with bows and arrows. Rug is 45 in. by 80½ in.   A—$1300

Ganado rug, 32 in. by 61 in., in good condition. Rug made by Daisy Mano, colors red, white and gray. Ca. 1920.   G—$1100

Navajo rug, Klagetoh area, measuring 38 in. by 57 in.   A—$300

Navajo rug, small, 20 in. by 40 in. Natural wool colors in gray, black and tan. Nice condition.   G—$350

Storm pattern rug, 4 ft. by 6 ft. excellent condition. Ca. 1940.   G—$1900

Yei rug, 4½ ft. by 6½ ft., with colors beige, brown, orange, vegetal-red, rust and blue. There are five central figures surrounded by Rainbow figure. Rug is ca. 1910. C—$2100

Two Grey Hills rug, measuring 40 in. by 70 in. A—$1250

Navajo rug, 2½ ft. by 5 ft. Pattern is double-diamonds with geometric border.   G—$350

Pine Springs rug, 30 in. by 56 in., colors tan, gray and white. Nice design and perfect condition. Made in 1976 by Florence James. Burnwater Post tag still attached.   G—$1225

Eye-Dazzler rug, 43 in. by 64 in., natural wool colors and red aniline dye. Handspun wool, and ca. 1920. C—$1700

TRANSITIONAL 2ND PHASE BLANKET, 41 in. by 62 in. Colors are a faded red, white, yellowish, brown and buff. There is a stain on one side, and condition is fair. Ca. 1880-85. C—$900

Photo courtesy Rob Swan Townshende, California.

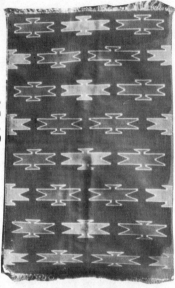

GERMANTOWN RUG OR BLANKET, black, white, blue and green designs on red ground. In poor condition, ca. 1890. C—$2400

Photo courtesy Jack Barry.

Extremely large TERRACE/STRIPED CHIEF'S BLANKET, in colors reddish, black, yellow and white. It measures 60 in. by 93½ in.; in good condition, with several minor, old repairs. From the transitional period, and ca. 1880-1895. C—$3600

Photo courtesy Rob Swan Townshende, California.

GERMANTOWN RUG OR BLANKET, blue and green designs outlined in white against red ground. Ca. 1890, good condition. C—$3200

Photo courtesy Jack Barry.

NAVAJO RUG, 24 in. by 46 in., in seven colors. From the Shiprock area, contemporary, and tagged. D—$250

Photo courtesy of American Indian World, Ltd., Denver, Colorado.

GERMANTOWN RUG OR BLANKET, green striping, white, black and blue designs against red ground. In good condition, ca. 1890. C—$2900

Photo courtesy Jack Barry.

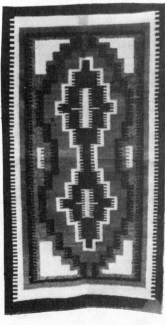

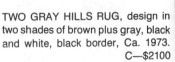

TWO GRAY HILLS RUG, design in two shades of brown plus gray, black and white, black border, Ca. 1973. C—$2100

Photo courtesy Jack Barry.

YEI/YEBECHAI RUG, about 60 in. by 8 feet, plus. Tight weave, and very good condition; colors predominately black, white, burnt-orange and red. Ca. 1920. C—$1750

Photo courtesy of Rob Swan Townshende, California.

307

Left: YEI RUG, figures in white, buff and gray against rich brown ground, border in black. Ca. 1973.

C—$800

Photo courtesy Jack Barry.

Right: YEI RUG, figures in red, yellow, white and blue-gray against gray ground. Ca. 1973.   C—$900

Photo courtesy Jack Barry.

Left: RUG, natural & vegetal dyes, ca. 1973.   C—$1000

Photo courtesy Jack Barry.

Right: PICTORIAL RUG, natural and vegetal colors, ca. 1973.

C—$1100

Photo courtesy Jack Barry.

Navajo rug, a fine large weaving in splendid condition. It is done in black, white, gray, red and rust and measures 58 x 84 in. This exceptional rug is ca. 1940. $2200

Pat & Dave Summers, Native American Artifacts, Victor, NY

Navajo rug, Eye-Dazzler, in colors of brown, gold, white, red, black and tan. Size is 38 x 72 in. This exquisite rug with very fine weave is ca. 1910. $700

Pat & Dave Summers, Native American Artifacts, Victor, NY

Navajo rug, Eye-Dazzler, in colors of red, white, gray and rust. This fine weaving is 34 x 58 in. and ca. 1925. $425

Pat & Dave Summers, Native American Artifacts, Victor, NY

Navajo rug, natural white, gray and dark brown. It has a concentric diamond pattern bordered with a fret design in red, natural white and dark brown. Size, 66 x 121 in. and ca. 1915.   Museum quality

James Reid, LTD, Santa Fe, New Mexico

Navajo rug, done in all-natural colors of white, brown, tan and camel. This classic weaving is 46 x 76 in. and is ca. 1920.

$600

Pat & Dave Summers, Native American Artifacts, Victor, NY

Navajo rug, Lightning pattern, in colors of brown, white, black and gray. Size is 30 x 57 in., with very fine weave. This well-done rug is ca. 1920.

$625

Pat & Dave Summers, Native American Artifacts, Victor, NY

Germantown Sunday saddle blanket, 24 x 29 in., in six colors. It is in top condition and ca. 1895. $450

Courtesy John Isaac, Albuquerque, New Mexico

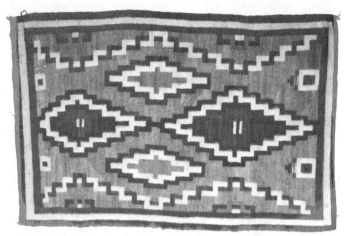

Navajo rug, Crystal pattern in colors of gray, red, white, brown and orange. It is 38 x 59 in., year 1920, from Crystal, New Mexico.
$450

Pat & Dave Summers, Native American Artifacts, Victor, NY

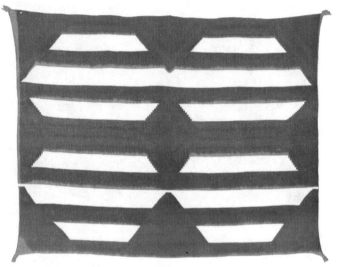

Blanket, Chief's pattern, Germantown third phase, done in white, black and red. This rare weaving is ca. 1880-1890.   Museum quality

Morning Star Gallery, Santa Fe, New Mexico

Crystal weaving, natural shades of brown with red and yellow ochre in storm pattern. This Navajo work has fine weave and fair condition. It is 34½ x 70 in. and ca. 1915.   Museum quality

James Reid, LTD, Santa Fe, New Mexico

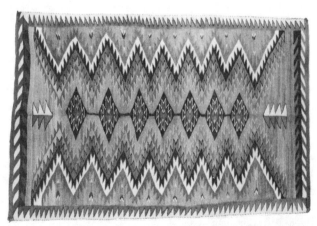

Rug, Navajo, 48 x 74 in. It is pre-World War One and a dazzler with exceptional weave. At some points in the design there are as many as 40 color-changes across the width of the rug with each change having an individual outline. Natural gray background with white, red, golds, black and yellow patterns. $3000

Sherman Holbert Collection, Fort Mile Lacs, Onamia, MN

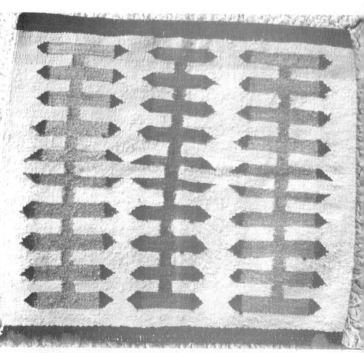

Saddle blanket, Navajo, blacks, grays, rust and red on tan-cream with black top and bottom borders. It is 28 x 30 in. and ca. 1940s. $150

Pocotopaug Trading Post, South Windsor, CT

Weaving, Germantown Yei, 2 ft. 8 in by 6 ft. This work is done in nine colors on a gray background and is ca. 1920. It is in mint condition. $4200

Courtesy John Isaac, Albuquerque, NM

Saddle-blanket, Navajo, twill weave, 27 x 29 in. Done in reds, black and buff, it is ca. 1930s. $100-$125

Pocotopaug Trading Post, South Windsor, CT

Crystal rug, Navajo, 5 ft. 2 in. by 8 ft. 10 in., very good condition. It is red and natural shades of white, beige and dark brown, with a central design and geometric border. With pleasing pattern, it is from the 1930s.
                    Museum quality

James Reid, LTD, Santa Fe, New Mexico

Regional Navajo rug, 43 x 58 in. It is black-bordered with colors of red, black and two shades of gray against white. Ca. 1920. $400-$600

Terry Schafer collection, Marietta, OH

Mr. Al R. Packard does business as Packard's Indian Trading Company, of Santa Fe, New Mexico. He is a third generation Indian trader, in Santa Fe since 1929. The writer was referred to Mr. Packard as being one of the most knowledgeable persons in the country on the subject of American Indian weavings, old and new.

Mr. Packard kindly consented to offer six tips on buying a Navajo rug, with two additional observations. These involve esthetic values and where to buy. Used with permission.

A PERSON BUYING A NAVAJO RUG SHOULD LOOK FOR THE FOLLOWING:

1) *Symmetry:* Place the rug on a floor without any background design. This way one can tell whether the edges and design are straight or crooked. If there is not an unobstructed area to throw the rug on, then fold the rug in half (warp end to warp end) and see if the width at each end is close to the same.

If there is a two inch or more difference on a 6 ft. long rug, then it will look crooked on the floor. Two inches would not matter on a twelve foot rug but even an inch would matter on a 4 ft. rug.

2) *Stains:* Although nearly all Navajo rugs have identical designs on both sides, the buyer must be sure to examine both sides. Occasionally there will be a rust, grease, ink, coffee, urine, etc. stain on one side but won't show through. An unethical dealer or weaver would throw the rug down with the unstained side showing.

3) *Cotton vs. wool warp:* Since the warp in a Navajo rug is completely hidden the buyer must pull the weft apart to tell whether the warp is cotton or wool. Wool warp is preferred and generally only an expert can tell the difference. However, wool is never quite as white as cotton, and cotton warp really looks and is cotton string.

4) *Weft packing:* For a long lasting rug, be sure that the weft is packed tightly together.

5) *Weft thickness:* The finer the weft threads are spun the sharper the design will be. Also, the finer the weft the more expensive the rug.

6) *Design:* The "one of a kind" designs in Navajo rugs offer endless patterns and colors. Peoples tastes differ also, so choose a rug of your own liking.

Do not look for absolute perfection when buying a Navajo rug. Using a primitive loom combined with natural human error cannot result in a perfect product. This is what makes Navajo weaving a true work of art. Buy it for what it is and treat it and enjoy it as you would a painting on your wall.

Buy at a reliable store, preferably an Indian Arts and Crafts Association member. Mexican imitations are saturating the market and although they don't compare with a true Navajo rug they can fool the uniformed buyer.

(A.R.P)

CHAPTER XVIII

SILVER AND
TURQUOISE JEWELRY

Probably no other category of contemporary Amerind art forms has so captured the attention of the general purchasing public as has jewelry. Silver and turquoise necklaces and bracelets and rings went for surprising sums in the 1970's and 1980's. Few buyers cared, or cared to check, whether the items were either well-made or authentic American Indian-made.

Behind the in-fashion publicity and money came the sharpsters. They proved, if nothing more, that Taiwan has some excellent crafts-people and that modern plastics can be made to resemble the shapes and colors of natural turquoise. More than one disenchanted buyer proudly called in an insurance agent to cover a $1500 squash-blossom, and found that the acquisition was indeed a good item—at one twentieth the price.

A few years have passed and three major changes have occurred. Many of the offending merchandisers have gone out of business, and consumer-protection agencies have gained some clout. Collectors and buyers have become more street-wise, educated, in the ways and means of purchasing good items.

And the Amerind artisans have themselves come to understand that craft quality in design and manufacture provide both a livelihood and a continuation of buyer/collector demand. It is the general opinion of dealers in contemporary jewelry that very good pieces are still available at reasonable prices; in other words, the investment aspect has not been lost.

Following is information pertaining to a special class of older Indian jewelry known as "Old Pawn". The background story of Old Pawn is fascinating; this, and the description of Old Pawn pieces, along with prices, is courtesy Don C. Tanner's Indian Gallery, 7007—5th Avenue, Scottsdale, Arizona. Reprinted by permission.

OLD PAWN—THE REAL INDIAN JEWELRY

"Old Pawn", when correctly used in conjunction with Indian jewelry, means a piece made by an Indian craftsman, acquired, worn, treasured and finally pawned by an Indian and sold by the trader when it becomes "dead". The term "old pawn" has a romantic appeal. It represents native ideals, craftsmanship, tradition, and intrinsic worth.

The pawn system today is still used as it was back in the late 1800's. However, the number of traders has diminished markedly due to increased legislative controls and the use of the monetary system. The pawn system began with the Reservation traders and became an integral part of the Reservation economics. Since most business was transacted by barter and exchange, money per se meant very little. Silver coins could be hammered, melted and cast into jewelry that could be worn, exchanged, or used as collateral for a loan. Guns, saddles, blankets, buckskins, baskets, and robes could be pawned also, but jewelry was most common.

The Southwest Indians used the pawn system regularly, primarily as collateral for a loan to get them by between sheep shearing seasons, lamb crops, pay checks, etc. In addition they would pawn their jewelry in order to keep it safe when they didn't need it. It also served as the Indian's visible bank account, displaying his worth. During the summer months there were the ceremonials and to appear at their best they made every effort to redeem their pawn, even though custom allows the Indian to take out their ornaments without redeeming them, after which they were conscientiously returned.

The Indian's personal jewelry is generally of the best quality. However, some will try and pawn their least valuable jewelry first. The pawn dealers usually have their own set of standards of what they will or will not accept. The pawn dealers then gain a reputation among the Indians by which they know what they can or cannot pawn.

There are some characteristics of "old pawn" Indian jewelry that one can recognize and should be familiar with.

The early jewelry was made out of hammered coins or by casting. In the 1940's most silversmiths were using sheet silver which didn't have to be melted or hammered. The older pieces tend to be heavier and massive compared to the newer jewelry. Old jewelry that has been worn should have a patina or light to dark gray coloration caused by the skin acids, etc. This can be done chemically so again one must exercise caution in their selection.

Some bracelets were originally made as plain silver bands and then the stones were set afterwards. Wire bracelets were made by hammering the wire to the desired size. This can be seen by the different thicknesses and twists of the wire.

Old jewelry was made by designing the bezel to fit the stone. Newer jewelry is the opposite. Some stones were used first as earrings and pendants, then reset in bracelets or rings. Consequently, small holes can sometimes be seen in the reused stones.

The real "old pawn" is becoming a scarce item. However, it is still available in limited quantity through reliable dealers. We see "old pawn" jewelry as an intimate relic of a people and a culture which is slowly and inevitably disappearing into history. This fact alone makes legitimate "old pawn" jewelry valuable in today's market place.

The information that follows—Indian Silversmithing; Navajo, Zuni and Hopi Silverwork; Santo Domingo Beadwork—has been reprinted with the kind cooperation and permission of Mr. Armand Ortega, owner of the Indian Ruins Trading Post at Sanders, Arizona.

Armand Ortega is a well-known and respected Indian trader, the product of four generations of life among the Indians of the Southwest. His expertise in the field of native American arts and crafts stems from this life-long experience, during which he learned the intricacies of turquoise, became fluent in the Spanish and Navajo languages, and developed a deep understanding and respect for Indian culture.

The Zunis began their silversmithing in the 1870's with most of the other Pueblos learning the art by 1890. Each tribe, influenced differently, developed its own special style. The Zunis worked initially as stone cutters and became well-known for their expertise and skill.

Much of the jewelry was originally made by the Indians for their own adornment, and the amount worn signified personal wealth. As the White traders close to the Indians began to see and appreciated the jewelry, they encouraged the craft and supplied turquoise, silver, and finer tools in order to refine the designs and increase quality. The Indians have never mined silver and only mined small quantities of turquoise. White traders today continue to supply them with the materials for their craft.

The first Indian jewelry marketing venture was initiated by the Fred Harvey Company in 1899, selling Indian jewelry on Santa Fe trails and at railroad station shops. Harvey provided silver and turquoise to the area trading posts and paid local silversmiths for finished work. This introduction of Indian jewelry to tourists from across the nation was a contributing factor in the popularity of hand-made jewelry which has grown over the years.

With more silversmiths than ever improving designs and workmanship, it is easy to see how the once crude craft has developed into the art it is today.

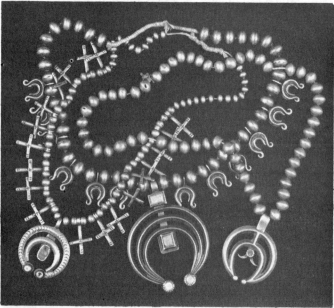

Three Navajo silver Naja necklaces, all ca. 1900. These came out of "Dead Pawn" before World War II. $1800-$4500, each

John C. Hill Antique Indian Art, Scottsdale, Arizona

Necklace, Navajo, hand-made silver beads with a 1946 silver half-dollar pendant: The pendant was worked to present a convex surface on the head side of the coin. Interesting and well-made necklace. $125

Sherman Holbert Collection, Fort Mille Lacs, Onamia, MN

INDIAN SILVERSMITHING

Silversmithing is a relatively recent Indian craft which began its development in the late 1850's. The Navajo, the first to engage in silversmithing, used the silver ornaments of the Spanish explorers as a basis for many of their designs. Conchas, originally from the bridles of Spanish horses, influenced the familiar concha belt. The squash blossom is an elongated version of the Spaniards' pomegranate ornament.

NAVAJO SILVERWORK

The work of the Navajos is generally massive and simple in design. The Navajos are expert silversmiths and enhance their silver work with turquoise stones. Along with their silversmithing, the art of sandcasting silver was begun long ago by the Navajo tribe. Recently they have started overlay silverwork with the inlay of chips of turquoise and coral in contemporary designs.

Bracelet pair, heavy silver wire bands, silver hollow balls, with blue-green turquoise nugget suspensions. Wrist-rings are 2¼ in. in diameter and set is 3¾ in. long. Southwest, ca. early 1900s. $90

Private collection, Ohio

Navajo woman's bracelet, silver and turquoise. The stone in this piece is untreated natural turquoise. $500-$750

Private collection

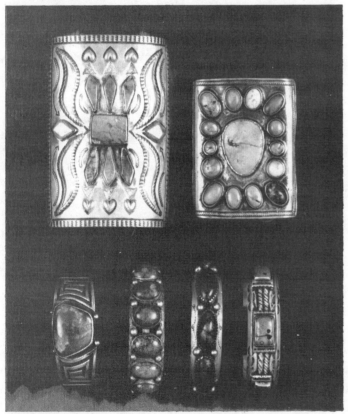

Silver and turquoise jewelry.
Top, Navajo and Hopi Ketohs or bow-guards. Bottom, early Hopi (left) and early Navajo bracelets, these ca. 1910-1940s.

$375-$950, each

John C. Hill Antique Indian Art, Scottsdale, Arizona

Zuni mosaic inlay ring, man's size. This example was made from the silver contained in one U.S. silver dollar. $175-$250

Private collection

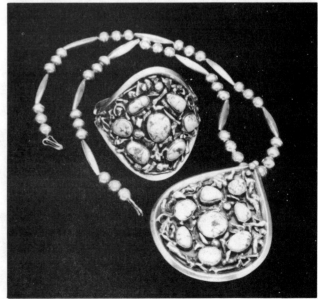

Jewelry, Navajo, silver and turquoise set. Necklace, 3¼ in. in diameter, bracelet 2¼ in. in diameter. Attractive and matching, there are seven stones in the bracelet and eight stones with 48 handmade silver beads in the necklace. Ca. 1970. $575, set

Sherman Holbert Collection, Fort Mille Lacs, Onamia, MN

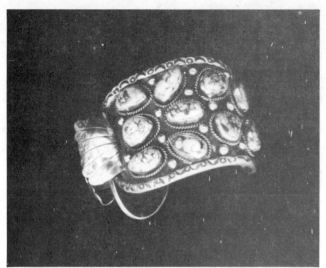

Bracelet, Navajo, silver and turquoise, 3 in. in diameter. Ca. 1970, the bracelet is beautifully made with 13 attractively mounted turquoise stones while the silver has an intricate pattern. Piece was made by Rose Fransiscus and is stamped with her mark. $495

Sherman Holbert Collection, Fort Mille Lacs, Onamia, MN

Navajo woman's necklace, silver in floral design with turquoise. Private collection $800-$1400

Necklace, Navajo, squash blossom, 20 in. long. A very attractive small necklace with 11 well-matched turquoise settings. With hand-made beads this ca. 1940s piece has nice patina. $425

Sherman Holbert Collection, Fort Mille Lacs, Onamia, MN

Concho belt, Navajo Second Phase, Transitional, excellent silverwork on leather. It is ca. 1900. $9500

Crown & Eagle Antiques, Inc., New Hope, PA

Concho belt, Navajo First Phase, silver on leather, very well made. It is ca. late 1800s. $10,000

Crown & Eagle Antiques, Inc., New Hope, PA

Navajo turquoise and silver bracelets, from the period ca. 1920s-1940s. The workstyle and materials are very fine. $150-$600, each

John C. Hill Antique Indian Art, Scottsdale, Arizona

ZUNI SILVERWORK

The emphasis on the stones rather than the silver characterizes Zuni craftsmanship. The Zunis are expert in cutting and setting stones in clusters, delicate needlepoint, and inlays of turquoise, coral, jet and shell. Setting and cutting stones was well-known to the Zunis long before they began working with silver.

Butterfly pin, Zuni, inlaid with jet, turquoise, mother-of-pearl and spiney oyster shell. This large pin is 4 in. across and ca. 1940s.

Crown & Eagle Antiques, Inc., New Hope, PA $900

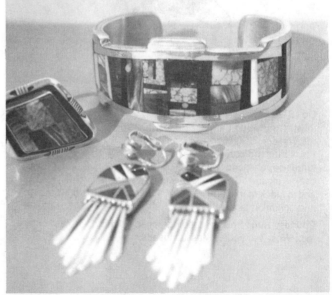

Contemporary Zuni jewelry, silver set with various precious and semi-precious materials. This set includes inlay bracelet and ring, plus earrings. $1100-$1700, set

Private collection

Belt, choice Santo Domingo 26-concha dime sampler belt of silver coins on black leather. Each ¾ x 1 in. concha is of individual design. Mid-20th century, it is signed CRZ. Ex-coll. Coriz. $500

Pat & Dave Summers, Native American Artifacts, Victor, NY

317

HOPI SILVERWORK

The overlay technique of the Hopi was developed in the 1930's. The Hopi had previously copied many of the Navajo and Zuni styles. With encouragement from the Museum of Northern Arizona, they developed their own overlay technique. Using many of their distinctive pottery designs, Hopi overlay is executed by cutting out a design in silver and attaching it to another layer of oxidized silver, allowing the design to stand out.

OUTSTANDING ZUNI INLAYED PIN, 4⅜ in. long. Made by the master craftsman Lambert Homer Jr. The pin was originally in the Wallace Collection and was made in 1951.
Pin is the form of a silver Rainbow god, inlayed with Blue Gem turquoise, pink and white shell, red coral and black jet. On pin back is etched "C.G. Wallace, Zuni", and in print, "Zuni, N.M.", and in black marker, "IOG 100". The inlay fitting is outstanding and condition is excellent.   G—$2500-$3500
Courtesy Hugo Poisson, photographer; Edmunds of Yarmouth, Inc.; West Yarmouth, Massachusetts.

SANTO DOMINGO BEADWORK

Santo Domingo bead work is an ancient art which originally made use of handmade tools and original techniques. Turquoise and coral as well as assorted shells are used in their bead making. The material is drilled and the stones are then strung on cord and rolled or ground to the shape and size of bead strands desired.

OLD AND RECENT SILVER AND TURQUOISE JEWELRY

Southwestern Indian **turquoise necklace,** 19½ in. long, consisting of raw stones and finished beads which alternate along the length. Blue turquoise, and very old piece, probably from early historic times.   C—$850

Single oblong **turquoise pendant,** 1½ in. long, drilled at smaller and thinner end. From a prehistoric Southwestern site, and accompanied by other bone artifacts. C—$110

Navajo chunk necklace, 1900 or before. Jaclas attached, and with handmade heishi; all turquoise is a natural green. One sing attached. Rare piece; necklace has both age and quality.   G—$1900

Navajo man's pawn belt, with six conchas, each 3 in. by 3½ in. Buckle and conchas set with turquoise; belt also has seven butterflies and is ca. 1930's.   G—$1695

Silver necklace, Navajo, about 25 in. long, with beads hammered from old silver dimes. Central pendant of silver-mounted turquoise. Ca. 1950's.   D—$800

Old Navajo bracelet, 2¼ in. at widest point. It contains 49 pieces of good turquoise set in silver; beautiful blue stone, excellent condition.   G—$650

Sheet-silver bracelet, 1½ in. wide and set with turquoise nuggets. This is an old piece.   G—$375

Tlingit **silver bracelet,** by Leo Jacobs of Haines.A—$195

Solid silver cockroach, 3 in. long and 2 in. wide. Item has eyes of inlayed turquoise, and is quite old and unusual.   G—$185

Silver wrist **bowguard,** recent Zuni, stamped silver on leather. Large carved central plate, well done. D—$365

Pawn silver, **Navajo concha belt;** piece has five conchas, five butterflies and buckle. All inlayed with turquoise and with original leather backing; early period.   G—$1225

Squash blossom necklace, Navajo, all silver with naja, and blossoms on each side. Necklace has a double row of beads, and is ca. 1950.   G—$525

Assorted Indian silverwork and turquoise:
Concha belt,C—$1100, Concha belt C—$675, (Ca. 1940)
          Cluster bracelet, C—$825

Navajo **Concha belt,** with six hand-stamped silver conchas on leather, with turquoise. Seven hand-stamped butterflies with single stones. Belt has multi-stoned buckle, and piece is ca. 1930.   G—$1900

Bolo tie fastener, Navajo, with pawn ticket attached. Fastener has two turquoise stones and is dated 1970.
G—$185

Sunburst cluster bracelet, Zuni, very nice piece and ca. 1940.
G—$795

Navajo concha belt, with eight hand-stamped conchas and buckle.
G—$1550

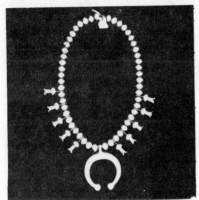

Heavy Navajo man's old SILVER SQUASH BLOSSOM NECKLACE, made with U.S. and Canadian dimes. No sets; fastened, necklace is 15 in. long and Naja is 4 in. wide. Has abalone piece tied to top. Sandcast Naja. This is a pawn piece from Teec Nos Pos Trading Post, Navajo reservation and ca. 1915.   C—$1200

S.W. Kernaghan photo; Marguerite Kernaghan Collection.

OLD NAVAJO SILVER AND TURQUOISE BRACELET, with circumference of bracelet 6¼ in. and stone measures 1¾ in. long 1¼ in wide. A very fancy silver setting surrounds the turquoise, the stone along the edges give an appearance of being spotted, with dark blue and a lighter blue. At bottom of bracelet back are etched two words, "Joann" and "Becent". Outstanding workstyle and in excellent condition, the piece is ca. 1920s.   G—$1300

Courtesy Hugo Poisson, photographer; Edmunds of Yarmouth, Inc., West Yarmouth, Massachusetts.

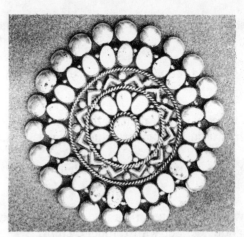

ZUNI CLUSTER PIN, measuring approximately 3 in. by 3 in. The turquoise stones are from the Lone Mountain mine; pin is signed on back in print, "Zuni" and in script, "Lee Mary". There are 23 tear-shaped stones on outer rim of the cluster, 10 on inner cluster, with one stone set in the center.

Lee Mary's work has been pictured in the Collectors Edition of *Arizona Highways* and in several other Indian jewelry books. Workstyle is outstanding and pin is in excellent condition. Pin was made in the late 1950s.
G—$1300

Courtesy Hugo Poisson, Photographer; Edmunds of Yarmouth, Inc., West Yarmouth, Massachusetts.

CONTEMPORARY JEWELRY

Silver necklace, contemporary Navajo, double beaded. Turquoise inlay of flying birds, crescent naja or pendant, also with chip inlay.
D—$900

Navajo pawn belt, woman's size, conchas 1½ in. in diameter. Buckle and conchas inlayed with turquoise; recent work.
G—$725

Concha belt, 32 in. in length, made of nine finely worked thin silver conchas and a rectangular belt buckle. No stones.
G—$510

Silver concha belt, made by Monroe Ashley, with thirteen conchas each 1½ in. by 2 in., plus buckle.   C—$600

Silver concha belt, disc-type conchas about 3 in. in diameter, with rectangular silver spacers. All with blue turquoise centers; contemporary Navajo.
D—$1600

Concha belt, made of nine sandcast silver conchas. Circular pieces, no stones, with belt buckle sandcast and in rectangular shape. Recent or contemporary item. G—$510

Silver bracelet, narrow, turquoise chip inlay, contemporary Navajo.
D—$70

Silver bracelet, ¾ in. wide, handmade and contemporary Hopi Indian.
D—$185

Silver bracelet, contemporary Navajo, with turquoise chip inlays.   D—$140

Silver bracelet, rope-twist style, contemporary Navajo.   D—$55

Silver bracelet, wide, man's size, contemporary Navajo. Piece has turquoise chip inlay, traditional designs. D—$210

Finger ring, handmade silver with two blue turquoise stones.   D—$70

Finger ring, ⅝ in. interior diameter, contemporary Navajo and handmade. Set with turquoise chips.   D—$95

Silver earrings, contemporary Navajo, handmade. D—$45

Silver earrings, contemporary Hopi, simple design in silver overlay.   D—$80

Silver pendant, 1⅞ in. long, contemporary Hopi handmade, with natural turquoise stone.   D—$145

Contemporary silver letter-opener, probably Navajo, and 8½ in. long. Handle is set with one large turquoise stone and one small stone. Very well-done work.   D—$80

Silver belt buckle, 2¼ in. by 3⅛ in., probably Hopi, entirely handmade.   D—$255

Silver bolo tie fastener, die-stamped silver, set with turquoise and red coral. Contemporary Navajo.   D—$250

Silver pendant, large size, contemporary Navajo. Traditional inlay designs; chip inlays of turquoise and red coral.   D—$325

Silver belt buckle, contemporary Navajo, with design in turquoise chip inlays.   D—$225

Solid silver Navajo cross, 3¼ in. wide and 5¼ in. high. Nice inlayed turquoise center; this is a well-done sandcast piece.   G—$160

Silver pin, 3 in. long and sandcast; contemporary Navajo.   D—$75

Silver cross-form pendant, 2 in. high, recent Navajo in origin. Piece set with several small turquoise stones.   D—$120

Bolo tie fastener, sandcast silver, 2¾ in. high, and with elongated natural turquoise stone. Solid silver front, with tool-marked designs.   D—$325

Silver brooch, 1¾ in. in diameter, set with natural turquoise stones; contemporary Hopi.   D—$220

Silver hat band, contemporary Navajo, with a dozen and a half miniature concha plates on leather strip. D—$160

Bolo tie fastener, contemporary Hopi, large, all silver.   D—$225

Sandcast silver belt buckle, 3 in. long, contemporary Navajo; double-naja motif, and graceful lines.   D—$210

CAST-SILVER BRACELET, 6½ in. in circumference, with a magnificent Blue Gem mine turquoise stone. Stone is 2 in. long Bracelet was made in the early 1950s and the craftperson did an outstanding job. Three silver bands support the stone and bands have been etched.
On the back of the turquoise is a silver plate ¾ in. by 1¼ in. and on which has been worked on intricate design. Bracelet in excellent condition.   G—$1800-$2400
Courtesy Hugo Poisson, Photographer; Edmunds of Yarmouth, Inc., West Yarmouth, Massachusetts.

KEYCHAIN PIECE or small pendant, 2 in. high, of sheet silver and small round greenish turquoise stone. A tourist item, and ca. 1955. C—$25
Private Collection.

Here are three examples of Indian-owned and operated arts and crafts businesses. All carry a selection of silver and turquoise jewelry.

Hopi Arts & Crafts Guild
P.O. Box 37
Second Mesa, Arizona   86043

Navajo Arts & Crafts Enterprise
P.O. Drawer A
Window Rock, Arizona   86515

Pueblo of Zuni   Arts & Crafts
P.O. Box 425
Zuni, New Mexico   87327

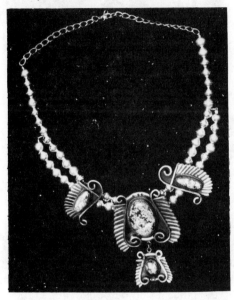

SILVER AND TUR-QUOISE NECKLACE, with one large and three smaller stones. All silver, contemporary styling.   D—$1300
Photo courtesy Howard Shaw, Casa Kakiki Sunland Park, New Mexico

The following information on turquoise is courtesy of Mr. Armand Ortega, owner of the Indian Ruins Trading Post, Sanders, Arizona, and reprinted by permission.

TURQUOISE—THE SKY STONE

To the Indians, turquoise has the life-giving power of sky and water and is held in high esteem. This beautiful blue gem that the earth has given is their sign of wealth as well as a symbol of protection from the forces of evil.

The "sky-stone" has been part of Indian cultures for centuries. The oldest well-documented record of the use of turquoise was the discovery of two turquoise ornaments at southeastern Arizona's Snaketown ruin estimated to have been made before 300 A.D. Turquoise deposits found in the West have shown evidence of prehistoric mining. It is said that turquoise mining predates any other kind of mining in the United States.

Technically, turquoise is a mineral belonging to the copper group and is found in arid regions of the Southwestern United States and parts of Asia. It is formed by the action of water which deposits it in veins in existing rock. This mother rock creates the markings or matrix which appear in the turquoise as thin black lines, brown or black blotches, iron pyrite or bits of quartz, and gives each stone its own natural beauty.

The color of turquoise varies from light blue to deep blue and green. As well as color variations, turquoise has many grades. Of each mine producing turquoise, only a small percentage is of high-grade gem quality. High-grade stones are those with greatest density, hardest consistency and deepest color, as well as those with the finest matrix pattern or "spiderwebbing" as it is commonly called. Turquoise is sold by carat weight with high-grade stones costing considerably more per carat because of their quality and scarcity.

As turquoise grades go downward, the hardness decreases accordingly and the color seems to get higher. These medium-to-lower-grades of turquoise are more abundant than the high-grade stone and most often stabilized to increase durability and deepen the color of the stones. Naturally, stabilized turquoise is less expensive than the higher grades but commands a greater price than unstabilized stones of the same grade.

Much confusion exists as to the merits of stabilized turquoise. Many people are under the impression that stabilization alters the true stone, covers faults, and makes it less valuable. On the contrary, proper stabilization of turquoise enhances the color and durability of the stone so that it will resist cracking and retain its sky-blue color through the years.

People are suddenly becoming suspicious of stabilized turquoise, when for many years turquoise and most other precious and semi-precious stones have been treated in similar and equally advantageous ways.

Turquoise is a relatively soft mineral and stabilizing does just what it implies—strengthens the stone. This added durability makes the turquoise easier for silversmiths to work with and assures the consumer that daily encounters with water, oils and moisture will no longer turn the stone a dull green.

Stabilization is scientifically done while turquoise is in rough form using material of a resinous nature which seals the pores of the turquoise while in a vacuum. No foreign or unnatural color is added, since the stabilizing process itself deepens the natural color of the stone.

There is a very old turquoise mine at Cerrillos, southwest of Santa Fe in New Mexico. The material was traded in prehistoric times even into present-day Mexico. Mining there began sometime in the early A.D. centuries.

Other well-known turquoise mines are: Castle Dome, Kingman, Number Eight, Carrico Lake, Fox, Villa Grove, Valley Blue, Battle Mountain, Globe, Lander Blue, Lone Mountain, Morenci, Bisbee, Blue Gem, Poe and Stormy Ridge.

The following provides additional accurate information about turquoise, including several little-known aspects of this attractive gemstone. This material has been provided by Edmunds of Yarmouth, Inc., of West Yarmouth, Massachusetts, and is reprinted by permission.

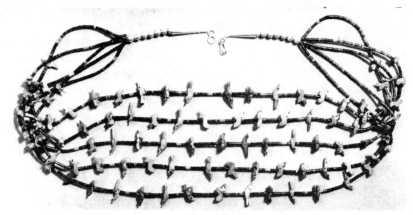

FINE TURQUOISE AND TORTOISE SHELL NECKLACE, length 32 in. end to end. Fetishes of turquoise are in the form of birds, turtles and bears. Hand-carved by Juanite Chapella, with stone from the Kingman mine. There are 100 fetishes on the necklace, workstyle is outstanding and condition is excellent.

Juanite Chapella had Atsidi Chon (Ugly Smith) of the Standing House Clan as an ancient grandfather. Atsidi Chon was one of the teachers of Slender-Maker-of-Silver.

G—$4000-$4500

Courtesy Hugo Poisson, Photographer; Edmunds of Yarmouth, Inc., West Yarmouth, Massachusetts.

BEARCLAW NECKLACE, silver and turquoise, with two bearclaw inclusions. D—$1200

Photo courtesy Howard Shaw, Casa Kakiki, Sunland Park, New Mexico.

A SHORT STORY OF TURQUOISE
By Edmunds of Yarmouth, Inc.

"Turquoise" comes from the French word meaning Turkish, indicating the origin (Middle East) of the stones. Turquoise is said to bring success in love and money. It is also the birthstone for December. Turquoise has not only found popularity in this country, but goes back to the early civilizations of foreign lands. Queen Zer of the first Egyptian Dynasty owned turquoise jewelry.

Turquoise is found in many locations all over the world. Most of the Southwestern states (Nevada, Arizona, New Mexico, Colorado) produce turquoise ranging in quality from low grade to gem. The mines around Nishapur, in Iran, yield the high quality stones known to us as Persian turquoise. Low to medium grade turquoise is also found in Africa, Australia, China and Tibet. The Indians of the Southwest were mining turquoise centuries before the White man came to the area. Now the White man mines the stones and the Indians buy from the traders.

Turquoise is cut usually in dome shape. The stones are usually cut so that the finished gem includes some of the matrix in which the turquoise is found. The matrix can be brown, black, yellow, red or even white in color. Many people judge a stone by how much matrix is in the stone. However, some people find the matrix more attractive. One form of matrix which is very popular today is that known as "spiderweb". In this type of turquoise, the matrix is formed in very fine lines which show patterns similar to lifelike spider webs.

Turquoise, especially the lighter blue stone, is a porous stone. Therefore, we recommend removing a turquoise ring before washing dishes, bathing, or washing hands, as the soaps and oils may change the color of the stone. Many Indian rings, especially Zuni inlay pieces, can have their stones loosened by prolonged exposure to water. Zuni rings are almost impossible to size, as heat is sizing the ring would harm the stone.

In the past few years turquoise has become very popular. We see the stars wearing it on television, and people from all walks of life wearing it on the street. The jewelry comes in many forms. It can be bought for babies; as silver spoons, diaper pins, bib-pins. It can be bought for grandmother; as bowls and flatware as well as the more common earrings, rings, bracelets, and necklaces. The men haven't been forgotten either, as bolas and belt buckles, tie tacs, rings, bracelets, watchbands, money clips, and cigarette cases are being made.

Like anything else where there is money to be made, people will try to sell anything. There are White men making jewelry that looks like Indian jewelry, and many have even signed the pieces. This is unfortunate, so be sure the person you are dealing with can guarantee that what you have purchased is American Indian made. Beware of plastic sold as turquoise, or inferior turquoise mixed with plastic, or dyed turquoise sold as genuine turquoise. Be sure the person you are dealing with will stand behind the merchandise. Matrix can be faked as well as the stone itself, by using iodine and also shoe polish.

To prove that so much of the Indian jewelry that is on the market today is not Indian made, that is a fact: The Indians only realize one to two percent of their income from making jewelry; the rest of it comes from sheep herding and harvesting their crops.

ZUNI INLAY NECKLACE AND EARRINGS, with total necklace length about 21 in. Jewelry is set with turquoise, jet, coral and mother-of-pearl. On the back of the larger half-moon is scratched the name of the maker, "Margaret Chico."

A limited edition of hand silk-screened tiles were made from this outstanding piece in 1975. Workstyle is exceptional and condition is excellent.　　　　G—$4500

Courtesy Hugo Poisson, Photographer; Edmunds of Yarmouth, Inc., West Yarmouth, Massachusetts.

TURQUOISE JEWELRY

Heishe turquoise choker necklace, contemporary Santo Domingo Pueblo, and 13 in. long, looped. Made of graduated-size natural turquoise beads.　　D—$230

Navajo nugget necklace, with treated turquoise; nuggets strung with white heishe.　　G—$795

Turquoise nugget necklace, strung with shell heishe, with coral bead spacers and bear claw capped with silver and turquoise and set as pendant. Contemporary Southwestern.　　G—$135

Navajo nugget necklace, turquoise strung with gray heishe; nuggets machine-drilled.　　G—$925

Turquoise nugget necklace, 14½ in. long, fastened. Graduated-size natural stone, deep blue. Machine-drilled, hand-shaped and polished.　　D—$1550

Navajo turquoise necklace, two strands of nuggets and strung on gray heishe.　　G—$825

Navajo turquoise necklace, single strand natural stone strung with white heishe.　　G—$775

ABOUT CONTEMPORARY JEWELRY

G.S. Khalsa, of Albuquerque, New Mexico, is an experienced and perceptive dealer in fine contemporary Indian jewelry. Mr. Khalsa consented to offer some tips on buying contemporary silver and turquoise jewelry. Used with permission.

"In recent years, American Indian jewelry has become the focal point of American Indian art and crafts. Since its emergence in the eighteen hundreds. Indian jewelry has been sought after and collected.

Navajo woman's necklace, silver and turquoise, naja with inset small stones. This is a fine work of art. $1200-$1800

Private collection

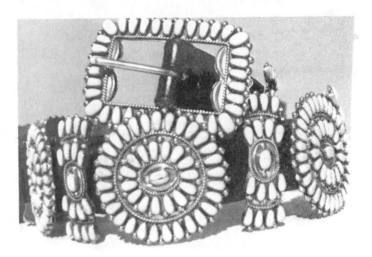

Zuni man's belt, silver and turquoise, matching blue stones.$1500-$2500
Private collection

Old Navajo squash-blossom necklace, silver and turquoise. The silver in this example is quite heavy. $1500-$2200

Private collection

Navajo Concho belts, ca. 1930s. These fine early works are of heavy gauge silver and high-grade old turquoise, both on the original leather.
Each, $2500-$3500

John C. Hill Antique Indian Art, Scottsdale, Arizona

"The great demand for Indian jewelry was at its peak in the early 1970's. The market subsequently became flooded with cheap imports, mass-produced styles and junk turquoise, including plastic imitations.

"Because of the growing skepticism as to the authenticity, the fever for American Indian pieces subsided as the decade wore on. At present, the market is stabilizing and once again growing in popularity worldwide.

"The average buyer or collector who wants to buy quality American Indian jewelry (whether it costs $5 or $5000) has the responsibility to discriminate between authentic, handmade American Indian jewelry and contemporary Southwestern-style jewelry.

"Southwestern-style is usually machine-made, cast jewelry made by non-Indians. For those who are unsure about how to pick authentic, handmade American Indian jewelry, here are some simple guide-lines and information.

"The three major silversmithing tribes are Navajos, Zunis and Hopis. Navajo jewelry is easily distinguishable because it features a more elaborate silver work, incorporating a leaf or feather motif. Sometimes their work does not include stones, such as sandcast jewelry. Sandcast jewelry is made by pouring hot molten silver into a mold carved out of volcanic rock.

"The Zunis, on the other hand, are expert lapidaries. Stone-on-stone inlay, needlepoint, and cluster work usually predominate their silver work. It should be noted that some Zunis are doing a Navajo style, as, too, Navajos are doing more and more inlay and cluster work. Nevertheless, the work is authentic.

"Hopi silver overlay is an altogether different style. The Hopi craftsman uses two layers of silver. The bottom layer is oxidized black. On the top layer, a design is drawn and cut out, then overlayed on the bottom. The final texture to the oxidized layer is achieved by etching lines into the black.

"The finished jewelry has a satin-brushed look quite different from Navajo or Zuni style. Stones are rarely incorporated into the design. Although Hopi jewelry is frequently imitated by the Navajos, the imitation may be inferior in quality and lower in price.

"The most important aspect to consider in buying American Indian jewelry is your choice of retail dealer. Your dealer must be reputable, honest, and willing to guarantee in writing the authenticity of each piece of jewelry. Large in-store inventories or memberships in jewelry associations do not necessarily guarantee the dealer's integrity.

"A bona-fide dealer has the responsibility to know and share with the customer all pertinent information about his merchandise: Who is the silversmith? Where is the stone from? What quality of stone is it? It is no longer valid to simply name the tribe. Be aware that phrases such as 'Zuni-style' or 'Indian-style' do not guarantee that the piece is authentic or handmade. Well buffed and nicely displayed jewelry is a good indication of how much the dealer respects what is being sold.

"When making a purchase, be sure the jewelry is 'clean'. The silver work should be neat, bezels around the stones ought to be seamless, and the soldering carefully done. There should be no sharp edges on the silver work. Insist on natural turquoise stones that are cut and polished, but not treated.

"The term 'natural' means genuine. Genuine stones may be real turquoise, but it may be that the stone is of very poor quality and treated to look better. It is considered acceptable that Zuni inlay jewelry and Santo Domingo heishe use stabilized turquoise, which provides the hardness needed for the delicate lapidary work involved. In Navajo silversmithing, insist on natural stones.

"Some simple rules of thumb to determine the relative quality of natural turquoise are hardness, intensity of natural color (either blue or green), hardness of the matrix (does it chip out with your fingernail?), and the ratio of turquoise to matrix.

"In Zuni channel work, a clean piece will not have filler to gap the distance between poorly cut stones and the silver. The surface of the entire inlay should be very smooth with a brilliant sheen to it. When looking at needlepoint or cluster work, the uniformity of shape and color of the stones determines quality.

"To appreciate American Indian jewelry is to become a part of the rich heritage and culture of the American Indians. The 'complex simplicity' of their lifestyle is expressed in their artifacts, sophisticated in design and workmanship, yet reflecting perfectly the individualism and undying spirit of Native Americans. So many of us long for such simplicity of spirit, and for the intimate communion with Nature from which it is spawned.

"The charm and desirability of authentic American Indian jewelry is that it looks and feels like it is made from a perfect mixture of the Southwestern landscape and a human spirit, overflowing with the joy of life." (G.S.K.)

Suggested Reading

Arizona Highways, issue of August, 1974

Arizona Highways, issue of March, 1975

Bahti, Mark, *A Consumer's Guide To Southwestern Indian Arts and Crafts;* Indian Pueblo Cultural Center, Albuquerque, New Mexico

Gillespie, Alva H., *How To Invest In Indian Jewelry,* Diamond Press, Albuquerque, New Mexico

Rosnek, Carl and Stacey, Joseph, *Skystone And Silver-The Collector's Book of Southwest Indian Jewelry*

CHAPTER XIX

OTHER AMERICAN
INDIAN COLLECTIBLES

The material in this chapter is a wonderful assemblage of authentic Amerind items. They are listed in no particular order and without regard to materials, regions or age. The listings either did not fit conveniently into other chapters or the information arrived after individual chapters were closed. Many are one-of-a-kind.

Probably only the Plains-style war club has enough entries for a separate heading. So it is practically impossible to locate a particular item for price-comparison, at least on first reading.

This section is probably treated best as a broad survey of Amerind creations for casual reading and general knowledge.

AMERIND COLLECTIBLES

Osage **hand-woven wool sash,** 54 in. long including fringe. Colors are red, white and blue, and in nice condition.
D—$85

Old **Indian powder horn,** 6½ in. long, with rawhide carrying thong. Wooden end-plug set with large brass tacks which added decoration. Plains Indian, probably mid-1800's.
A—$160

Sioux war club, with rawhide-wrapped handle; fine example.
A—$270

High quality **beaded saddle blanket,** with bells, fringed, and in excellent condition. Sioux.
D—$2350

Chippewa martingale, on cloth with beaded panels. Piece is 26 in. by 44 in., with patterns in floral design. Excellent condition.
G—$1195

Apache rawhide **quiver and assorted arrows.**
A—$410

Paiute buckskin covered **cradleboard,** moderately beaded. Yarn decorated sun shade.
G—$575

Wool blanket with beaded strip 2 in. wide and 80 in. long, and with four large colorful rosettes.
G—$260

Saddle blanket, possibly Crow Indian, and needs repair.
A—$200

Club with beaded handle, stone head with one chip missing; handle is thin and 12 in. long, fully quilled. Piece has four cone dangles.
G—$320

Indian Wars weapon, 1873 Springfield carbine, tack-decorated stock.
A—$455

Leather awl case, Apache, 12½ in. long. Piece has rows of small tin bells on yellow leather, with yellow and blue beadwork.
A—$145

Santee Sioux **horse bridle,** with red and navy trade cloth; canvas-backed, with nice floral designs.
G—$410

Crow bridle with German silver bit; engraved and inlayed German silver with flat headstall. Beaded in typical Crow designs; leather formerly dyed red. Rare piece, excellent condition.
G—$795

Kiowa war club, rawhide wrapped; hide cracking. Ex-museum piece and quite old.
G—$150

Sioux bow with two bone-tipped arrows.
G—$220

Sioux **dog travois,** sticks and rawhide laced platform. Fine display or museum piece, high quality.
G—$285

Beaded **horseman's gauntlets,** Plains Indian and probably Nez Perce, with very small designs in beads on back. Fair condition and ca. 1890.
D—$345

Northwest Coast **silver salad fork and spoon,** both 9½ in. long. Native-incised handles.
G—$325

Sioux **war club** with rawhide wrapped handle, stone head; an old and good piece.
G—$315

Sioux beaded **cradleboard cover,** with trade cloth sinew sewn. Geometric design on white back. Colors of beads are red, blue, green and yellow.
G—$585

Peyote fan, pheasant feathers with finely beaded handle.
G—$80

Buckskin knife and awl case, 8 in. long and 2 in. wide. Small knife and awl included, both with carved handles in shape of bear's head. Tin cone dangles on tassles. G—$285

Northwest Coast **painted hide** with effigy figure painted on it in brilliant blacks and reds. Very decorative and fine art work. G—$1800

Northwest Coast **carved halibut hook,** 10 in. long. G—$210

Dance wand, may be Ghost Dance period; 15 in. overall length. Top is comprised of two small horns and handle decorated with beaded horse hair. G—$325

Tepee bag, probably made from cradle cover. Designs are Sioux, Cheyenne and Crow motifs. Piece is 15 in. by 23 in. Fully beaded on front and in excellent condition. G—$800

Haida **argillite carving,** depicting miniature totem pole. Item is 13 in. high and shows mythical creatures. Ca. 1930 (?). C—$850

Quilled contemporary breastplate, 12 in. by 20 in. Done in Blackfoot design and excellent work. G—$635

Taos Pueblo **complete bow set,** with bow case and quiver, painted cedar bow that is sinew strung. Painted war arrows without feathers. Items are ca. 1860-70. D—$1000

Cheyenne buffalo hair **medicine case,** ca. 1900. D—$145

Apache **arrow quiver,** 15½ in. long, made of soft leather and about 3½ in. wide. Unusual, and good condition. C—$300

Gueverra **long bow** with four cane arrows with fancy foreshafts. Set is ca. 1870. D—$350

Beaded case, 3 in. by 4 in., with geometric designs in green and white, with blue, yellow and pink. One beaded fringe missing; Sioux. A—$95

Fish effigy made of yellow-gray shale, drilled at dorsal fin region, from Virginia. Piece is 2⅛ in. long, good condition. C—$65

Sioux **bow and quiver case** with bow and arrow. Made of moose hide, and has beaded edge with fringe and strap. Good condition. Piece is ca. 1920. G—$450

Martingale, Blackfoot, and loom-beaded. Has red, white and blue ribbons, hawk bells and tin cone danglers. Fine condition. G—$475

Apache saddle bags with intricate cutout designs backed with red trade cloth. Made of rawhide and with long fringe. Such items are seldom encountered. G—$2250

Cheyenne **baby cradle** with fully beaded hood, and with bottom part made of calfskin. Good condition, and ca. 1880. G—$645

Old Russell Green River **trade knife,** complete with leather sheath. Rare piece, with a polished antler handle; knife is 9 in. in length. G—$200

Leather partially beaded **case for rifle,** probably an early flintlock or percussion weapon. Case is 4 ft. 1 in. long, and may have been used by a Mountain Man trapper, though certainly Indian-made. Old tag states that piece was collected in Idaho in 1907. C—$825

War club, stone head, hide-wrapped handle, good condition. D—$260

Sioux painted **parfleche box,** 11 in. by 9 in. by 7 in. G—$110

Painted pottery tile, 4¼ in. wide and 5¼ in. high, with painted Kachina face on front. A—$80

Plains Indian **knife and sheath,** the sheath 9½ in. long, the knife blade 5¼ in. long, with bone handle. Sheath well-beaded and nicely fringed; alone, $155. Knife White-made and used, possibly hide-skinner's tool, blade well-worn. Knife alone, $55. Presented as a set, but knife and sheath obviously mismatched. C—uncertain value

Sioux **saddle blanket,** with 6 in. beaded panels, and with bells and heavy fringe. Excellent condition. G—$2250

Plains Indian **parfleche container,** 6¼ in. by 9½ in., painted at one time. Good condition. D—$155

Indian **carrying net,** collected in California, over 20 in. long. Woven with wide spaces, each about 2 in. square. Used for transporting unwieldly loads; natural fibers. C—$145

Bison hide, painted with various designs; very fine work and may show a "count" of years and events. Condition average. D—$1200

Bow and arrows, old set, bow 3 ft. 4 in. long, and with five arrows. Condition not good; feathers missing from arrows, and string from bow; arrows iron-tipped. Set found in old house and had been exposed to elements for many years. C—$425

Parfleche container, nicely decorated, medium size. A—$240

Flesher, from Taos Pueblo, 15 in. long. Piece has wooden handle, inset metal blade, and in fine condition. Ca. 1890. G—$145

Nez Perce **corn husk pouch.**   A—$95

Plains **"egg-head" skull-cracker club,** good condition.
                                                  D—$250

Sioux **saddle blanket,** fully beaded on hide, and 36 in. by 80 in. Piece has canvas center and yellow fringe; beads are on blue background with fine geometric designs and four different colored horses. Perfect condition and ca. 1910.
                                                  G—$2200

Plains Indian **knife sheath** about 12 in. long, and about late 1800's. Small beadwork designs, geometric pattern, one side.
                                                  D—$275

Beaded **knife sheath,** fringed and some beadwork missing; leather is parfleche, good condition.   D—$250

Pair of beaded **horseman's gauntlets,** wide-cuffed. A—$210

Bolo tie fastener, 2 in. high; shell inlayed with jet, turquoise and coral in the form of a quail. Exquisite work by Eliot Quelo, and signed.   G—$1100

Columbia River **basalt carving,** 23 in. tall.   A—$335

Large and fine Plains Indian woman's **hair-pipe breastplate,** many beads, all with beautiful patina. Ca. 1880. C—$1900

Nez Perce **"sally-bag",** 7 in. by 10¾ in.   A—$300

Cherokee **plaited mat,** made of river cane.   A—$25

Old Sioux **quill and deer hair roach;** good condition.
                                                  D—$165

Original **lance with point,** California desert region; lance is 52 in. long, with obsidian point about 3 in. long, still secured with original lashings. Unknown age, but old.
                                                  D—$450

Squaw axe, trade iron, 5 in. high. Excellent condition, and blade has flower-like stamping.   A—$75

Wood comb, 9 in. long, with 13 long wooden teeth. Piece has early chip-carving and abalone shell inlays. Northwest Coast.   A—$45

Tubular pipe, of a reddish-yellow quality stone, 3⅜ in. long, just less than 1 in. in middle diameter. Highly polished, in the vague effigy of an unknown animal. Probably a late B.C. piece, from Archaic and Woodland site in the Midwest.
                                                  C—$725

Silver and turquoise concha belt, 34 in. long. Conchas elongated, with much stampwork and well-set with turquoise. Spacers in butterfly shape; ornate buckle, eleven worked silver pieces in all. Good overall tooling. A—$700

Birchbark basket, rectangular, 7¼ in. long and 3⅜ in. wide, with floral designs in dyed quills. Historic, Great Lakes area. Probably Canadian Indian.   D—$170

Beaded belt, 30½ in. long, beaded on leather and with tying thongs. Geometric designs done on blue field, with colors red, yellow and black.   A—$180

Silver and turquoise squashblossom necklace, large, all beads made from liberty dimes. Naja with 7 large stones and 10 "blossoms", each with 2 stones. Well-made piece.
                                                  A—$625

Carved bullet, 45-70 cartridge, unfired, with lead bullet portion carved to represent human face. Believed to be Indian work; shell casing of brass has heavy patina. From Kansas, estimated to be late-1800's.   C—$45

Trade-silver cross, 2½ in. high, with back touchmarked "Montreal", and front hand-stamped. Suspended on necklace consisting of black beads with silver beads at intervals.   A—$165

Kachina doll, 8¾ in. high, painted wood, and recent.
                                                  D—$75

Silver ketoh or wrist bowguard, leather, with turquoise stone in silver attached. Silver plate measures 2½ in. by 3½ in.   A—$180

Trade-iron arrowhead, 2⅞ in. long with squared stem serrated on edge for lashings.   C—$25

Shell necklace, 18 in. long, made of thin disc-beads of clamshell. Necklace somewhat resembles puka shell; well-made.
                                                  A—$60

Apache bow and two arrows; arrows without points. Bow was once painted and is 42 in. long. Documented; pre-1901.
                                                  A—$215

Two Pomo arrows, cane shafts with wooden tips; each, 36 in. long, and in very good condition.   G—$55 ea.

Rawhide quirt, intricately braided, and contemporary.
                                                  G—$145

Bridle and reins, bridle with some beadwork and lined with trade cloth (on leather); rawhide reins 3½ ft. long. C—$470

Medicine weasel, pelt stuffed with sweetgrass; piece has beaded eyes and nose.   G—$305

Sioux **war club** with large stone head and ca. 1900. D—$125

Cheyenne **knife sheath,** fully beaded with five colors of beads; piece is 2¾ in. wide and 7 in. long. Sinew-sewn rawhide and buckskin, and ca. 1910.   G—$400

Sioux "skull-cracker" war club, wooden handle covered with rawhide, with stone head. Piece is 17 in. long, in good condition, and ca. 1900.   G—$290

Fine old Haida silver spoon.   A—$365

Umatilla "sally-bag".   A—$85

Sioux cradle cover, fully beaded top triangle with later added Hudson Bay blanket wrap. Good early colors; high quality.   G—$600

Birch-bark container, Canada and Upper Great Lakes area. Made from folded sections of bark; container has reinforced top and is 14 in. long. Worn but good condition. C—$145

Parfleche knife case, probably Sioux, painted and old; knife goes with case.   D—$385

Large frame of Basket-Maker artifacts—projectile point flakers, cordage, yucca strings, rope, and so forth. Shelter finds from New Mexico.   D—$145

Plains Indian bow-drill outfit, pump-style with short bow, cord and wooden drillstick. Probably late 1800's. C—$260

Rawhide knife sheath, Western Plains, 6½ in. long and made of very heavy leather. Well-done, authentic, old.   D—$150

Hopi painted bow, sinew-strung and with four small game arrows. Items are ca. 1890.   D—$275

Crow Indian beaded knife sheath, 7¾ in. long, not in good condition. Many beads are missing; design uncertain.   C—$70

Columbia River region stone club, 13½ in. long, about 3 in. wide, with a polished handgrip. Purpose unknown, but may be related to the "slave killer" monolithic axes. May be an unfinished piece as it is rather thick in proportion to length.   C—$310

Pair of Cheyenne beaded saddle blanket strips. A—$460

Pair of hair ties, braided and quilled, good condition.   D—$125

Sioux pemmican hammer, rawhide covered handle with granite stone for base; item shows much age and use.   G—$260

Horse martingale, Blackfoot, 12 in. by 48 in., and fringed with 4 in. of basket beads with hawk bells at ends. Piece collected in the 1930's.   G—$610

Kiowa war club, bound with rawhide; old piece. D—$200

Plains-type war club, 1800's. Stone fully encased in rawhide with rawhide-wrapped handle. Some beaded decoration, but probably added later.   G—$315

Northern Sioux saddle bags, buffalo hide with large beaded panels and a heavy fringe; piece has connecting beaded strips and is ca. late-1800's. Scarce, and quality item.   G—$2200

Tsimshian basketry hair receiver.   A—$75

Corn husk bag, 11½ in. long by 13½ in., with geometric designs on one side only. Nicely woven and sturdy, and probably ca. 1950.   C—$125

Cheyenne baby carrier, fully quilled hood and partially quilled sides. Full size, and ca. 1870.   G—$2750

Parfleche container, envelope-type, with triangular red and green designs. Piece is 17 in. long, 12¼ in. high, and with wraparound thong fastener.   C—$475

Crow saddle blanket, made of old tepee canvas as base with beaded strip of cloth. Good condition, and ca. 1880.   G—$830

Nez Perce corn-husk container, probably for small personal items; unrolled length 17 in. Unusual wool embroidery on sides, and a recent piece.   C—$345

Pomo cane arrows, California, with hardwood foreshaft that is sinew-tied. Ca. 1880.   D—$60 ea.

Plains Indian bow with three iron-tipped and feather-vaned arrows, all good condition.   C—$325

Sioux umbilical fetish.   A—$160

Unusual Catlinite napkin ring, 2 in. in diameter, said to have been traded on an Army post in mid-1800's. Probably once part of a set. Carving on outside depicts a Western Army post.   C—$125

Old Sioux tobacco cutting board in the shape of a turtle or possibly a beaver pelt; piece has brass tack eyes. G—$235

Zuni bear-hunting fetish, made of fur, feathers and beads. A rare item and ca. 1870.   D—$130

Plains Indian fan, probably Prairie hen feathers (several missing), handle of sinew and some beadwork. D—$65

Pair of beaded gauntles gloves, possibly Crow, with slight damage.   G—$260

Mojave painted bow with one painted arrow; ca. 1870-80.   D—$275

Gila River effigy, 4 in. wide and 8 in. long, good condition with some restoration.   G—$825

Warm Springs **beaded leggings.** A—$120

Skokomish **slate spear,** 12 in. long; a ceremonial item and ca. 1860. D—$120

Salish **woven tumpline,** Columbia River area, wide leather band and braided rawhide straps. About 20 in. long, fastened. C—$175

Nez Perce **corn-husk martingale,** 18 in. wide and 31 in. long; rare, and in good condition. ca.1900. G—$825

Sioux **umbilical lizard,** worn but in good condition.G—$240

Pair of **hair ties** with beadwork and feather down; small brass dangles or tinklers. D—$75

Sioux **miniature tepee,** 14½ in. high, with nine thin lodge poles. Leather covering for the structure has the remnants of fringe at bottom, so many have been taken from a worn-out shirt or dress. Unusual, fine condition. C—$370

Mono **cradleboard,** with woven red and green sash straps and a decorated hood. G—$495

Horse bridle, trade cloth, with good designs, beadwork in Plains Indian style. A—$385

Cheyenne **beaded sheath and knife,** buckskin. Knife is trade-steel, edge well-worn, and with antler or bone handle. D—$265

Old **Navajo shirt,** with approximately 400 hand-made silver buttons. G—$845

Old **dance sash,** 44 in. long and 12½ in. wide, with trade beads the length. Fine condition. G—$400

Pallette or slate ornament, 3⅝ in. in diameter, made of thin slate. This interesting late prehistoric artifact probably originated in or near Tennessee where the type is found. Old information on the artifact states it was found near the Old Erie Canal, Defiance County, Ohio.

Museum quality

Larry Garvin collection

WOODEN-HORSE STICK, 24 in. in length. Plains Indian, and ca. 1880.
G—Museum Quality

Nedra Matteucci's Fenn Galleries, Santa Fe, New Mexico

Modoc quiver, bear-skin, with ten sinew-wrapped feather drops. It is rawhide-sewn and 26 in. long. From northern California, this ex-museum piece is ca. 1880-1900. $325

Morris' Art & Artifacts, Anaheim, California; Dawn Gober photograph

Great Lakes region charm bags, various sizes, designs, ages and materials. All ca. 1830-1870. $150-$2000, each

Private collection; photo by John McLaughlin

Cornhusk artworks, Nez Perce, fiber, yarn and hide. Upper left, woman's hat, ca. 1920, $400 (general, $300-$1000). Sally-bag, pouch, lower left, ca. 1880, $1500 (general, $300-$1500). Center, bag, ca. 1890, $500 (general, $200-$1000, exceptional up to $2500).
Upper right, bag, ca. 1910 $400
Lower right, belt-pouch, ca. 1930 $500

Private collection; photo by John McLaughlin

NOTE by the collector regarding cornhusk items: "In general the following are considered when appraising cornhusk bags: Type, condition, beauty, size, fineness of weave and age. Age is not a major consideration; even modern pieces are highly sought"

Figure by Fletcher Healing, 10 in. high, colorful and well-done. $425

Courtesy John Isaac, Albuquerque, New Mexico

Unknown artifact, solid copper, possibly a non-utilitarian object of some sort. It has very squared edges, is 2½ in. long, and is in very good condition. It was a personal find by the owner in Barron County, Wisconsin.
                    $75-$100

Dennis R. Lindblad collection, Chetek, Wisconsin

Copper fishhook, a scarce and unusual find by the owner in Barron County, Wisconsin. It is 2½ in. long. $50

Dennis R. Lindblad collection, Chetek, Wisconsin

Prehistoric artifacts.
Left, Adena gorget, banded slate, LaGrange County, Indiana. $225

Center, salvaged gorget or pendant, note broken-out hole at top center, from Michigan. $145
Right, copper celt, 3¾ in. long, Kent County, Michigan. $225

Larry Lantz, First Mesa, South Bend, Indiana

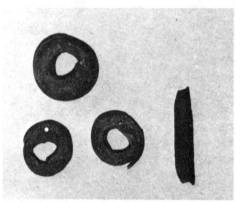

Rolled copper beads and a clasp, largest bead ½ in. in diameter. These were personal finds by the owner in Barron County, Wisconsin.
$50, group

Dennis R. Lindblad collection, Chetek, Wisconsin

Corn-husk bag, Umatilla, ca. 1870-1880. It is 8 x 9½ in., very finely woven; data on old tag reads "Collected near Umatilla Ring, Oregon / 1880". The reverse has a different pattern. Exceptional item.
$875

Larry Lantz, First Mesa, South Bend, Indiana

"Adoption Papers", unique Seneca Wolf Clan item. Paint on rawhide, signed by Chief Shongo, July 4, 1942. Size 31½ x 38 in., ex-coll. Casterline. $400

Pat & Dave Summers, Native American Artifacts, Victor, NY

House wall or foundation material, clay tempered with pine straw or needles, state of Louisiana. Building material of any kind from prehistoric times is unusual. Study value

Wilfred A. Dick collection, Magnolia, Mississippi

Fossils and a small turtle shell that evidence prehistoric human reworking and polishing. These early objects were probably picked up as curios and collectibles; all are from known prehistoric sites in Mississippi.
$1-$50, each

Wilfred A. Dick collection, Magnolia, Mississippi

Ghost Dance club, 9¾ x 20 in. It has two buffalo horns bound with rawhide and is well-decorated with white, green, blue and red beads and feather quill. This very interesting piece is ca. 1880s. $750

Sherman Holbert Collection, Fort Mille Lacs, Onamia, Minnesota

Elk hide with beaded strips, Plateau, beadwork in colors of black, pink and blue and with ermine drops. Ca. 1890s. Museum quality

Morning Star Gallery, Santa Fe, New Mexico

Picture frame, basketry, Thompson River Salish, 6 x 9 in. This unusual piece is ca. 1890-1900. $75
Pocotopaug Trading Post, South Windsor, CT

Duck decoy, Southeast Woodland, unknown age. It is 4½ in. wide and 12⅛ in. long. With hand-carved head, the straw body is bound with twisted cord. As-new condition. $50

Sherman Holbert Collection, Fort Mille Lacs, Onamia, Minnesota

Freshwater pearl necklace, rare, from Mississippian period. It consists of 80 small white pearls and came from near Elizabethtown, Tennessee.

Pat & Dave Summers, Native American Artifacts, Victor, NY $1700

Necklace, unknown origin and time-period, 19½ in. long. It is made of pipestone ground into small discs and laced together. It has a total of 188 disc-beads. $95

Sherman Holbert Collection. Fort Mille Lacs, Onamia, Minnesota

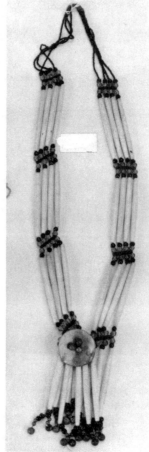

Breastplate, ladies, hairpipe, ca. 1920s-1930s. It is 28 in. long and made of 37 hairpipes, 95 large black beads, 69 large gold beads, and with harness leather dividers. There are also 13 round brass buttons, a bell, a Canadian coin dated 1910, an abalone button and four strands of black beads at the neck. $850

Sherman Holbert Collection, Fort Mille Lacs, Onamia, Minnesota

Bowl game, Chippewa, bowl 11½ in. in diameter. Ca. 1940s. The game consists of hand-carved wooden bowl, game pieces and puzzle bag for same, plus counters. Bowl, ex-colls. Owen and Blessing. $450

Sherman Holbert Collection, Fort Mille Lacs, Onamia, Minnesota

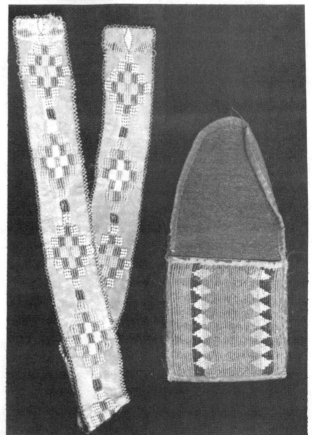

Sally bag, Wasco. These bags vary greatly in size. This one is typical, about 4 x 10 in. They usually have figures on them but some were produced with geometrics. Older specimens have condors (they look like butterflies), skeletal human figures or very intricate geometric designs. Values are determined by size, condition and design. Better examples sell for $3000-$4000. Size range is 3 x 4 to 6 x 15 in. Example, ca. 1880.

Private collection, photo by John McLaughlin $1500

Woodlands beadwork.
Left, Kickapoo belt, 1800s, 2 x 26 in., seed-beaded in geometrics. $385

Right, Sauk charm bag, ca. 1865, loom-beaded with cloth backing, 4 x 4 in. $650

Larry Lantz, First Mesa, South Bend, Indiana

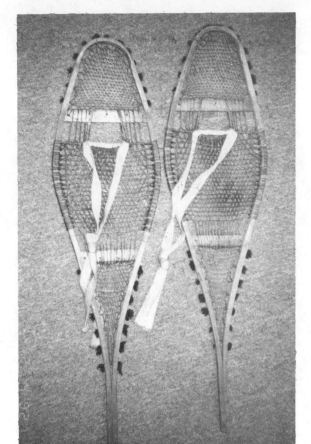

Skookum doll, old, 6 x 18 in. While many tribes made these as tourist items, they are collector items in their own right. The word "Skookum" in Chinook means powerful or great, while an older meaning was ghost or spirit. This came from the Northeast but Skookums can be found across the country. $125-$200

Marguerite L. Kernaghan collection; photo by Marguerite L. and Stewart W. Kernaghan, Bellvue, Colorado

Indian-made snowshoes, Great Lakes region type, 37½ in. long. $135, pair

Wendy Wolfsen collection, Michigan

MEDICINE BAG, Cheyenne, 6 in. wide and 14 in. long, with fringes. It is of unlined hide, sinew-sewn and bead design indicate the owner might have belonged to the Cheyenne Warrior Society because of the four (black bead) horseheads with red arrow emerging from their mouths. (Sacred arrows?) Other designs are geometric; hide strap across bag top. Piece is ca. 1880.   C—$1600

Photo courtesy Bill Post Collection.

BUFFALO-HORN "SKULL-CRACKER", 17¾ in. long. Piece had been brought to Springfield, Oregon in the 1930s by a family who came from South Dakota, purchased by them on the Pine Ridge reservation. This would be a Sioux item.   C—$425

S.W. Kernaghan photo; Marguerite Kernaghan Collection.

335

Moosehair embroidery, Iroquois, very rare, done on black cloth. It is 13½ x 14 in. and ca. 1850. $800

Pat & Dave Summers, Native American Artifacts, Victor, NY

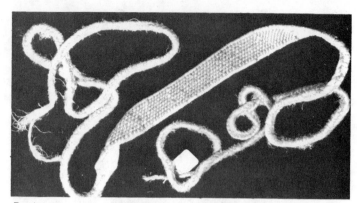

Burden strap or tumpline, Salish, mountain sheep wool and plant fibers. Shoulder strap is 2 x 18 in. with 4 foot ties at each end. Late 1800s, museum tag reads "Puget Sound". $425

Larry Lantz, First Mesa, South Bend, Indiana

Black slate knives, left and right, Oswego, NY. $25 each
Center, semi-luncate knife, granite, 4 in. long, from Connecticut.$300

Pocotopaug Trading Post, South Windsor, CT

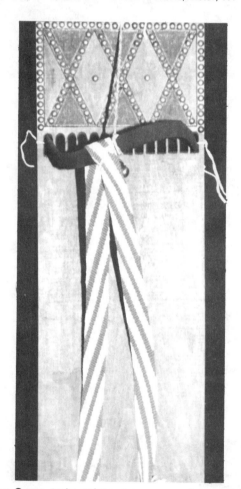

Baby carrier, Osage, tacks, paint and yarn on wooden board. It is ca. 1900. $1000

Private collection, photo by John McLaughlin

Assorted adornments or ornaments, consisting of stone beads, drilled obsidian crescent, undrilled obsidian, and jasper pendants. From the Columbia River area these are ca. AD 1600-1800. $100

Morris' Art & Artifacts, Anaheim, California; Dawn Gober photo.

Chopper-type hand (?) celt, early, from North Carolina. $65

Private collection

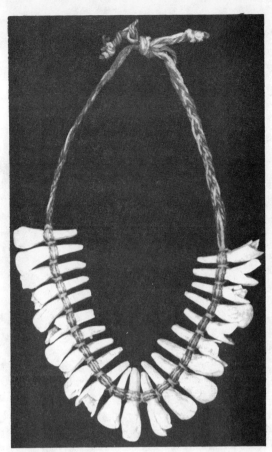

Buffalo tooth necklace, Sioux, collected from Mandan, North Dakota, in the late 1800s. Each tooth is individually tied with braided trade yarn. $350

Larry Lantz, First Mesa, South Bend, Indiana

Fabric sample, extremely rare, made of shredded sagebrush. Made prior to 700 BC, this came from a rockshelter in Oregon. Material like this was used for sandals, sleeping mats and the like. $200

Pat & Dave Summers, Native American Artifacts, Victor, NY

Oil painting by Louis Shipshee, 24 x 30 in., mint condition.

$450

Courtesy Dr. Fred Belk, Corrales, New Mexico

Ceremonial cape, child's size, Winnebago, made from 45 ermine skins.
Note the tails; mid to late 1800s, rare item. $650-$750

Larry Lantz, First Mesa, South Bend, Indiana

Restored club, ancient head and new wooden handle. The stone clubhead was found in western Kansas. Club head $50
New wooden haft $35

Lee Hallman collection, Telford, Pennsylvania

Alabaster turtle figure by Doug Hyde (Nez Perce, Chippewa and Assiniboin) and 13½ in. tall. The sculpture is ca. 1985. $6000

Dennis R. Phillips / Fine American Indian Art, Chicago, IL

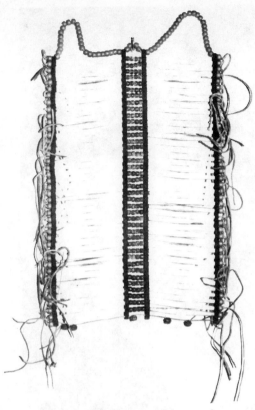

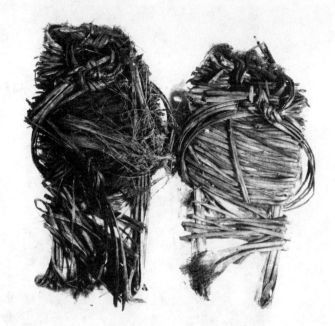

Pair of WOVEN FIBER SANDALS, from a cave shelter in New Mexico. Twelve pair came from this particular site, on privately owned land. Material is yucca plant fibres, and sandals are Anasazi culture.

C—$135-$185

Photo courtesy Wayne Parker, TX

Sioux man's BREASTPLATE, of leather thongs, bone tubes and large beads. Piece is 20 in. high and 12 in. wide, ca. 1900.

$1850

Photo courtesy Winona Trading Post, Santa Fe—Pierre & Sylvia Bovis.

Three YEI BI CHAI MASKS: The Navajo medicine man is extremely important during ceremonies. The Yei Bi Chai dance is held during the winter months as a major curing ceremony. The Yei Bi Chai dancers appear during the last two nights of the nine day ceremony. The Yei represent supernatural beings who have great powers.
The Yei masks are made of buckskin from deer which have been suffocated with sacred meal. The full masks are worn by male dancers. These masks are approximately 18 in. long and 14 in. wide; ca. 1920.C—$1950 each

Photos courtesy W.J. Crawford. The Americana Galleries, Phoenix, Arizona.

Rock art at Indian Petroglyph State Park, near Albuquerque, New Mexico. These figures were pecked into the dark basalt lava, probably by the Pueblo peoples ca. AD 1100-1600. There are many animal and human figures plus unknown designs.

Lar Hothem photo

CHAPTER XX

ESKIMO, ALEUT
& ALASKAN INDIAN
ITEMS

Today two main but related groups—with roots stretching far back into prehistory with the Umnak people—inhabit the Alaskan region. They are the Aleuts, who inhabit the Alutian Islands, and the Eskimos. The word "Eskimo" was a non-complimentary term applied by a Northcentral Amerind group, and it meant something like "Eaters of raw fish".

Eskimos on the coastal areas called themselves "Inuit", while more inland Eskimos were the "Nunamuit". Technicalities aside, all groups were almost totally dependent on fish, birds and animals.

There are two other Alaskan-area Indian peoples who still make traditional arts and crafts. There are the Athbascan Indians (of inland and coastal areas) and the Tlingit-Haida (southern coastal parts).

Some contemporary painting and sculpting is done, but the emphasis is on items made of ivory, bone, soapstone and woodworking, plus some basketry and clothing. Much work is characterized by combining simplicity and clean, almost stark, but dramatic lines in the best artistic fashions. Some nephrite (jade) is mined northeast of Kotzebue, Alaska, and is made into small objects.

At Little Diomede Island, near the International Date Line and not far from the USSR's Siberian coast, a pair of walrus tusks is valued at about $200. However, if the native carvers make the ivory into small art objects, the same ivory can eventually return nearly $2000.

Not many people, compared with other Amerind items, as yet collect Alaskan-area and Eskimo artifacts and artworks. It would appear to be a very good area to explore. The most valued material is ivory, which usually comes from walrus tusks; sometimes whale teeth are used, more rarely the single tusk of the narwhale. Included here is some very interesting information about walrus ivory, which will aid in identifying the type used in making certain collectibles.

Special thanks are due Mary Lou Lindahl, General Manager of Alaskan Native Arts & Crafts, INC., for permission to reprint these facts on ivory, plus other material as noted.

For catalog, write (and enclose a couple of stamps) to:
Alaskan Native Arts & Crafts, 425 D. Street, Anchorage, Alaska 99501. The Co-op employs only native craftspeople, and their Trademark is "ANAC".

WALRUS IVORY

Alaskan ivory comes from the walrus that inhabit the Arctic Ocean and Bering Sea areas. Walrus herds generally migrate north in the spring and at that time villages along the coast harvest the animal for a variety of uses. Although the walrus provides the main meat supply for many villages the year round, it is a renewable resource, in the same sense that cattle are, and the impact of the Alaskan Native on the walrus herds is far below the herd growth level. The walrus is in no danger of becoming extinct.

The ivory tusk of the walrus protrudes downward from the upper jaw, extending as much as three feet. The tusk has three layers: an inner core of light tan, dark tan and white; a second layer of soft white, and an outer shell that, when properly worked, can be polished to a brilliant sheen.

The ivory is found in three basic forms, identifiable by coloration.

1. New ivory—that which has been recently harvested, is the gleaming white color described above.

2. Old ivory—like that commonly found along beaches, is usually tan or brown from exposure to the elements.

3. Fossilized ivory—is often very dark from having been buried in the permafrost for many years.

The Alaskan native peoples, in comparison with better-known Amerind groups, have a significantly smaller output of traditional arts and crafts. However, the art forms are so unusual that there is usually little difficulty in assigning an Eskimo, or far northern, origin.

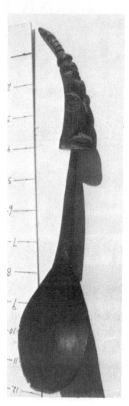

Left:
Spoon with detachable ivory carved handle, rare decoration, from Alaska.
$1000, the two

Private collection

Barbed bird point carved from ivory, 2 in. long, from Alaska. This is a carefully made piece with delicate serrations or barbs. $75

Private collection

OLD ESKIMO & ALEUT ITEMS

Small ivory **Eskimo bear fetish** or toggle, 1⅛ in. long. Ivory is a rich amber color; small hole drilled in shoulder region for cord. Perfect condition, and very old.   C—$125

Steatite (soapstone) Eskimo **bowl oil lamp,** oblong, 13 in. long and 9 in. wide, 3¼ in. deep. One small end has a groove which held a twist of moss for a wick. Bottom almost perfectly flat.   C—$240

Rounded **fish lure,** Eskimo, carved from bone or ivory, and 4 in. long. Curved iron hook set into body; hole drilled at front end, both to represent eyes and to hold fishing line.   C—$150

Eskimo **lidded basket,** 13 in. in diameter and 9 in. high. Good condition, and ca. 1900.   G—$250

Portion of Eskimo **compound harpoon,** carved from bone. Piece is 4⅜ in. long, has socketed base, drill hole for cord, and cut-out notch in top for harpoon head section. Plain, but very well made and good lines. Old.   C—$115

Eskimo **tobacco container,** nicely beaded, and ca. 1900.   G—$200

Small **bone Eskimo comb,** very old, 2¾ in. wide and 1¾ in. high. Few teeth are broken, but very well made.   C—$80

Small **ivory effigy,** or decorative toggle, Eskimo. Piece is just over 1 in. long, cylindrical, and in the shape of the upper portion of a walrus.   C—$140

Eskimo basket, 5 in. high by 10 in. and 12½ in.   A—$50

Bone meat hook, Alaska, 14½ in. long and with a sharply angled ivory inset to form holding barb. Used to catch and strip blubber when butchering large sea mammals.   C—$425

Eskimo **chipped bear point,** made from material resembling chert 3¾ in. long. Stemmed, shoulders rounded, edges show extensive wear so may have also been a working blade.   C—$60

Eskimo **baleen basket,** made from the fibrous material in the mouth of some whales, used to screen plankton. Piece is 4½ in. in diameter and 4⅛ in. high. Several small ivory animals on lid; all in good condition.   G—$475

Carved-ivory snow goggles, from an early group. About 4½ in. wide and 1½ in. high, with drill-holes at ends for fastening cords. Eye-slits are straight lines; very unusual and well-carved item. Prehistoric.   C—$700

Old pre-Eskimo **whalebone mask,** from northern Alaska. It has typical inset eyes with vision slits, protruding and elongated nose and mouth opening. Piece is 8¾ in. high, and in average good condition.   C—$800

Eskimo **walrus ivory hunter's tally.**   A—$300

Eskimo or Aleut **ivory chisel,** with ground-down orca or killer whale tooth set in bone handle. Very rare item.   C—$425

Eskimo **wooden point scabbard,** a hallowed holster-like device used to protect sharp harpoon tips when stored. Piece is 4 in. long, 1¾ in. wide at base; may have been carved from driftwood. Good condition.   C—$75

Walrus-tusk adz-blade, from very early Alaskan coastal site, without handle. Tusk section is 8¼ in. long.   C—$230

Eskimo **wooden fire-making set,** with curved fire-bow, pointed and worn drill-stick, and fire-base with drilled holes for friction starts. Unusual items, and in good condition.   C—$130

Eskimo **ulu** or woman's knife, with bone handle.   A—$45

Eskimo **ulu,** with walrus design carved on handle.   A—$130

Eskimo ivory **hairpin or perforator,** 4⅛ in. long and polished from use. Incised-line decorations.   C—$55

Ivory bow **wristguard,** attached to inside of lower arm holding bow to protect against bowstring slap. Piece is 4½ in. long and drilled front and rear for fastening.   C—$235

Pre-Eskimo **microlith blade,** 1⅜ in. long, evidencing ultra-fine chipping, nearly 20 flakes to the inch. Very thin tip; may have served as a barb for harpoon, but actual use unknown.   C—$40

Ivory harpoon tip, Alaska, from Dorset site, 3¼ in. long. Double barbs on each side, and in good condition. C—$170

Eskimo doll, of carved wood, about 5 in. high. May be from early 1900's; miniature skin parka, probably made of seal-gut.   C—$160

Eskimo **snow shovel,** bone blade and about 48 in. in length. Good condition and ca. 1900.   G—$285

Alaskan artifact, ivory thumb-guard with incised lines, for use with bow and arrows. $95

Private collection

Sealskin boots, Eskimo, 10 in. long. Made of caribou hide, the pair has snowshoe straps and is beaded with fur tops; from the 1920s. $385

Larry Lantz, First Mesa, South Bend, Indiana

Ivory carving, possibly a miniature totem pole, Tlingit, 8 in. high. Made of walrus tusk, it is ca. 1920-1940. $300-$400

Pocotopaug Trading Post, South Windsor, CT

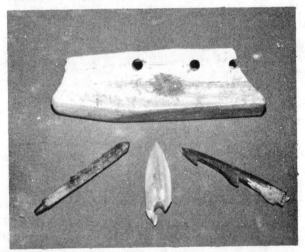

Alaskan artifacts.
Top, section of ivory or bone sled runner, drilled for attachment to sled runner frame. $100
Harpoon points, $35, each

Wilfred A. Dick collection, Magnolia, Mississippi

RECENT ESKIMO & ALEUT ITEMS

Eskimo **baleen "wolf-scarer"**, a long, flat object attached to thong and swung in a circle; makes a vibrating, whistling roar.
A—$55

Eskimo **lidded basket,** 4 in. in diameter, 3¾ in. high. Coil-weave, natural plant fibers.
C—$230

Eskimo **fossilized ivory bracelet.**
A—$85

Pair of Eskimo **leather mittens,** 14½ in. long with extension for thumb. Coastal Alaska, in fair condition.
C—$200

Pair of Eskimo **sealskin boots,** thigh-length and man-size, with waterproofed seam stitching. Good condition, and unusual.
C—$595

Miniature skin mukluks, footgear, from St. Lawrence Island.
A—$45

Eskimo **fur doll,** from Yukon Delta.
A—$60

Aleut basket, Alaskan islands, of braided grass 11 in. in diameter. Has braided carrying strap, and is probably a light-weight collecting basket.
C—$425

Walrus **ivory carving,** depicting a snowy owl.
A—$60

Eskimo **miniature skin kayak.**
A—$50

Miniature umiak or woman's boat, actually used by families to hunt and travel, 17 in. long, and gut-covered wooden frame. There are four tiny paddles, each about 5 in. long.
C—$400

Scrimshaw **walrus ivory box.**
A—$95

Eskimo **walrus-tusk etching,** soot-impregnated thin incised lines, illustrating wintertime activities. Tusk section is just over 13 in. long, decorated both sides. Not signed, and probably ca. 1930's. From Point Hope, Alaska.
C—$875

Carved seal, of fossilized ivory, set on base.
A—$90

Walrus **ivory cribbage board,** Eskimo, and ca. 1930.
A—$340

Walrus tusk **ivory cribbage board,** 13½ in. long and lacking game pegs. Fine condition, ivory and golden tan brown.
C—$330

Attu **lidded basket,** miniature style, with fine weave.
A—$775

Eskimo **lidded basket,** 11 in. in diameter and 12 in. high; basket has a swirling stairstep design, and is in good condition.
G—$335

Eskimo **basket,** measuring 5½ in. by 13 in.
A—$60

Small **Eskimo doll,** with carved-ivory face.
A—$65

Eskimo **carved soapstone fish,** done by Tom Mayac.
A—$75

Eskimo **baleen basket,** with ivory seal and bear.
A—$300

Eskimo carving of a drummer, done on walrus jawbone.
A—$160

Eskimo **yo-yo,** braided sealskin with a baleen handle.
A—$45

Eskimo **lidded basket,** polychrome geometric design, 4½ in. in diameter and 4½ in. high.
G—$150

Two walrus **ivory carved seals,** set on soapstone base; done by Tom Mayac.
A—$45

Eskimo **basket,** 4½ in. in diameter and 3 in. high. Basket has geometric designs, and is in good condition.
G—$95

The following are recent auction results, all concerning Eskimo items. The material is courtesy Rod Sauvageau, Trade Winds West Auction Gallery, Vancouver, Washington. Used with permission.

Eskimo skin parka.
A—$345

Eskimo basket, large, 13½ in. by 15½ in.
A—$105

Eskimo whalebone mask, by Alex Frankson of Point Hope, Alaska. Piece has ivory teeth and eyes, with baleen pupils and jade labrets.
A—$185

Eskimo bracelet, ivory on fossilized ivory; a fine carving with gold nugget.
A—$200

Eskimo adz, long-handled and with stone blade and oogruk lashing.
A—$170

Ivory carving, unusual, of Eskimo man hunting walrus with a gun. Polychrome, and ca. 1890.
A—$575

Eskimo caribou hunter's belt, with teeth, beads, and cartridge case suspensions. Belt has 248 sets of caribou front teeth.
A—$2100

Eskimo bracelet of fossilized ivory, with finely carved relief of polar bears.
A—$205

Eskimo storyboard, with many carved figures attached.
A—$1250

Two Eskimo harpoons and an ivory harpoon point. One lot.
A—$270

Walrus ivory cribbage board, by Joe Ignatius. A—$390

Eskimo bolas, set of 14, used for hunting birds. A—$55

Eskimo miniature sled, made of caribou jaw, with baleen bottom.   A—$60

Eskimo applique skin mat, 38 in. diameter, and an exceptional piece.   A—$1075

Eskimo tom cod jigging outfit, complete with baleen line, ivory weight and lure.   A—$70

Eskimo whalebone snow shovel.   A—$170

Eskimo carver's box, filled with items relating to carving.   A—$310

Eskimo fish net and line made of hide.   A—$270

Eskimo skin boots, very old.   A—$120

Eskimo kayak paddle, full size.   A—$115

Eskimo cup, made from the jaw of a walrus.   A—$125

Eskimo small-game harpoon, fine piece.   A—$120

Two Eskimo bow-drills.   A—$240

Eskimo doll, fur and wood, from the Kuskokwim River Delta.   A—$45

Eskimo baleen woven box, with ivory lid and bottom.   A—$335

Carving, Eskimo, St. Lawrence Island. Ca. 1970, it is 2¼ in. wide and 10¼ in. long. This unusual carving is mounted on a cross-section of a fossil ivory sled-runner and depicts a hunter spearing a walrus. A very fine Eskimo art piece. $750

Sherman Holbert Collection, Fort Mille Lacs, Onamia, Minnesota

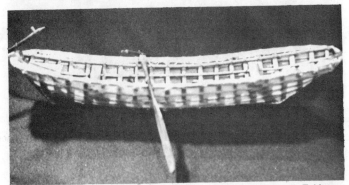

Model whaling or general-purpose boat, sealskin over wood, Eskimo. This unusual piece is 15½ in. long. $290

Pat & Dave Summers, Native American Artifacts, Victor, NY

Basket, Eskimo, body made of whale baleen and with ivory animal head handle. It is 6 in. high and 7 in. in diameter. Ca. 1940s. $1500

Crown & Eagle Antiques, Inc., New Hope, PA

CONTEMPORARY ESKIMO & ALEUT ITEMS

The material that follows is a selection of typical and authentic artifacts and artworks from the Alaskan region. All examples are from the current Alaska Native Arts & Crafts catalog; used by permission. Values are ca. 1980.

Game sled, weight two pounds, with walrus ivory sled on base made of fossilized ivory.   G—$170

Ivory birds, from 1½ in. to 4½ in. in length. Artists include works by Peter Mayac and by Kokuluk. Birds have wings etched in India ink and colored beaks and feet; ivory birds can be purchased with or without bases.
Smaller birds, G—$110
Larger birds, G—$165

Whalebone mask, from Point Hope, Alaska, 9 in. high and 6 in. wide. Use of bone shows that very few parts of the whale go to waste.   G—$115
(Price range on plain to elaborate masks is $80-$135)

Masks, made of caribou skin, with wolf or fox trim; these are made in the community of Anaktuvuk Pass in the Brooks Mountain Range. Size is 9 in. high and 5 in. side. The masks began as a Halloween prank many years ago, but have since become art objects to the trade. G—$45-$95

"Strong Man" mask, by Willie Marks of Hoonah. Mask depicts an ancient legend in which a youth is strong enough to save his village from sea demons. Item, 9 in. high and 7 in. wide.   G—$135

Ivory pendant, of fossilized ivory, constructed and etched by Lincoln Nayapuk of Shishmaref. Pendant is a cross-section of fossil ivory, 2½ in. across. Pendant has gold chain.   G—$69

Medium coil grass basket, from Kuskokwim Delta village of Kipnuk, showing use of both dried grass and seal gut. This membrane is very thin and strong; it is woven as an overlay to the grass. Quality depends on how well the seal gut is tied back into the grass.   G—$142

Miniature harpoon, by Eric Tetpon of Shaktoolik, and 14 in. long. The detachable ivory head is tied to the wooden shaft with sinew.   G—$40

Ivory owl, by Keith Oozeva, from recently harvested walrus ivory. All three layers of walrus ivory tusk can be seen. Owl's eyes are darkened with India ink and wing outlines are etched and counter-sunk.   G—$52

Dyed grass and seal gut basket, 11 in. in diameter and 10 in. high. Basket handcrafted from marsh grasses collected in the summer months; patterns are whipped into the basketry by using dyed grass and sometimes dyed seal gut. Made by Mrs. Milton Mandigo of Chefornak. G—$195

Soapstone carvings on various themes, all hand-carved:
Soapstone bird, 6 in. long, by Levi Tetpon,   G—$22
Soapstone kayak, 5 in. long, by Walton Tetpon,G—$42
Soapstone bear, 10 in. high, by Robert Tevuk,G—$230

MUSK OX PRODUCTS

For contemporary fashion-clothing items made from the soft, brown underwool of the musk ox, write:

Musk Ox Producers' Cooperative, 604—H Street, Anchorage, Alaska 99501

Suggested Reading

(By the Editors), *Indians of the Americas,* The National Geographic Society, 1955

Ivory drum handle, probably Eskimo, from Alaska. $65
Private collection

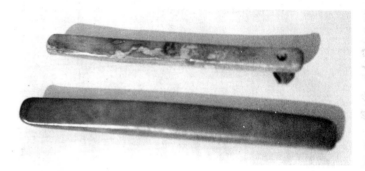

Alaskan artifacts.
Top, ivory sinew-twister, polished.
Bottom polished bone or ivory tool. $60-$90 each
Private collection

Alaskan artifacts, as follows:
Top row, bone point, slate point or knife, and slate harpoon head.
Center left, ivory fixed barb point.
Bottom row, ivory barbed bird point and ivory spear point.$30-$125 each
Private collection

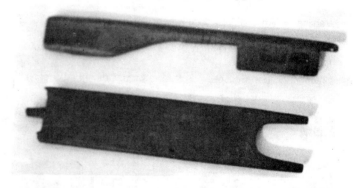

Alaskan artifacts.
Top, fishing-net gauge, ivory.
Bottom, fishing-net gauge, made of bone. $65-$90 each
Private collection

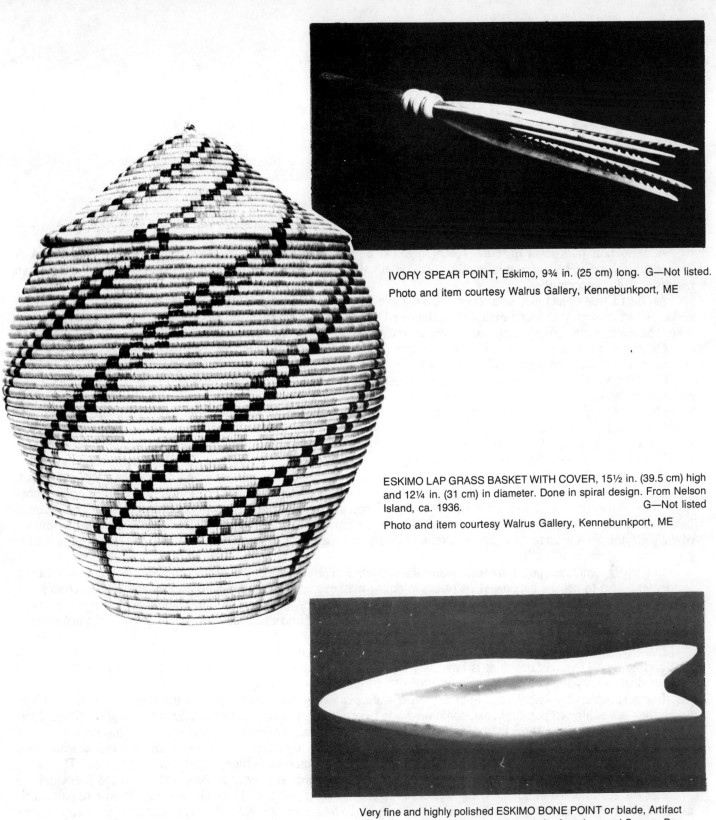

IVORY SPEAR POINT, Eskimo, 9¾ in. (25 cm) long. G—Not listed.
Photo and item courtesy Walrus Gallery, Kennebunkport, ME

ESKIMO LAP GRASS BASKET WITH COVER, 15½ in. (39.5 cm) high and 12¼ in. (31 cm) in diameter. Done in spiral design. From Nelson Island, ca. 1936.   G—Not listed

Photo and item courtesy Walrus Gallery, Kennebunkport, ME

Very fine and highly polished ESKIMO BONE POINT or blade, Artifact is 4½ in. in length. It is a type that can be found around Spence Bay in the Arctic. There, frozen ground conditions (perma-frost) help to preserve organic materials almost indefinitely.   C—$28

Photo courtesy Howard Popkie, Arnprior, Ontario, Canada

347

CHAPTER XXI

WHAT ARE AMERIND COLLECTIBLES REALLY WORTH

Here is a look at the four major sources for prices used in this Guidebook. They are each, in their special way, valid interpretations of value.

A, or auction, puts down an actual, recent, high bid. Since bidders are often present for a pre-viewing, many catalogs do not fully describe the piece sold, or the small details that can make a big difference in bids. Regional and human factors also are important.

An East Coast object may be auctioned on the West Coast at a lower price than in the "home territory", and vice-versa. Or, an item may go much higher than the usual because of keen competition evidenced by spirited and high bidding. The auction may cover a large and respected collection, in which case the prices are likely to be higher than usual.

Or, bad weather may keep important out-of-state collectors away, with bids then somewhat lethargic. On the whole, auction prices should "average out", and be a fairly close indication of item values.

C, or collector prices, would seem to be the most accurate, because the owner has had time to study objects and make comparisons. Contributors were in all cases asked to set a "fair market value", and most did. The collection, in his or her collecting field(s), tends to keep abreast of "going rates". While the collector attempts to purchase and evaluate realistically, other angles can be considered.

People and interests change. In a few cases, collectors got into Amerind objects and then, for whatever reasons, kept the collection but did not continue active collecting. In such cases, the "C" listings were below current market rates and were either dropped from the book or, with the collector's permission, were corrected to reflect current set prices and ranges.

Correspondingly—and the psychology of pricing enters strongly here—several collectors sent photos and descriptions of items that may have been somewhat over-valued, based on the nebulous concept of fair market price. No changes have been made by the writer in this area unless the figure seemed outlandishly high, and then, only with the permission of the collector. So it is up to the reader to evaluate the merits of any one piece and relate that to the given figure—quite a learning experience in itself.

Collectors sometimes pay more for an item to complete a type collection. There's another side to prices, in that collectors tend also to get the bargains, fine pieces at below market averages. In some instances—and all collectors know of them, especially that they always seem to happen to someone else—purchase to value ratio would be a few cents on the dollar. Such windfalls are probably reflected occasionally in the Guidebook, being lower priced, but examples would not be common.

D, or dealer, is a good source of study, for in most cases dealers are in the field of Amerind collectibles for both love and money. Love, because that is how they choose to spend a great deal of time and effort. Money, because to exist as dealers they must average a certain profit to continue the business.

Further, dealers, probably more than any other source-category, must be aware of what collectors want, and how much they are willing to pay for items, common-grade to select. Many dealers offer a wide range of good pieces. Most concentrate in one of the three major Amerind collecting time-spans, prehistoric, historic or contemporary.

G, or gallery, is a special classification, and the writer defines a gallery as a business which is concentrated in a limited Amerind collecting field. That area is irrelevant, and a characteristic is high-quality, authentic pieces. The owner or manager may also be very knowledgeable in his or her own right, and tends to deal with advanced collectors.

For the beginner—and not referring necessarily to classifications of A, C, D, or G—it would be wise to pay nearly as much attention to the seller as to the desired object itself. To be a good purchase, the item must offer both authenticity and high quality, both of which should also be reflected by the seller.

For example, America is loosening up a bit, getting away from traditional antiques shops, dealers and second-hand stores in pursuit of collectibles. All and more have been combined in the great buy-sell-trade arenas called flea markets.

True, tremendous bargains can be obtained when the wise collector spots a good Amerind piece at a giveaway price. Sometimes a tremendous buy turns out to be "hot stuff", stolen goods. Then the collector is left with an item that cannot be displayed or sold, or even admired with an easy mind.

In all categories of Amerind collectibles, but especially those from prehistoric and historic times, there is a chance that damage has occurred. Very minor damage can merely be taken as a sign of authenticity, depending on the type; however, major damage detracts from value. Sometimes, major damage has been concealed by a variety of methods. This may not have been done to deceive, and the seller may not even know that a piece has been restored.

No matter how the item came to be restored and no matter how well the work has been done, the piece is still not as valuable as a complete and original specimen. And it should not be sold as such or paid for as such. Check out the various methods that have been used in any area you are interested in collecting, for restoration can be quite subtle.

Regarding Amerind collectibles as a whole, a friend has some interesting observations: "The goal is to get a superb piece in excellent condition, and at a good price. Steady buying in the $1-$10 range, the purchases are just a hobby. In the $10-$100 range, it is still a hobby, but a serious one. And in the $100-$1000-and-above range, the buyer is involved with fine art—or had well better be!"

Attribution can be tricky. In buying an historic Amerind item that is said to have been owned by a known historic figure—or a contemporary object made by a "name" craftsperson—be sure all documentation is in order. Be sure the documentation is also authentic.

Be equally certain that if the item is being sold as having been in a long-time collection, that that is factually the case. Many large collections are sold at public auction by specialized auctioneers. Buying from them, you can be sure of the source, and you are also buying, at competitive prices, directly from that collection.

Collector demand in a specific area can send prices nearly beyond the financial reach of average collectors. The high prices of good pieces are partly the result of competition, plus some inflation. Also add to this the fast-growing awareness that genuine Amerind items of prehistoric, historic and recent times are limited in number, while collector demand increases.

Only in the area of recent and contemporary jewelry—silver, turquoise and other valuable metals and stones—does the material itself make up a significant part of the value. Otherwise, and with a few exceptions, the actual material is of limited worth.

What, really, is the value of several pounds of deer hide, the quills from a few porcupines and the sinew from a bison? And yet, all worked into a Plains Indian dress, the current owner has quite a treasure.

The real worth of the majority of Amerind items is a different sort of worth, and has to do with a number of factors. One of the things that definitely intrigues collectors is that everyday materials were treated in unique ways. They were made into items quite different from those known to our prevailing culture.

Beyond the importance of the basic form, decoration of almost any kind, if harmonious with the form, adds to value. In short, and a repetition of what the whole Guidebook is about, collecting good Amerind pieces is collecting good art. A Picasso, for instance, is not valued at ten dollars worth of paint and canvas.

As the value of the basic material increases, this contributes to overall value today. Ivory is generally more valuable than bone and gem-quality flint more valuable than listless, drab chert. Even in White-made goods, an iron and steel-bladed pipe-tomahawk is more valuable than an all-iron head. The better the material the higher the price.

For the book, price ranges are helpful in that they give an idea of upper and lower price structures. The actual price is even more useful, in that there is no doubt what the piece sold for or is currently valued at. As to terms used, the words "piece", "specimen", "item" and so on are used interchangeably throughout the Guidebook.

People in the field of Amerind collectibles, with only a few collecting area exceptions (old baskets), tend to be vocally aware of the problem of fakes. The writer acknowledges similar feelings, but there is a danger that people who are just starting collecting may feel that every other piece is nonauthentic, questionable, etc. Sweeping statements have been made regarding the supposed percentage of fakes in certain collecting areas, and each expert has a different expert opinion.

Several things need to be said. The problem of spurious specimens, bad pieces, is not confined to the field of Amerind collectibles, not will it be. Artifacts and artworks "in the style of" earlier periods, and for which a market demand exists, have been around for thousands of years. This is so from coins and stamps to furniture and glass and paintings.

Unless one has many years of in-depth experience, an encyclopedia-like knowledge of all other collecting areas, and a computer's capacity and speed of summation, few accurate comparisons can be made. All collecting fields of things that are worth collecting will have the problem. But—the chances of a person being "taken" decrease in direct proportion to that person's knowledge of what is being collected.

Keeping in mind several key characteristics of Amerind-made collectibles—that they are and were largely created in unique forms and styles, and with a great deal of time spent in that making — what might be some good collecting areas for the future?

In the prehistoric field, chipped artifacts predominate. Prices tend to be high for large blades and those of exceptional materials. Often overlooked are the mundane tools like scrapers, which may evidence both excellent materials and workstyles.

Some hardstone tools are probably under-priced, but the type varies with the locality. Good axes are now high and will certainly go higher. Slate forms, especially the less dramatic specimens, are probably a good bet. Items like effigy slates will one day approach the prices of average birdstones.

In the historic Amerind fields, there are of course two types of collectibles, those made by Whites and those made by Amerinds. Both have appreciated greatly in the last decade, with collector focus on items used for war or hunting, in the trade iron field. Strike-a-lights might be good, plus any trade objects entirely or partly made of copper or brass.

Smaller historic Amerind pieces of good beadwork ought to be solid buys, if only because more collectors will be able to afford them in the future. Some plainer containers, basketry and pottery, are still priced at reasonable levels. Often pieces made for the early 1900's tourist trade have excellent quality.

In the contemporary collectibles field, jewelry is still very much in demand. There are so many aspects to this field that only very general guidelines can be given. First, learn as much as possible about good silver, turquoise and shell. If the contemplated object is a poor-grade piece, it is not a bargain no matter how many times it has been sale-discounted.

Also, buy only what appeals to you personally, jewelry you can live with easily and proudly. Last—and even the experts repeat this time and again—buy only from a reputable source. This above all is your guarantee of quality at a fair price.

There are two fields of contemporary collectibles that the writer feels have been somewhat overlooked. One is good baskets by non-famous makers; the other is good weavings by competent makers.

The amount of time—exclusive of gathering and preparing the materials—that goes into a 6 in. diameter basket is amazing. Faye Stouff, Chetimacha Indian basket weaver of Route 2, Jeanerette, Louisiana, advised the writer that at least three days are required to make one of her smaller pine-needle coiled and split-stitch lidded baskets. In the opinion of the writer, the work of this craftslady—and many similar Indian artisans—will triple in value in the next few years.

Weavings, in terms of time/price, are much the same on a larger scale, with the average non-famous weaver working at something like half the national minimum-wage rate. Reading between the lines of statements made by a number of authorities, here are some things that are happening in the basketry and weaving areas.

The Indian craftspeople have recognized they are spending a great deal of time on work that yields very little monetary return; almost anything else, workwise, pays much better. Contrary to some popular beliefs, most Indians in this country do not make a living with arts and crafts. Probably fewer than five percent are so-involved.

In a number of cases, only a few skilled older people are still at work, and their productions will not be found in the market-place in quantity. That's now, and in the future. It would probably not be a bad idea to concentrate on collecting items made by the smaller Amerind groups. This not only helps support such craftspeople, but their work is often superior to more publicized creations.

Good-quality jewelry, by all signs, is still a good buy, whether from the standpoint of use or investment. In fact, when the U.S. dollar sinks drastically on the international currency market, there are a number of people who place excess funds in quality Indian jewelry.

Pieces purchased are often in the $500-$1000 range, and so do not diminish the supply for the typical collector or casual buyer, or unduly elevate prices. For top-quality pieces, it has always been a seller's market, always in demand.

There was some concern when the Guidebook was being put together that auction (A) values would predominate. There is a feeling among some collectors that auction prices tend to be higher than average. "After all", a collecting friend said, "Don't forget that the winning bid is one 'raise' above what every other bidder thought the item was worth".

Perhaps so, but auctions still, on average, do not noticeably price items beyond a fair market value. In fact, the writer is aware of non-publicized, single-item sales between advanced collectors, or dealers and collectors, that are well above several type categories listed.

As to what American Indian items are really worth, there is a stock reply that insists any one piece is worth whatever the seller can get for it. Not really, because both seller and buyer may have reached monetary (or trade material) agreement on a value, but that may still be high or low for the type.

It is, the writer suggests, the medium figure (of many such similar-item exchanges) that can give a reasonable idea of fair market value. And the collector goes on from there.

CHAPTER XXII
HELPFUL AGENCIES

The average person interested in contemporary and traditional American Indian materials might like to know something about two very relevant agencies. One is professional, the other governmental.

The trade organizations is the Indian Arts and Crafts Association, commonly referred to as I.A.C.A. or IACA. The United States government agency is the Indian Arts and Crafts Board of the U.S. Department of the Interior. Both have kindly given permission for use of pertinent facts. IACA is dicussed first.

INDIAN ARTS AND CRAFTS ASSOCIATION

The Indian Arts and Crafts Association is a national non-profit association of traders, museums, collectors, individual Indian craftspeople, tribal co-ops and guilds.

Primary purposes of IACA include the promotion of Indian arts and crafts and the maintenance of high ethical standards. Other activities include national advertising, twice-yearly wholesale markets that attract nation-wide buyers, seminars, publications, legislative support (see, later), consumer information materials and awards.

Available from IACA, and recommended by the author, are: A set of ten informational brochures on such subjects as buying weavings, jewelry and pottery, cost $5.00 a set; the current IACA Directory of Members and Buyers Guide, cost $10.00 each. The brochures mainly cover Southwestern items, while the Directory is national.

The IACA is active in introducing and supporting legislation that provides stiff penalties for misrepresentation of Indian arts and crafts.

Members are pledged to guarantee honest representation of any and all items they sell. Any member who, after a complete investigation of both sides, is found to be in violation of the IACA Code of Ethics, is ejected from the IACA. The information gathered is turned over to the appropriate authorities if there has been possible violation of federal, state or local law. All complaints are handled on a confidential basis for the protection of both parties.

Finally, the IACA acts as a clearing house for information that individuals, organizations or firms may request on Indian arts and crafts.

In short, if a business displays the IACA seal of membership, that means the personnel will honestly and correctly represent its merchandise as to nature and origin. The IACA additionally sponsors regular seminars by Indian craftspeople and other recognized experts on both Indian arts and crafts and cultures.

Following, reprinted in full, is the IACA Code of Ethics. All members of the Indian Arts and Crafts Association agree to adhere to these principles.

IACA CODE OF ETHICS

1. To honestly represent American Indian arts and crafts as to nature and origin within the realm of their control and to offer return privileges for articles found by the Indian Arts and Crafts Association to have been misrepresented.
2. To abide by all Federal, state, and local, and tribal laws pertaining to Indian arts and crafts, artifacts, and natural resources.
3. To abide by ethical business conduct regarding advertising, appraising, pricing, and guarantees offered.
4. To respect and support ethical business activities of all Indian Arts and Crafts Association members.
5. To encourage consumer confidence in the authenticity of articles identified with the IACA seal.
6. To cooperate with law enforcement agencies and the IACA in the investigation of crimes involving Indian arts and crafts and to promote proper identification of Indian arts and crafts.

Anyone may obtain the Directory of Members simply by writing and requesting same, at $10.00.

Write to: Indian Arts and Crafts Association, 122 La Veta NE, Albuquerque, New Mexico 87108   (505)265-9149

As another example of IACA work, the Association has recently drawn up Guidelines for ethical appraisal practices. The recommended guidelines section alone has twelve key parts, while eleven containments are suggested for the actual appraisal report.

The purpose of the IACA Appraisal Guidelines is "...to provide a needed service to our clients and to encourage public trust in the objectivity and competence of appraisals performed by IACA members".

Finally, in its role of introducing and supporting legislation, the IACA has been instrumental in amending New Mexico's Indian Arts and Crafts Sales Act, which is considered by many to be one of the few state legal Indian arts and crafts acts with "teeth". It is Chapter 334, 1977 Laws, 1st Session of the 33rd Legislature, State of New Mexico.

According to a past IACA Executive Directory (personal communication): "This is now one of the better laws in the U.S. This can and is being used as 'model legislation' in other states which need to up-date and improve existing statutes, and to guide introduction of legislation in other states with no laws."

The Act includes a legal definition of terms commonly used (Indian handcrafted; natural turquoise), required duties of arts and crafts dealers, unlawful acts (mainly, misrepresentation), and possible penalties for such unlawful acts.

Included is possible action by the state attorney general ("... civil penalties not to exceed five thousand dollars per violation.."), as well as a private right of action. This last means the damaged party can sue for damages in district court.

Legislation of the sort just mentioned will, both in short-term and long-range, help assure the buyer that he or she is getting exactly what the item is supposed to be. Such legislation offers three-way protection, to the authentic Indian-made goods and the Indian craftspeople, the reputable dealers, and the buyer.

Another helpful agency is **THE INDIAN ARTS AND CRAFTS BOARD OF THE U.S. DEPARTMENT OF THE INTERIOR.** Established in 1935, the Board promotes the development of Native American arts and crafts—the creative work of Indian, Eskimo, and Aleut peoples.

The Indian Arts and Crafts Board concentrated on stimulating what Indian arts and crafts existed, and engaged in aiding production, in marketing and public awareness. Eventually, advisory groups—such as the Navajo Arts and Crafts Guild, and the Alaska Native Arts and Crafts—were soundly established.

A demand for authenticity and quality increased, and training programs were set up. These concentrated on individual craftspeople, with teaching by example. The reason is well-expressed in this extraction from the Board's recent Fact Sheet:

"This is because, in any art of any culture in history, it has always been impossible to separate absolutely the influence of the whole culture from the unique influence of the individual. An artist expresses both background and a special view of it in the work, and an individual whose work is good inspires and stimulates many others in the immediate community and beyond."

The Board actively assists artists and craftspeople to develop co-operative marketing organizations and to advance professional careers. A special emphasis has been placed on helping Native leaders regarding the preservation and evolution of Native culture in the years ahead.

The Board's Advisory Staff has played a major role in helping Native craftspeople and organizations counteract a wave of misrepresentation of imitation Indian-type crafts products that occurred as part of a fashion craze for things Indian. The Board served as a clearinghouse for information, and successfully gained the co-operation of state and local consumer protection officials, various Federal agencies, newspapers—all to heighten consumer awareness to discriminate between genuine and imitation products.

As a result of these efforts, major distributors began to show a much greater sensitivity to honest representation in their marketing. The staff's continuing effort is to help Native people to register trademarks in the U.S. Patent and Trademark Office, so that their work can receive full legal protection when it is marketed.

The Board's Museums, Exhibitions and Publications Staff administers three Indian art museums. These were founded in the 1930s and 1940s by the U.S. Department of the Interior's Bureau of Indian Affairs, with advisory assistance from the Indian Arts and Crafts Board.

Each of these museums operates in a similar way. There is a permanent exhibition of historic tribal arts of the immediate region, plus a series of changing displays devoted to works by outstanding Native American artists and craftspeople. Sales shops offer the customer some of the finest contemporary artworks to be found.

The museums operate year-round, and there is no admission charge. They are:

MUSEUM OF THE PLAINS INDIAN
P.O. Box 400
Browning, Montana   59417

SOUTHERN PLAINS INDIAN MUSEUM
Highway 62 East
P.O. Box 749
Anadarko, Oklahoma   73005

SIOUX INDIAN MUSEUM
P.O. Box 1504
Rapid City, South Dakota   57701

The sales shops at the museums are operated, respectively, by the Northern Plains Indian Crafts Association, the Oklahoma Indian Arts and Crafts Cooperative, and the Tipi Shop, Inc. These highly successful Native American arts businesses are independently operated, provide their own management and handle their own affairs. They buy works directly from the artists and craftspeople. The works are then offered to the public, either at the individual museum, or through mail order.

The Indian Arts and Crafts Board's Washington, D.C., office helps the buyer of Indian art in several ways. The Board periodically publishes, and updates, a Source Directory dealing with American Indian crafts organizations and individual workers. This lists only Native American owned and operated arts businesses throughout the United States.

Copies of the Source Directory can be obtained on request by writing:

General Manager
U.S. Department of the Interior
Indian Arts and Crafts Board
1849 C. Street NW
USDI Room 4004
Washington, D.C.   20240-0001
(202)208-3773

In addition, the Washington office also issues a Bibliography listing major books on contemporary Indian arts titles. Single copies of the Bibliography will be sent, again, free, on request. Write the General Manager of the Board at the Washington address.

The writer recommends that the person interested in contemporary Indian arts and crafts obtain both the IACA Directory of Members and the Board's Source Directory. And books listed in the Bibliography can be found either in a library (another fine source of Amerind information) or at a bookstore.

The writer also recommends the Indian Craft Shop in Washington, D.C. This retail-only, no mail-order business (operated by Government Services, Inc.) has Indian and Eskimo arts and crafts, these obtained from cooperatives and artists and craftspeople. Hours are 8:30 AM - 4 PM, Monday through Friday. The address is:

Indian Craft Shop
1050 Wisconsin Ave. NW
Washington, D.C.   20007
(202)342-3918

The **U.S. Department of the Interior's Bureau of Indian Affairs** also deserves mention here. The Bureau, in 1962, established the Institute of American Indian Arts. The purpose, as recommended by the Board, was to provide heritage-centered instruction to Indian youths with artistic talent.

Today, the Institute has achieved an international reputation for creative and innovative education. Now chartered as a junior college, many of the Institute's graduates are in the assertive vanguard of Indian artists and craftspeople.

The Institute has two public exhibits called Student Sales Shows, with a gallery of sales items priced by the students. The exhibits are held in May and December, both in the second week of the month. The Institute of American Indian Arts is located on Cerrillos Road in Santa Fe, New Mexico.

The Institute of American Indian Arts is also responsible for the Traveling Exhibit, called "One With the Earth". The Exhibit consists of fine contemporary Indian art, as well as historic pieces from the Institute's Honors Collection. The Exhibit includes pottery, sculpture, painting, beadwork, weaving, basketry and other creative works.

In the 1960s, fine Indian works of many kinds began to decorate the offices of the U.S. Department of the Interior. Appreciation spread until even U.S. embassies abroad used Indian art in their decor.

The Traveling Exhibits have toured Europe, the Far East, and South America. And now, full circle, the Exhibits are being shown in Native American communities.

The buyer/collector, it can be seen, has some valuable and powerful agencies which are extremely interested in seeing that American Indian arts and crafts are fairly and accurately represented at all times. Beginner and advanced collectors alike are advised to make use of the available information.

CHAPTER XXIII
DIRECTORY

The Directory is intended as a guide to both selected businesses and further sources of information.

The criteria for inclusion of a shop, dealer or gallery in this section is that each has, in some important fashion, contributed to putting this book together. Each has been instrumental in providing factual data, photographs, necessary permission for use of material, or all three.

Some of the enterprises are long-established, others are relatively recent. Some keep regular business hours, others are by chance or appointment. As a further help, a brief notation is given regarding the main line of American Indian collectibles for that business. Besides those listed, other items are usually carried as well.

Before making a long trip, it would be best to call ahead and determine hours, current stock, special collectibles you might want to see, and so forth. A few businesses are mainly wholesale dealers to the trade, and will be so-noted. You would need to be a dealer to purchase there; however, your favorite shop can handle your order as intermediary.

The Directory to business handling American Indian material has been set up on a state basis, alphabetically.

COLLECTORS

JOEY WHITLOCK, 45 Co. Rd. 351, Moulton, AL 35650, (205) 350-2645, Stone and flint artifacts, the Atl-atl

DAVID HRACHOVY, P.O. Box 1069, Cedar Glen, CA 92321, (909) 337-9953, Plains Indian weaponry and accoutrements

MARGUERITE L. KERNAGHAN, 511 La Escena Drive, Bellvue, CO 80512, (303) 493-4471, All American Indian artifacts

STEVEN D. KITCH, 631 Wilson Ave., Pueblo, CO 81004, (719) 542-1136, Paleo Points from Co, NE, NM and NY

PHILIP L. RUSSO, 59 Lake Ave., Danbury, CT 06810, (203) 792-9885, Indian Artifacts

JOHN & SUSAN MAURER, 370 Tucson Dr., Fayetteville, NC 28303

MICHAEL SLASINSKI, 7201 Danny Drive, Saginaw, MI 48609, (517) 781-1152, Woodland Indian tools and implements, masks

WILFRED A. DICK, Rt. 4 Box 14-C, Magnolia, MS 39652, (601) 783-3400, All Indian artifacts

DR. FRED BELK, P.O. Box 4, Corrales, NM 87048, Unlisted, Antique American Indian art

HOTHEM HOUSE, Lar Hothem, P.O. Box 458, Lancaster, OH 43130, (614) 653-9030, Ohio fluted points, prehistoric artifacts; books

JAMES BRUNER, Rt. 1 Box 39, Keota, OK 74941, (918) 966-3779, Oklahoma artifacts

LARRY G. MERRIAM, 8716 Old Brompton Road, Oklahoma City, OK 73132, (405) 721-0484, Midwestern and OK flint artifacts, Paleo period

G. THOMAS NOAKES, 107 Gilshire Dr., Coraopolis, PA 15108, (412) 269-7965, Plateau, Southeast U.S. and Great Lakes regions

GARY L. FOGELMAN, RD 1 Box 240, Turbotville, PA 17772, (717) 437-3698, Northeastern U.S. artifacts

LEE HALLMAN, 166 W. Broad St., Telford, PA 18969, (215) 723-9471, Indian artifacts of PA and the Northeast U.S.

ALVIN LEE MORELAND, 1234 Hayward, Corpus Christi, TX 78411, (512) 855-2321, Prehistoric American and Mexican Indian artifacts

GRADY PATRICK McCREA, 12637 McCrea Road, Miles, TX 76861, (915) 468-6161, Early Texas artifacts

WILLIE FIELDS, Rt. 2 Box 625, Hallsville, TX 75650, (903) 668-3273, Scottsbluff culture

DENNIS R. LINDBLAD, 1628 8th Street, Chetek, WI 54728, (715) 924-4373, Ancient copper artifacts, historic trade goods

MERT COWLEY, 611 22¾th St., Chetek, WI 54728, (715) 924-4668, Early Wisconsin artifacts

ROBERT D. LUND, 918 Cleveland St., Watertown, WI 53094, (414) 261-2147, Wisconsin artifacts

DEALERS

CADDO TRADING COMPANY & GALLERY, Sam Johnson, Rt 2, Box 669, Murfreesboro, AR 71958, (501) 542-3652, Moundbuilder art

INDIAN RUINS TRADING POST, P.O. Box 46, Sanders, AZ 86512, (602) 688-2787, Contemporary silver and turquoise

PIERRE G. BOVIS, P.O. Box 460, Tombstone, AZ 85638, (602) 457-3359, Plains Indian material

INDIAN ROCK GALLERY, John W. Barry, P.O. Box 583, Davis, CA 95616, (916) 758-2561, Contemporary Southwestern pottery

MORRIS' ART & ARTIFACTS, Cliff Morris, P.O. Box 4771, Anaheim, CA 92803, (714) 533-0391, Northwest Coast artworks, historic Plains period

THE CURIO SHOP, Robert Vincent, P.O. Box 1013, Anderson, CA 96007, (916) 365-6458, North and South American Indian culture

FREYA'S COLLECTIBLES, Alan McClelland, 114 Banff Ave. / P.O. Box 1362, Banff, Alberta, Canada TOL OCO, (403) 762-4714, Central and Northern Plains, beadwork

TOH-ATIN TRADING COMPANY, P.O. Box 2329, Durango, CO 81301, (303) 247-1252 or (303) 247-8277, Wholesale; old and contemporary art

POCOTOPAUG TRADING POST, Alan or John Atkins, P.O. Box 577, South Windsor, CT 06074, (203) 644-4476, Prehistoric to historic items, related books

DENNIS R. PHILLIPS, 1819 W. Thome Ave., Chicago, IL 60660, (708) 869-6367, Pottery, weavings of the American Southwest

EDMUNDS OF YARMOUTH INC., P.O. Box 788, West Yarmouth, MA 02673, (617) 775-9303, Contemporary material

PLAINS INDIAN ART, 609 Greenway Terrace, Kansas City, MO 64113, (816) 361-1599, Plains Indian items, many types

CASA KAKIKI, P.O. Box 111, Sunland Park, NM, (915) 584-0195, Contemporary jewelry

HYDE'S, P.O. Box 2304, Santa Fe, NM 87501, (505) 983-2096, Historic, Plains Indian

JOHN ISAAC, 2036 S. Plaza NW, Albuquerque, NM 87104, (505) 842-6656, Southwestern textiles, baskets, pottery, kachinas, beadwork

KHALSA TRADING COMPANY, 1423 Carlisle NE, Albuquerque, NM 87110, (505) 255-8278, Contemporary jewelry

MORNING STAR GALLERY, Joe Rivera 513 Canyon Rd., Santa Fe, NM 87501, (505) 982, 8187, Pre-1900 art from all North American tribes

PACKARD'S CHAPARRAL TRADING POST, 61 Old Santa Fe Trail, Santa Fe, NM 87501, (505) 983-9241, Old and contemporary items

TOM NOEDING, P.O. Box 153, Taos, NM 87571, (505) 758-2376, Southwestern Indian artifacts

NATIVE AMERICAN ARTIFACTS, David Summers, P.O. Box 104, Victor, NY 14564, (716) 924-5167, Full line of historic and prehistoric artifacts

PORT OF CALL, Frank Bergevin, 65 Church Street, Alexandria Bay, NY 13607, (315) 482-6544, American Indian art and antiquities

BACK TO EARTH, Larry Garvin, 17 N LaSalle Drive, South Zanesville, OH 43701, (614) 454-0874, Artifacts, fossils, jewelry, books

CROWN & EAGLE ANTIQUES, INC., Mrs. Lynn D. Trusdell, Rt. 202, P.O. Box 181, New Hope, PA 18938, (215) 794-7972, Highest quality jewelry, rugs, pottery, stone and beadwork

JAMES O. APLAN, HC 80 / Box 793-24, Piedmont, SD 57769, (605) 347-5016, Plains Indian items

CRAZY CROW TRADING POST, 107 North Fannin, Denison, TX 75020, (214) 341-7715, Plains and historic pieces

FIRST MESA, Larry Lantz, P.O. Box 1256, South Bend, IN 46624, (219) 232-2095, Historical and prehistoric artworks

DON C. TANNER'S INDIAN GALLERY, 7007 5th Ave., Scottsdale, AZ 85251, (602) 945-5416, Old pawn jewelry, other varieties

JOHN C. HILL ANTIQUE INDIAN ART, John C. Hill, 6990 E. Main St., Suite 201, Scottsdale, AZ 85251, (602) 946-2910, Rugs, blankets, baskets, old pawn, kachinas, pottery

THE AMERICANA GALLERIES, 3901 East Anne Street, Phoenix, AZ 85016, (602) 268-3477, Ancient and primitive art

THE ANSEL ADAMS GALLERY, Village Mall / Box 455, Yosemite National Park, CA 95389, (209) 372-4413, Contemporary selections.

WHISPERING PINES GALLERY, 8243, La Mesa Boulevard, La Mesa, CA 92041, (714) 460-3096, Historic and other material

JAY EVETTS, Yoder, CO 80864, (303) 478-2248, Navajo blankets, early rugs, historic pottery

SHERMAN HOLBERT COLLECTION, Sherman Holbert, Fort Mille Lacs, Star Route, Onamia, MN 56359, (612) 532-3651, Historic American Indian artifacts and artworks

CANFIELD GALLERY, Kenneth Canfield, 414 Canyon Road, Santa Fe, NM 87501, (505) 988-4199, Antique Indian art, Plains artworks, Southwestern pottery

NEDRA MATTEUCCI'S FENN GALLERIES, Alexis Buchanan, 1075 Paseo Peralta, Santa Fe, New Mexico, (505) 982-4631, American Indian Art

JAMES REID, LTD., Kellie M. Keto, Curator, 114 E. Palace Avenue, Santa Fe, NM 87501, (505) 988-1147, Antique Indian art, Southwest furniture and paintings

RAY TRACEY GALLERIES, Nancy Welker, 135 W. Palace Ave., Santa Fe, NM 87501, (505) 989-3430, Works of Navajo jeweler Ray Tracey, other quality arts

MANITOU GALLERY, 1718 Capitol Ave., Cheyenne, WY 82001, (307) 635-0019, Original Indian materials

OTHER

ROBERT C. CALVERT, 363 Avondale Rd., London, Ontario, Canada N5W 5B4, (519) 455-4002, Canadian artifacts; hobbyist

ANDENT, INC., Ellis J. Neiburger, DDS, 1000 North Ave., Waukegan, IL 60085, (708) 244-0292, Ancient copper artifacts; research

PIEDMONT ARCHAEOLOGICAL SOCIETY, Rodney M. Peck, 2121 Quail Drive, Harrisburg, NC 28075, (704) 786-6294, The Southeastern U.S.; publications

THE EASTERN COWBOYS, Jay Sadow, 4235 North 86th Place, Scottsdale, AZ 85251, (602) 945-9804, Arts and Crafts of 60 Indian Nations; distributor

KACHINA SHOP
Denver Museum of Natural History
City Park / 2001 Colorado Blvd.
Denver, Colorado 80205
(303)370-6312

One of the fine pleasures of collecting American Indian items of any kind is learning more about them and the people who made them. Books are an important source of information; following is a sourcelist of booksellers who carry a selection of books on Indian-related subjects.

COLLECTOR BOOKS
P.O. Box 3009
Paducah, Kentucky 42001

BOOKS AMERICANA
P.O. Box 2326
Florence, AL 35630

Hothem House
P.O. Box 458
Lancaster, OH 43130

AMERICAN INDIAN BOOKS
9868 Diamond Point Drive
St. Louis, MO 63123

Auctions are one very good way to obtain exceptional American Indian items, and here are three that have such sales on a regular basis. Write for information on Indian-item mailing lists.

AUCTION HOUSES

GARTH'S AUCTION, INC.
2690 Stratford Road
Delaware, OH 43015

SOTHEBY, PARKE BERNET, INC.
980 Madison Avenue
New York City, 10021

OLD BARN AUCTION
10040 St-Rt. 224 W.
Findlay, OH 45840 (419) 422-8531

AMATEUR ARCHAEOLOGICAL ORGANIZATIONS

The archaeological societies are excellent for learning more about American Indians and their cultures, especially the earlier peoples. The cost of belonging is nominal; while many have regional names, membership is nationwide.

These non-profit organizations concentrate on education, and the dissemination of facts about prehistoric lifeways. Each of the societies puts out a quarterly journal, and these alone are reason enough to become a member.

Most states and regions have such archaeological groups. Six of the major organizations are listed here, from East to West, and some areas between the two. You may write, at no obligation, to the society that interests you. Thus you can easily learn what the society is and does, and how to become a member.

THE CENTRAL STATES ARCHAEOLOGICAL
  SOCIETIES
6118 Scott
Davenport, IA 52806

EASTERN STATES ARCHAEOLOGICAL
FEDERATION
RD #2, Box 166
Dover, Delaware 19901

GENUINE INDIAN RELIC SOCIETY, INC.
3416 Lucas-Hunt Road
St. Louis, MO 63121

OHIO ARCHAEOLOGICAL SOCIETY
5210 Coonpath Road
Pleasantville, OH 43148

OKLAHOMA ANTHROPOLOGICAL SOCIETY
1000 Horn Street
Muskogee, Oklahoma 74401

OREGON ARCHAEOLOGICAL SOCIETY
P.O. Box 13293
Portland, Oregon 97213

COLLECTOR'S WHO'S WHO

Your attention is directed to a hardcover book series called *Who's Who In Indian Relics*. (Early editors were Hubert C. Wachtel, Dayton, Ohio and more recently, Cameron W. Parks, Garrett, Indiana; recent editor is Ben W. Thompson, Kirkwood, Missouri). In the writer's opinion, these books are invaluable in collecting fields for the prehistoric and historic time-spans.

Each book (with No. 8 published, Nos. 1-7 are collectors' items in themselves) is a North American guide, with biographical data, to hundreds of major collectors. Amerind items range from the early prehistoric to contemporary goods. Many thousand fine artifacts and artworks are shown.

For futher information, write:

Janie Weidner
Who's Who Editor
P.O. Box 88
Sunbury, OH 43074

And for a variety of display frames:

Indian River Display Case Co.
13706 Robins Rd.
Westerville, OH 43081
1-800-444-1280

PUBLICATIONS

There are three publications in the field of American Indian items that the writer does not hesitate to recommend. These periodicals cover artifacts, handicrafts and artworks of many kinds. You may write directly to the publications, as listed below, for subscription information.

Editor
THE INDIAN TRADER
P.O. Box 1421
Gallup, New Mexico 87305

Editor
AMERICAN INDIAN ART Magazine
7314 E. Osborn Dr.
Scottsdale, AZ 85251

Editor
PREHISTORIC ANTIQUITIES
P.O. Box 53
North Lewisburg, OH 43060

SOME FINAL NOTES...

To remain faithful to materials sent by contributors, and to demonstrate the variety in words, spelling of key terms has not been standardized. In fact, there is often no single "correct" version.

A good example is "heishe" which appears in half a dozen slightly different ways. The guideline has been that such words must resemble one another only to the extent that there is no confusion as to the intended meaning.

If anyone who contributed to the book was not thanked in the Acknowledgement section or listed in the Directory or credited with photographs that were published, you have the writer's apology in advance. Any such oversight will be corrected in subsequent editions.

This book is periodically revised and updated, and there is a need for additional photographs for each edition. If good photographs of quality artifacts and artworks are available, there is a strong possibility that the pictures can be used. For such contributions, please contact the author in care of the publisher.

Since *North American Indian Artifacts* first appeared, in 1978, great changes have taken place in the collecting field. An accurate summary of what has happened in the past fifteen years would, ideally, require comment from individual experts in each of the collecting categories and in subdivisions of each category. (In fact, this might be a good thing to do for the next edition.) It is now enough to say that very many additional collectors have entered the field, and at all levels of monetary ability and knowledge.

There has developed a great awareness and appreciation of American Indian collectibles, again at all levels and in all areas of the country. It is true that some valuable items can cost hundreds of thousands of dollars, but hundreds of thousands of items cost only a few dollars.

All areas of Amerind collectibles have increased in value, partly due to the influx of new collectors and a growing recognition of the uniqueness and special beauty of the pieces. Those people who studied carefully and bought wisely have seen their acquisitions increase in value many times. Still, an overall guide and a purpose of this book, is to consider the investment aspect as secondary to the enjoyment aspect. Ancient or modern, the piece should be something that provides solid satisfaction just in having it around, in seeing and touching and displaying. Such an enlightened attitude honors both the maker and the owner.

At the early end of the collecting spectrum, one can acquire the oldest human-made items in all of North America. In the latest context are those artists and craftspeople who are today working in materials not used in more traditional times, but whose sculptures and jewelry and paintings add a new dimension to the world of artistic accomplishment. The field, in short, has broadened and grown.

There will be many more changes in the next fifteen years, and hopefully all this will be reflected in the pages of *North American Indian Artifacts.*

Lar Hothem

GLOSSARY
POINT & BLADE TYPES

⅓ Approximate size

Dovetail (St. Charles) Blade

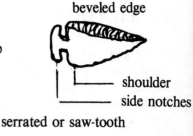

Leaf shaped
Adena cache blade

Fluted-base points

Folsom
(Paleo)

Triangular
Arrowhead
(unnotched)

Clovis-type

Late Arrowhead
Triangular, notched

Northwest Coast
Gempoint

Woodland Period

Hopewell point or blade
(notched)

Adena point or blade
(stemmed)

PROJECTILE POINT PARTS

Triangular
blade
(no notches or stem)

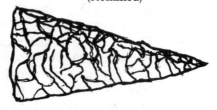

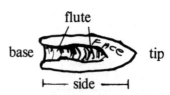

flute
base   tip
side

beveled edge

shoulder
side notches

serrated or saw-tooth
edge
barb
stem

break area

corner notch

Archaic E-notch
beveled blade

Serrated edge
point or blade

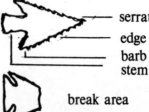

Late-Paleo
stemmed & shouldered blade

Bifurcated-base
point or blade
(Archaic)

358

COMMON AXE TYPES
Scale: 1/6

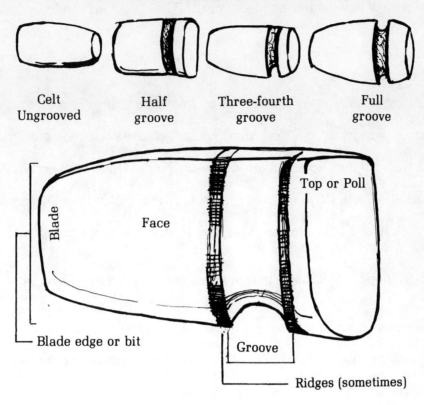

Celt
Ungrooved

Half
groove

Three-fourth
groove

Full
groove

Blade

Face

Top or Poll

Blade edge or bit

Groove

Ridges (sometimes)

GLOSSARY
For Points & Blades

AUTHENTIC—Point actually made in prehistoric times.

BEVEL—Blade edge that is sharply angled, formed by rechipping or resharpening edge.

BIRFURCATE—Point base split into double lobes with indentation similar to notches on sides.

BIRDPOINT—Small (less than 1 inch) late prehistoric arrowheads, either stemmed or notched at base.

BLANK—Otherwise finished point or blade but without base notches or stem put in.

CACHE BLADE—Quantities of points or blades found together in an underground depository or in a mound. Adena cache blades (large, leaf-shaped) are common in the Midwest.

DUO-NOTCH—Point with double set of notches, but rare. A few duo-tipped points also exist.

FAKE—Modern-made point passed off as authentic and old.

FLUTE—Channel-chip taken from both faces of Paleo point, extending towards tip. Shaft end fitted grooved portion and allowed deep penetration in target animal.

FRACTURE-BASED—Special chipping technique that knocked off long thin slivers of flint from point edges. Usually done on base bottom, occasionally on lower shoulders. May have been a chipping "short-cut".

GEMPOINT—Smallish points made of very high grade (colorful and/or translucent flints), commonly found in the Pacific Northwest.

GLOSSY—Flint with high surface sheen, usually denoting quality.

GRINDING—Base of point of blade with sharp edges ground off and smoothed. Evidently done so binding thongs were not cut.

HAFT—Means a method of fastening to shaft or handle, generally notches or stem. A "hafted shaft scraper" once had a handle.

NOTCHES—Matching indentations in point base area, may be in base, at point corners or sides.

OBSIDIAN—Common in western regions, this natural volcanic glass exists in shades of red, brown and black.

PATINA—Surface coloration or thin deposits from soil chemicals; in short, how point exterior differs from interior flint.

PERCUSSION FLAKING—Large flakes removed by direct or indirect blows from flaking hammer.

POT LID MARKS—Conical depressions in flint that prove the item was once in a fire. Heat caused moisture in tiny hollows to expand and blow out a section of flint.

PRESSURE FLAKING—Controlled flaking that used finger pressure to create delicate work, edge retouch, deep notches, etc.

QUESTIONABLE—Point or blade is probably not "good", i.e., is a fake.

REPRODUCTION—Modern point made without intent to deceive, as exercise in chipping skill.

SERRATIONS—Saw-tooth projections on blade or point edges.

STEM—Hafting method at base where flint extends in a central column.

TIP-BASE—The top and bottom of point or blade.

TRANSLUCENT—Chipped material that transmits a certain amount of light; usually means high quality.

WARPOINT—Small, late prehistoric general-purpose arrowheads with triangular configuration, without notches or stem.